Studies in
Myth, Orality and Folklore in World Literature

Studies in Myth, Orality and Folklore in World Literature

Edited by
Vandhana Sharma

ATLANTIC
PUBLISHERS & DISTRIBUTORS (P) LTD

Published by

ATLANTIC

PUBLISHERS & DISTRIBUTORS (P) LTD

7/22, Ansari Road, Darya Ganj, New Delhi-110002
Phones : +91-11-40775252, 23273880, 23275880, 23280451
Fax : +91-11-23285873
Web : www.atlanticbooks.com
E-mail : orders@atlanticbooks.com

Branch Office
5, Nallathambi Street, Wallajah Road, Chennai-600002
Phones : +91-44-64611085, 32413319
E-mail : chennai@atlanticbooks.com

ISBN 978-81-269-1800-3

Printed in India at Glorious Printers, A-13, D.S.I.D.C.,
Jhilmil Industrial Area, Delhi-110095

Dedicated to

My Daughter Matngi
and
My Husband M.K. Sharma

सत्यमेव जयते

GOVERNOR
JAMMU & KASHMIR

RAJ BHAVAN
Srinagar-190001

Foreword

I am happy to learn that the School of Languages and Literature, Shri Mata Vaishno Devi University is bringing out a book on the proceedings of the "International Seminar on Myth, Orality and Folklore in World Literature (with special reference to Rabindranath Tagore)", which was organized by this School in March 2012.

I gather that the various sections of the volume, titled "Myth, Orality and Folklore in World Literature", examine the range, depth and variety of the terms "myth", "orality", and "folklore" and how these are used in the writings of Rabindranath Tagore; reflect on the studies in regional myths, folklore and oral narratives of India; present an interesting mosaic of myth and folklore in Indian writings; examine the most representative literary endeavors in British and American literature on this subject and present selections from Canadian and African literature.

I compliment Dr. Vandhana Sharma, Director, School of Languages and Literature, Shri Mata Vaishno Devi University, for bringing out the projected volume.

3rd October, 2012
Srinagar

N.N. Vohra
Chancellor,
Sri Mata Vaishno Devi University

Preface

The present anthology is the outcome of an International Conference on Myth, Orality and Folklore in the World Literature (With Special Reference to Rabindranath Tagore) organized by the School of Languages and Literature, Shri Mata Vaishno Devi University, Katra, Jammu & Kashmir from 29-31 March, 2012. An overwhelming response of scholarship provided an exhaustive and all-encompassing perspective to the theme of the conference, thereby, establishing the generic similarity of myth, orality and folklore in all literatures of the world, across space, time and culture.

The corpus of myths and rituals with its roots in the oral traditions and folklores has always made life more worthy. The writers worldwide turned to myths and mythology to juxtapose the past and the present in order to depict the predicament of mankind and to probe the mythicality of human existence. The book offers a selection of the most representative literary luminaries, but the substantive foci is Indian writers, leading the reader to explore and uncover for himself the unrepresented and less represented areas. It comprises five parts and each part is linked with the other part with its overt emphasis on the strand of myth, orality and folklore beginning with the great universalist Rabindranath Tagore, moving on to the other regions of India and finally to the other literatures of the world.

Rooted, as it is, in the concept of World Literature at the 150th birth centenary celebrations of Rabindranath Tagore, who has left a bountiful repository of the homogeneity of literatures, the book starts with essays which study the range, depth, variety and complexity of the terms myth, orality and folklore and how these terms resonate with rich evocations in the literary oeuvre of Rabindranath Tagore. The book focuses on various facets of mythopoeic vision of Gurudev who learnt as much from the socially outcaste *Baul* minstrels as from the progressive Western arts. Indranath Chaudhuri in his paper, delivered as keynote to the conference, has dealt with the history of myth, and asserts that in Indian context oral, tribal or folklore are neither the residue of the past, nor the behaviour of the uncivilized, but it is the continuity of a rich culture and also a process of making the present more worthy, and along with *shastra* it gives a complete picture of Indian culture and thought. Mohit K. Ray in his paper, delivered as the valedictory address maps out the variety and complexity of Tagore's use of myth, orality and folklore with copious illustrations from the writings of Tagore. Jasbir Jain's scholarly enterprise is on oral narratives across time, through a wide selection of narratives from the "katha", the folktale, and its contemporary use and selections from Tagore seeking to problematise the "listener" in the narrative. Mahua Mukherjee unveils the new horizons of Indian dance forms which were revived by Tagore and their application in Gurudev's songs. Neeru Tandon examines the process by which the discourse of folklore and myth is used to en-textualize and re-contextualize the oral tradition in West Bengal through a discussion of Tagore's *Chandalika* and *Gandhari's Prayer*. Santosh Gupta analyses myths, legends and folktales in Tagore, Karnad and Ghosh, while Sanjoy Saksena studies myths and Tagore's *The Home and the World*. Ajay Kukde chooses to examine glimpses of Bengal in the stories of Tagore, while Saiket Banerjee looks at Tagore as the librettist of orality.

Then there are papers that herald tacitly the studies in regional myths, folklore and oral narratives of India. Samina Khan analyzes *Nautanki* with its folk dimensions in Northern India and Safdar Hashmi's role in popularising street theatre form to create social and political awareness in different parts of India. Vandhana Sharma explores the farmland myth of Jammu and traces the hero's journey in Dogri play *Bawa Jitto*, while Mrinalini Attri analyses the socio-cultural context of Dogri folk-ballads. Indira N. analyses the jatayu myth in the poetry of Sitanshu Yashas Chandra Mehta who gave a new turn to Gujarati poetry. Catherina Moss presents a case study of folklore of the Lepcha community in India with special emphasis on the relation of the community to the land, its creatures and the supernatural realm.

These are followed by essays which present an interesting mosaic of myth and folklore in Indian writings. Shashi Khurana projects the degeneration of a distinct mytho-fictional genre sustained by women through oral narratives in her study on Mrinal Pandey's short story "Girls" and the novella *Devi: Tales of the Goddess in Our Time.* K.S Vaishali revisits myth-making as an act of feminist resistance in the short stories of Mahashweta Devi. Geetanjli Multani studies the polemics in Chitra Banerjee's rendering of the tradition of myth in two of her famous novels, *The Mistress of Spices* and *The Palace of Illusions.* Prakash Chandra Pradhan contextualizes myths of the *Mahabharata* to bring out Tharoor's vision in *The Great Indian Novel.* Geetanjali Rana and Anita Bhela analyze myth and reality in the plays of Girish Karnad and Vijay Tendulkar, while Pulakesh Ghosh maps out the use of myth, orality and folklore in the short stories of R.K. Narayan.

Then we cross the geographical frontiers of India, go abroad and present essays that examine the most representative literary endeavours in British and American literature beginning with "American Hero's Passage to India" by Alan Johnson where Johnson compares and contrasts America's conception of mythic frontier landscape with other mythic stories. J. Hansford Vest addresses the trickster figure as a primary foundation of Native American mytho-orality centered ethnocriticism. Rashmi Attri analyses Irish legends in her study of *The Countess Cathleen,* and Ravi Bhushan provides a critique of William Golding's fiction by exploring the myth of universal human nature. Shahla Gauri analyses Ishmail Kadare's use of myth in *Spring Flowers* and *Spring Frost* for presenting and understanding the present state of affairs in Albania. K.B.S. Krishna analyses the myth in Harper Lee's *To*

Kill a Mocking Bird, and Isha Malhotra revisits the myth of androgyny in feminist writing.

Finally we offer selections from Canadian and African literature where Sonia Khajuria analyses the myth of a doomed woman artist in Margaret Atwood's *Surfacing* and *Lady Oracle.* Jatinder Kaur moves to black novelistic literary tradition by analysing myth and orality in Gloria Naylor's novels, while Rupali Gupta unveils the myth of harem in her study of Fatima Mernissi's *Dreams of Trespass.* Vaishali Sharma and Vandhana Sharma analyse the character Demoke in Wole Soyinka's magnum opus *A Dance of the Forests* as the Yoruba god, Ogun, who embodies the paradox of creation and destruction.

I would like to conclude that this was admittedly a daunting task of exhibiting a tiny fraction of infinite diversity in the realms of myth, orality and folklore in the world literature. I am deeply indebted to all the contributors for their well researched papers. I am hopeful that the book will be useful to the students and teachers of English Literature and will be a prized possession for any library—personal or institutional.

Vandhana Sharma

Acknowledgements

I am indebted to many colleagues, friends, and institutions and to the patience of my family. I want to begin by thanking the supreme Goddess who gave me capability and energy to accomplish the daunting task of organizing an international conference. It is pleasure to acknowledge the assistance of several people in the organization of the conference and the preparation of this book. My thanks go to Prof. R.N.K. Bamezai, Vice Chancellor of Shri Mata Vaishno Devi University; Ms. Roop Avtar Kaur, Registrar; Mr. S.K. Sadhotra; Mr. Vinod Sharma, Ms. Saitu, Dr. Neeru, Dr. Shivani and many more for all their support. I acknowledge the financial assistance provided by Tagore Commemoration Scheme under the Ministry of Culture, ICPR and UGC.

My debt is due to the participants in the conference who promptly submitted their papers for publication and conscientiously answered the editorial queries. My sincere thanks go particularly to Prof. Jasbir Jain, Prof. Alan Johnson and Prof. Jay Hansford Vest for all their valuable observations and suggestions during the conference. A special word of thanks to Prof. G.K. Das for all his guidance.

I am grateful to Prof. Mohit K. Ray, for his close attention to this project. His detailed and judicious comments improved the draft immensely.

I am thankful to my students, particularly Vaishali, Simranpreet, Quleen and Priyanka for all their editorial assistance.

Last but not least I express my thanks to Dr. K.R. Gupta and Mr. Harjeet Singh, Atlantic Publishers and Distributors, for bringing out the book in an amazingly short time.

Vandhana Sharma

Contents

1

Myth, Orality and Folklore in World Literature with Special Reference to Tagore

Indra Nath Choudhuri

> The thing truly worth seeing in world literature is the way human beings express their joy in literature and the abiding form in which the human soul wishes to reveal itself through the diversity of this expression.
>
> Tagore in his essay on "World Literature"

Myth, orality, folklore, world literature and Tagore the range of the theme of this international conference is all-encompassing and extremely wide. Any critical analysis of a theme or a book for Tagore is an act of worship. In his essay on the Ramayana, Tagore writes, "True criticism is an act of worship, *puja*. The true critic is a worshipping priest, who merely gives expression to his own mingled wonder and adoration or that of public at large" (10). Is not the Greek criticism of Homar or the Roman criticism of Virgil a *puja*? T.S. Eliot declared that the greatness of literature cannot be determined solely by literary standards. The concept of *puja* is not an extraneous issue in criticism, but very much a part of history. This keynote is an act of worship, *puja* of the theme of the conference.

Tagore in his essay "The Religion of the Forest" says that Râmachandra, the great hero of our epic, had his initiation to the spiritual life from Vashishtha, the life of inner peace and perfection. But he had his initiation to war from Vishvâmitra, who called him to kill the demons and gave him weapons that were irresistible. Tagore says that reconciliation between these two forces is possible through creation (518-19). Creation is the harmony of contrary forces—the forces of attraction and repulsion. When they join hands, all the fire and fight are changed into the smile of flowers and the songs of birds.

While explaining myth, Levi-Strauss says that mythical thought progresses from the awareness of oppositions toward their resolution and the element which brings resolution according to Tagore is creation. The Sanskrit term for Creation is *srishti*, meaning a manifestation or formation of something that remained occult. Time and space both lay latent in the timeless eternity. The phenomenal creation was only a projection of this transcendent eternity into time and space.

Some of the modern critics of myth have stressed that the myth is essentially related to creation. Says Mircea Eliade, "myth tells how, through the deeds of Supernatural Beings, a reality came into existence, be it the whole of reality, the cosmos, or only a fragment of reality—an island, a species of plant, a particular kind of human behaviour, an institution. Myth then is always an account of a 'creation'" (5-6). C.G. Jung similarly says that "myth is formed around a figure that may be a god a man or a process that repeats itself throughout man's history whenever creative phantasy is freely manifested" (18).

The miracle of creation is to bring conflicting forces into the harmony of the one. The power which accomplishes that is known as the archetype or eternal cosmic principal or what Levi Strauss says "universal law of human thought" (10). It is not a shift from myth as a narrative story to myth as a way of thinking. Both are very closely interrelated. It is first an idea or archetype (*satyadharma*) which becomes the basis of a story to be woven around the idea or thought and hence any mythical story (*devatakhyan*) rests on an idea or an archetype. It is explained by Jung as "the collective unconscious" and he strongly feels that when a man loses his mythical heritage he has really lost his soul (18). Myth as said by Frank Karmode, "short-circuits the intellect and liberates the imagination" (4), which helps in deriving its universal significance by reconstituting an original event or explaining some fact about human nature and its worldly or cosmic context.

The question of reference or history of myth is still unresolved. In ancient Greece, two main theories were put forward to explain myths and they are followed even today by some scholars. One is known as Euhmerist theory, called after its originator Euhmeros (300 B.C.) who saw in myths apotheosis of historical events related to human beings and thus Zeus was taken as an actual king of Crete, a human hero, who had overthrown the regime of Kronos and who was deified later by men and turned into a myth. Regarding the origin of Vedic God Indra, R.N. Dandekar has taken a Euhmeristic view, for according to him Indra was originally a war hero of the Vedic Aryans. The other Greek theory upheld by the poets Epicharmus (6th C.B.C.) and Theagenus of Rhegium (5th C.B.C.) and condemned by Plato in his *Phaedrus* saw in myths, personification of various natural phenomena and thus Zeus was the sky, Poseidon stood for water and like that. Much before that it was Yaska (7th C.B.C.) in a passage connected with the identification of Vrtra in his book of Vedic etymology, *Nirukta*, showed that from the very beginning there had been two main schools of interpreting Vedic mythology, the historical school, i.e. of the *aithihasikas*, and the naturalistic schools, i.e. of the *nairuktas*. The former believed that Vrtra was a demon, a son of Tvashtr, the later, on the other hand, held that Vrtra is cloud personified or Indra is light personified (*Megha iti naituktah. Tvashtro asuraiti iti aiitihasika, Nirukta*, 2.5.17).

But let me say in passing, as said by Sri Aurobindo about Vedic gods that they are no mythic barbarian gods of clouds, sun and shower, no confused allegories of wonderstruck savages, but the objects of worship to men far more inwardly civilized and profound in self-knowledge than ourselves.... They had read the riddle of death and found the secret of immortality; they had sought for and discovered the One and known and worshipped Him, in their glories of his light and purity and wisdom and power (284).

No doubt the ancient society, not primitive society, was the myth's proper milieu but it will be wrong to follow the Anthropo-ethnological school of scholars like A. Lang, E.B. Taylor, E. Durkheim, Levy Bruhal and call it pre-logical and nothing but "savage thought". In fact, it is not savage thought but collective unconscious as Jung explains. For instance, the shaman calling out like birds and animals was not in a state of "possession" but signified at—one-ness or return to a prelapsarian (biblical time before the fall from grace) state of unified consciousness. For Kerenyi, "The going back to the origin and primal time is basic feature of every mythology." This is what Mircea Eliade calls sacral time. It is from this point or place beyond time, that society receives all its functions and sanctions and matters is not when they taught but what they taught and hence "mythological events cannot be judged historically" (Baynes, 790) because the power of the myth resides in a "more-than-historical reality" (Ransom, 65).

The word for myth in Indian context is *purana* and they are episodical. Here history changes into *purana*, so one cannot find a unity which one derives out of a cause and effect relationship. The *purana* keeps up its subterranean historical origin, but goes on adding, multiplying and expanding its body, aiming to bring home the archetypal meaning of the enduring totality. So *Mahabharata* is *itihasa* as well as *purana*. While explaining the term history as given in *Nirukta*, Yaska explains that the war between Indra and Vritra is not a historical happening but a symbolic event (*upamaarthena yudha varnabhavanti tatro upamarthena*, 2.16.2), however historical stories like Harishchandra, Nachiketa, etc. are also to be found. In other words, *itihasa* in the Indian tradition is both history as is understood in the West and at the same time it is mythical history. Amarkosha defines *itihasa* simply as *puravritta*, i.e. events of the past (1.6.4) but the Indian tradition of Dharmashastra has given a specific connotation to the term *itihasa* which stands for a particular class of literature. The *Mahabharata* defines it as "*Dharmartha kama mokshanam upadesha samanvitam, puravritta samayuktamitihasam prachakshate,*" i.e. *itihasa* is the narrative of the past but, at the same time, it contains teaching on *dharma* (religious and moral duties), *artha* (necessities of life, i.e. means of material prosperity), *kama* (fulfilment of desire) and *moksha* (emancipation). Since *itihasa* does not assert "so it was" but it also reminds us that "so it has been" hence *itihasa* literally ("thus verily it has been") is a narrative of past events, the recitation of which is a part of the process of self-renewal and regeneration. In the Indian view the "so it was" aspect remains neither relevant nor real: the most it can achieve is to stimulate one point in a continuum whereas the "so it has been" view remains continuously relevant and real.

In *itihasa,* the emphasis is not on the happenings, however true they may be, but on some teaching, on some ideal. Hence, in Indian tradition *itihasa* is coupled with *purana*, "that which is old and is still new" or "that which renews the old" and hence timeless and eternal.

From the ancient time in India, *purana* stands for that this is new at the same time ancient, eternal and primordial. Shri Krishna is known as *Purana Purusha*, *The Bhagvad Gita* says, "*Ajo nitya shashvatoym puranah*" (unborn, eternal, ever existent and primeval is He). In the *Rgveda* the same epithet is used for Usha—"*Punah punarjayamana purani*" (being born again and again she is primeval) (Choudhuri, 112). Malinowski calls it "a living reality".

Tagore uses the pauranic myths of Ahalya and Uravasi, in his two poems, to give an eternal archetypal meaning by juxtaposing the old with the new consciousness of the modern period. Ahalya recovers from a millennium of sleep, "full youth bathed in a new childhood", "blossoming on a single stock; rising like the dawn/ from the blue waters of oblivion" is a myth of renovation of desolateness into life nourishment—an imaginative identification with the vast germinations that fertilise the earth or the human mind. On the contrary, the myth of Uravashi as described by Tagore in his poem "Uravashi, as an Incarnate Eros", is "neither mother, daughter nor wife." She is the eternal beauty which is now lost in the modern world of falsehood and deceit. The pathos evoked by her unavailability in the world as it is—"*phiribe na phiribe na*", she will not come back, not come back—is not to be found in the epics or the ancient texts. In two other poems, Tagore imagines the beauty of the universe as divided into two separate forces—one represents by Urvashi and the other by Lakshmi, the two fair women who rose in the beginning of time from the churning of God's dream. Urvashi stands for that aspect of beauty which is seen in the flowering frenzy of nature and which, in the shape of a woman, haunts startles and waylays man. Lakshmi, on the other hand, is the spirit of plenty in nature and of motherliness in humanity, leading men not to the bower of passionate tryst but to the temple of the divine love, wealth and prosperity. The archetypal meaning is clear that life consists of these two opposites and true creativity knows how to unite them into one entity to make life a thing of true joy and happiness and contentment.

As myths are symbolic, it has multiple meaningfulness; it is not unilinear but multilinear; it is not a fact but an experience of the self (the microcosm), his culture (mesocosm) and the universe (macrocosm). It is not a thought-out word but an experienced one, the being of the things themselves (Ghose, 19). This experience gives a perspective which is not limited by the personal or historical subjectivity but is fostered by centering and unfolding of the individual in integrity and hence the Indian mythical discourse has a holistic world view. It maintains that human affairs do not become intelligible until they are seen as a whole.

There are instances to highlight the point that Indian mythology seen in totality leads us to the conclusion that no part can truly be appreciated unless the whole is understood, and everything can be appreciated only in the light of human destiny. Just to cite one example about the significance of a myth in India is that the story of the myth entertains as well as instructs. Ego sustains man's separation from the Divine and with this separation being primarily responsible for the human fascination for wrong values, disenchantment with such fascination is an inevitable part of the process of progress.

Dhruva in his previous life was a young aspirant, yet the luxurious life of a prince fascinated him for a while. He was born as a prince only to be disillusioned and to return to the sunlit path of quest with greater determination (Das, 10).

The myth or the *purana* has a self-renewing, eternalising aspect which appeals to the Indian mind. The story within a story or the "chain-tale" is a uniquely Indian form of narration used in the *Mahabharata* which makes the story timeless prototype of human existence. There are stories within stories and the thread of the main story is taken up after many narrations. Sometimes the main story seems almost forgotten or lost, but then it is taken up again which makes the narration move on the level of flux and timelessness. So the stories are primordial and eternal, indefinitely old as well as infinitely new.

In the Indian context, it is the myth-making function of history that underlies its dynamic force in moulding the social life, morality and culture of a people. Accordingly, the mutable man is called *Nara*. The man who develops an urge for some creative action becomes *Narottma*, the superior man—the inhabitant not of one country and age but of all countries and ages, the maker of enduring myths and traditions and the bearer of the ultimate values ever projected towards which the whole creation moves. Then there is man, the deity—the goal towards which the whole creation moves. He is the eternal man, *Narayana*. So Kalhana, the famous Indian historian following the tradition of historiography says that the historian, resembling *Prajapati* (creator) must possess the divine perception of the past (Choudhuri, 113). Tagore by referring to *Ramayana* and *Mahabharata*, in his essay on "The Ramayana" says that they are also history but not the history of actual events, for such a history is limited to a particular period of time, but the history of timeless life of India. Other histories change at time passes; this history has known no change. Within these two vast poetic edifices is enthroned the history of that India strove for, worshipped and purposed.

One cannot deny that the operative sensibility of most of the writers of the world has retained the mythic origin of their historic sense, and as a result the critical idioms developed in literature probe the mythicality of human existence. It has become now all the more necessary because the status of words like "truth" and "reality" has turned out to be problematic. Myth has now been accepted as a meaningful unit of the literary text. Tagore's example is very apt in this respect. He says in his essay "Silent Poet, Untaught Poet"; that it is nonetheless true that on a quite night, moonlight does seem to be asleep. Let them discover every minute scientific fact about the moonlight, let them even demonstrate that it is not a substance at all; people will still say that the moonlight sleeps. Which master scientist will dare call that a lie?'

The next logical question is how this mythic knowledge is communicated? All the important Indian texts whether *Vedas*, *Ramayana*, *Mahabharata* and others were initially narrated in the oral tradition and still orally narrated by the story tellers and *dastagoi* of India in the folk form. *Mahabharata* was narrated first by Vaishampayana, then Ugrashrava Lomaharshini, then Sanjaya but the original teller was Vyasa. *Ramacharit Manas* has three pairs of questioners and responders: Parvati, Garuda and Bharadwaja are the questioners and responders are Shiva, Kaka Bhushandi and Yajnavalkya. These answers are sacred truths as they are "*santan ke vachan*" (words from saints) spoken orally at the four banks of the river. The fourth narrator is Tulsi Das himself who cleverly transposes all the queries of his readers to the story through these three questioners and becomes a part of the oral narrative structure. He uses the authorial voices of Shiva, Kaka Bhushandi and Yajnavalkya for engendering in the listener an ever-deepening understanding of life, death and destiny. These voices elevate the story which is a narration of events of at least one eye-witness, and thus turn history into *purana*.

The Indian narrator of the oral culture describes events for the exteriorization of the worldly process, and therefore selects a vantage point in the time past or the time present or the time future which enables him to frequently change his axis in time as well as space. This mobility gives him a holistic vision; time turns circular for him, and he talks with his total existence which may be described as orchestration of all the senses. On the contrary, written culture is based on a cause and effect phenomenon, has a linear development, and deals primarily with visual symbols. The axis of the Western narratology is in the written text, and fixity is its main characteristic. Vedas are unique in this respect. Initially, it was all oral but at the same time fixity became its main characteristic. In fact, because of auxiliary literature like *Shiksa*, *Nirukta*, *Vyakarana*, *Kalpa*, etc., the Vedas offer an example of the written culture into the oral culture, and because of this infixion it becomes the literature of the power class. Oral is for masses and does not believe in fixity.

Malleability is the characteristic of oral culture. The Indian oral culture takes the help of *itihasa* or *purana* or narratology to explain the Vedic truth. So the *Mahabharata* is the *panchama* Veda. Here you have many different versions, many discrepancies, stories within stories, innumerable legends and episodes, inconsistencies, irregularities but nothing affects the core which remains intact. The core or the nucleus serves as a string holding together numberless legends, episodes, discussions and dialectic portions. Here history changes into *purana*, so one cannot find a unity which one derives out of a cause and effect relationship. The *purana* keeps up its subterranean historical origin, but goes on adding, multiplying and expanding its body, aiming to bring home the archetypal meaning of the enduring totality (Choudhuri, 110-11). So the *Mahabharata* is *itihasa* as well as *purana*.

Now the question is what the relationship between the oral and the written is? Are they binary opposites? Is there tension between them? Is the written privileged or placed in status in a hierarchical order? The moment we address these seemingly simple questions, a complex field opens up.

Both oral and written become the basis to serve as instruments of communication and dialogue between different levels of society and across regions but it would be fallacious, however, as explained by A.K. Ramanujan, to assume a notion of linear development between the written and the oral or classical and folk. It is more profitable to imagine a history of texts that is made up of written and oral forms contained within cycles of transmission that move up and down through time resulting in manifold possible recompositions within a "simultaneous order" of texts (Ramanujan, 187-216).

Aditya Malik reiterates the "simultaneous order" of oral and written tradition and says that oral tradition in Indian context is not restricted to folk tradition and folklore. While folklore and folk narratives are indeed recited, spoken, sung and performed—orality itself is not confined to folk traditions. In fact, in classical and Sanskrit traditions, one finds a prevalence of the oral word, in spoken and sung form, both in an epistemological sense—sound as vibration (*nada*) carries knowledge and metaphysical meaning as well as ritual efficacy (*mantra*)—and in a per formative sense. Many Sanskrit texts, for example, *Puranas* and *Mahatmyas*, use narrative framing devices that involve a speaker and an audience in dialogue with one another. Even more so, several important Hindu religious texts such as the *Rigveda* and the two great epics, the *Mahabharata* and *Ramayana*, are not only orally recited and transmitted for millennia, but once written, as is the case with the latter two texts, continued to show signs of having originated out of a possibly oral "core" that coalesced into their current written form...(Malik). Kapila Vatsyayan by referring to Amartya Sen and also taking the cue from a sloka of the *Mundakopanishad* speaks of the two birds on the same branch as the "experience" (*bhokta*) and the "seer" (*drasta)*—and one cannot live without the other (*Mundakopanisad*, 3.1.1) and then rounds up the issue by stating that the oral and the written are like two birds on the same branch: if the oral is sacred, so also is the written word. Let me quote what did she actually say, "May I draw attention to Nobel Laureate Amartya Sen's book *Argumentative Indian*? He has delved into the primary sources and other dialogical traditions. However, most humbly, may I say, these dialogues were also oral! This is quite nearly a case of considering *shruti* the word heard as primary and the *smriti* the word written as secondary. The oral and the written are two birds on the same branch: if the oral is sacred, so also is the written word" (24-26).

It is not easy to draw a line between myths on the one hand and legends, folklore and facts of a remote past on the other. The primordial roots still visible in the oral tradition and folklores have been vital in the growth of the corpus of Indian myth and ritual.

Folk in the Indian context is *loka* and the *loka* and *shastra* (folk and elite) contrast is contrary to the Western contrast between great and little Tradition. India does not believe that non-literate cultures are "Knowledge blanks" which need to be filled in with the modern knowledge of different discipline and dominant cultures. A.K. Coomaraswamy, who many decades ago had written a seminal article "The Bugbear of Literacy", speaks not against literacy but instead that elementary or functional literacy cannot be considered sole criteria for evaluating the total human potentials (10). The argument holds good even today.

Cultures are never "blanks". In some matters, e.g. in the ecological management practices used by tribals are far superior to anything we could teach them. The tragedy is that modernism has imposed a single perspective in dealing with human culture and today this kind of fixed perspective is challenged by the indeterminacy of experience. The search for the one truth in the many is at odds with the relativist experience of anthropology (Choudhuri, 196).

In reality, traditional Indian mind thinks that *loka* or *desi* and *sastra* or *margi* contrast represents two different expressions of the same tradition and not of different tradition.

These folk literary approaches are not liquidated or co-opted by core literary tradition but assimilated as alternative models of human expressions or as parts of the whole (Choudhuri, 196-97).

In this way, classical Sanskrit literature describes, on one side, the core regions, Dakshina-patha, Kuru-Panchala, Madhyadesa, Gandhara and on the other peripheries like

Naga, Shabara, Dasa and Kirata to share the making of Indian literature.

The main narrative viewpoint of Indian literature consists of a classical core trinity. But there is no denial of the fact that the periphery in Indian literature is very vital and hence in Banabhatta's *Kadambari* or Bharavi's *Kiratarjuniam*, the periphery always comes and speaks in classical texts. For example, in classical literature, Shiva appears as *Shabara* in *Kiratarjuniam.* Bana has a Chandala girl as an important character woven in his story. Similarly, the modern writers use folk extensively in explaining the modern predicaments (Choudhuri, 83).

The focus of classical regional trinity was to create something vital with the help of the periphery, and in the process, both the geographical region and the social sense were brought into focus, but by keeping it outside the framework of the caste system in society. These two literary expressions of core and periphery are always taken together in Indian literary context but of course not as a monolithic unity but as diverse structures complementing each other. Tagore by quoting a *baul* song explains that the distinction and unity are complementary to each other. A school of Vedanta philosophy which admits the truth of what is known as the principle of *bhedabheda* to indicate a belief that *bheda* or "distinction"; and *abheda* or "unity" can co-exist and be in intimate relation with each other. Substance and attribute, universal and particular, whole and parts, joys and sorrows may seem to be different from, or even opposed to, each other, but really there is no incompatibility between them, for they can be reconciled in a unity which pervades the difference and is its very being. "Our joys and sorrows are contradictory", as says Tagore in "An Indian Folk Religion" when self separates them in opposition. But for the heart in which self merges in God's love, they lose their absoluteness. He explains this by quoting a *baul* song:

> I am the boat; you are the sea, and also the boatman,
>
> Though you never make the shore, though you let me sink, why should I be foolish and afraid?

> Is the reaching the shore a greater prize than loosing myself with you?
>
> If you are only the heaven, as they say, then what is the sea?
>
> I lie in you, whatever and however you appear.
>
> Save me or kill me as you wish, only never leave me in other's hands. (*Hiriyanna*, 95-96)

Orality or folk is never marginalized in India. It is always an alternative tradition and alternative is not to be understood as "the opposite". If you want to draw a white line, you need a black or grey or any dark colour background, so it is a mistake to say white is the opposite of black or grey or blue. We have to make use of black or grey or any dark colour to bring out white in all its distinction.

Here in India the glory of "mainstream" literature rests not by marginalizing but by accepting oral or folk as complementary. In the folk stories of the marriage of Shiva and Parvati, the words of praise for Shiva are *shastra* oriented but the words of praise for Parvati who is the mother of the universe, are folk in content.

Similarly, the notion of Shakti *puja* belonging to Anga, Banga, Kalinga and Kamboja regions gets absorbed into the Puritanical Brahminical orthodoxy of the classical core regions which felt psychologically assured to relate itself with Tantric Hinduism. These are examples of many such contacts between the classical creative mind and the culture of excluded peoples and classes.

To give another example of such contacts is the loom of a weaver or the wheel of a potter which are used to explain many intricate literary and philosophical theories. This process of socio-cultural interaction is a dominating factor in India's literary scene that swept all the regions, and with the passage of time, created different important literary movements including the *bhakti* movement, which fostered a sense of identity in the use of languages and cultural specificities, and the historical functioning in the context of the community. But, at the same time, the pan-Indianness of the content structure of *bhakti* once again established the fact that the unitary vision of art and literature consisted of profound speculations contained in the systems of Sankhya, Vedanta, and Yoga philosophy and transformed into the living harvest of the people's literature. In this way, *loka* and *shastra* were merged together to reveal the essence of Indian philosophical discourse.

In Indian context, oral, tribal or folklore are neither the residue of the past, nor the behaviour of the uncivilized but it is the continuity of a rich culture and also a process of making the present more life worthy and along with *shastra* it gives a complete picture of Indian culture and thought.

Abanindranath Tagore came also to regard the folk arts and village crafts as the finest repositories of Indian tradition.

It was a conscious attempt to appropriate the popular in a sanitized, idealized form within the scope of the reconstructed tradition—to create for Indian art both the legacy of a classical past and the pride of an uncorrupted living tradition.

Works Cited

Arora, U.P. *Motifs in Indian Mythology, Their Greek and Other Parallels*. New Delhi: Indika Publication House, 1981.

Aurobindo, Sri. *On the Veda*. Pondicharry: Sri Aurobindo Ashram Publication Department, 1997.

Baynes. *Mythology of the Soul*. New York: Publication Rider, 1969.

Choudhuri, Indra Nath. "Indian Narratology", *Comparative Indian Literature: Some Perspectives*. New York: Sterling Publishers, 1992.

Choudhuri, Indra Nath. *Traditions of Folk in Literature, Folklore and the Alternative Modernities*, (ed.) Nandini Sahu, New Delhi: Author Press, 2012.

Choudhari, Indra Nath. "The Concept of Regionality in the Indian Literary Context", *The Genesis of Imagination*. New Delhi: Sterling Publication, 2001.

Coomaraswamy, A.K. *The Bugbear of Literacy, Middlesex*, Permanent Books, 1979.

Das, S.K. and Chaudhuri, Sukanta. (ed.), *Selected Writings on Literature and Languages: Rabindranath Tagore*, OUP India, Oxford India Paperbacks, 2001.

Das, Manoj. *Myths, Legends, Concepts and Literary Antiquities of India*. New Delhi: Sahitya Akademi, 2009.

Eliade, Mircea. *Myth and Reality*, Waveland Press, 1998.

Ghose, Sisir Kumar. "Myth: Old and New", *Lost Dimensions*.

Hiriyanna, M. *Indian Philosophical Studies*, Kavyalaya Publishers, 1972.

Kermode, Frank. *Mystical Intentions in Modern Literature Introduction* Trans. by Eric Gould, Princeton University Press, 1981.

Malik, Aditya. *Oral Traditions and Folklore*. Koninklijke Brill NY, Leiden, 2010.

Ramanujan, A.K. *Where Mirrors are Windows: Towards an Anthology of Reflections*, Oxford University Press, 1989.

Ransom, John Crowe. *God Without Thunder: An Orthodox Defence of Orthodoxy*. Archon Books, 1965.

Strauss, Levi. *The Raw and the Cooked*, Penguin Publication, 1992.

Tagore, Rabindranath. "The Religion of the Forest", *Creative Unity, The English Writings of Rabindranath Tagore*, Vol. 2, Sahitya Akademi.

The statement by Jung is referred to by Sisir Kumar Ghose, Lost *Dimension*, 18.

"Two friendly birds are sitting together on the same tree. One (who is the bhokta or experience) is tasting the fruit and the other (who is only a drasta, seer) only beholds without eating." *Mundakopanisad*, 3.1.1.

Vatsyayan, Kapila. Paper on "Pluralism and Diversity in South Asia", Presented in the SACEPS World Conference on "South Asia: Democracy, Sustainable Development and Peace", New Delhi, February 2011.

2

Tagore's Use of Myth, Orality and Folklore

Mohit K. Ray

Myths are as old as human civilization. They belong to the oral tradition and have strong potential for emotional impact. There is so much power and life in the myths that they have easily survived the onslaughts of time. A myth, according to Roland Barthes, "is not defined by the object of its message, but by the way in which it utters this message" (*Mythologies*, 109). During the Renaissance, myths were seen as symbolic representations of profound truth and in the twentieth century modernist writers started using myth as a trope to impose significance on their writings. Eliot draws on fertility myths, Yeats draws on the Celtic myths and Pound draws on Odysseus myths.

Tagore was brought up in an atmosphere which was thick with interactions of Indian and global myths. Although Tagore draws mainly on Indian classical myths, the 'myriad-minded' poet never remained confined to one particular storehouse of myths. His use of myth, orality and folklore is pervasive. Steeped as he was in the rich literary tradition of both India and Europe his writings register creative use of both indigenous and global myths and his imaginative re-creations of them register the assimilation, adaptation, celebration, interrogation, and creative rewriting of the ancient myths and folklore. With the alchemy of his genius he assimilates them into the matrix of his verbal artifacts and alerts us about their contemporaneity, combining "a sense of the timeless as well as the temporal and of the timeless and of the temporal together" (Eliot).

Even a cursory look at the writings of Tagore shows how abundant and varied is his use of the legends of the *Mahabharata*, the *Ramayana*, gods of the Hindu pantheon in their different forms and roles—Lord Shiva, Nataraja, Krishna, Kali, Lakshmi, Saraswati, Ganesha, Kubera and others—legends of Buddha and Christ, universal myths of journey motifs, the child-voyager, etc.

Tagore's use of myths is so masterly that the texts resonate with rich evocations and associations of familiar popular memory of myths and tales, stirring nostalgia for a lost world of the past, lending to the richness of meanings and suggestions. The myths as used by Tagore are at the same time as much organically functional as they are aesthetically decorative.

With equal felicity Tagore draws on Indian folklores and fairy tales, and his admiration for folk literature is evident not only in the way he draws on it in his poems, songs and plays, but also in the book of insightful essays entitled *Lokasāhitya* or folk literature and village literature. His imaginative recreations of them highlight their contemporary relevancc.

Let us start with Tagore's use of the *Ramayana*. Of the many references to the *Ramayana* that are scattered over the entire gamut of his writings we can just pick up two to see the point. Take for example, the play *Raktakarabī* (*Red Oleanders*). In the Prologue to the play, Tagore refers to the *Ramayana* myth and suggests that the play *Raktakarabī* re-enacts what Tagore considers the essence of the *Ramayana* myth: the conflict between the evils of mindless materialism and the human values of agriculture. He believes that Rama with Sita represent the agricultural civilization while Ravana and his *raksasas* stand for possessive materialism. The problem is as topical today as it was in the age of the *Ramayana*. Here Tagore reinterprets the myth to define a contemporary situation.

To take another example, let us consider the poem, "Bane o Rājye" (In the forest and in the kingdom. *RR* 1:550). In the

Ramayana, there is a reference to *svarnasīta* (the golden Sita). The passage runs like this:

> Hrdi krtvā tadā sītamayodhyām prabibesa ha/Istayajno narapatih putradvayasamanvitah/Na sītāyāh param bhāryām babre sa raghunandana/ Yajne yajne ca patnyartham janakīkancanibhavat. (Uttarakānda, Canto 99, verses 7-8)

[After the *yajna* Rama entered Ayodhya, engrossed in the thought of Sita along with his two sons, and started living there. Although Sita was not there, Raghunandana did not marry a second time. At the time of *yajna* whenever there was any need for the ritualistically married wife he used to get an image of Sita made in gold.]

In the *Ramayana,* the golden Sita is a material object and is meant to serve a material need only. But in Tagore's poem, the golden image of Sita is used to reflect the personal tragedy of Rama, his loneliness which he silently carries in his heart. In Tagore, in other words, the golden Sita is no material object but a metaphor. As in the case of the *Ramayana* so in the case of the *Mahabharata.* And this is most drastic and radical in his treatment of the Karna myth. Let us first see how the character of Karna is depicted in the original *Mahabharata.* In the *Sabha Parva,* which includes the harassment of Draupadi after Yudhisthira has lost everything including Draupadi in the game of dice, the title to Draupadi goes to the Kauravas. Drunk with pride and arrogance, they drag Draupadi to the court and want to strip her naked in public to spite the Pandavas. The scene acts as an objective correlative to reveal the true colour of the characters involved. In course of the proceedings when Duryodhana bares his thighs and makes obscene gestures to Draupadi in the presence of all the dignitaries as Dushasana is about to strip her naked, we find Karna enjoying the harassment of Draupadi. He keeps on smiling in approval of the act in wild glee. The relevant aspect of the image of Karna that we get in the *Mahabharata* is that he is a great hero, a valorous warrior but extremely proud and arrogant and a vainglorious braggart.

In the thirty-seventh chapter of the section on *Karna Parvva* [the Book of Karna] Karna says: "Let Dhananjaya behold today the might of my arms, when I will be shooting shafts winged with *Kanaka* feathers in hundreds of thousands. Today O Salya, I shall shoot shafts with great energy for the destruction of the Pandavas and the victory of Duryodhana with my physical prowess" (*PCR*, 98). Not only that. He says: "If Yama, Varuna, Kubera and Vasava, with all their followers coming hither, unitedly protect the son of Pandu [Arjuna] in this great battle, what need of many words, I will still vanquish him with them" (*PCR*, 101).

About Karna, Krisna tells Arjuna: "Towards the Pandavas he is always of wicked soul and sinful behaviour, and cruel and of wicked intelligence.... That Suta's son of wicked soul, from exceeding pride, always disregards the sons of Pandu" (*PCR*, 208). And Krishna goes on to say that Karna is at the root of all the atrocities done by Duryodhana to the Pandavas. It was he who was behind Duryodhan's attempt to burn the Pandavas to death. It was he, again, who was behind the game of dice which caused untold miseries to the Pandavas. In brief, whatever tortures Duryodhana had inflicted on the Pandavas, were at the instigation of Karna. And later when the wheel of Karna's chariot gets stuck into the ground and he asks to be given time to lift it, on the ground of righteousness Krishna sharply retorts that he is not fit to ask for anything on religious ground; he has, in fact, forfeited his claim to religious concession, because all along he has committed sacrilegious things. Krisna then narrates atrocities one by one and puts Karna to shame. Krisna tells Karna:

> By good luck it is, O son of Radha, that thou remembers virtue! It is generally seen that they that are mean, when they sink into distress, rail at Providence but never at their own misdeeds. Thyself and Suyodhana and Dushasana and Sakuni, the son of Suvala, had caused Draupadi, clad in a single piece of raiment, to be brought into the midst of the assembly. On that occasion, O Karna, this virtue of thine did not manifest itself. When at the assembly, Sakuni, an adept in dice,

vanquished Kunti's son Yudhisthira who was unacquainted with it, whither had this virtue gone? When the Kuru king (Duryodhana), acting under thy counsels, treated Bhimasena in that way with the aid of snakes and poisoned food, whither of this virtue of thine gone? When the period of exile into the woods was over as also the thirteenth year, thou didst not make over to the Pandavas their kingdom. Whither had this virtue of thine then gone? Thou didst set fire to the house of lac at Varanavata for burning to death the sleeping Pandavas. Whither then, O son of Radha, had this virtue of thine gone? Thou laughedst at Krishna (Draupadi) while she stood in the midst of the assembly, scantily dressed because in her season and obedient to Dushasana's will, whither, then, O Karna, had this virtue of thine gone? When from the apartment reserved for the females innocent Krishna (Draupadi) was dragged thou didst not interfere. Whither O son of Radha, had this virtue of thine gone? Thyself addressing the princess Draupadi, that lady whose tread is as dignified as that of the elephant, in these words, *viz.* "The pandavas, O Krishna, are lost. They have sunk into the eternal hell. Do thou choose another husband!" thou lookedst on the scene with delight. Whither thou, O Kana, had this virtue of thine gone? Covetous of kingdom and relying on the ruler of the Gandharvas, thou summonedst the Pandavas (to a match at dice). Whither then had this virtue of thine gone? When many mighty car-warriors, encompassing the boy Abhimanyu in battle slew him, whither had this virtue of thine gone? If this virtue that thou invokest was nowhere on those occasions, what is the use then of parching thy palate now by uttering that word? Thou art now for the practice of virtue, but thou shalt not escape with life..." (*PCR*, 277-78). On hearing these Karna "hung down his head in shame and gave no answer" (*PCR*, 278).

In sharp contrast to this image of Karna as a wicked, deceitful, cruel, scheming, boorish "villain", Tagore presents

Karna in the long dialogic poem, "Karnakuntisamvād" (*Sañcayitā,* 395-403) as a very dignified and noble person, hungering for the love and affection of his mother whom he had never seen before and extremely loyal to his duties as a hero and a general of Duryodhana. He resists all the temptations of victory, fame and kingdoın and the royal status for the sake of the religion of a hero. In the concluding lines of this dialogic poem, he accepts his fate stoically and prays to his mother, "Before you leave just bless me that I should never fall from the rightful fate of a hero by succumbing to the temptations of victory, fame or kingdom".

In recreating the Karna myth, Tagore possibly draws on Bankimchandra's assessment of Karna in *Krisna Karnasaṃvād*. In chapter eight of *Krisnacaritra* Krisna talks privately to Karna and tells him almost everything that Kunti tells him in *Karnakuntisamvād*, and there, too, Karna resists all the temptations and Bankimchandra concludes: "*Karnacaritra ati mahat o manohar*" (The character of Karna is very great and beautiful). (*Bankim Racanāvalī* [*Collected Works of Bankomchandra*] Vol. 2, p. 486).

The image that Tagore constructs is a re-creation of the Karna myth as he tries to present him as a very pious person and a noble man full of tender human sentiments, although abandoned by his mother at birth and suffering ignominy at every stage of his life. He becomes an embodiment of Renaissance humanism, a tragic hero, a fallen angel, and "more sinned against than sinning". In other words, Tagore's recreation of the Karna myth may be seen to be in keeping with the *zeitgeist,* as an aspect of Bengal Renaissance. Incidentally, Peter Brook in his *Mahabharata* film draws on the image constructed by Tagore.

Tagore uses the source materials from the *Mahabharata* in many of his poems; "Gāndhārir Ābedan" (The Appeal of Gandhari, *Sañcayitā,* 375-95), "Bidāy Abhiśāp" (Curse at Parting, *Sañcayitā,* 201-13), etc. and everywhere the myth is recreated in the light of Renaissance ideal of humanism and human values. In "Gāndhārir Ābedan", Gandhari appeals to Dhrtaraāstra to control, and if possible, reject, Duryodhana and prevent the impending war. It is painful to reject one's son, but she argues in the spirit of Renaissance humanism that the highest form of justice demands that the person who punishes suffers equally with the person who is punished: *Danditer sāthe/Dandadātā kā̃de yabe samān āghā te/Sarvaśresṭha se vicār*).

In "Bidāy Abhiśāp", the dialogue between Kaca and Devayani focuses on the human weaknesses of Kaca who comes from heaven to receive some particular lessons from the father of Devayani and falls in love with her and evokes the feelings of love in her. At the time of parting when Kaca disowns his love and refuses to marry Devayani she lashes out at him and brings out the hypocritical elements in his character. She says:

> Don't you know that love is aware of the other's mind? A fully bloomed flower remains hidden in the foliage, but how can it hide its fragrance? Many a day whenever you lifted up your face, looked at me, heard my voice your whole frame spelt the throb of your heart—as at the slightest movement a diamond radiates its scintillating light. Haven't I seen it? You are caught; you are, therefore my captive. (*Sañcayitā,* 209).

Then she curses him before he goes back to heaven from where he came. In the re-creation of the myth, the departures from the *Mahabharata* are many the most important of which is the repeated assassination of Kaca by the demons and his revival by Shukracharya, Devayani's father. Tagore leaves out all the elaborate details of the episode and focuses on the human relationship, or more precisely, the human relationship between Kaca and Devayani and the psychological complexities of the relationship. A dull, uninteresting and largely unconvincing story suddenly comes to life with Tagore's recreation and reinterpretation of the myth.

There are many other uses of the *Mahabharata* in Tagore's works; there is neither space nor necessity to discuss them in detail. Suffice it to say that in every instance Tagore leaves the indelible mark of his genius by recreating them and reinterpreting them by an effective use of the symbolic mode.

In the same way, myths related to the various deities of the Hindu pantheon are recreated in terms of modern sensibility. Take for example Lord Shiva, the Hindu God of destruction. Shiva is also *Natarāj*, the great dancer. Tagore equates the rapturous dance of Shiva to the cosmic dance, the dance of the celestial bodies in a beautiful song, the rhythm and sound pattern of which replicate the dance of Shiva which it describes. Even the cycle of seasons is seen to keep up the rhythm of the dance of Shiva. Sometimes, again, Tagore presents Shiva as an ascetic engrossed in meditation. In "Sannyāsi" (The Ascetic, *RR* 3: 303-04), this asceticism is seen as a preparation for the purity of love, love purged of all dross through purgatorial fire. Sometimes, Tagore would invoke the stern spirit of Shiva, known as his Rudra image for strength and ability to burn everything that is mean and nasty. There are innumerable references to Shiva in Tagore and different uses of the image only show that for Tagore the traditional myth of Shiva is only the starting point that triggers off his imagination and helps him luxuriate in creating, recreating and reinterpreting the image to adapt the myth to modern sensibility.

Another important deity of the Hindu pantheon is Krisna [*krsna*], and the pan-Indian culture is suffused with cult of Krisna in various forms of which his image as the romantic lover of Brindaban is possibly most popular. Sometimes again he is seen differently as a solace to the suffering multitude, a shrewd diplomat, the charioteer of Arjuna, and sometimes again a symbol of peaceful death. In *Bhānusimher Padāvalī*, written when Tagore was just about twenty-one years old, he evokes the romantic relationship between Radha and Krisna. In one of the poems written in the style of the Vaishnab verses of medieval Bengal the love-lorn Radha wants to embrace death, because death to her is as beautiful as Shyama (Krisna), and she believes that death will remove all her agonies and give her peace. Death will offer deathlessness. She addresses death as Shyāma (pronounced as *śyama*); "Shyāma tohāri nāma" (Shyama is thy name only). This is a very significant departure from the mythical image of Krisna. The departure elevates the poem to a transcendental level and Krisna becomes a metaphor suffused with enormous symbolic suggestions. He gives similar symbolic significance to the flute of Krisna, to the image of Krisna as a shepherd boy playing on a pipe. The entire world is a flute which is played on by the Supreme Being, the Beauty incarnate. The call of the flute creates a feeling of nostalgia, the ecstasy of separation and the eternal longing for union with the beloved. The simple mythical image of Krisna is transformed into a rich universal symbol of magnificent dimension of multiple perspectives.

Other mythical deities are also treated similarly. The goddess Kali becomes the metaphor for the motherland, Saraswati becomes the symbol of divine inspiration, Lakshmi becomes a symbol of the spirit of aesthetic beauty, grace and the wealth of the mind, and also the spirit of vitality as Urvashi (pronounced as *urvaśī*) is used as a symbol of erotic beauty and pleasure. Furthermore, in the poem "Urvashi" Tagore luxuriates in describing the physical charm of Urvashi and depicts her as a celestial "la belle dame sans merci". Nevertheless, she is also a tormented soul. In a fine expression of modern feminist sensibility, Urvashi tells Arjuna in the poem "Nāṭ āka" (*RR*, 3:7-9) that she does not like heaven because the gods are devoid of any desire and her real fulfillment consists in her being desired, and she, therefore, asks Arjuna to greet her with his desire: "You welcome me with your desire and the nectarean tears which one cannot find in heaven. Tagore in fact interrogates and modernizes the very mythical concept of heaven as an ideal abode. In the poem "Amartya" (Unearthly, *RR*, 3:555-56), Tagore says that he has no desire to go to heaven (*Āmār mane ekṭuo nei baikunṭher āśā// Aikhāne mor bāsā/ye māṭite śiure uthe ghās,* [I don't have the least intention to go to heaven.], and explains why: he is fascinated by the beauty of the earth in its multifarious forms. In "Svarga hate vidāy" (Farewell to Heaven, *RR*, 1:512-15), the persona feels unhappy that there is no touch of sorrow in the denizens of heaven at his departure from heaven. He resents their impervious indifference. He prefers the earth, because, he realizes, and that he is a stranger to heaven while he is a son of the earth: "The earth is not heaven; it is motherland. That is why if somebody leaves even for two minutes after staying for two days the earth weeps". This reminds one of Goethe's poems "Prometheus" where Prometheus says that that there is no reason for him to honour Zeus: "I honour you? What for? Have you ever soothed my pains when I was heavy laden? Have you ever dried my tears when I was frightened?" In contrast to the cold, pitiless heaven Tagore's earth is human.

Tagore recreates the myth of the earth by giving it human attributes and by seeing it as an affectionate, helpless mother. In one of his letters Tagore presents earth as a distressed mother reflecting; "A daughter of the gods though I am, I do not have the powers of a god. I love, but I cannot protect. I begin, but I cannot complete. I give birth I cannot save them from the hands of death" (Chinnapatra, N. 18. Visva Bharati 1319, BS). Tagore's deep attachment to earth and his love for the beauty of earth manifested in the sights and sounds of nature go a long way in accounting for his recreation of the myth. The myth of earth has some affinity with the Greek Demeter myth, but the essential difference lies in Tagore's humanization of the earth. One can discover similar echoes of many other Greek myths such as charon, an old man of formidable and squalid appearance, who, recreated, becomes for Tagore *jīvandevatā* or the presiding deity of his life, and the river is sometimes seen as the symbol of life, sometimes again it is seen as marking the frontier line between life and death. Incidentally, the image of the boatman which abounds in the writings of Tagore fits squarely with the cultural ethos of Bengal which is a land of rivers where the boatmen occupy an important position, and boatmen's songs constitute a significant body of Bengali folklore. Tagore's symbolic use of the boatman thus evokes the folklores of Bengal. Not only that. Transcending the folklore tradition Tagore sometimes looks upon the boatman metaphorically as the boatman for the stream of his life. In the poem No. 140 "Ore mājhi,/ ore āmār mānabjanamtaritr mājhi,/ Śunte ki pās dūrer theke/ Pārer bā̃nśī utche bāji" (*RR*, 2:303) [Oh boatman, Oh the boatman of the boat of my human life, do you hear the call of the flute coming from afar?] Or, "I must launch out my boat. The languid hours pass by on the shore—Alas for me" (English *Gitanjali* Song No. 21). Sometimes, again, almost echoing Tennyson's "Crossing the Bar" he would say: "The ocean of peace is lying in front of me. Please put out the boat, Oh my boatman" (*RR*, 3:895). The boat becomes a simple symbol of transport, a vehicle to ferry between life and death: "Who are you Oh the boatman who always ferry between two shores! (*RR*, 2:212).

In mythology the king is an archetypal figure, a vibrant and formidable image of regality, royal grandeur, power and mystery. In the Western mythology, the king is the supreme power of the land; he is God's representative on earth, and God is the king of heaven, the king of all kings. Tagore modernizes the myth when in addition to the traditional attributes of the archetypal king, variously used in *The Post Office, The King of the Dark Chamber* and *Phalgunī* Tagore looks upon God as the king who gives unity to the whole universe and is a perennial source of infinite joy and has given a flute,—the musical talent—to play his tune. Sometimes, paradoxically, he would address God as "duhkhrāter rājā" [King of the Doleful Night]. But the paradox is solved when we realize that in Tagore's vision of life sorrows and sufferings only humanize the soul and draw out the essential goodness and the pristine purity of a person and, in the process bring one closer to God. It is a kind of purgatorial fire through which one must pass through before reaching paradise: "Unless you burn the incense stick it does not emit fragrance; unless the burn the lamp it never emits light" (*RR*, 4:75). Needless to say, both the incense stick and the lamp are metaphors for persona of the poem, presumably the poet himself. At another point Tagore says, "When we see sorrow in the light of the fullness of truth, we see it not as sorrow but only as a form of joy" (*RR*, 11:526).

Let alone the divinities and the king, Tagore's treatment of historical personalities who have acquired a mythical halo about them over the centuries is also marked by modern sensibility. His treatment of Christ spread over a number of essays and poems is marked not by any ecclesiastical or Episcopal or conventional Christian approach but by broad humanism of which he sees Christ as a significant exponent. In the fairly long poem, "The Child" (*EWT*, 1:477-85), possibly the only poem which was originally written in English and subsequently translated into Bengali Tagore describes in detail a pilgrimage by all kinds of people to Bethlehem where the "mother is seated on a straw bed with the child on her lap". The journey as described by Tagore is very different from Eliot's poetic account of the journey in "The Journey of the Magi". In Tagore's poem we come across all kinds of people, where "[m]en begin to gather from all quarters,/ from across the seas, the mountains and pathless wastes,..." (*EWT*, 1:479), including "the dissolute, the thief and the man who makes a trade of his God for profit and mimics the saint" (*EWT*, 1:480). Obviously, Tagore uses the Christ myth as a literary trope to give us a transcript of the contemporary social scenario and malaise of the modern world, and thus makes a significant departure from the traditional accounts of the journey of the magi with his unequivocal emphasis on humanism and with his clarion call: "Victory to Man" (*EWT*, 1:485). In the poem, "Mānabaputra" (Son of Man, *RR*, 3:93). Tagore recreates the Christ myth in the context of violence and hypocrisy rampant in the world today. In this poem, Christ is made to realize that his job is not yet over. Those who killed him have now gathered at the precincts of temples and inciting people from the temple altars to violence: Those who killed him that day standing in the shade of the religious temple, are born again in numbers and they are calling the killer soldiers in the tone of chanting incantations of worship and telling them, "Kill them, kill". In his several writings on Christ—"Yīśucarit" (The Character of Jesus), "Khrstotsab" (Christ Festival), "*Mānabsambandher Devatā*" (God of Human Relationship), "Badodin" (Christmas). "Khrstaprasanga" (Observations on Christ), Tagore's emphasis is invariably on humanism, and he draws parallels between the teachings of Christ and the teachings of the Upanishads. For example, he says: "Humanism of man does not consist in the grandeur of the empire or in the practice of rituals. But the truth that God is manifested through man makes him true (*RR*, 11:508). Again, "In the Vedas one name of God is '*ābih*'; that is manifestation is his nature. He has expressed himself through his creation, and that is religion". And again, "Through his birth as man Christ has established that God and man are one" (*RR*, 11:517). And again, "Those who are great among men stand on equal footing with all men at a point where a communication is established between their souls and the cosmic soul of the all pervasive, the Supreme Being" (*RR*, 11:524). In brief, Tagore recreates the myth of Christ, contextualizes it to the modern world and assimilates it into his own philosophy of life.

He believes that we all are children of God (*amrtasya putrāh*). This leads to the idea of unity of man. He believes in the Greek notion, *hen kai pen* (One and the Many) which is echoed in the Upanishadic idea of *ekoham bahusyām* (I am One, I shall be Many), and the Roman idea of *omne ens unum* (All in One). Thus, all human beings are manifestations of the Supreme. The individual self, the narrow self who is confined to the body always longs for union with the universal self, the Supreme Being. This becomes possible only when the individual man comes out of the cell of his narrow self.

The same approach marks his recreation of the Buddha myth. In "Buddhadev" (*RR*, 11:469-73), Tagore invokes the spirit of Buddha certainly as a voice of protest against violence, greed, material ambition and all kinds of meanness, but more importantly as an exponent of the truth, humanism and the unity of man. Tagore presents Buddha as a complete man, the universal man who realizes his unity with all men of all time across space and culture and whose consciousness is not fragmented by limitations of nation, culture, space and time. Tagore says that the real manifestation of man consists in truth, and he goes on to say that according to the Upanishad "one who sees himself reflected in every creature, is the one who actually sees": "Ātmavat sarvabhūtesu ya paśyati sa paśyati". Through his reinterpretation of Buddha, Tagore reaffirms his philosophy of the unity of man and the universality of mind.

Tagore's explorations of myth, however, are not confined to divinities, religious teachers or historical personalities. Sometimes he would even mythicize a character dear to his heart. The case of Kalidasa is an example. Kalidasa is a major influence on Tagore's romanticism, an influence that he assimilated into his blood stream, and naturally Kalidasa figures repeatedly in the poetry of Tagore. Sometimes Tagore would try to recreate the romantic atmosphere of Kalidasa's poetry as in "Svapna" (Dream, *RR*, 699-701) and imagine himself as a character of that time; sometimes, as in "Kālidaser Prati" (To Kalidasa, *RR*, 1:578.) He would treat him as a god, a denizen of Alaka in heaven, the archetypal poet, and who accompanies the dance of Shiva with his song, and pleased with his song Gauri would decorate him with her ornaments. Sometimes again, as in "Kumārasambhavagān" (The Song of Kumārasambhava, *RR*, 1:579) he would imagine Kalidasa singing the story of Kumārasambhava to the divine couple (Shiva and Uma). Sometimes, again, as in "Mānasaloka (The World of the Mind, *RR*, 1:579) he would imagine Kalidasa as the personal poet of Lord Shiva, on the peak of the mountain, Kailas: "In the solitary world of the peak of Mānasakailās you were the private poet of Lord Shiva in the courtyard of his temple".

Although Tagore made an extensive use of classical and medieval myths, he was not an escapist. There is no reason to believe that he had lost touch with the contemporary reality. On the contrary, his antennae were always out to register every movement that took place in the intellectual, cultural, religious and social spheres of his time. His use of the legends and folklores of Punjab, Rajasthan and Maharashtra may be regarded as his contribution to cultural nationalism. "Bandī Bīr" (The Captive Hero, *RR*, 1:646-49). "Prārthanātita Dān" (Gift Exceeding the Prayer, *RR*, 1:652), and "Śes Śiksā" (The Last Lesson, *RR*, 1:657-60) are some of the dialogic narrative poems drawn on the legends and folklores of Punjab celebrating the moral courage and outstanding heroism of the Sikhs. Similarly, "Nakal Gad" (The Artificial Fort, *RR*, 1:661-62), "Horikhelā" [The Play of Colours, *RR*, 662-65], "Bibāha"

(The Marriage, *RR,* 1:666-68) highlighting glorious tales of bravery are drawn on the legends and folktales of Rajasthan. Again, the legends and folktales of Maharashtra which have always been popular in Bengal are poetically evoked by Tagore in many poems of which particularly notable are "Pratinidhī" (Representative, *RR,* 1:665), "Bicārak" (The Judge, *RR,* 667) and "Sibājī Utsav" (Shivaji Festival, *RR,* 3:917-21). Tagore's references to the heroes and their valorization in the colonial context prevailing at that time reminds one of Yeats's spirit of nationalism and his celebration of the heroes like Cuchulian, Fergus and Diamond.

Sometimes Tagore would revive old legends and folklore and reformat them to reflect on the social malaise and mobilize public opinion against the narrow superstitions and bigotry. Some such poems are: "Śuci" (Purity, *RR,* 3:75-77), "Premer Sonā" (Gold of Love, *RR,* 3:80-81), "Snān Samāpan" (End of Bath, *RR,* 3:82-83), "Pratham Pūjā" (First Worship, *RR,* 3:83-87) where Tagore uses the medieval legends of Ramananda, Kabir, Rabidas and others to argue against untouchability, an old social malaise and pleads for humanistic values, to treat man as an independent of caste, colour and creed. The theme of untouchability is treated elaborately in "Chandalika" (pronounced as "Canḍālikā") [*RR,* 6:1130-58] a fine dance drama based on a Buddhist legend. In fact, Tagore, a great admirer of Buddha has written quite a few poems and plays using Buddhist legends. Some of these are: "Abhisār" (A Secret Journey to Meet One's Beloved, *RR,* 1:626-28), "Pūjārinī" (The Female Worshipper, *RR,* 1: 623-25), "Śrestha Bhiksā" (The Best Alms, *RR,* 1:613-15), "Mūlyapr āpti" (Receipt of the Price, *RR,* 1:638-39), "Nagarlaksmī" (The City Goddess, *RR,* 640-41), "Pratiśodh" (Revenge, *RR,* 4:760-67), "Mālinī" (*RR,* 5:483-516), "Rājā" (The King, *RR,* 6:303-62), "Naṭīr Pujā", "Chandalika", and "Shapmochan" pronounced as *śāpmocan*) (Lifting of the Curse, *RR,* 5:687-710). "Mukti" (Freedom, *RR,* 3:79-80) strikes a different note where inspired by the song of *kirtanī* (Vaishnab ascetic and a singer) Bajirao Peshwa leaves for a life of asceticism on the day of his coronation.

If use of myths constitutes a significant aspect of Tagore's writings, no less important is his use of folklore. Tagore's interest in folklore may be attributed to two major factors. First, as a romantic poet he had strong fascination for the distant past, the distinctive elements of human characters rather than their universality, and for the simplicity of the people who lived close to nature, like the Wordsworthian men. That is why he was more interested in the village life than in the city life, more interested in village culture than in city culture. It is not for nothing that though born in one of the most respectable families of Calcutta where his grandfather was "a partner in empire", he spent most of his life at Santiniketan, a village situated more than 200 kilometers away from Calcutta and willingly suffered all the disadvantages of living in a village in terms of comfort and communication. The second reason is that when in course of his looking after the zemindari estate he used to spend days and months on the Padma he came in close contact of the villagers and their simple way of life, their joys and sorrows, their trials and tribulations. He loved them; he had developed a strong emotional bond with them. The foundation of Sriniketan with the programme of rural reconstruction is a result of this experience. In his writings, in the stories and poems and plays, even in many songs and dances we meet characters who are drawn from the folk experience. We can have an idea of the theoretical foundation of his contribution to folklore from his very perceptive essays in the book "Lokasāhitya" (Folk Literature, *RR*, 13:663-734) which contains (i) an essay on nursery rhymes, (ii) a collection of nursery rhymes and (iii) an essay on folk literature, among other things. Tagore says that the kind of aesthetic pleasure that we derive from nursery rhymes lies outside the standard categories of aesthetic pleasure or *rasa*. The kind of smell that we get when the earth is tilled or the smell of the body of a child cannot be compared with the fragrance of a rose or perfume or incense stick. It has a primitive beauty and appeal, and so is the case with nursery rhymes which are at the same time very old and ever new. Tagore says that these rhymes contain many remnants of lost history, many scattered fragments of ancient memory. It is not possible to reconstruct them archaeologically into a whole, but our imagination does try to be familiar with that world which is very distant and yet very near. Tagore also examines some nursery rhymes to show how, though dreamlike, a rhyme is true, and in what sense, and the strength on which some rhymes, though logically incoherent, become profoundly meaningful. And he goes on to point out how almost in every rhyme, even in its trivial wordings we get a picture of some aspect of the cultural life of Bengal, some familiar folk tune, some touch of domestic chores, some glimpse of social life or family life of Bengal. Tagore argues that in their nature nursery rhymes are like myths. He says that these rhymes are clouds lightly floating in the sky of the human mind. At one moment they come together and take some strange shape, and assume another form the next moment. Not only that. Both the nursery rhymes and the clouds are always in a flux, colorful and afloat. They are apparently meaningless. But as the clouds come down in rains and give life to the corns, similarly the rhymes fertilize and sustain the heart of a child.

Furthermore, Tagore believes that as a tree draws its sustenance from the subterranean soil, sending its roots to the depths of earth similarly it is the folk literature going deep down in the people's experience and firmly rooted in the cultural heritage of a people that sustains the elite literature of a people.

Now from theory to practice. All the stories of "Lipikā" (*RR*, 7:779-848) are told in the folktale tradition, so that we have age-old paradigms, simple plot outline and simple narrative style, though marked by Tagore's modern sensitive approach and romantic imagination. "Parīr Paricay" (The Identity of the Fairy), "Bidūṣak" (The Jester), "Rājputtur" (The Prince), which though written in the folktale tradition uses the quest myth and the myth of the voyaging boy. "Suorānir Sādh" (The Desire of the Favourite Queen) and "Kartār Bhut" (The Ghost of the Master) are some of the examples. There are poems like "Rājār Chele o Rājār Meye" (The Son of the King and the Daughter of the King) which is a fairy tale in verse.

Some other works exploring the myth of the voyager are the poem "Bīr Puruṣ" (The Child Hero, *RR*, 2:27-28), and the drama, Tāser Deś (The Land of Cards, *RR*, 6:1159-90).

It should be evident from the foregoing discussion that the writings of Tagore are replete with his abundant use of myth, orality and folklore in all their varied aspects and aesthetic richness which is simultaneously both decorative and functional. One cannot really make watertight compartments of myth, orality and folklore, as orality seems to subsume both myth and folklore. Myths and folklore must have found their place first in orality before the neotic process of acquiring, accumulating, storing and disseminating began, and the myths and folklores were reduced to writing. Incidentally, it was only in 1846 that William John Thomas introduced the term "Folk Lore" into the English language through an article entitled "Folk Lore" published in the *Athenaeum*, and "Folk Lore" includes ballads, fairy tales, legends and folk songs among other literary forms. Even a myth the story of which must have been told over and over again with variations across space, time and culture yet never losing its emotional impact on the readers/auditors may be rightfully regarded as part of folklore.

Tagore's masterly use of myths predates the publication of *Ulysses* and *The Waste Land*, and in this respect he may be seen as a pioneer of modernism. But that would be putting him in a strait jacket. Tagore, "the myriad minded" poet and a versatile genius opened up new and ever widening horizons in literature leaving practically nothing *en route*. Spell bound one can only exclaim, "Here is God's plenty".

Notes

1. I am grateful to my colleague, Dr Rama Kundu, Former Professor of English, Burdwan University for making many valuable suggestions and contributions when the paper was in progress.
2. Unless otherwise stated all the translations from the Sanskrit and the Bengali texts are by the present author.
3. The original Sanskrit and Bengali passages have not been usually quoted to avoid the burdensome use of the diacritical marks. However, one can look up the original passages, if

interested, by following the references given along with translated texts.

No diacritical marks have been used for the names of gods and goddesses, literary figures and historical characters or words where standard spellings are in practice, e.g. Shiva, Kali, Mahabharata, Ramayana Bankimchandra, Rabindranath, etc. In doubtful cases, the correct pronunciations have been indicated in diacritical marks in brackets.

Works Cited

Barthes, Roland. *Mythologies*. London: Paladin Grafton Books, 1988.

C.I.E. Vol. 8. Calcutta: Oriental Publishing Co. *n.d.* Cited as *PCR*.

Cuddon, J.A. *Dictionary of Literary Terms and Literary Theory*. 4th ed., England: Penguin Books. Rpt. 1999.

Drabble, Margaret. *The Oxford Companion to English Literature*. 6th edition. Oxford, 2000.

Poona, Bhandarkar Oriental Research Institute, 1954.

Rabīndra-Racanābalī. 15 Vols. (*Collected Works of Tagore*). Centenary edition. Kolkata: Government of West Bengal, 1961. Cited as *RR*.

Ramayanam of Adikavi Maharsi Valmiki. 2 Vols. Trans. (Bengali) Acarya Dr Dhyanesh Narayan Chakravorti. Calcutta: New Light, 1996.

Routledge Encyclopedia of Narrative Theory. Eds. David Herman, Manred Jahn and Ryan, Marie-Laure. London and Newyork: Routledge, 2004.

Tagore, Rabindranath. *Chinnapatra* (Torru Letter) No. 18 VisvaBharti, 1319 BS.

Tagore, Rabindranath. *Sañcayitā* (*Collection of Poems*) Kolkata: VisvaBharti, 2009. Originally published in 1931.

Tagore, Rabindranath. *The English Writings of Tagore*. 8 Vols. New Delhi: Atlantic, 2007. Cited as *EWT*.

The Karnaparvan, being the eighth book of the Mahabharata. Ed. Parashuram Lakshman Vaidya.

The Mahabharata of Krishna-Dwaipayana Vyasa. Trans., Pratap Chandra Roy.

Wiener, Philip. P. *Dictionary of the History of Ideas*. 4 Vols. eds. *et al* New York: Charles Scribner's Sons, *nd*.

3

The Listener in the Tale: Orality, Tradition and Modernity

Jasbir Jain

Orality as a feature of communication embodies in it both traditional and modern characteristics. Timeless and unanchored, it freely travels from age to age, country to country and genre to genre. In India, we have a powerful oral tradition which still persists in various forms. Oral discourse displays several characteristics. One may expect it to be located in power structures with the speaker exercising some authority over the listeners. This too is easily reversed in the storytelling which takes place in domestic environs. The shift from temple to home transfers its impact. But in each "telling", it is the telling which is significant. It can be additive and accumulative. The teller has full freedom to insert his point of view and political and moral ideas.

Ferdinand de Saussure, using the linkages between signifier and signified, used the words "langue" and "parole", in order to differentiate between speech and its use. But he failed to take cognizance of the fact that language is much more than mere traffic between two different modes such as speech and writing. It embodies a full knowledge system and religious discourse. It is anchored firmly in its time and environmental surroundings. Further, language and silence, both are necessary survival and sustaining features of human life. The written word acquires fixity in a particular context, while the spoken word contains within it the potential to rise above the moment.

Rabindranath Tagore's use of orality can be traced in three different ways: one, his mystical and devotional poetry impacted by his observation and fascination for the Baul singers, second, his embedding of it in his narrative and dramatic forms, and third, in those narratives which include a strong didactic element, along with playfulness and concerns of other sentient beings. I shall briefly dwell on the influence of the Baul singers both on his thought and his poetry before discussing in detail the form of the oral story and Tagore's use of it. In his early life, when he took on the responsibility of managing their Estates, he had an exposure to the life of the common people. It is here, in the 1890s, that Tagore wrote some of his finest songs. His letters of this period are full of descriptions of the people he observed and the dreams he dreamt infused with magic and magicians. In a letter dated 4 July 1890, he describes a young girl he had seen stepping out of a boat, one who was a combination of innocence and womanly charms and he wrote that he had never imagined such women existed in the villages of Bengal. It was this image he carried forward to his short story "Samapti" (Ray, 24). The village folk believed in the agency of the supernatural, in trances, in the powers of nature. He moved close to nature with all its spontaneity, unstructured presence and emotionality. He felt that love is the foundation of all religion.... "Let me sympathise with the happiness, sorrow and pain of all creatures.... Birds resemble us to some extent and in one respect there is a little difference between them and us...in the way we both show spontaneous tenderness for our offspring. Banabhatta was able to feel this similarity in compassion through his imaginative faculty and gave expression into it, as in the phrase 'one touch of nature makes the whole world kin'" [38, letter dated 22 March (1894)].

Time was another significant preoccupation with Tagore, an aspect which contributes simultaneously to the Indian perception of time as well to the continuity of orality despite its many transformations. One felt liberated and "outside the current of time". When living outside Calcutta he felt, "time is quadrupled because I live in my inner world where time may be stretched or compressed and clocks do not work in the usual way. Duration is measured by intensity of feeling; the emotions of the moment seem endless.... And then it seems to me that subdivisions of time and space are figments of my mind. Each atom is immeasurable and each movement infinite" (Letter dated 24 June 1894, 39). One must remember that this idea is manifested through a personal experiential response well before Bergson's *duree* (though they were both contemporaries). In this letter Tagore also recounts a Persian story he had read about this idea of time in which a *fakir* invites a king to take a dip in a bathtub filled with magic water. The king, on doing so, found himself in a strange country (39). A similar timelessness is manifested in the oral tale where mobility of space is another concern. During this period, he was reading *Arabian Nights* and his writing impulse was motivated by folk literature. The piece he mentions is "Womens' Rhymes".

Amit Chaudhuri in his Introduction to *On Clearing a Space* refers to an essay "Chhelebhulano Chhara" (1894) approximately meaning children's rhymes or rhymes meant for children. Chaudhuri believes this essay to be a conscious effort on Tagore's part "to relate himself to the important nationalist projects being undertaken in Bengal at the time, the attempts to create, for want of a better word, a 'low' or oral history...." (Chaudhuri, 22). Several of Tagore's contemporaries and predecessors were similarly engaged in building up archives of the local material. The idyllic environs in which Tagore chose to locate Shantiniketan, is another assertion of his appreciation of, and communication with nature.

Tagore's writings on Indian civilization and discourse refer over and over again to a mystical relationship with nature, limited not only to the ascetic but one which includes the average person as he responds to his surroundings. In an essay "The Message of the Forest", he emphasizes the fact of continuity between the past, the present and the unknown and unpredictable future. He zeroes down to the forest, which permeates our classical literature (which is its earlier forms was oral, narrated and passed on by word of narration or recital).

The forest gave them "shelter and shade, fruit and flower, fodder and fuel", and made it easy for them to know their own lives and its connection with the larger universe ("The Message" 386). Even Rama during his exile was not really in exile ("The Message", 396), he was only distanced from the seat of power.

It as this continued realization of the connection between man and his environs, the presence of the divine in nature, the non-ritualistic and secular religion of nature and the roots of these in Indian tradition, that attracted Tagore to the orality present both in tradition and his environs, one which favoured communication, spread of knowledge and co-existence. These ideas are further expanded in his long essay "Religion of Man", Hibbert Lectures delivered at Manchester College, Oxford. Incidentally, it is contemporary in time to Freud's essay "Civilization and Its Discontents" and outlines the contrasts/opposition in the two world views, an essay in which he explores the meaning of religion, reality and human consciousness. But what is even more significant are the four appendices suffixed to this work, two of them by Professor Kshite Mohun, in which the Baul tradition is expounded upon and the focus is on the freedom of the soul from worldly shackles that these singers sing about. It is a cult very much in the Bhakti tradition common to both ascetics and householders, not adhering to any scriptures, not affiliated to any temples with their songs passed on from father to son. They represent a common wealth and adopt a 'sahaj' style—one which is free of all complications.

The other side of this oral tradition emerging from the same environment is the prose narrative, a katha, which is more worldly, at times allegorical and didactic, catering to practical wisdom based on moral edicts. This inherits its tradition from the embedded cycle of narratives in the *Kathasaritsagar* and the two dominant epics. These represent an accumulated folk wisdom and the focus shifts from the individual consciousness and its relationship to a mystical and spiritual reality to rules of guidance for everyday behavior. This does not rule out observations on abstract values such as freedom, knowledge and desire. At one level, there is an overlapping concern with compassion, a reaching out to the other, and to the practice of dharma. Character development in heroic terms is not its concern, instead it is the moral element which seeks dominance. Humour may occasionally feature in it. And when it is transferred to such modes as "Hari Katha" or "Gandhi Katha" it borders between hagiography and biography but here too, despite the fact that they narrate mythical stories, they do not indulge in any mythopoeia. The writer/narrator enjoys anonymity and the narrative a fluid continuity. The form of the "Katha" similarly has travelled all over the world. As Vishnu Prabhakar has observed it has travelled from India to Iran, to Arabia, to Turkey, to Rome and has been adopted freely by Boccacio, La Fonte and a host of others (Vishnu Prabhakar, "Introduction" to the Hindi *Kathasaritsagar,* 7). It is a tradition shared by Buddhism in the *Jataka Tales*, *Hitopadasa* and is also reflected in the fables of *Panchtantra.* Arshia Sattar in her "Introduction" to the volume of *Kathasaritsagar* (English) comments upon the social range of the characters and "framed" narratives by which she implies the box-like frames with one story being embedded in another or emerging from another. Sattar is of the view that it caters to the four *Purusartha* and of these primarily *artha.* (*Kathasaritsagar*, compiled 1070 CE). "Vrat-Kathas" are another subcategory which combine the supernatural with a didactic purpose for prescribing a moral code. They invoke fear of wrongdoing, with punishment following close on the heels of any violation of the norm. Orality encompasses a large number of narrative forms in prose literature ranging from myths, legends, fables to fairy tales, each differentiated from the other by its dominant grounding either in the supernatural or in historical happenings, and being about animal or narratives full of commonsensical advice. There is more often than not a happy ending with fulfillment for the seeker after due trial. My focus, however, is on the "Katha", the folktale, and its contemporary use. For that purpose, I propose first to take a story from *Kathasaritasagar* before turning to three of Tagore's stories: "The Parrot's Tale", "Samapti" and "The

Hidden Treasure". Each is of varying length, drawing its affinity from a different folk genre.

In the *Kathasaritsagar*, the tales are brief but continued from one to another, form a whole cycle of stories. Information and explanation are asked for and provided. The narration varies from first person to third person. A story is framed in time, such as "One Day", "Long Time Ago" or "Once Upon a Time" and "Such are the Times". The listener is always in the tale. At times the narrator is or has been on earlier listener and is now recounting the story. For instance in a story titled, "The Garden of the Goddess", the narrator wanders along the banks of the Godavari and comes across a beautiful garden. He then asks the caretaker about the origins of the garden. Then the caretaker tells him what he had heard, thus begins another story told by a Brahmin born in a place on the banks of Narmada. In his adult life, he aspires to win the Goddess Durga, where he proposes to sacrifice himself. She forbids him to do so and directs him to a more constructive role of planting trees. If one reads this story carefully one finds several things—the narrator has a sub-narrator, who has another one. They are also listeners. Then geographical connections between Godavari and Narmada are made, further the traditional form of worship through sacrifice is substituted by a more constructive devotion which spreads happiness and pleasure. The didactic element and the socio-cultural subversion are very subtly conveyed in the tale. It actually has no beginning and no ending—the narrator wanders into that area and after hearing this story goes home slowly carrying with him a sense of wonder. There is no defined protagonist, and no climax or anti-climax takes place. There are several other stories which follow the same pattern such as "The Mouse Merchant" where a man growing up in poverty and dependence learns to use his mind, takes up a dead mouse barters him as cat food for a handful of gram, which he offers to tired wood-carriers who in turn part with some wood, which he sells and sets up a shop, grows rich and returns to marry the daughter of the merchant from whose floor he had picked up the dead mouse. These stories narrate incidents which contribute to character building and cultivation of positive, socially productive qualities.

Before moving on to Tagore, there is another folk narrative, one needs to look at—the "Tota Kahani" which too has come down to us in many forms and under different names, a cycle of stories of speaking birds, where they are used as messengers, spies and guardians, where it is the "forbidden" route which attracts opposition, struggle and conflict. In this cycle, storytelling becomes an essential strategy for survival. Tagore's "The Parrot's Tale" inherits this legacy, though he puts it to a different use. The "Tales of a Parrot", oral versions of which many of us must have heard as children, are in Persian and have come to us through translation from *Nakshabi's Tuti Nama* (1330) (by Muhammad Kadiri, translated into Hindustani by Saiy'd Haldar Baksh and into English by George Small, London: W.H. Allen). They are believed to have been originally composed in Sanskrit under the title *Shukusptati.* Oral literature travels freely across languages and geographical boundaries and can withstand multiple transformations. It is evident that both additions and subtractions are constantly at work and local colour and idioms come to inhabit it. But these constant and relatively easy transformations also comment on the nature of oral literature—one, it is its story which is important; two, it relates to a culture and is much more dialogic than written literature as it constantly interacts with its listener/audience moulding itself to what is familiar and interesting. The element of fantasy or the supernatural is also comfortably accommodated within it and is used as a source of inspiration and education. Birds and animals that can speak and keep watch over human action help to establish human oneness with nature.

"Tuti-Nama" is a continued cycle of stories centred on Ahmed Sultan and the education of his seven-year-old son. In this story, a parrot challenges himself to prove his worth to man. A statement of the parrot proves to be prophetic and consequently he is made the Sultan's business advisor. During one of business trips, the Sultan places his wife under the birds, a Tota and a Maina's, guardianship. When the Sultan's wife wants permission to clandestinely meet her lover, the Maina restrains her. Khogista infuriated wrings the Maina's neck. By this the parrot is put on his guard and refrains from advising her. But he develops a different strategy to keep her at home. That night and each successive night, he gets her absorbed in listening to a story, embedded in the main narrative, and thus becomes a narrator not only for his own survival but also to fulfill his duty to his master and impose a check on his mistress. The power of storytelling is foregrounded against the background of patriarchal control where the freedom of the woman is curtailed not through physical power or coercion but through storytelling.

Tagore's "The Parrot's Training" also known as "The Parrot's Tale" focuses on a similar trait by illustrating it through a reverse tactics by exposing the foolishness alike of the king and his courtiers. Although knowledge production is recognized as a necessary social need, the way they set about it is ridiculous: "Once upon a time there was a bird. It was ignorant". The measure of its ignorance is measured by his inability to recite scriptures. So he is to be taught for which his environs need to be improved. A cage of gold is provided, his freedom and natural chirpiness are curtailed. "Culture, captured and caged!" The highest value is attached to wealth, knowledge comes as a poor second ("The Parrot", 379), a pundit is appointed to teach the bird, scribes are hired to copy from books. A lot of employability is generated. Progress in every direction takes place; the goldsmith makes money, the scribes become rich, the hired people build their own palaces, but alas the bird does not still recite scriptures. In all this glamour, the bird is forgotten. And when finally remembered, it could hardly breathe with its throat choked with the leaves from the books. But whenever it fluttered its wings, it was checked. The birds wings were soon clipped and his tiny feet clamped. And the bird died. This simple tale is loaded with several episodes each exposing the stupidity of the manner in which values are perceived: money, religion, education, production, and freedom. "The Parrot's Training" is a comment on the world gone wrong where hollowness of values dominates, with pretensions and appearances, self-interest and wasteful production acquiring the upper hand.

"The Hidden Treasure" is a much longer story, truly cyclical in its span as it covers several generations, with listeners and narrators changing with every generation and secrets, mysteries, adventures generating their own excitement. The story moves from present to the past, from Mrityunjaya to his grandfather Harihar, to the visit of a sannyasi who handed over a map along with a verse filled with clues. This paper with its promise of wealth became a cause of disruption in the family; it is hidden and later passed as to Harihar's son, still later stolen and then again the grandson comes across another sannyasi. The search thus continues; Mrityunjaya follows the sannyasi into a forest, and into cave, where he discovers that the sannyasi is none other than his grand uncle, in pursuit of the same treasure. There is enmity and suspicion and Mrityunjaya finds himself alone in a dark cavern, unable to find a way out. The sannyasi rescues him on the condition that he forgets about the treasure but being a greedy man, he yields to temptation when confronted with the treasure and its gold. He wallows in his wealth for sometime but not for long. Soon the hungers of the body and the soul begin to call him and true wisdom dawns on him. His utmost need is for light, for the open sky and freedom ("THT", 320). Once again, it is the critiquing of greed and the pursuit of worthless pleasures which is critiqued, prioritizing the value of freedom.

Orality in its narration is audience geared, with the listener intervening with a query or an acknowledgement, or an expression of wonder and surprise. It is an open structure in every way. The ending is always temporary and a turn in the course of events and its multiple embeddings open out other doors, some of which are not fully explored. The subject is highly mouldable can be used with alternative patterns. Tagore's story "Samapti" was written during the years he spent on his Estate and is woven around a young girl he had seen stepping out of a boat. Although transferred into a romantic tale and domestic environs, it retains the other features of a tale. A young man who has just completed his studies and is now ready for marriage but when he goes to see the girl chosen by his mother, he chooses the girl who he had spotted while landing from the boat. This creates the first loop in the story. The second loop is when the girl's father is unable to come and Apoorvakrishan has also to overcome the resistance from his own mother. All this while, the concerned girl, on account of her uninhibited behavior has collected a reputation of being carefree, unusual and mad. But unknowingly she has crept into the young man's heart. Finally, when the marriage takes place, the girl rejects him, resenting the bonds of marriage. There is an attempt at running away and Mrinmayi sets out in search of her father. But the boatman brings her back to her husband's house. The fourth shift occurs when Apoorva offers to escort her to her father' place of work, where they stay for a few days. Both are equally guilty of disobedience. But while the narrative takes several loops, Mrinmayi doesn't draw any close to him. He goes away to Calcutta; she to her mother's home where for the first time she misses him but waiting to be summoned by his wife he doesn't come home even during his holidays. Finally, it is the agency of his mother and his married sister, who lives in Calcutta, which brings the two together. The reader notices that the attention shifts from Apoorva to Mrinmayi, to the women in Apoorva's family and the normative expectations from gender and social roles are upset; that Mrinmayi loses her laughter and spontaneity, before her womanly love can be aroused. First Mrinmayi's father is absent, then Apoorva goes into self-exile, thus clearing away the space for female action, turning them into active agents. In the process of the narration, all three major participants in the narrative shift from their earlier positions, each yielding place to the will of the others and by the end gender roles are redefined. The title "Samapti" meaning "conclusion" or "The Closure" but it is not really a closure, it is a new beginning. The absent reader/listener is all along present in his interaction with the sociological and psychological frameworks. In this story, the form of the oral tale has been appropriated and made meaningful for contemporary society. Somewhere, hidden in its depth, are the seeds of the postmodernism narrative.

The listener is present in Mahasweta Devi's "Kunti and the Nishadin" even in a more concrete manner where orality is concerned. The story is in the form of a confession, where the tale of the barber bursting to tell his news which he has been forbidden to talk about, is adopted for social purposes. In the original tale, the barber burdened by his secret knowledge, embraces a tree and shares his secret with it. In "Nishadin", Kunti, the mother of the Pandavas, is similarly burdened not by any secret knowledge, but by the guilt experienced through her own relationship with her sons, Draupadi and herself. The confession in the forest is both an act of introspection and of an unburdening. But ironically enough, it does not lighten her burden. Devi's attack is on injustice and inequality and she weaves it round this confession and the listener, who is supposed not to listen or to be aware of this. "Nishadin" is a tragic story and has moved further away from any consolatory or happy ending such as the one we have in "Samapti". Structurally, it works through several segments, moving to and pro between the past and the present, between deeds done and not done and Kunti's realization of the wrongs she has done to others as well as the self-denial which has made her what she is. "Nishadin" is interlaced with a repeated mention of the need to confess when no one can hear, to confess in whispers. Narratively, the plot is structured along contrasts and opposition—the contrast between the well-built Nishadins and Kunti's emaciated body, between their sense of freedom and joy and her guilt and on unwilling subjugation to penance, between the moral laws of Rajyavritta and Lokavritta, between the children born of legitimate unions and the offspring fathered by outsiders. There is also a repetitive stress on Kunti's need to be alone, to confess but not to communicate, her treating of the Nishadins as less than human, acts which render her confession incomplete. These different pulls act as divisionary lines in the memory segments. The final confrontation takes place when a nishadin approaches her and reminds her of the Pandava's betrayal of hospitality when they set fire to their cottage having trapped the tribal woman with her five sons. It is at this point, through the spreading forest fire that the confession actually materializes, once again other directed and not self-directed by Kunti. Here both myth and narrative are transformed, shifted to a larger discourse reversing the very motion of morality and of power and exposing the shallow limits of self-knowledge. Orality has been modernized and used by writers all over the world to create parables, long narratives, and to capture the complexity of reality. It has been used by writers as widely different as Jorge Luis Borges and Githa Hariharan. Both these writers have resorted to it in work after work. It is a major component of feminist as well as political writing, and it is visibly an underpinning of many postmodernist works. Its progress from a simple village tale to cultural narratives and to a way of combating the overwhelming mechanization of our life is as amazing as its continuity through the ages.

Works Cited

Chaudhuri, Amit. Introduction, *On Clearing a Space* New Delhi; Black Kite in association with Rupa & Co., 2008.

Devi, Mahasweta. "Kunti and the Nishadin" in *The Politics of Literary Theory and Representation: Writings on Activism and Aesthetics*. Ed. Pankaj K. Singh. New Delhi: Manohar, 2003.

"Devotional Songs" *The Essential Tagore*. Edited by Fakrul Alam and Radha Chakravarty Kolkata Vishvabharati; 2011.

Nakshabi. *Tuti-Nama, The Tota Kahani or Tales of a Parrot* Translated by George Small from Saiyid Haider Baksh's Hindustani version translated from Muhammad Kadiri's Persian version. London: W.H. Allen & Co, 1875.

Prabhakar, Vishnu. Bhumika (Intoduction). *Katha Saritsagar* (Hindi). Ed. Vishnu Prabhakar. New Delhi: Sasta Sahitya Mandal. 2010.

Samapti (Hindi translation from the Bengali original) *Rabindranath Ki Kahaniya.* Translated by Kanika Tomar. 2 Volumes. New Delhi; Sahitya Akademi. (1991) 2010.

Sattar, Arishia. Introduction *Kathasaritsagar* (English). New Delhi: Penguin, 2003.

Somdeva. *Katha Saritsagar* (English). Ed. Arshia Sattar. New Delhi: Penguin, 2003.

Tagore. Rabindranath. *The Religion of Man. The English Writings of Rabindranath. A Miscellany*. Edited by Sisir Kumar Das. New Delhi: Sahitya Akademi (1996), 2008.

"The Hidden Treasure", *The Hidden Treasures and Other Stories* in *Rabindranath Tagore Omnibus*. New Delhi: Rupa & Co., (2003), 2010.

"The Message of the Forest". *The English Writings of Rabindranath. A Miscellany*. Edited by Sisir Kumar Das. New Delhi: Sahitya Akademi (1996), 2008.

"The Parrot's Training", *The Hidden Treasures and Other Stories* in *Rabindranath Tagore Omnibus*. New Delhi: Rupa & Co. (2003) 2010.

"Zamindar" (1890-1897). *Selected Letters of Rabindranath Tagore*. Eds. Krishna Dutta and Andrew Robinson. Cambridge: CUP. Asian Edition. New Delhi: Cambridge 2005.

4

Folk Dance and Rabindranath Tagore

Mahua Mukherjee

The world knows Tagore through literature and yet he is also a genius in dance and music. The rhythm of dance supports his philosophy. Dance and music completes his personality and thus perfects his art forms. He expressed his views about Fine—Arts—"Music and Fine Arts are the best media of national self-expression. The country which does not have its own music or arts remains inarticulate forever" (A Tribute, 102). Tagore expressed himself in one of his famous poems:

> My Heart Sings
> My HEART sings at the wonder of my place
> In this world or light and life,
> at the feel in my pulse of the rhythm of creation
> condensed by the swing of the endless time.
>
> I feel the tenderness of the grass in my forest walk.
> The wayside flowers startle me;
> That the gifts of the infinite are strewn in the dust
> Wakens my song in wonder.
> I have seen, have heard, have lived;
> In the depth of the known have felt
> the truth that exceeds all knowledge
> which fills my heart with wonder and I sing.

(English Writings, 355)

During 19th century, Neo-babu class were the pioneers of British rule, products of Anglo-Indian trade. They owed no account to culture. This displacement was most apparent in Bengal which was the seat of the foreign culture, foreign government and foreign trade as Calcutta was the capital of India till 1911. Thus, all native artistic creation had stopped. At this crisis of Indian culture, the Tagore family took the lead in the movement of creative assimilation that had been initiated by Raja Rammohan Roy. Rabindranath Tagore was the supreme artist in a family of artists. His urge of creation was furnished by the need of all life. In him were combined the sense of values of the aristocrat and the simplicity, directness and universality of the child of the soil. He was the worshipper of rhythm. So he created the rhythm of joy, established rhythm of life, the rhythm of India—the dance.

Rabindranath's life was intriguing. His mastery was shown in the unity he gave to his life, the unity of a lyric, for his life was as deep in emotional realization, as broad in conception as rhythmic, as rich in metaphor, as evocative of meaning and as sweepingly imaginative and as profound in perception. His life was a whole a single creation. His pencil, pen and ink scribbling and sketches and his paintings and compositions in coloured inks, show a masterly control of line and a sort of a mystic abandon to colour and form, which makes his contributions in this domain of very great significance in the history of Modern Art in India. At the same time, he also inspired and directed the revival and full development of the Art of Dance in Modern India.

The amazing versatility of Rabindranath sometimes makes one wonder what really in his greatest contribution as a man of letters; his poetry or his songs or his novels and short stories or his dramas or his essays and sermons or his dance—dramas. Apart from that we all dancers of India remember him for his greatest contribution in dance, for launching an institution. So we can say Rabindranath was a dance-education. He tried throughout his life to make people educated and aware about music and dance and for this established Visva-Bharati at Shantiniketan. There is no doubt that Tagore's pre-eminence as a poet and writer will continue to be recognized down to the ages but at the same time his contribution in the field of dance is equally note-worthy.

Before Rabindranath Tagore, dance as an art and profession was looked down in the middle-class society of India particularly Bengal. As a result, dance had no respect in British ruled India. Dance and its standard as a mode of entertainment declined, and it got restricted only to lowly perceived 'Nachwali' performers. Rabindranath realized the importance of Fine Arts and its necessity for the society as a major part of education. Thus, he founded the Shantiniketan School in 1901. In 1921, he started the college of Music and Dance in "Visva-Bharati" for higher studies and gave dance and music equal importance with the other subjects of learning. In the beginning, his efforts were far from being appreciated rather it was condemned. His heart was overwhelmed with the pure joy of rhythm. He patronized classical dances which had been revived and established by that time and folk dance forms.

Tagore with dance performers

In the villages of India, various types of dances were prevalent, but the lack of respect and patronage resulted in the extinction of many forms of folk dances. Gurudeva put all his effort to revive the folk dance forms and late Gurusaday Dutta also initiated the movement for the revival of that forms. He first organized folk congress in India. Rabindranath Tagore was in favor of the ancient Indian system of education, yet he never discarded the realities of the Indian social environment of the twentieth century. His constant endeavour was to amalgamate the ancient ideal with present-day society of urban and village population. After the foundation of Visva-Bharati, many seasonal festivals of village were re-introduced, like—Halakarshan, Sharodotsava, Maghotsava, etc. and were celebrated regularly. In 1915 at Shantiniketan and in 1916 at Kolkata Gurudeva himself danced in "Falguni" drama as a blind Baul. He absorbed and stylized all the influences, Eastern and Western, that came in his way and made something out of that which is entirely his own. His universality lies in introducing foreign folk dances as well as Indian folk dances at the Visva-Bharati where he introduced Gallop and Lancer dance of England. In "Taser Desh" the song "Sankochero bihabalata" was choreographed in the forms of primary Judo exercise. Russian folk dance, Hungerian folk dance, Japanese dance, Kandy dance of Ceylon were introduced in the dance of Shantiniketan.

Mrs. Bruner danced in her own Hungerian style in "Gitotsab" of Autumn Festival. Dr. Timbers was in Russia with his family before joining Visva-Bharati where he and his wife learnt few folk dances. Santidev Ghosh was very much impressed and he learnt these dances from Mrs. Timbers. Later he performed dance on Maghi Purnima, the 2 February 1932 in this Russian style with Rabindra Sangeet. In 1940, a Japanese student, named Maki was present at Shantiniketan during the performance of *Chitrangada*. In this dance-drama, he performed the character of Madan the cupid. His choreography was a blend of Japanese and European dance forms.

In 1923, Gurudeva was mesmerised by the rural dance of girls in a village of Saurashtra. The girls were singing while sitting on the ground with a 'dhol' and pair of 'Mandira' in hands. Tagore brought one such family who is expert in Mandira dance to Shantiniketan. The teen-aged girl of a family danced Mandira Nritya at the songs of her parents. This event inspired Rabindranath to write song, "Duihate Kaler Mandiraje" and Nandalal Bose had drawn the picture of the dancing girl in "Amrakunja".

Prof. Jahangir Vakil came to Visva-Bharati in 1924 along with his family from Bombay to teach English. His wife could dance "Garba" popular in women's folk society in Gujarat. Rabindranath and Pratima Devi requested her to teach the girls "Garba". The girls of Shantiniketan learnt "Garba" and used to perform occasionally. In his time nobody knew the name of Mohiniattam. Today it is regarded as a classical dance, public was apathetic towards this dance due to its degradation as a 'street-vulgar dance'. Vallathol Narayan Menon has done his best to re-establish its place and now Mohiniattam has got its own appropriate place as a classical dance side by side Kathakali. With the co-operation of the king of Cochin, Tagore appointed O. Kalyani Amma as a teacher at Shantiniketan, where she taught Mohiniattam. As a result, Mohiniattam rose at the beginning of the 19th century but got almost extinct by the middle of twentieth century. When at the middle of twentieth century its restoration process began, Rabindranath was the first person to patronize it by allowing teaching of this discarded dance form of Kerala at Shantiniketan. O. Kalyani Amma taught '*Swaram*', '*Koikottikoli*', etc. This dance piece with Tagore song "Ogo Bodhu Sundari" was created by Santideva Ghosh by the style, taught by O. Kalyani Amma. Hence, students of Shantiniketan have been the first who learned Mohiniattam in modern India. The same we can see in case of Manipuri dance.

Tagore patronized the dance form based on Gaudiya Vaishnava religion which was practiced in rural Vaishnava temples and monasteries [Akhdas] of Manipur, and he gave that dance form a classical recognition. It was after an overwhelming experience of '*Rakhal Nritya*' in Machimpur village of Shyllet in the year 1919 when the village girls performed dance at his bunglow, Tagore decided that he would introduce Manipuri dance in Shantiniketan. In 1926 Manipuri dance was included in the syllabus of Shantiniketan. After learning some dance postures Tagore applied and choreographed on the rhythm of his song—"Aay Aay Re Pagol Bhulbire Chal Apnake". Thus, by the initiative and interest of Tagore, regular dance classes were started at Shantiniketan and Manipuri dance got institutional recognition too. Rabindranath further expanded Manipuri dance across Gujarat and even to Shillong. Ambalal Sarabhai, a prominent merchant of Shillong met Rabindranath and after hearing about the description of the Manipuri dance performance in "Natr Puja" and "Nataraja" acting at Shantiniketan, he decided to include Manipuri dances in the syllabus of his family school. Ambalal came in contact with a Manipuri dance guru Nabakumar Singh through Rabindranath and inspired by Tagore he took him to Ahmedabad with him. In this way, Rabindranath played a great role in the spread of Manipuri dance in Gujarat and Maharashtra. Till now most of the renowned Manipuri dancers apart from Manipur are Gujarati and Bengali.

Same picture can be seen in case of Kathakali. Kathakali got its formal recognition from modern urban educational institution in 1930, after establishment of Kerala Kalamandalam by poet Vallathol Narayanna Menon. Inspired by Tagore, Vallathol established "Kerala Kalamandalam" in 1930 and "Kalakshetra" was established by Rukmini Devi Arundale in 1936 respectively for Kathakali and Bhasratanatya. Thus, Rabindranath showed the path of establishing Indian and universal cultural institutions. Hence, he named his institution '*Visva-Bharati*'. "Visva" means universe and "Bharati" means Saraswati—the goddess of knowledge. Rabindranath applied Kathakali in his own form of dance at Visva-Bharati and arranged for training of students. Thus, he helped poet Vallathol's endeavour to go a long way. We cannot ignore the role of Santideva Ghosh (a student of Visva-Bharati) in this aspect. At that time none was aware of this dance. Sri Ghosh came to know about the male dancers of Kerala through a foreign magazine. Let us quote him—"In a French magazine I got the opportunity to go through the good pictures of male dancers of Kerala. I expressed my desire to an ex-student of early Visva-Bharat residing at Travancore. In reply he wrote that boys of their villages practice a specific type of dancing and acting. If the dance appeals to me then, he would arrange for learning this male dance." Again Santideva commented—"After listenting me Anujan Achhan (ex-student of Santiniketan) suggested that I need not to go Travancore, because Kerala's profound poet Vallathol Narayanan Menon has established a school for learning Kathakali in a village in Cochin, just a few months ago. Same male dance about which I have heard from Travancore would be taught there. The name of the dance is Kathakali and the name of the institution is '*Kerala Kalamandalam*'—the next day we went to the place 10-12 miles east of Trichur, where the construction of this institution is going on. The name of the village was Mulkunnathkav" (*Gurudeva Rabindranath*, 47-49). Within two to three months Santideva learned the tala-based dances like—Kalasam, Sari, etc. and in Shantiniketan he combined these dances with the other forms like Baul, Manipuri, etc. and choreographed with Tagore Songs—"Oi Bujhi Kal Boisakhi".

This detailed historicity makes us understand how the different rural art forms were recognized as classical art forms through evolution and included in institutional syllabus especially in Visva-Bharati. We can also realize the contribution of Rabindranath in promoting Kathakali dance in its developmental stage and as a result, universities of Bengal (Visva-Bharati and Rabindra Bharati) included Kathakali in their syllabus which is a rare example in entire India.

In January 1931, Santidev Ghosh went to the village fair of Jayadeva Kenduli, there he saw the high standard, talented Baul dancers. According to his description—"their dance was based on codified system of beats and rhythmic footsteps with noticeable variations. The manly bold form attracted him; he tried to imitate the dance form" (*Gurudeva Rabindranath*, 49). By this experience he choreographed Tagore's songs based on 'Baul' tune—"E Bela Dak Poreche". After this he performed "Fagun Haoay Haoay" with '*Ektara*' [one stringed instrument of Baul] in Calcutta. At a function organized by Gurusaday Dutta, for the first time he saw '*Raibenshe*' dance by the

'*Doms*' at Birbhum and the performance of Muslim male dancers from Mymensingh on Jari songs with handkerchiefs in their hands. These two bold manly dance forms left a permanent impression on his mind. He requested Gurudeva to allow him to learn "Raibenshe". Gurudeva Tagore allowed and arranged training for seven days and later Santideva and Banabehari performed a blend of "Raibeshe" and "Jari" with the song—"Ebela Dak Poreche". To him, dance was a medium of knowledge and education. He said—"I am the envoy of wonderfulness, I myself dance and make others dance. I laugh and make others laugh, I sing, I draw. The amazing soul of nature which plays in multi-form, in lyric and music, in dance, paintings, multivarious friction of joy and sorrow, in conflict of good and evil. I am the bearer of this multicoloured form of the truth. I wanted to be the associate of the youthful boys and girls at the courtyard of the rising and setting sky of this Ashram. My success lies in awakening them in joy by dancing, singing in time with the rhythm of the joyous nature."

The following tables highlight the application of folk dance forms at Visva-Bharati during Rabindranath Tagore's time.

Table 1: Application of Folk Dances of Bengal in Gurudeva's Songs

Song	Dance Style Applied	Dancers
Ebala dak poreche	Baul	Santideva Ghosh
Fagun haway haway	Baul	Santideva Ghosh
E bala dak poreche	Rabenshe and Jari	Santideva Ghosh Banabehari Maity

Table 2: Application of Folk Dances of Gujarat

Song	Dance Style Applied	Performers
----	Saurashtra dance	Gujarati dance
Gujarati Songs	Garba	Girl students of Santiniketan
(Inspired by Saurashtra dance 'Dui hate kaler Mandiraje' – the song was composed by Tagore)		

Table 3: In Tagore's Time Kathakali, Manipuri, Mohiniattam All These Rural Dance Forms [at present all are recognized as classical dance forms] were also Used in His Dance Items and Dramas

Sl. No.	Songs	Forms	Artists	Characters of dance drama
1.	Oi bujhi kal boishakhi	Kathakali	Santideva Ghosh	—
2.	Songs of Shyama	Manipuri	Nandita	Shyama
3.	Shyama	Kathakali	Kelu Nair	Prahari
4.	Shyama	Kathakali	Kelu Nair	Bajrasen
5.	Natir Puja [1st production]	Manipuri	Gauri Devi	Srimat, directed by Pratima Devi and Nabakumar Singha
6.	Natir Puja [Later production]	Kathakali, Baul, Manipuri	Lalita Sen [Tatu]	Srimat, directed by Santideva Ghosh
7.	Ogobodhu Sundari	Mohiniattam	Students of Santiniketan	—
8.	Taser Desh [Earlier production]	Manipuri, Kandy and Kathakali	Students and Teachers	All characters
9.	Taser Desh [Later production]	Kathakali and other Indian folk dance forms	Students and teachers	All characters

Table 4: Application of Foreign Folk Dances on Tagore's Compositions

Dancers	Style	Characters/Songs
Tagore taught from London's dancers	Lancer and Gallop	In 'Manmoyee' drama—'Ay tabe Sahachari'
Elmherst and Tagore	1923	In Basanta drama—'Ore Pathik'
Mrs. Timbers taught the student	Russian dance technique	Santidev Ghosh performed with Tagore song in Maghi Purnima
Mrs. Bruner	Hungerian Style	Ami Chini go Chini tomare
Dr. Timbers	Russian and other European dance styles	'Sapmochan' dance – drama in 'Aruneswar' character.

Dancers of Santiniketan	Judo-Karate style	'Taser Desh'—Dance drama, song – Sankochero bihobalata
Mr. Maki	Japanese and European style	'Sapmochan'—Aruneswar character
Mr. Maki	Japanese and European style	Churiwala
Mr. Anangalal	Kandy Style	'Shyama'—Katal role
Mr. Anangalal	Kandy Style	In 'Varsamangal'.
Mr. Maki	Japanese and European style	Arjun in first show and Madan in next show at 'Chitrangada'

Table 5: Special—Application by the Artists of Shantiniketan

Forms	Instruments	Performers	Production
Application of Chinese, Japanese and Indian mask	Application of Chinese, Burmese, Japanese and Indonesian instruments	Artists of Santiniketan	Rabaner Kanda – based on Ramayana

Works Cited

A Centenary Volume Rabindranath Tagore [1861-1961], Sahitya Akademi, 4th Printing, 1992.

Chaudhuri, Ahindra. "The Professional Theatre in Bengal". *Sangeet Natak Journal*, Vol. XXXVIII, No. 2, 2004.

Ghosh, Santideva. *Gurudeva Rabindranath O Adhunik Bharatiya Nritya*, Ananda Publishers Ltd., Kolkata 1963.

Ghosh, Santideva. Music and Dance in Rabindranath Tagore's, Education Philosophy, Sangeet Natak Akademi, 1978.

Javeri, Darshana and Devi, Kalavati. *Shastriya Manipuri Nartan*, Manipuri Nartanalaya, 1993.

Kumar, Mohit. *English Writings of Rabindranath Tagore—Poems by Rabindranath Tagore*, New Delhi: Atlantic Publishers and Distributors, 2007.

Mukhopadhyay, Mahua. *Bharatiya Nritye Troyee, Jaideva*, Chaitanyadeva O Rabindranath, N.E. Publishers, 2003.

Mukhopadhyay, Mahua. *Lokoritya O Rabindranath, Rabindra Bharati Patrika*, New Series, Vol. XIV, Special Tagore Issue, 2011.

Ray, Lila. "The Plays of Tagore", *Sangeet Natak*, Vol. XXXVIII, No. 2, 2004.

Sen, Pulinbihari and Roy, Kshitis. [ed.] *Rabindranath Tagore: A Tribute*, Sangeet Natak Akademi and Hope India Publication, New Delhi & Gurgao, 2006.

Venu, G. and Nirmala Paniker. *Mohiniyattam: The Lasya Dance*, Natana Kairati, 1995.

Venu, G. and Nirmala, Paniker. *Mohiniyattam,* Published by G. Venu Chittore House: Trivandrum Kerala, 1995.

Guide to Pronunciation of the Bengali words and phrases used in the paper:

Aay aay re pagal bhulbire chal apnake: āy āy re pāgal bhulbire cal āpnāka
Akhdas: ākhḍās
Ami Chini go Chinitomare: āmi cini go cini tomāre
Amrakunja: āmrakuñja
Aruneswar: aruneśvar
Ay tabe Sahacari: āy tabe sañcārī
Baul: bāul
Chitrangada: citrāñgadā
Duihate kaler mandiraje: dui hāte kāler mandirāje
Ebela dak poreche e belā ḍāk pareche
Ektara: ektārā
Fagun haoay haoay: phāgun hāoāy hāoāy
Falguni: phālgunā
Gitotsab: Gītotsab
Kalakshetra: Kalāksetra
Kathakali: Kathākali
Maghi purnima: māghī pūrṇimā
Maghosava: māghosava
Mandira: mandirā
Manmoyee: mānmayī
Nachwali: nācoyālī
Nataraja: naṭarāaja
Natir Puja: natīr pūjā
Ogo bodhu sundari: ogo badhū sundarī
Oi bujhi KalBoisakhi: ai bujhi kāl baiśākhī
Ore Pathik: ore pathik
Raibenshe: rāibenśe
Rakhal Nritya: rākhāl nṛtya
Sankochero bihabalata: saṅkocera bihvabalatā
Sapmochan: śāpmocan
Sharodatsava: śārodotsab
Srimati: Srīmatī
Taser Desh: tāser deś
Varsa mangal: Varsāmangal

5

En-textualizing and Re-contextualizing the Oral Tradition, Myth and Folklore in Tagore's Dramatic World

Neeru Tandon

Unlike in Western theatre, folk performance is a composite art in India. It is a total art with fusion elements from music, dance, pantomime, versification, epic ballad recitation, religion and festival peasantry. It imbibes ceremonials, rituals, belief and social system. It has deep religious and ritualistic overtones and again, it can surely project social life, secular themes and universal values. As veteran folk media scholar Balwant Gargi rightly said:

> Folk theater represents the people in their natural habitat, with all their contradictions and multifarious activities. It gives a glimpse of their style of speech, music, dance, dress, behavior, humor, proverbs, wit and wisdom. It contains a rich store of mythological heroes, medieval romances, chivalric tales, social customs, beliefs and legends. In order to understand the colorful diversity and unity of India, it is important to see the folk theater in its natural setting. Folk drama is unself-conscious, spontaneous, boisterously naive. The classical theatre is rigid, complex, sophisticated. The folk is unhewn, the classical chistled. The folk sprawls, the classical demands mathematical exactness. One is rural,

> the other regal. Folk theatre can make a whole community take part; the classical is for the chosen few. The folk has mass appeal and caters to the lowest common denominator, the ordinary man; the classical is for the elite and demands previous knowledge from the spectator. The folk theater has a universality which the classical lacks. Folk art (singing, dancing, acting) crosses the borders of class, religion, and country. The classical often imposes these barriers because of its esoteric nature. (*Theatre in India,* 2)

Motifs from folk tales, myths, and popular epic poems are being re-appropriated by urban cultural forms—both popular and elite—to articulate new identities and subject positions. Myths are supposed to be the concrete embodiments of ideas and not vehicles. The bearers of folklore continue to be conceptualized as "them"—villagers or at least men and women of lower strata. Such cultural productions are clearly marked by a vested interest in maintaining the exotic for cross-regional domestic, particularly metropolitan, as well as foreign consumption. Folkloric tales were often oral in nature. Even when translated, like the *Panchatantra* or the *Jataka Tales,* their original oral nature can be detected in the many repetitions, which are valuable in creating rhythm and cadence. They give birth to various myths. Noted writer Mariam Karim writes about it in her article "Myth, Folklore and Society":

> In a country like India religion and mythology are closely interlinked even today and each region has its own myths and beliefs that form an integral part of the cultural, social and even political life of people. Tales everywhere are considered to play a very important role in the development and sustaining of cultures. It is interesting also to note that psychologists and theorists of socio-cultural evolution maintain that folk and fairy tales, and now our modern folklore of cinema and television help us define our own values and guide us in taking life's major decisions, especially those pertaining to our emotions. Jungian psychology would explain this

> through the creation of unconscious psychological patterns or mental archetypes. (3)

If we look back, we find that under British initiative, the study of folklore was advanced primarily by British civil officers and European missionaries. The ideals upheld by the Folklore Society (established in London in 1878) were of enlightened parochialism. Its journal *Folklore* voiced the late nineteenth century ideals of disciplining through knowledge. Later on Empire Theory of Folklore was reaffirmed by E.S. Hartland in his Presidential Address in 1990 which was voiced by Edward W. Brabooke and Charlotte Burne in *The Handbook of Folklore* (1914).

The second phase of the folklore movement was introduced by Bengali scholars of nationalistic tendencies. Rabindranath Tagore was the pioneer during this period. From 1885 to 1899 he published four essays showing the importance of folk literature. These four essays were compiled in his book *Lok-Sahitya* (Folk-Literature) in 1907. Rabindranath Tagore once said, "I want to keep an exhibition of folk culture at Santiniketan." Rabindranath Tagore realized that Indian society was "permeated by religion and living myth, endowed with a psychic landscape having its own concept of orality, folklore, time and space"(Ghosh, 36).

He tried to portray this unique reality through modes and methods indigenous to Indian culture. Tagore patronized others and he himself collected a large number of folklore materials from his vast estate in East Pakistan. He himself wrote, "when I was at Seaildah, I would always keep close contact with the Bauls (mystic folksingers) and have discussions with them, and it is a fact that I infused tunes of Baul songs into many of my own songs" (Ghosh, 38). The Asiatic Society of Pakistan in Dacca gave recognition to folklore and published research articles on the subject in its journal. *The Mohammadi*, the *Mahe-Nau*, and the *Saugat*, three important monthly journals of East Pakistan, published frequent articles on folklore. Conferences and folk festivals were held in different parts of the country. Folk festivals including dramas, folksongs, and exhibitions of folk arts and crafts became important features of government-sponsored exhibitions and fairs all over the country. Radio Pakistan in Dacca allocated time and money for broadcasting folk songs and dramas. In addition, scholars were invited to take part in the regular discussion programs of folklore in Radio Pakistan. Under the able guidance of the late Abbas Uddin Ahmed, eminent folk singers such as Momtaj Ali Khan, Bedaruddin Ahmed, Sohrab Hussain, Abdul Latif, Abdul Alim and Ferdousi Begum collected folk songs with their tunes directly from oral tradition, to broadcast on the air. Almost all of them directly or indirectly acknowledged the impact of Tagore and his literature.

Folklorist William Bascom states that folklore has many cultural aspects such as allowing for escape from societal consequences. In addition, folklore can also serve to validate a culture (romantic nationalism), as well as transmit a culture's morals and values. For Tagore, folk represents cultural past, rural simplicity and unadorned childlike innocence. Tagore's explicit distancing and implicit identification with the creative process of folk literature secured a special place for him in the contemporary literary world. Dr. Dusan Zbavitel, professor of Indology in the Oriental Institute of Czechoslovakia, writes that "It is my firm belief that without staying in the countryside for as long as he did, Rabindranath could never have become what he was, either as a man or a poet". Tagore's example was followed by the leading Bengali journals. Bangiya Sahitya Parisada, a Bengali literary society, was established under his encouragement in 1895. The *Sahitya Parisada Journal*, from the year of its inception (1895), began publishing folklore materials collected from the various regions now comprising East Pakistan.

No doubt folklore in Tagore's world comes to represent the authentic voice of the folk, a living museum from which Bengal's history may be excavated. Tagore was of the view that rhymes play a very significant role in folklore and orality. At the same time he admitted the truth that we cannot find details of their composers and no one asks the date on which they were written. Because of this spontaneous universality of popular rhymes, they are age-old even if composed today, and remain fresh even if they are thousand years old. It is worth mentioning here that Tagore has a relation with Kashmiri poetry and folklore too. Famous Kashmiri singer and composer Mahjoor enlarged the canvas of Ghazal, widely referred to local flora and fauna and made his Ghazal the chief vehicle of his thought. He believed that traditional performing art being functional, inter-personal and having a contextual base would be able to carry the message of change, development and growth. He loved various colours of life and depicted the hues of nature in his Ghazals. This attracted the attention of Tagore and he called Mahjoor 'the Wordsworth of Kashmiri poetry'.

Noted folk media expert Shyam Parmar observes that the communication needs in India are much greater than the resources we have to meet them today. While the mass media have been constantly expanding, the traditional media have been playing an important role in this field due to our peculiar needs. The folk literature mainly exists in four forms.

1. Folk Story
2. Folk Song
3. Proverbs and Sayings
4. Folk Drama

Tagore tried his hands in almost everything. He wrote many stories with folktales, used proverbs and sayings in his dramas and stories. Many of Tagore's songs were influenced by the Baul songs and later on the Bauls also got influenced by Tagore songs. You can see that the relationship between the Bauls and Tagore is like a full cycle. Manipur dance was not known beyond the borders of Manipur until Tagore discovered this beautiful dance about 1920. The poet adapted the Manipur dance to his own poetic style of song and composed several dance-dramas. The major dance-dramas by Tagore are: *Mayar Khela, Chandalika, Balmiki Protiva, Taserdesh, Chitrangada, Shyama, Kaalmrigye*, etc.

This paper examines the process by which the discourse of folklore and myth is used to en-textualize and re-contextualize the oral tradition specifically in West Bengal through a discussion of two dramas of Tagore: *Chitrangda* (1892), which was published in English as *Chitra* in 1913, and *Gandhari's Prayer* (1897). I selected these dramas by considering the mode in which orality is inscribed. One of the plays attempts to re-constitute oral lore from a popular epic composed in the medieval period, and the other re-inscribes a myth that is part of folk ritual into a new genre through the mediation of folklore discourse that is responsible for the first step in en-textualizing the myth.

Tagore dispelled the social taboo once attached to dancing and regained full social acceptance by putting it back on the centre stage. Along with the indigenous Indian dance forms, both the classical and the folk forms, he used the 'other dance languages' which have had roots not merely in a national but in a transnational culture. Tagore chose the icons of marginality—warrior, untouchable, and courtesan—as protagonists in his women-centered dance dramas and presented the folk stories studded with folk songs and dances. Tagore's dance dramas occupy a position where religion, poetry, music and dance, merge into one another. In Tagore's dance dramas, plain speech progressively develops into heightened speech and then draws itself up into emotionally charged songs and the corresponding action is transformed artistically into dance. Songs and dances in these dramas are an extension of the dialogues and action, not having any separate role to play. Unlike previous Bengali dramas, Tagore's dance dramas emphasize a fusion of lyrical flow and emotional rhythm tightly focused on a core idea of orality, myth or folklore. In them, he has freely adopted in his own way the style and techniques from Manipuri, Katthak, Bharat Natyam, Kathakali, folk dances and even European dances like the ballet, as and when necessary.

His portrayal of women in dance dramas like *Chandalika* or *Chitrangada* is a reflection of the idea of the 'new woman' that had emerged from the time of the Bengal Renaissance. In *Chandalika*, Tagore uses an ancient Buddhist legend for his play, but treats it in a highly imaginative way, giving it a modernist interpretation. Through material desire Prakriti reaches a spiritual desire. Ananda's request, "Give me water" besides indicating his physical need symbolizes water's regenerative image common in many religious traditions. In the Indian context, a holy man asking for water from an untouchable violates a social as well as a religious norm. To receives and to give food or water were sacrilegious for both. The monk's extraordinarily radical request awakens Prakriti's awareness of her own innate self. Through the universal image of water, Tagore intertwines the ideological revolution reflected in the social, religious, and political scene of his own time.

Chitrangada, *Natir Puja* (The Dancer's Prayer) and *Shyama* were Tagore's other answers to eliminate the social taboo associated with dancing on stage. He wanted to convey that dance is an expression of emotions in spiritual ecstasy. In *Chitrangada*, the situation is significantly different. Tagore has beautifully recast the original story in the play with certain changes, but maintaining its full mythical significance. Chitrangada, the warrior princess, falls in love with Arjuna, the warrior prince. But Arjuna rejects her as she is Kurupa, a woman devoid of feminine charms to attract him. So with the help of Madana, the god of love, Chitrangada dons the mask of Surupa, the beautiful, seductive woman ready to entice men like Arjuna. Yet she is suffocating under this guise of the 'true woman'—the eternal feminine. As soon as Arjun hears about the warrior princess, he loses interest in Surupa, the beautiful woman that Chitrangada had become in her desire for Arjun as a lover.

She wants Arjun as an ideal companion equal to her in all respects, someone who would respect her for who she is. Yet she is also conscious of her multifariousness; in Surupa, the alter ego of Kurupa, we find the desirous woman who changes herself to woo her beloved man, she acts as the agent rather than a goal and her decision to change herself is her own; as Kurupa, Chitrangada also exercises her choice and agency when she determines the time when she would unmask herself before Arjun and reveal her true identity. Chitrangada becomes the exemplary woman in tune with her own identity, her desires and her womanhood. She possesses the power and agency to determine her own fate.

In *Gandhari's Prayer* (1897) also known as Mother's Prayer we find a different presentation of an Indian mother. Its story has been taken from the well-known great Indian epic *The Mahabharata*. K.R. Srinivasa Iyengar said, "This play is a study of a mother and her son, the great and magnanimous mother of the Kurus and her eldest ill-fated son Duryodhana. Both Dhritrastra the father and Gandhari the mother know that Duryodhana is wrong, but the father compromises, while Gandhari will not. She is a great character" (Rabindranath Tagore, 138). Dhritrastra cannot see the malicious intentions of Duryodhana and therefore pays no heed of Gandhari's prayers.

Ghandhari as mother is reluctant to accept the evil and unjust behavior of her own son. She makes an earnest request that Dhritrastra as king should renounce their son Duryodhana. She can foresee the end of Duryodhana. She loves her son but opposes his evil deeds. She actually symbolizes universal motherhood, broadmindedness, morality, integrity, uprightness, magnanimity and detachment. She says to her husband, "The son is dancing with joy by picking up honey coated poisonous fruits of sin. I request you to punish him." Tagore has beautifully handled the *Mahabharata* myth of Gandhari who by virtue of her morality and magnanimity has become an ideal woman and myth of Draupadi who by virtue of her special position in the lives of Pandavas and Sri Krishna catches attention.

Karna and Kunti (1897), another play by Tagore deals with the mythical story of *Mahabharata*. Here Tagore had brought into focus the conflict between illegitimate childhood and unmarried motherhood. As a result of Kunti's invocation of the Sun god in the days of her virginity, Karna came to her womb as the blessings of the Sun god. Karna was born, but unmarried Kunti gave him to holy Ganga and a Charioteer Adhiratha brought him up as her son. I will like to refer here the Myth of Panchkanya—as I find that Tagore somewhere is greatly influenced by this myth and presented Draupadi, Kunti and Ghandhari in a new context in his work of art. See his Chitrangada, Prakriti or Binodini—all share some qualities of these panchkanyas. Scriptures mention five women as ideal wives:

> Ahalya Draupadi Sita,Tara Mandodari tatha,|
>
> Pancha kanya smarenityam, maha pataka nashanam ||

("Mediating on the merits of the five great ladies, namely Ahalya, Draupadi, Sita, Tara and Mandodari, helps destroy even the greatest of sins!!")

In some texts, we find name of Kunti in place of Mandodari. Now if we re-contextualize it we find Ahalya was raped, Draupadi had multiple husbands. Sita was accused of having sons by another man.Tara was married to her younger brother-in-law after her husband was killed by him and Kunti was an unmarried mother.

If you read their lives, one thing is for sure, none of them was a "compliant, malleable" wife. They were not the picture perfect "pativrata" depicted in novels, movies and popular folklore. None of these women stood by and took what family and society gave them at face value. In fact, they held on to their dignity as women despite what family and society threw at them. Ahalya refused to accept social exile for being raped. She was duped into thinking she was having sex with her husband. How can that be her fault? Instead of slinking away into a forest retreat to cry over her dishonour, she stood firm, staying in the very ashram where she was shamed and carrying on her good work despite society's censor. In the end, Rama, considered to be the model of duty and embodiment of correct behaviour, came out on her side and declared her blameless in this incidence. At no point did Ahalya seek anyone's assistance in her fight against injustice. When we re-contextualise we find several questions like when Rama could declare Ahilya as sati and blameless, why the same principles could not be applied on Sita?

Sita was a headstrong woman, one who successfully argued her case with Rama and her in-laws to follow Rama into exile. Why couldn't she argue when she was blamed? It was not a simple task in those days to live the life of a single mother, and yet, she successfully brought up two sons in the ashram of sage Valmiki. At no point did she ask for assistance from her parents, compensation from Vibhishan or compassion from Rama.

Kunti was an unmarried mother and several myths are attached with her as a mother. Her daughter-in-law Draupadi had the characteristics of great wives as listed in the Puranas—dignity, patience, diplomacy, resourcefulness, drive to succeed, looking out for the family, etc. I find Tagore's heroines greatly reflect Draupadi. She had five sons, one by each of the Pandavas: Prativindhya, Sutasoma, Shruthakeerti, Satanika, and Srutasena. She has been described in the *Mahabharata* to be extraordinarily beautiful—undefeated by any woman of her time in terms of beauty. She is one of the Panch-Kanya (The Five Virgins) of Ancient Hindu Mythology along with her mother-in-law Kunti.

Draupadi emerged as a beautiful dark-skinned young woman together with her sibling Dhristadyumna from the sacrificial fire. Draupadi's life was full of woes. She was mocked and subjected to all sorts of unkind remarks all her life, yet she lives through it all with queenly dignity. Draupadi fanned the fires of revenge whenever her husband's seem to "cool off" in the twelve year exile. But she is no war monger, when compassion was called for, she was the first to relent and forgive Guru-putra Ashwasthama. Her keen sense of justice and "rights" kept her husband's from veering off into sentimentality under family pressure. Loyal to her husband's till the end, she demonstrated how "divided love" can unite a family. Hers was the toughest task as she had to keep together five different personalities and focus their energies towards a great goal. Indeed, Draupadi was the embodiment of "karma—action".

The main myth and related folktales with Draupadi and her five husbands are unique. There are several folktales. Upon hearing of the Pandavas' supposed death at Varanavata Draupadi set up a swayamvara for Draupadi intended to bring Arjuna out into the open. Draupadi was confident that Arjuna alone could accomplish this task. Karna came forward but on Krishna's signal, Draupadi stops Karna, saying that her *varmaala* (wedding garland) is not meant for a charioteer's son. Arjuna came and did the needful. Then Yudhishthira, the son of Kunti, beholding his younger brothers, understood what was passing in their minds. And that bull among men immediately from fear of a division amongst the brothers, addressing all of them, said, "The auspicious Draupadi shall be the common wife of us all."

Another tale runs like this that while in exile, Kunti, mother of the Pandavas often advised her sons that they share everything they have (or obtain through *bhiksha*, i.e. alms) equally amongst themselves. Upon returning home with Draupadi, on purpose, Yudhishthira addresses his mother first "Look mother, I have brought *bhiksha* (alms)!" Kunti, unmindful of what Yudhishthira was referring to, unassumingly asked her son to share whatever it is with his brothers. Thus, in order to obey their mother's order all five accepted Draupadi as their wife. When Krishna visits the family, he explains to Draupadi that her unique position as the wife of five brothers results from a certain incident in her previous birth. She was born as Nalayani (daughter of Nala and Dhamayanthi). She had in that lifetime prayed to Shiva to grant her a husband with five desired qualities. Shiva, pleased with her devotion, tells her that it is very difficult to get a husband with all five qualities that she desired. But she sticks to her ground and asks for the same. Then Lord Shiva grants her wish saying that she would get the same in her next birth with five husbands, she was shocked and asked Lord Shiva is it a boon or curse, Shiva replied back saying "My child do not get worried, you will regain your virginity each and every morning you take bath, till the end of your life you will live with virginity". Hence, she gets married to five brothers each who represents a given quality: The just Yudhishthira for his wisdom of *Dharma*; the powerful Bhima for his strength that exceeded that of a thousand elephants combined; the valiant Arjuna for his courage and knowledge of the battlefield; the exceedingly handsome Nakula and Sahadeva, for their love that put even Kama, the God of Love, to shame. Over here Pandava's represents to Five Virtue's not as human beings. It is interesting to note that Karna, Kunti's illegitimate oldest son, had all five of the desired qualities in question, but was brutally rejected by Draupadi due to his caste status.

As per the *Garuda Purana*, Draupadi is the incarnation of Bharati-Devi, The Consort of Lord Vayu. As per *Narada Purana* and *Vayu Purana*, Draupadi is the composite *Avatar* of Goddesses Shyamala (wife of Dharma), Bharati (wife of Vayu), Shachi (wife of Indra), Usha (wife of Ashwin), and Parvati (wife of Shiva), and hence married their earthly counterparts in the form of the five Pandavas. Enraged at a jest by Parvati, Shyamala, Shachi and Usha, Brahma cursed them to human birth. Parvati thought of the solution wherein they would be born as one woman, Draupadi, and hence share the earthly body for a smaller period of time. They requested Bharati to be with them in their human birth. Draupadi's characteristic fight against injustice reflects Parvati or her Shakti, Kali, inhabiting Draupadi's mortal flesh at times. At other times, Draupadi was docile and even waited to be rescued (as in case of Jayadratha and Jatasura) showing the qualities of other goddesses like Shachi and Usha. Other times, she showed astuteness in hiding their true identity and asking Vayu's son Bhima to kill the evil Keechaka, like Bharati would. Draupadi was also avatar of Goddess Shree, who was joint wife to five Indras, who incarnated as the Five Pandavas.

The Puranic description of womanhood seems to be more in keeping with realities of today. This was just an example. We have various folk forms in our country, which are very much alive today. We can see it in our cultural heritage. All these need careful investigation, study and documentation after serious investigation; their characteristics have to be studied. Whether people see it or not, mythology and folklore are still prevalent in today's society as it is kept alive in literature. Many modern writers look to the past to help describe the present. Literature may not always agree on the same message, but it can always comment on today's society through its words and symbolism and the use of mythology and folklore.

Works Cited

Crooke, William. "The Popular Religion and Folk-Lore of Northern: India". *Journal of Asiatic Society of Bengal.* 2 Vols. 1983.

Gargi, Balwant. *Theatre in India.* Theatre Arts Books, 1962. http://www.yakshagana.com/re-mar02.htm

Ghosh, Arjun. *A History of the Jana Natya Manch: Plays for the People.* New Delhi: Sage Publications, 2012.

Iyengar, K.R. Srinivasa. "*Rabindranath Tagore*", Volume 1 of The Literary Criterion Publications on Indian Men of Letters. Bombay: Popular Prakashan, 1965.

Karim, Mariam. "Myth, Folklore and Society". *Contemporary Literary Review India*, Saturday, November 5, 2011.

6

Overflowing the Boundaries of Form: Legends, Myths and Folktales in the Works of Rabindranath Tagore, Girish Karnad and Amitav Ghosh

Santosh Gupta

Modern Indian writers have searched for suitable narrative modes, sources and devices as they have dealt with the radical shifts, significant issues and transformations in India in the twentieth century. Many writers have probed into the indigenous narrative sources for representing the continuities as well as discontinuities in the historical and cultural spheres. Among such writers Rabindranath Tagore stands foremost, who expressed his appreciation of the folktales and local narrative strands, which he found in the street singers, peasantry and domestic servants, who despite their illiteracy, were familiar with the ancient wisdom contained within the orally transmitted simple tales and legends. There have been several other writers who have used the folktales and other Indian narrative streams, along with the written literary traditions. The inclusion of the legend, myths and tales from these non-canonical streams has widened the sphere of Indian literature, reflecting the plurality and diversity of the country's many cultural strands.

Rabindranath Tagore's interest in folktales began at an early age; he began collecting the Bengali folktales from 1883 onwards, and, in 1907 published essays titled "Lok Sahitya" where he paid great tribute to the folktales and stories women told to children, to please and control them; he considered the folktales to be, as Shukla says, "a 'continuation of the epic tradition', disseminating much of the philosophic concepts and religious values contained in them" (109). However, towards the latter part of his career, Tagore used a Buddhist legend that critiques one of the Hindu society's age-old practices—of untouchability, derived from its caste-divisions; the story expresses the humanistic vision of the lowly placed social groups that Buddhism gave in ancient India....

In *Chandalika,* Tagore takes up a story that represents Anand, Lord Buddha's disciple and his meeting with an untouchable girl. Tagore explores the story's contemporaneous relevance on the persistence of this ugly practice in the twentieth century. This play, written in 1937, places the young woman's transformation at the centre of the entire action, moving away from the popular historical or social drama of the time and uses the psychological drama of the girl's experience to generate sympathy for the suffering humanity.

In a similarly innovative drama, Girish Karnad in the 1980s uses a folktale centered on women as narrators and as characters, in the play *Naga-Mandala* (1999); Karnad had used for his earlier plays myths from the *Mahabharata* or historical figures as in *Yayati* (1961) and *Tuglaq* (1964). In the *Naga-Madala*, he uses a non-naturalistic stage form as he weaves women's story into modern social milieu.

Amitav Ghosh's novel *The Hungry Tide* (2008), written mainly in the realistic mode, incorporates a folktale popular among the community of fishermen, wood cutters, honey-collectors and peasants in the Sunderbans region. The Bonbibi's tale forms the basis of a religious cult of the forest goddess; these men and women have unquestioning faith in the deity's powers, benevolence and kindness. Ghosh's use of this tale raises political, cultural and moral issues, and also pertains to contemporary environmental problems by creating parallels and contrasts between the different stories told simultaneously, through a craftsmanship and structure that is extremely skilled.

In these three texts by some of the most remarkable of modern Indian writers the legends and folktales taken from the cultural groups that are, for the most part, placed marginally in the mainstream society, comparative perspectives emerge, that question hegemonic patriarchal structures, subverts the dominant moral and religious attitudes, and, also provides meaningful insights. It is an interesting common feature in all the three texts that there is a centrality enjoyed by the women characters, adding to the experience of marginality in a more authentic manner.

Tagore's play *Chandalika* dramatizes the young untouchable woman, Prakriti's transformation with the emergence of her awareness of her 'human' self, its potential for love, desire and self-seeking which the conventions of social suppression had denied to her, and to the whole class of the untouchables. This story, which describes the liberating impact of Lord Buddha's message to an untouchable, belongs to a group of similar Buddhist legends related to other marginalized figures who are given a new hope of moral regeneration, a freedom from degraded social exclusion and rehabilitation; such legends deal with prostitutes, dacoits and the so-called 'sinners'. Although these legends have existed in written form, their popularity among Indian masses has been mainly through their repeated oral retelling.

In using the Buddhist legend Tagore evokes a subversive, critical view of the Hindu religion's emphasis of caste as being the primary construct of human identity. Through this story it also presents the continuity of the evil up to the twentieth century. During the 1930s, there was already in India a public discourse asking for the eradication of untouchability. Through the fiction, poetry, and repeated discussions of the social problem by writers like Premchand, Mulk Raj Anand, T.S. Pillai, M.K. Gandhi and others, a public awareness of the inhumanity of this practice was generated; a Bombay made film *Achchut Kanya* (1936) which was very popular, also evoked widespread sympathy for the sufferings of women from the lower castes. Tagore's play also contributed to this discourse through an ancient legend, and the use of music and songs, rather than a direct realistic portrayal of the problem as were done by most of the others debating the issue.

The play begins with a euphoric Prakriti who is waiting for the Monk at the village well, where she had met him earlier. She tells her mother about impact of that meeting. When she expressed her unwillingness in giving him water for fear of polluting him, he had told her, "You and I are of the same family. All water that quenches thirst and relieves need is pure" (Tagore, 1994:170). The water that she pours to Ananda becomes a regenerative force. Prakriti finds her new birth takes place, creating a human self; "She says that the water drowned my family, my caste and my birth" (Tagore, 1994:170). Her human identity that so far has lain dormant, buried under the layers of the socially constructed images, now pushes forth moving towards a greater self-realization and assertion.

In the opening scene of the play, between Prakriti and her mother, two distinct discourses are found conflicting with each other. The mother admonishes the excited daughter who wants to forge the reality of social divisions and hierarchies, to reflect the traditions constructed by Hindu religion and society represents the custom-bound anti-humanistic ideas. The daughter feels compelled to look beyond the existing system to a more humane, egalitarian and liberal social order, where the periphery could relate to the centre more equally, she represents a hope for change in the orthodox social system.

The Buddhist legend in Tagore's play becomes a story also of the moral regeneration of Prakriti, as she undergoes a conflict within her passions and the urge to become free of desire itself. Full freedom, as Buddha has taught, comes to human beings once they annihilate their desires and learn the values of compassion, non-violence and surrender the ego. Attracted to the Monk, Prakriti feels a strong desire for his closeness to her and she wants to call him back to her. Prakriti's insistence forces her mother to work up a magic spell on Ananda. As he approaches the hut, Prakriti looks into the magic mirror to see him. She looks at the pain and self-loathing of Ananda reflected on his face, as he is forcibly brought there by the magic and realizes how her wish to possess Anand would destroy his piety and her own self. She breaks the magic mirror, releases Anand and is once again "saved", this time from the passions within her. These moments represent another human struggle, between the egoistic notion of power over the person one loves, and a more moral, spiritual understanding of self, other, and of love. The internal moral struggle of Prakriti depicts the female self becoming free of gendered ideas of passion, and reaches a human self as it gains an insight into the spiritual aspects of love.

This play evolves a form of relationship between characters that is not based on an action or external conflict. The destabilizing emotions within Prakriti's own self lead to the moral and psychological changes which generates sympathy for her. Her liberation from her desires provides her the knowledge and understanding of Buddha's message to humanity. Saved now from her own passions, at the end of the play, she feels a sense of joy, looking forward to a new life.

The central role of the untouchable female in the play disturbs the patriarchal hegemony of the society and its images of caste domination. This play represents the mature vision of the dramatist, who had begun to look beyond Hinduism to the marginalized, little cultures within India, with greater respect. Ashis Nandy argues that in the post-1920s Tagore became conscious of the "politics of culture", and he became open to "an inclusive concept of India" (78). By writing about the Buddhist legend, and center-staging Prakriti, Tagore portrayed women's potential for spiritual and moral awareness which he had explored in his earlier writings, in fiction and drama.

The folktale used by Girish Karnad in *Naga-Mandala* belongs to the female domain as it has become a tale women narrate amongst themselves on the day of a particular fast; it is a *vrat-katha*. Karnad explains in the "Introduction" he wrote for the *Three Plays*, that he took two orally narrated tales, which "are narrated normally by the older women in the family or the group also when children are being fed in the kitchen or being put to bed. The other adults present on these occasions are also women. Therefore, these tales, though directed at the children, often serve as a parallel system of communication among the women in the family" (36).

Women's narratives circulating amongst them have different tone, stance and understanding of their position within the patriarchal system. These tales subvert male dominance, value system as women share certain views and experiences that are otherwise not expressed. They express "a distinctly woman's understanding of the reality around her, a lived counterpoint to the patriarchal structures of classical texts and institutions" (Karnad, 1999:36). Here Karnad links the role of textual strategies in narratives to the questioning of institutions that may be contained within these states.

It was during the early phase of his literary career that Girish Karnad became conscious of the Indian writers "need to evolve their own narrative forms and styles if they were keen to write about the historical, political and cultural issues faced by Indians. Experiments with stage craft, theatre and playwriting in the west provided some interesting possibilities" (31). But adopting the stage and writing style of Ibsen, Shaw or Jean Anouilh could not provide a fully satisfactory form of self-expression. In the writing of his own plays, he went back to ancient Indian myths and epic stories, traditions of folk stage practices, and drama. The restriction of the actors to the drawing room, as the naturalistic theatre did, seemed totally contradictory to the "geography of the homes" of the Indian playwright, where, Karnad says, "most meaningful action actually took place in the kitchen or the courtyard" (31). His plays moved beyond naturalistic drama to include the elements of ancient drama, folk performances and other indigenous little traditions. These shifts towards the indigenous form of performances and literary art suited the dramatist own probing into the socio-cultural situations.

The *Naga-Mandala* exposes in an ironic mode the double moral standards of the Indian society and male hypocrisy through the story of a young couple. Soon after her marriage Rani is left alone inside the house while her husband Appanna leaves the house during day-time locks her inside to prevent her from making any social contacts. The play begins with another formal frame where a group of narrators and listeners form a small society of their own.

The play opens in a deserted temple located on the outskirts of the village. The space within the temple is filled up when a traveler happens to stop by, and as female shaped "flames" from the village homes collect there to gossip amongst themselves. This space outside the village marks the outer fringe of the village, and the women's group a marginalized group; this space provides them a freedom that is used by the flames to come forth with the strange story of a Naga take on human shape and woo the lonely and pretty Rani. The heterotypic aura of this space opens up the marriage of Rani—Appanna to a critical mockery, as several other characters enter the play—the Naga in the shape of Appanna, Kappanna, a village youth looking for his beloved, and the village community. Not strictly governed by the social pressures, here, in the temple those women as narrators and as characters enjoy a different kind of self-confidence and understanding of the woman's ambivalent attitude towards the lover as Naga.

When Rani is loved by Appanna at night she is bewildered by the contradiction in his behavior but she is also happy. The initial fear and horror of sexual relationship reflect the repressive psychological atmosphere of her socialization, but soon her initiation leads to greater maturity, a sense of responsibility and an ability to take her own decisions. This play, like Tagore's, puts the women's psychological growth and self-awareness at the centre of the action, which is closely related to the patriarchal values of marital relations, its emphasis on female purity. This relationship expresses the repressive adult sexual mores where the erotic aspect of love is often reduced to a crude functional relationship. With a compassionate and mild humour the chastity test scene further depicts the hidden complexities within familial and conjugal relations (Karnad, 1994:54-55).

Tagore and Karnad have taken tales that represent silenced marginalities, the world of women, and the outcastes. Lower social status brings in them an insight that the dominant group cannot obtain—an insight and sharing in the pain of other, seen in Rani and Prakriti both in their sensitivity to the pain and feelings of others—even towards the men who may have hurt them. Subversive role of the folk tale is turned into creating meaningful relationship and formation of selfhood. The *vrat-katha* provides a "female context and content" in the "phallocentric social world", for within the play Karnad associates the oral narrative tradition to the "women's subculture...in the re-telling of the existing myths and folktales", as I have argued elsewhere (Gupta, 1999:251). These tales contain subtle psychological understanding of the complex and tenuous relationships between men and women. There is strong human approach marked with humor.

In Amitav Ghosh's *The Hungry Tide* (2008), this role of women in balancing the needs of economy, human lives and the world around them becomes more powerful and dominates the novel. The folktale of Bonbibi that runs parallel to the many other stories within the novel not only becomes a mode of reflecting upon the man-made problems and injustices, it provides the moral viewpoint that a world grappling with serious environmental and ecological problems needs urgently. The novel explores myths and various other narratives forms, and develops a polyphonic multi-layered narrative in which realistic depiction of some characters, historical tales, and myths about the Ganges and the natural world jostle together.

In the main narrative frame which consists of Kanai Dutt's visit to Lusibari, a small village in Sunderbans, to meet his mashima Nilima Bose, his few encounters with other characters including one with a tiger, bring about an important change in his own personality, the linear mode of narration is used. He is given the notebook written by his uncle, Nirmal Bose, whose last wish was that the matter written in it be read first by none other than Kanai. The many stories related to the region unfold, including a myth related to the Ganges, the worship of Bonbibi and the story of the struggle between the poor people who try to develop a colony of their own, with the State Government.

Nirmal Bose's account was written in a frenzied manner, when he felt his end coming. As a young student, he had believed ardently in the need for a revolution to create an equal world. With this enthusiasm he had joined the Communist Party (of Bengal) to work for a transformation of the Indian society devoid of the classes and caste systems. His over enthusiasm became embarrassing when the Party came into power and he was tactfully sent away to the remote region of Sunderbans with his wife, Nilima. Now as he is about to retire from his service as a school teacher, he becomes involved in a small movement of the poor fishermen and other displaced groups, of that area; some of them have come from Bangladesh as refugees; these landless poor try to occupy one of the islands in that area, called Morichjhapi and establish a colony of their own. The Morichjhapi event in 1979 gained notoriety as the State Government of Bengal came down heavily upon these unauthorized, hence illegal settlers, and evacuated them by using brutal force. Nirmal happened to be present there; he witnessed these operations and felt compelled to write down these details, so that the events could be known to others. He wants to preserve the truth in public memory, which has been pushed to the periphery and is almost a forgotten event.

The shock of the political action and the people's suffering almost kills the old man. But he takes it as his moral responsibility to record the incident as he had witnessed it, and to write about the marginalized and displaced poor. Although his friends from Calcutta who visit the place, knowing well that the experiment will be destroyed soon, remind him of the Party's willingness to "break some eggs to make an omlette" (Ghosh, 2008:191), for Nirmal those human beings needed support and protection, so that they could live their lives with dignity.

As Nirmal watched helplessly these events take place he felt compelled to write as a moral obligation towards these people. The writer should/could take a stand, he felt; somewhat similar to the realization that Ghosh himself had come to after he had witnessed the anti-Sikh riots in New Delhi in 1984. Ghosh describes this moment of realizing his role as a writer in the essay "The Ghosts of Mrs. Gandhi" (61-62). Ghosh writes that in general writers don't join processions, but, he says "What do you do when the constitutional authority fails to act? You join and in joining bear all the responsibilities and obligations and guilt that joining represents" (61). Ghosh had joined a procession at that time and had decided to write about these violent events in public life, to make his own voice heard. As a writer Nirmal takes upon himself the duty to write the account of the event, whatever he knew personally about these peasants, refugees and the landless poor who had pinned all their hopes upon this collective effort to build house for themselves. He records these events which others around him might be all to willing to forget. Keeping the memory of that event becomes a moral role he can play.

In his notebook, the narration moves at several levels: the political event at Morichjhapi in 1979 is interspersed with Nirmal's conversations with Kusum and Horen, the two local persons with whom he has become somewhat friendly. In talking with them Nirmal gets to know about the deep faith these villagers have in Bonbibi, the forest goddess, and the curious story of her birth, her travel from an Arab country to Bengal, her fight with a demon, Dakshin Rai and her victory. This folktale runs throughout the account of Nirmal, and in the novel, as other characters also refer to the faith, its form of worship and main tenets of belief.

The strong faith that these villagers have in the protection provided by Bonbibi helps the local men and women who live in constant threat to their life and survival. The firm faith of these people surprises the characters like Nirmal, Kanai Dutt and Piyali Roy, a marine scientist who has come from the U.S. to study the dolphins in the Bay of Bengal region. As the form of worship, their prayers and shrines become known many unique features of the cult are revealed to these characters.

One of the most important features of the Bonbibi worship is its hybrid character; in the prayer Horen offers at the shrine, Nirmal is surprised to hear words from three different languages: Persian, Arabic and Bangla (Ghosh, 2008:246).

Nirmal attributes this mixing of languages to the history of travellers to this region; he calls the area a "door-mat" of India because several nationalities have entered India through this point. But the mixing of different cultures, religious and regions is inherent in the tale itself, for this goddess was born to a Sufi Saint, living in Mecca, and she was given a divine instruction to protect the helpless people in the region of tide—Bhatir desh, i.e. the Sunderbans (Ghosh, 2008:246). Her story transcends several borders of space and religious for her protection is provided to all believers, irrespective of the believer's community or religion.

The folktale of Bonbibi provides within *The Hungry Tide* an insight into the wisdom and benevolence of these local forms of worship. The benevolence and generosity of the goddess is unlimited, granting relief even to the enemy, Dokhin Rai, and allowing him to share some part of the forest. Of her devotees she asks for a purity of heart, and self-discipline—in their minimal, need—based use of the resources of land and sea. The demon is required to keep within his limit. There are no other rituals or offerings besides a full faith in her. The rule of the Goddess runs parallel to the political government's powers that rules the state, but which has failed to provide the poor citizens with their basic requirements for their well-being. The conflict between the ruler and the ruled runs in contrast to the kind governance and faith the people have in Bonbibi's providence.

In this tale, the relocation of ecological, environmental pressures become part of a faith that is complete. No other state or human agency enjoys such faith in their efficacy or such a following. This folktale, like many others in different regions in India, is part of the "accumulative tradition", circulating in communities more through oral narration, although they may be scripted in some written texts by some academic, knowledgeable person. Bonbibi's tale was written in Bangla by a Hindu writer Krishna Ram Das in 1686, when it was called Rai-Mangal and later in Arabic by Abdur Rahman. The origin remains unknown, though it can be related to the entry of Islam through Sufi Saints in Bengal, as the historian Richard Eaton maintains.

The faith that protects the villagers enables them to undertake the risky tasks necessary for their survival. The lives and beliefs of these marginal communities exist in a mutual relationship, overcoming the divisions and borders created in the mainstream world. Muslim worshippers sit together with the Hindu and offer their prayers to the goddess, at her shrine, where other figures are also worshipped. Such a flexibility of practice reflects the vibrancy, fluidity and openness to contingent reality when religious travel across regions. This flexibility in religious practices and mutual tolerance form the core of the survival strategies used by these groups. Living in the forgotten backwaters of South Asia, these groups are labeled "peripheral" in political dealings; they face threats to their survival totally unarmed with technology, equipments of any support system from governmental agencies. But their direct dealings with natural phenomena, predatory animal and undeveloped economic system teaches them the secrets of nature that the developed societies cannot learn. Fokir's intimate knowledge of the sea surprises Piya with its utter reliability and accuracy. Kanai initially treats Fokir with a great deal of arrogance, comparing the very different educational and economic levels that they have. But when he gains an insight with that man's moral fiber, his human concern for Piya and his self-sacrifice, Kanai's attitude changes tremendously. Through these encounters and changes, Ghosh successfully creates the need for a change in the society's larger perceptions of these communities and their indigenous knowledge systems.

These local groups gain moral values and integrity of character that fills them with a greater concern for human beings as well as animals. Bonbibi's worship strengthens their ability to deal with danger, and learn to be satisfied with little. In the modern consumerist culture pervading the entire world their bare and hard lives seem shocking. But they possess strength of emotions; show loyalty, trust and complete love for one another that none of the city dwellers (in the novel) has known.

In portraying the village community of the Sunderbans region, Amitav Ghosh brings them into the bigger world—which has, otherwise, forgotten them. By also depicting in detail the story of Bonbibi the deep faith these communities have in her kindness and protective care, Ghosh implies a critical comparison with the other belief systems governing modern man's life. The non-modern, peripheral ethic "has a longer, deeper memory." In these people "faith is more lived out than articulated; and tolerance or forgiveness is given expression in the actualities of living, not in ideological or even theological propositions" (Nandy, 2003:46). In the modern world these values have become difficult to locate, yet all the more needed for peaceful coexistence.

Bonbibi's worship demonstrates through action how co-existence with the "other" can be worked out and maintained. The borders of geographical spaces and cultural spheres can be made sources of writing, and maintaining peace rather than of dividing and destroying the other. Annu Jalai looks upon the folktales as containing special social and political significance in the post-colonial societies fighting with one another over borders and spatial divisions. Similarly, the sharing of natural resources can be done in an ethically responsible manner, by treating the natural world with reverence.

The most significant message of the belief comes in its insistence upon a restrained use of the resources, and tolerance towards animal world, howsoever predatory and violent. Such an outlook shows the wisdom of the village communities who respect the world of nature, use it but do not abuse it. Maintaining such a restraint would require a moral discipline that the modern, global capitalist world seriously lacks.

Works Cited

Ghosh, Amitav. "The Ghosts of Mrs. Gandhi", *The Inam and the Indian, Prose Pieces*. Delhi: Ravi Dayal Publisher, 2002.

Ghosh, Amitav. *The Hungry Tide*, Noida (India): Harper Collins, 2008.

Gupta, Santosh. "Naga-Mandala: A Story of Marriage and Love", *The Plays of Girish Karnad: Critical Perspectives*, Jaydip Sinh Dodiya. New Delhi: Prestige Books, 1999.

Jalais, Annu in *"Bonbibi: Bridging the Worlds"*, http://www.indiafolklore.org/images/7/7a/ifl28.pdf/accessed on 7.3.2012

Karnad, Girish, "Introduction", *Three Plays: The Plays of Girish Karnad: Critical Perspectives*. Ed. Jaydip Sinh Dodiya. New Delhi: Prestige Books, 1999.

Karnad, Girish, "Naga-Mandala", *Three Plays*. Delhi: Oxford University Press, 1994.

Nandy, Ashis. *The Illegitimacy of Nationalism: Rabindranath Tagore and the Politics of Self*. Delhi: Oxford Univ. Press, 1994.

Nandy, Ashis. *The Romance of the State and the Fate of Dissent in the Tropics*. New Delhi: Oxford India Paperback, 2003.

Shukla, S.K. *Rabindranath Tagore—Educational Philosopher and His Work*, New Delhi: Omega Publishers, 2008.

Tagore, R.N. "Chandalika", *A Tagore Reader*. Ed. and translated by Amiya Chakravorty. New Delhi: Rupa & Co., 1994.

7

Myths and Tagore's *The Home and the World*

Sanjoy Saksena

Tagore made extensive use of myths in his fiction because they came handy in validating history. For our purposes it is metahistory or fiction as it finds expression in *Ghare Baire*. The centrality of myths in traditional societies cannot be denied, they not only determine our behavior and beliefs but account for our intense communication at a spiritual level often brought about by common vibes. Tagore's use of myths becomes problematic in the novel because they are interpreted and given a slant through re-contextualization or mis-contextualization for selfish ends by the anti-hero. Myths contain beneath them the essence of truths which are fluid for they depend on their context. The point is that beneath a myth there is no standard or fixed truth for a lot is left for us to interpret. To follow any definite method of critical enquiry is to restrict one's critical incursions and explorations. David Carroll, a Freudian scholar, says:

> Literary criticism is neither "objective" nor universal Any critical method has limitations because it must necessarily be organized around certain principles, the hypothesis, which act as its center of origin.
>
> (*New Literary History*, 513)

I have tried to take this wholesome advice and not confine myself to any ready-made method, charter my own course independently. It is the freedom to interpret that is turned into license and then misused by Sandip that generates the problems. Tagore was aware of the misuse of myths among the Hindus for fishy ends and he tries to expose this social and religious evil that carried within it serious troubles for the masses, including those who belonged to the elite classes. Rationality in religion had become popular among the educated Hindus after Raja Rammohan Roy but a lot remained to be achieved in the form of reform. One of the main reasons for Tagore's wide use of myths in his novel was to reveal the manner in which myths were being employed to the detriment of the national cause by some of those who had managed to reach the forefront of the freedom struggle. Tagore does not even spare the archetype of the mother in the Jungian sense and fuses it with the representation of the mother in the Hindu myths, then he goes on to deconstruct the two together by pressing the clever Sandip into his fictional service. Thus, Freud and Jung are both employed in the novel for displaying the degradation of the character of educated Hindus, many of whom subscribed to the modern myth and concept of Mother India. It is this subversion of the myths and archetypes by Tagore that makes *The Home and the World* a soul destroying experience for the traditional Indian imagination that refuses to critique the hidden side of its countrymen's and leaders' character. Tagore himself was a Zamindar and of the paternalistic kind, therefore, it is but natural that his sympathy should be with Nikhilesh. In fact, it has been speculated that Tagore himself is Nikhilesh in the novel and that the hero's opinions are those of the author himself, if only because in the conflict that followed the *Swadeshi* movement Tagore found himself similarly placed. The choices that stared at Nikhilesh also haunted Tagore. It would be erroneous to presume that Tagore was against nationalism but he certainly could not rush in to support strident nationalism in its perverse form at the cost of several other issues and problems that besieged his motherland.

The *Swadeshi* position was that the nation was above everything else. It was this everything else, which often included thousands of poor people, which Tagore was not willing to sacrifice or ruin for blinkered nationalism; on the contrary he tried to highlight that which was being senselessly sacrificed and destroyed by the *Swadeshi* movement. The contradiction between the *Swadeshi* and the European enveloped a much wider problem: the conflict between modernity and retrogressive tradition. Modernity after all came to India from the West and it came at a time when the Indians were technologically and attitudinally behind the Europeans. The choice before Tagore and his even more influential contemporary Gandhi was the choice between progressiveness and general backwardness. Gandhi whether right or wrong was more certain about his opinions but Tagore kept on dithering, lost in the searing experiences that he underwent in Bengal. The compromise that they reached was an uneasy one for even the religious and social reform movements were either a direct consequence of European modernity or a reaction against it that resulted in serious critical introspection on rational lines. The potent evident form of reaction was patriotism and nationalism, ideas that had traveled from Europe and assumed an Indian color. All *Swadeshis*, including Gandhi at a later stage, were confident when they chose nationalism but Tagore remained uncomfortable with their notions as the novel, *Ghare Baire*, itself bears out. Tagore's discomfort with nationalism manifested itself in some of his essays and he till the end believed that the English would become a part of the synthetic Indian culture and settle down in India the way the Huns, Mongols, Uzbegistanis, Afghans, Arabs, Turks, Persians, etc. had done in the past. Gandhi called Tagore "The Great Sentinel" and a true watch dog as he refused to accept the dominant prevailing political opinions and social codes of conduct that were being followed by the general mill of the Indian society, whether feudal landlords or the general mass of people. *The Home and the World* sought to expose that face of India that in social eclipse, was being suppressed to encourage a particular politics of gender and in support of the *Swadeshi* movement whose means did not justify the ends. The novel highlights that anti-colonialism which had overtaken Bengal from 1905 to 1908 because it was not a sufficient precondition either for independence or emancipation from general backwardness because the British policy of divide and rule had made its wide ranging disastrous claims deep in the Indian psyche. The Hindu patriots by being overzealous were actually dividing the Indian society on communal lines, tearing apart the ruptured social fabric and playing into the hands of their colonial adversaries.

The question that one may ask is: Why is *Ghare Baire* replete with myths? Tagore uses myths extensively because they denoted a shared thinking and when it came to the sphere of religion their being held sacrosanct gave them immense power over the emotional masses. Indians were as a people, and still are, tradition minded. They have blind faith in myths and this makes them more susceptible to being taken for a ride or cheated, as it happens in this novel:

> Enlightened thinking or *logos*, writes Jurgen Hebermas, seeks to convince through "the unforced force of the better argument," while myth takes its stand on the authoritarian normativity of a tradition. Myth, in the words of an expositor of Barthes, is "another word for the *doxa*, a common, unexamined assumption rooted... in the prevailing political (or social) order." Basing ourselves on this philosophical and critical sense of the "myth", we may define it as a set of propositions, often stated in narrative form, that is accepted uncritically by a culture or speech-community and that serves to found or affirm its self-conception.
>
> (Heehs, 3)

When people believe in religious myths, the emergence of those who exploit such beliefs becomes a natural cultural corollary. Sandip fits the tricky bill and takes advantage of the "self-conception" that people have based on myths and religion. He gives Bimala a new identity that is a modified version of whatever she thinks she is. Since the belief in myths or self-conception based on myths is non-scientific inherently, it becomes extremely easy for him to pander and work his way up into the landlord's family, till he assumes a commanding position. He goes on transforming myths at will and plays on the sexual layers of meaning hidden, often providing them where they would be normally absent and transmitting them to Bimala. The logic and authority are bungled up and blended in such an intricate manner that truth becomes a casualty; the unscientific is presented as rational and such deliberately mixed-up rationale is swallowed as logical.

Many of those who were apparently on the Indian side were brown skinned carpet baggers, political adventurers, and looking avariciously for personal gains in the violence that ensued. The post-independence rhetoric presupposes that all Indians were one and that they were largely supportive of the *Swadeshi* cause whereas the fact of the matter is that outside Bengal few people had much to do with it, continued to live as they had in utter hopelessness under the colonial patronage. The violence that followed the Revolt of 1857 and the dire consequences that it invited for the revolutionaries had established the supremacy of the mighty British who in the succeeding years had become more ruthless by controlling. More than the Nawab of Dacca it was the new class of native educated elite that foresaw India's future in modernization that meant following the colonial modes of thought. If there was muslim communalism, there was Hindu communalism too! As for his own self Tagore was not opposed to those Europeans who were sympathetic in the way in which Mrs. Annie Besant was because India was unprepared to charter its own course of destiny in the community of world nations. The matter had become clearer after the outbreak of the First World War. The ignorance and poverty of the masses coupled with fissiparous tendencies never allowed Tagore to feel confident about India emerging as a truly independent and powerful nation on its nativistic strength.

To remove the general backwardness and to destroy the myth about the home being the rightful place of women, Tagore introduces Western thought and practices. Miss Gilby's presence in the novel and Nikhilesh's attempt to Europeanize his wife are indicative of the serious inadequacies that were the hallmark of most Indian women. The protagonist, Nikhilesh, himself tries to destroy the myth about women as being purveyors and guardians of Indian culture by espousing

Western ideas for social upward movement. In a world driven by science and commerce myths about the greatness of traditional women had to be destroyed, the veil of ignorance had to be shed and supplanted by progressiveness. The Miss Gilby episode in the novel shows how self-conscious the Bengali aristocracy was while it was struggling to Europeanize itself, even though many from the aristocratic fold were opposed to Westernization because the *Swadeshi* movement had gained a hold on its imagination and their closed minds did not approve of women's emancipation when around the same time Virginia Woolf was busy attacking the patriarchy left, right and center. It would be difficult to deny the Indian intelligentsia's ignorance of her writings because British newspapers and journals were being avidly read by the elite in Calcutta. The resentment to Miss Gilby's presence being emblematized by stone pelting by Naren and the necessity of all that she stood for as perceived by the so-called moderns being symbolized by Nikhilesh's personally escorting the lady—"taking things a bit too far". This may be considered as an invitation to European sexuality and often it was confused in those days, as it is even today, with libertinism. The point was to liberate women and the country by adopting Western modes of thought, infusing them inside the households, against the colonials.

In the beginning it was Bimala who keeps on warning Nikhilesh about the avaricious nature of Sandip and his enormous capacity for cheating under the garb of patriotism and friendship. To start with Bimala is described by Sandip as "a representative of that goddess-motherland". Gradually, she is identified as the goddess itself in flattery and for the sake of manipulation. It was Sandip who made Bimala the image of Mother India, a concept that was foisted initially by Bankim Chandra Chatterji, and he discussed matters concerning the liberation of India with her, often over-powering the impressionable woman with his deceptive rhetoric that the husband often dismissed with a smile. First, a communication gap and a difference of opinion is created between the husband and wife. Later, he plays his game of sexual chess, bringing in his followers to bolster his arguments in support of the *Swadeshi*. It was with the passage of time that the "veil of inhibition" was ripped away between the crafty lover and the puffed up beloved, the "zeal of lust" prevailing more and more strongly. Tagore does not leave the matter unclear and Sandip brazenly says on Bimala's face that "women have become enchantresses under duress" (Tagore, 52). Sandip was a past master in the art of seduction and he had become further emboldened by his success with the widow Kusum who voluntarily surrendered as well as the white girl whom he described as "fire-wood". The game plan was to make women accept "desire as a reality" and encourage them to take the road to modernity that too as he understood it in his own licentious way. The point of Sandip's larger argument was to create a praxis between conceptions of mother India, Durga, Kali and Radha in Bimala's mind, make her break inhibitions in which sexuality was bound to play as much a role as the release of feminine energy for apparent social, political and spiritual transformation. Deep down the motives were always unholy, unpatriotic and full of luxurious greed. It is the much touted capacity for spiritual transformation of the goddesses and their ability to change our lives for the better that has been utilized by Sandip to win over Bimala. A change does take place in the woman and the very first steps that makes *Ghare Baire*, outside the safe confines home, and into the deceptive world go in the wrong directions, lead her to perdition. What Tagore is trying to highlight is that the path to women's reform and national liberation was fraught with tricky problems that could come from directions where one expected them the least. Politically speaking, it is the supposed leader and patriotic liberator of India, Sandip, who poses the greatest threat to the causes that he is arguing for and openly espousing.

Sandip knows very well the progress he had made with Bimala, was also confident that the desire within her had made the woman fall into his hands, he was aware of the hesitation in her due to social repercussions and yet to achieve his goal he thinks in his own eccentric manner that he would "merge Bimala with his country". Thus, the merger of mother India and Bimala is due to a planned dishonest intellectual effort and not merely an accident that happens in the immature female mind:

> The same westward storm that has snatched away the veil of right and wrong from the face of the motherland, will raise the bridal veil off Bimala face—there is no disregard for her in that nakedness. The ship will sway on the waves of the ocean of people, the victory flag of Vande Mataram will flutter at its helm, roars and foaming waters all around—that ship will be our vessel of strength as well as that of love. There, Bimala will perceive such immense freedom that on its face, all her inhibitions will drop away without shame, unknown to her. Fascinated by this visage of destruction she won't hesitate to turn cruel. In Bimala I have seen the face of that gorgeous ruthlessness, which is the natural strength of Nature. If women could free themselves of the phony binds placed on them by men, I'd have truly witnessed Kali on this earth—she is the brazen goddess, she is heartless. I am a devotee of the same Kali; one day I'll drag Bimala amidst that devastation and invoke Kali. Let me make preparations for that.
>
> (Tagore, 84)

The point is that in Sandip's imagination sexuality, myths, religion and nationalism have coalesced, his attitude towards the three is ambivalent, maniacal, deceptive and corrupt. He wants to ravish mother India and its strategically created representation—Bimala, through convoluted rhetorical drives, perverse improvised symbolism and deceptive language. For him in sexual ecstasy the imagination takes flight and he himself partakes in secret pleasures, enjoys pain, thrills of female conquest and political surge. One of the ways in which Sandip wins over Bimala is by showering praises on her physical beauty, apart from the spiritual and dynamic qualities that she was made to imagine that she possessed. Bimala was aware of her lack of physical beauty because right since childhood she had been reminded of this in her parental house. Richard Moran says:

> One might, for instance, have reasons to be suspicious of pleasure itself, its role in culture, or the exaggerated claims for it, or one may have metaphysical scruples deriving from the idea that beauty can be no property of things in themselves but can only be a projection of our own sensibilities upon the world. In different ways, then, there can seem to be a certain extravagance built into the notion of the beautiful itself, as though it were internal to its invocation that it claims more for itself than it can deliver on.
>
> (Moran, 298)

It is the pursuit of pleasure, power and wealth that motivate Sandip to lavish praise on her looks and it is due to his exaggeration of her womanly graces that Bimala starts projecting herself as extraordinary. Her latent sensibility that had been suppressed at a young age comes to the fore and she tries to impose her beauty and other imaginary gifts of greatness on her subjects and husband. The husband does not repudiate her claims but on the other hand derives satisfaction in seeing that his wife had gained confidence in herself. Her husband tries to enhance her physical beauty by adding frills like more Westernized blouses and hair-styles after the European fashion. The notion of beauty itself undergoes a change and Western concepts start taking precedence: the internal invocation is challenged. Bimala till she is polluted by Sandip takes pride in her 'inner beauty' and purity. The beauty myth helps in building the mysterious superiority syndrome that she inhabits under her lover's influence. What Max Muller called the "disease of language" contributes towards building the profane myth that she herself becomes for her own self while suffering from narcissism. Wittgenstein broadly believed that myths, including those of beauty, could lead to paradoxical changes in character. Bimala's language itself undergoes a change, becomes more charged and she tries to alleviate herself and the desire present in her transcends language.

This is a precisely Freudian situation in which sadomasochism is present, one in which both Bimala and

Sandip swing like a pendulum between Eros and Thanatos. Both, Bimala and Sandip suffer from narcissism, the dicey patriot from a sense of inadequacy due to a lack of money and the woman from the limitations of her gender that she is fragilely out to conquer with cleverness under the influence of sexual attraction. Their limitations compel the growth of a restrictive inferiority which they try to surmount with shamelessness and intrigue, especially against Nikhilesh who is more balanced and devoid of flashiness in administering, intellectual matters and politics. If we study the subconscious template of Bimala that started taking shape when she was a child, we recognize that she was extremely conscious of her lack of beauty, and this gave rise to the urge to draw attention of others and dominate the scene, once Nikhilesh had given her more latitude than was required in those days. It is this subconscious template that ultimately leads to her loss of chastity and being cheated due to her blind faith in Sandip. After all, Lord Ram's wife Sita, mother of Luv and Kush, is considered to be the epitome of purity in Hindu culture. It was Sita who was a part of Bimala' self-righteous thoughts. The loss of purity in Bimala was the result of the over lapping of modernity, love for the motherland, erotic love, familial love and friendship. Sandip was almost a brother to Nikhilesh and later to his wife and it was after taking them into confidence that he could practice his guiles on them. There was always a suspicion about his activities deep down in the couple but they succumbed because he had managed to create a tunnel vision in Bimala; she saw what he wanted her to see once she had been smothered intellectually, over-powered emotionally and slowly sexually as well.

Tagore practiced restraint in describing sexuality and unlike D.H. Lawrence, who was one of his hostile reviewers, chose to be reticent. The development of secret sexual desires in Bimala for Sandip had pushed her into a state of self-hypnosis, a cloudy state of mind in which she could never perceive anything independently. Unconsciously, Bimala becomes more and more aggressive and she starts hiding matters from Nikhilesh, even despising his balanced understanding of the ugly situation that had arisen due to the *Swadeshi* politics. What Freud called "the pleasure principle" or translation of drives into need and actions dominate Bimala and Sandip, whereas Nikhilesh considers and reconsiders his actions, weighs them. Nikhilesh is conscious of the affair between his wife and friend but does not plot revenge or try to subvert the filthy *Swadeshi* politics: he merely wishes to purge it of its maliciousness and evils. He is a man with a conscience and believes in right action, there is no contradiction between thought and action in him most unlike his friend and rival Sandip for Bimala's affections. The life instinct within him does not motivate him into either illegitimate relationships or preventing his wife from attaining liberation from social mores or resorting to exploitative practices as a landed aristocrat. A simple exercise of brutal power that came naturally to the likes of him would have got rid of miserably poor and crafty Sandip. Nikhilesh fails to support the *Swadeshi* nationalism wherever he finds that it goes against the interests of the helpless rustics who have no workable alternative choices to eke out a living. He wants to float a shipping company, start a factory to meet the requirements of Indians but would not do anything that would lead to the growth of fissiparous tendencies among the Hindus and muslims or destroy petty traders selling European goods for their survival.

It is the life instinct within that makes him love Bimala, Westernize her dresses and manners, and act in the general interest of the poor. Bimala on the other hand is carried off her feet and as the novel starts tapering towards the end, caught in-between her sexual drives, guilt, arrogance, betrayal and, in Freudian language, death instinct; she is driven towards to borrow from Freud, once again, "the nirvana principle". The nirvana principle inherents a death wish and the desire inherent in it is compared to the blowing out of a candle which denotes rising above all pain and suffering. It is after being possessed by this death wish that Bimala decides to steal money and give away her jewelry: "All the time I felt if I died, all troubles would cease" (Tagore, 210). The words that Tagore employs to describe Bimala's psychological condition are "hypnotized" and "mesmerized", especially in relation to Sandip. And the man apart from being seductive also carries plenty of intellectual freight that he does not practice himself and convinces the woman to believe in him to enjoy life on her money, improve his chances within the politics of the *Swadeshi* movement. Bimala is caught up in the middle of conflicting demands, between Nikhilesh and Sandip, ideas that they stood for. It was as much Sandip's sexual overtures as his strong language that won the women to his side and towards the end of the novel Bimala makes Nikhilesh risk his life after the outbreak of communal violence. In the novel, Nikhilesh is critically wounded but in Satyajit Ray's film he is supposed to be fatally injured: dead. The paradox about the possibilities of survival is resolved and the flickering ray of hope is killed much to the audience's discomfiture. Bimala does not suffer from much moral anxiety, Sandip is untouched by it and Nikhilesh is possessed by it. It is the loss of moral anxiety that causes impulsive behavior in Bimala and Sandip, causes the debauch leader of the *Swadeshi* movement to behave like a confidence tricking criminal. Bimala loses control over herself and rationality falls a willing prey in the hands of Sandip once she is under the spell of libidinal drives that block her initial suspicion and caution. Even when she becomes conscious of Sandip's foul play and luxuriousness she glosses over the matter simply because the sexual drives had been kindled well inside her consciousness. Nikhilesh and his widowed sisters-in-law were aware of the germinating sexuality between Bimala and Sandip. One of them disapproves graciously, another one passes sly bawdy remarks and Nikhilesh adopts an ascetic attitude, tries to protest himself through self-denial, abnegation, isolation and by not taking an aggressive stand.

It is well known that Tagore was like his other influential contemporaries a part of Hindu nationalism and believed like Ranade, Tilak, Vivekanand and Sri Aurobindo that by singing the glories of ancient Hindustan he would be able to contribute towards rebuilding Indian pride and ousting the Europeans. It was only after his intimate experience of the *Swadeshi* movement that he became disillusioned. If the Nawab of Dacca was fanning communalism and playing into the hands of the British, the Hindu nationalists who were all for *Swadeshi* were behaving in a coercive manner even if it meant a big loss to the poor peasantry. It was this thoughtless intimidation of the peasantry, completely unmindful of the serious economic consequences that drove him to revise his opinions. He became critical of the muslims, Hindu nationalists, feudal landlords as well as the peasants who were often not driven by any moral compulsions. The poor peasants were hardly conscious of their national obligations and barely understood the larger aims behind the *Swadeshi* movement. Most of them wanted to subsist as they had done in the past and were averse to anything that was likely to jeopardize the shaky economic status of their families any further. Apart from communalism at that time, following the partition of Bengal in 1905, nationalism in Europe had led to the First World War. Tagore around that time had been traveling in the U.S.A. and Japan, lecturing distraught with its future scope. The subsequent reception of the novel was also affected very much by the savageries that were witnessed by huge numbers of the populace in Europe and elsewhere. *Ghare Baire*, therefore, became, in the succeeding years, a call for nationalistic restraint and for a comprehensive, balanced understanding. Sandip's personality is exposed in front of Nikhilesh when he confesses clearly. It is just that the man's inherent goodness and kindness come in his way when it comes to dismissing his dear friend:

> One thing, Nikhil, is for sure—in these times, it is women who will salvage our nation. This is not the time for us to differentiate between good and evil, right and wrong; today, unscrupulously and indifferently, we have to be ruthless and unfettered; we have to anoint sin with holy markers and let the women of the nation receive it cordially. Don't you remember what the poet has said?—
>
> Welcome sin, welcome oh beauty!
> Let the flaming tonic of your kiss
> Inflame my blood.

> Sound the trumpet of malevolence,
> Anoint my brow with infamy,
> Fill my heart with tumultuous,
> Dark, sinful murk, shameless.
> Shame on that piety which is incapable of being callously ruthless.
>
> Having said this, he stamped his foot twice very loudly. Startled, a lot of drowsy dust rose off the carpet and into the air. He stood straight with such pride after having scorned in an instant the very values, which are treasured across lands over the ages, that a shiver went down my spine as I looked at him. (Tagore, 28-29)

Not only Nikhilesh but Bimala is immediately made aware of what was in the offing and Sandip's success with the lady should be seen in this light for she knew too well all that was happening. She becomes a willing prey to Sandip's lust because despite all the resistance and the inhibitions, she allows herself to become his friend and ally. Nationalism was merely a cover-up and she betrays the confidence reposed in her by her husband. Sandip never tries to hide his desire for Bimala before her and it is his directness as well as mixing up of sexuality with nationalist politics that makes his task easier.

In *Ghare Baire,* Bimala is the heroine and both husband Nikhilesh and his friend Sandip are the satellites that revolve around her, affect her destiny. Bimala's lack of exposure to the outside world and rawness make her sensitive and prone to new ideas that are double edged and dangerous because of the corruption hidden beneath supposedly progressive intellectual and ideological activities. The triangle that forms between Bimala, Nikhilesh and Sandip leads to the growth of psycho-sexual conflict within the lady that has calamitous social and political repercussions for the people of the surrounding areas. Nationalism and the husband's desire to see his wife catch up with the forward thinking European women assiduously stirs the libido within the woman, to get trapped within the conflict between Eros and Thanatos. The reification of reality, the over lappings and transgressions of love for Mother India drive Bimala in directions that she cannot comprehend because inherent in this desire is the fixation for smooth talking Sandip. It is at this juncture that Thanatos or the death wish becomes paramount inside her encapsulated as it is within patriotism, tradition, sexuality and freedom. The paradox is infused with the urge to prove herself worthy as a champion of the *Swadeshi* cause and as a woman who is capable of making sacrifices no less than the chauvinistic men whom contemporary Bengali society held in high esteem. In Bimala the source of the death wish is libido itself and it is while being troubled by these contradictions that she girds up her loins to move forward, often with the aid of her doting husband who for all his generosity and sincerity is cheated heartlessly by his own close friend. Bimala imagines herself as an incarnation of Mother India and it is this delusion that eggs her on to participate in activities, emotionally and politically transgressive, fall for Sandip who is her pretentious 'worshipper', seducer and cheat at the same time. For a normal Hindu woman belonging to a conservative household due to the strong grip of traditional feminine morality, this would be inconceivable.

Tagore himself came from a family that took pride in its Europeanization to a fault, its women being liberated, howsoever reluctantly, and its men folk were reputed to be libertines like most Zamindars. To Europeanize in those days was a difficult proposition because it was not socially acceptable, certainly not within the four walls of the house, and the vast majority who did give themselves a try had done it with limited success. The Tagores were not Hindus in the strict sense for they professed Brahmoism, which combined within itself a limited amount Christian practices with traditional Hinduism, nor were they muslims. This gave them leverage to often ignore the social pressures, especially when combined with their wealth, and access to their colonial masters. Tagore, therefore, could write about the scandalous liaison between Bimala and Sandip, an immoral relationship, that Sandip's young followers failed to imagine as being true. Therefore, the novel that was serialized in *Sabuj Patra* and was considered spicy reading material and its critique of the *Swadeshi* movement considered of secondary importance by many readers. It was the possibility of scandal and immorality that titillated them and in this sense we can say that Tagore played up to the popular bourgeoisie taste in his own inimitable manner. "I need to do something self-destructive to be able to bear the ecstasy I felt" (Tagore, 20). This is at once a European response, one that an Indian woman from an orthodox Hindu family in the second decade of the twentieth century was incapable of on her own. It is death wish sans sorrow and suffering, the thrill of sin!

When Bimala and Sandip meet each other for the first time, the lady resents his transgressions which unfortunately have her husband's sanction confused as they are with forward looking social behavior. Sandip possesses a much stronger, deceptive and aggressive personality in comparison to Nikhilesh's who in turn keeps on generously giving him money, often even when he disagreed with his concocted reasons. Nikhilesh being a man does not have any sexual attraction towards Sandip which Bimala, being inexperienced of the outside world and safe within the confines of home, has. Sandip's outbursts against his dear friend and patron Nikhilesh together with his sexual attraction and guiles over power her and gradually she starts identifying with the aggressor, in the process forgiving his trespasses and absorbing his negative traits, immaturely rationalizing and sublimating all the while.

Tagore, in the novel, several times, describes contact between Sandip and Bimala in what Freudian parlance one may describe as erogenous zones and their psycho-sexual consequences, actions that have a direct socio-political bearing. The psycho-sexual becomes important because it makes Bimala and Sandip end as up dirty partners in the politics of the *Swadeshi* movement in which thousands were destroyed in and around the area that was within the scope of Nikhilesh's administration. Bimala's tragedy is less important in her personal domain and more so in the public sphere. Socio-politically even economically speaking, the tragedy caused by the psycho-sexual problems of Sandip, Bimala and Nikhilesh create disturbances that were to initiate terrible consequences for the poor and the uneducated folk who had little control over their own destinies. In his struggle against the English, Sandip makes Bimala his linchpin and not Nikhilesh who tries to be more compassionate as well as pro-poor.

Once Bimala has been eulogized and flattered as being a symbolic Mother India or a Mother Goddess like Radha, Durga and Kali by Sandip, she tries to live up to this image. She becomes sensitive to her husband's patronizing and imagines an active independent role for herself in the social and political issues that confront her people. Her logic is fuzzy and her vision is obscure, clouded by steamy concupiscence. Traditionally too the wives of Zamindars and landlords were looked upon by their subjects as mothers because they were considered to be the feeders, givers, protectors and the saviours. The concept of Mother India gained currency after Bankim Chandra Chatterji and was employed with great success by the nationalists after the Mutiny of 1857 to knit a splintered India together. Sandip capitalizes on this traditional mode of thought and deludes Bimala with intoxicating ideas about political independence and a rosy future to such an extent that she being a green horn, without any direct encounter of the outside world's chicaneries, succumbs and swallows his *Swadeshi* bait that is laced with self-indulgence, deception and political ambitions. As time passes Bimala loses self-control and starts suffering from penis envy, seeks a substitute in Sandip as a lover and accepts her subordinate position. The dynamic repression finds an outburst and she rises in her own self-estimate when compared to the mythic Durga and Kali, goddesses of power. She rises to such an extent that she starts behaving like one of those village women who, when possessed by the *devi*, go out of control in a trance. It is in such moments that one can locate a form of mother-fixation in Sandip, a resurgence and mutilated reappearance of the Oedipus complex. After all being a rich landlord's wife, Bimala had induced the people to describe and address her as Mother India, Durga and Kali, if only out of expectations for financial assistance and patriotic inspiration that they had from her. In Sandip's case, it was more financial and sexual gratification but he too feels dwarfed at times in her presence, often being unsure of the extent of her generosity.

Sandip played the motherly card to gain the lady's confidence and affections to exploit or shall we say exploit her. A common four-letter word in India is "mother-fucker". It was employed by Mulk Raj Anand with amazing success in his novel *Untouchable*. The point is that the origins of this four-letter word have their basis in reality and polygamy was common in pre-modern India. Mother-fucker has sexual denotations clearly but it is understood largely metaphorically, i.e. in the sense of spoiling, bungling, subverting, cheating and double dealing. Today, the four-letter word has gained perhaps greater currency and has lost its precise meaning but the sexual connotations have not been lost for living mother-goddesses abound in this country as they did in the past. Deification of women is endemic to Hindu society and the gullible one's are befooled and cheated by men by attributing divine motherly qualities to them. Bimala is convinced about being extra-ordinary by Sandip, brain-washed till sexuality and divinity blur in her imagination, combine to produce the tragedy in which her wealth and husband are lost. The psychodynamics that forms within Bimala shows that she transforms from a humble house-wife into a woman of high self-esteem, her prior submissiveness is overtaken by incredible deceptiveness and pushy assertiveness.

She imagines herself as an incarnation of power or *Shakti*, an agent of redemption, of freedom; and as Radha who is Lord Krishna's mistress and somebody else's wife in the Hindu mythology. Radha too is attributed strongly divine qualities and she is placed by many of her devotees on a higher pedestal than Lord Krishna himself. The myth thus supports Bimala's idea of being divine herself at the promptings of Sandip who is on the lookout for the pleasures of the flesh and lucre, both. This ideational pugnacity and cleverness is in defiance of her own reason that had been atrophied by the calculating, scheming and artful Sandip—his bombast and grandiloquent ideas for independence, women's emancipation and self-reliance. Sandip's ideas do not cut much ice with his friend

Nikhilesh who patronizes him but keeps his preferences clear, often at odds with those of his friend. Being an independent man Nikhilesh has no homosexual compulsions to pressurize him. If we believe as perhaps Freud did that an oedipal relationship between a mother and son is unavoidable. The possibility of a similar relationship between the mother-goddess and devotee sons always remains nascent. It is common in all cultures to attribute motherly qualities, or, to bestow or attribute the status of a mother to women who are rich and powerful by those who expect something in return from them. The receiver or recipient of kindness and generosity becomes a son or is assigned whatever the position of a poor son may be in front of his rich, influential and benevolent mother. Since such relationships are not natural or through blood, the possibility of sexuality being present in them is always there. In most cases, the possibilities of a strong sexual bonding and relationship can be ruled out for they are killed at a nascent or initial stage by the conscious mind.

Symbolism and signification work within a cultural context and those who are a part of that particular culture cannot easily escape the codes of conduct that the symbolic order or hierarchy has to impose. Human nature due to its inherent characteristics often goes beyond the limitations that are supposed to exist, breaks the sanctioned boundaries that the social order imposes as it happens in the case of Sandip and Bimala. The question arises: why does Sandip have to make Bimala imagine herself as a mythic mother-goddess and Mother India—a giver, provider and sustainer? Why does Sandip need to make Bimala fantasize about herself as being some kind of a mother to poor Indians, including himself? The answer is a simple one: it helps him pander to her womanly graces, ego and exploit her. With the aid of brash, aggressive and powerful speeches that are at bottom hollow and in which he himself does not believe, he manages to prove his genuineness that is at the core fake and he tramples her husband's cool, balanced and sincere thinking with his spurious ideas. With Nikhilesh he used his grandiloquent thoughts and appealed to his kindness. On the contrary, with Bimala he ends up demanding money that he spends on luxuries which he could not afford and on playing *Swadeshi* politics to gain prominence—creates a communal situation in which Nikhilesh is critically, almost fatally injured. Possessed by the demon of love and *Swadeshi* Bimala doesn't have imagination enough to realize that she had dispatched her husband to his death. Psychologically speaking, if Nikhilesh be the father and Sandip the son, then in this case the father's death can be pinned along with the mother on the son, the son more than the mother because he was the prime motivator. This confirms the Freudian theory of incest in which the son has a desire to kill the father and to possess the mother solely for his affections. In *Ghare Baire,* the imagined mother connives with the imagined son with little compunctions to restrain. Deification helps in India in gaining the hearts of men and women, and in the case of the latter in gaining sympathies and access to the extent that one can exploit them, with some cleverness, sexually. Sandip we are told in the novel was a known philanderer and a clever talking cheat.

Myths have therapeutic value in a religious society and people who subscribe to religion lend themselves happily to such therapies. Medication is administered and to be understood metaphorically. Religion implies faith and a willing suspension of disbelief—acceptance of the metaphysical as the truth itself. Therapy in the religious sense is not just considered necessary for those who have lost their faith but also for those who are possessed by it to make them more stoutly devout:

> When we use the word "therapy" we can refer to treatment not only of the body or psyche but of something more "religious" suggested by the word "soul". "Religious" as used here assumes the recognition of a universal entity that, as indicated by etymology, somehow binds things back to itself. This binding back provides the religious person with his or her reason for being, and traditionally the point of connection between the divine and the individual is the soul. If the soul is "sick", if connection with the reason for being is lost, therapy is called for.
>
> (D. Leeming, 115)

Religion in the hands of persons of low integrity or shall we say dubious doctors can be put to perverse ends. For our purposes it is Sandip who is the perverse physician who finds a patient in Bimala for himself. He gives myths and religious beliefs a twist and turn according to his dishonest requirements. He makes use of myths, as Barthes would suggest, because it is not the business of science to do so and capitalizes on mystification. He makes the cure itself a disease and it is this aspect that Leeming ignores in his learned essay that relies on psychology, myths and religion to explore our spiritual lives. Metaphors are given new meanings according to the false doctor's fancy and the content beneath the surface becomes damaging instead of being curative. His cures generate diseases of the mind and later of the flesh, money and politics. Patriotism becomes a camouflage and a Freudian obsession with sex is underpinned with ease. The sickness of the Indian soul for freedom and abolition of poverty is treated in such a manner that death and destruction become inevitable towards the end.

Sandip calls Bimala, Radha, and expects her to behave as Radha did with Lord Krishna in her intimate interface with him. Bimala, besotted, crosses the barriers that the commonly accepted norms of contemporary Hindu matrimony had placed on her because Radha too was a married woman and had fallen in love with Krishna outside her marriage. This provided the rationale for the relationship between Sandip and Bimala, justification for forming an illegitimate bond that the society would not accept even though in religion there was a shining example. As Radha, Bimala was to be Sandip's devotee and beloved, an expanded form of the Lord's energy and divine inspiration in the task of decolonization. In the Vaishnav faith that Tagore understood well and partially subscribed to Radha and Krishna have been taken as being a part of the same God, the Hindu supreme God understood as *Ardhnarishwar* because God in Hinduism is at once both male and female. Since Radha and Krishna become the expanded manifestation of the Supreme Being, Bimala and Sandip too tried appropriate the right to become a dynamic patent of the sublime because deep down there was deceit that required a convincing cover. Bimala cheats her husband and encourages him to go weaponless into the communal violence whereas Sandip heartlessly deceives both of them. Their being taken for ride proves how vulnerable the genteel folk were to double dealing, especially when indulged in by the educated fraudulent patriots. It is this profanity, double-cross and callousness that makes the triangular relationship pathetic, sad and phony. The sham works on the naïve and ignorant woman because she accepts Sandip's words at their face value once she is infatuated with him and conquered by his craftiness.

In *Brihad-Gautamiya Tantra,* Radha is described mythically as "Sarva-laskshmi-mayi" or as the one who embodies all wealth and it is this association with wealth that attracts Sandip the most towards his adoring lady patron. He becomes a conditioned soul and a devotee to rip-off Radha or Bimala, short change. It is with Radha and Krishna that the ecstasy of love is associated and celebrated. And it is this aspect of the relationship that becomes surreptitiously the tantalizing and scrambled motive. Radha and Krishna are incomplete without each other, they are the binaries that combine to form a divine whole of love and cosmic energy. Radha is referred to as Radharani or Queen Radha and Bimala is frequently referred to as Queen Bee or just Queen or Queen Radha by innuendo and a process of inclusion. Queen Bee is an appellation that is born out of a hybridity of thought that was present in all educated people and was used to flatter the lady, win her affections. Lord Krishna in various medieval texts assumes the position of a devotee to taste Radha's sweetness which is divine and exhibits his own divine potency. It is this transcendental consciousness that is at work within Bimala and creates within her an extremely high degree of devotion towards Sandip which actually leads to a change of heart in the edgy swindler who wears the mask of *Swadeshi* for he returns a part of the wealth that he had stolen from her husband's treasury and the misguided woman's jewelry. The true devotee of this self-professed Radha-Krishna duo in the novel is Amulya, true to the bone, pure hearted, and devoted to the cause of the nation—and he gives his life in their service as well as the cause that they apparently supported. However, the conman is won over by devotion and *Shakti* of the woman who decides to sacrifice her all for the sake of her country and lover.

The Vaishnav legend has it that Radha kept Lord Krishna under her control and in *Ghare Baire* Sandip feels small in Bimala's presence, admits his treachery and devotion to her, before, he takes leave of the lady and Nikhilesh. He feels her power/*Shakti*—"the death-dance" inside him, "weak" and "caged". The libidinal drives inside the lady prompt her to get more intimate with Sandip and she confesses it too while introspecting. The blame therefore does not lie entirely on Sandip for Bimala also ambitiously imagines a more prominent role for herself in the *Swadeshi* movement, in the society that kept its women in *Purdah*. Her differences with Nikhilesh were obvious to all family members, no less clear were her preferences for a man other than her husband, and she imagined herself as an individual who had a right to follow her own path in life perhaps due to the European influence that was invited by the master of the house willingly in the name of social progress. Northrop Frye tried to define myths in terms of the "great chain of being" through which human beings sought the so-called highest accomplishments of their desires and all things were supposed to ultimately coalesce into the divine. The binary opposite of the divine is the infernal and in the case of *The Home and the World* the two overlap and create an aporiatic space. It is this space that gradually drifts towards the vicious, upsets the balance and causes the tragedy. Frye's great chain of being becomes complex and transgresses the balance which mankind had consciously tilted in favor of the divine; and this conflict becomes an important centrifugal intertext in the novel as we delve into the layers of meaning.

Myth has it that Radha is also worshipped as a mother and because of over-lappings due to her prominence in mythology as Krishna's beloved, an element of the Oedipal invariably enters subterraneanly. It is this synthesis between her worship as a mother and beloved at once that emulsifies the sexual, activates it, because the goddess is understood in a multiple ways by the common people who would fain deny this ambivalence and amalgamation that are sometimes employed for dubious ends. It is this assorted ambiguity that Tagore as a novelist exploits and Sandip utilizes, mingles to his profit. Several exponents of Vaishnavism, especially during modern times, have warned the uninitiated about the possibilities of being misled by mischievous and motivated fabrications. The moment the element of *Shakti* or power in Radha is invoked, the motherly aspect of the goddess gains prominence. It is under Krishna's beloved's patronage that the devotees flourish—the same beloved that has become a metaphor for all mistresses among the Hindus. It is this fusion between the beloved, the mother, the powerful and the wealth showering that Tagore intends to play upon and he makes the parallel between Radha and Bimala's position ostensibly clear. The Hindu religious psychology is as complex as the mother-son relationship was for Sigmund Freud and it flourishes in the Indian social domain.

Sandip is always aggressive in his behavior when it comes to dealing with Nikhilesh and Bimala, as also others. Aggression is a way of getting past people and having his way with the people for Sandip. His sexual concerns and interests in Bimala become obvious once he gains proximity to her. Melford Spiro has candidly explained the crux of the matter on theoretical lines:

> It used to be that one had to be a Freudian to believe that nonsexual themes in ritual and myth might possibly be viewed as disguised expressions of sexual concerns. It now appears that only a Freudian might believe that undisguised sexual themes might be expressions of sexual concerns. And not only sexual. For the wide influence of Levi-Strauss' theory of myth also suggests that only a Freudian might believe that explicit aggressive themes in myth are really concerned with aggression.
>
> (American Anthropologist, 81)

Aggression for its own sake has never been the case and for our purposes the Freudian motives are abundantly clear for as Levi-Strauss would also suggest they reflect mental patterns. Sandip encourages violence between the Hindus and Muslims before rioting starts in Nikhilesh's territory and in neighboring areas. His aggressive behavior leads to aggression between the two major religious communities and the motives are out and out political. In Nikhilesh's fiefdom, violence is instigated by Sandip's men and the master is eventually destroyed. It is this aggression mixed with aggression that becomes a recurrent pattern of behavior in Sandip's case, his style as it were, that thrives on spirituality and nationalism as a cover up.

Durga in the general play of sexuality becomes a part of the erotic drama between the lovers, the gaps left by the novelist encourage such an understanding. The mythical Durga too is associated with Shiva and as his wife she becomes the embodiment of feminine power who wears, the god of wealth, Kuber's precious necklace. Hence, she for all her power becomes secondary to her husband as the destroyer of evil and possessor of wealth. She is another manifestation of Parvati, the divine mother and Shiva's consort, an aspect that makes an allowance for the Oedipal to enter among the devotees. It is not Nikhilesh but Sandip who appropriates the role of Shiva and the credit for making Bimala a representation of Durga goes to him as it did to Shiva. Sandip selectively manipulates, turns and twists the Hindu mythologies to suit his advantage. Often it his own subjective rendering and intermixing of the mythology that is fed into the impressionable and besotted Bimala's mind that is only too receptive because of her obsession with the man. The selection and rejection of mythological episodes is made at will, and then amalgamated to suit the wicked purpose of plunder of an affluent and influential family, including the people who live in the area within their direct administration. In the novel it is Sandip's smooth flattery and rhetoric that forces the transformation in Bimala. The myth is thus redined and defined, mixed-up for questionable purposes that are eventually served, though towards the end exposed as well in *Ghare Bhaire*. If we deconstruct Durga in *Ghare Baire*, and explore the layers of meaning embedded a strong Oedipal element is discernable because the total devotion of the devotees and worshippers makes the male devotees susceptible to the perfect beauty of the goddess. We could also imagine Sandip as the son who has a burning desire to possess the mother, Bimala, and destroy the father, Nikhilesh. Eros and Thanatos, both co-exist within the two lovers and they decide to play hot to their hearts desire in the inflamed political environment created by the *Swadeshi* movement. Durga is also employed in tantric rituals and the erotic invariably becomes a part of the rituals, though the Kali form is always more dominating.

Kali is divine consciousness (*Tatva*) of Shiva in potential energy form. Always naked and black in popular iconography, she is never seen independent of Shiva as *Kaala* or *Shakti* or power for he remains the substance and the goddess becomes the form. This relationship Sandip has at the back of his mind when he contemplates about Bimala. Apart from being a manifestation of power, Kali is also another form of Parvati who is considered in Hindu mythology as a devout wife. Hindu mythology at different times and places underwent changes that have been accepted haphazardly on a selective basis based on personal preferences. Kali is understood as having breast fed Shiva who appeared in the form of a child to stop her dance under intoxication caused by drinking the blood of her enemies. She is also shown iconographically as standing on her husband, whom she spares even in a violent form. She is violently fearless, *Abhaya*, and full of blessings. It is this violent frenzy that Sandip wants to create in Bimala who is religiously credulous and sexually charged for the sake of the nation and her lover. Wendel Johnson says that it is not only true that the language we use puts words in our mouths; it also puts notions in our heads. This is what a semantician has to suggest. It is these notions that Sandip is trying to arise in Bimala head and heart to succeed with her. The tantrics practice meditation on pure consciousness in which all inhibitions are given up and the focus is on the divine aspect of creation, preservation and destruction that takes place through the powers of the goddess.

In these spiritual rituals, the presiding deities are Shiva and Kali, the divine couple, and in their *tantric* worship figures their copulation. It is in their union that the birth of the universe is seen, including mankind, and this symbolism denotes the evolution of the mental and physical changes that takes place within the practitioners of *tantra*. It is this sexual element that Sandip wants to play on and help arise within Bimala so that she may see him as Shiva and nothing of the god in her husband Nikhilesh.

Since the divine energy unleashed by *tantric* practices is supposed to be wild and uncontrollable in Kali and only Shiva has the power to subdue her well into control, Sandip too imagines the role of Shiva for himself by making Bimala wild and sexually ignited in some perverse form of Hinduism that he cleverly manufacturers for gains through the woman. And controlling Bimala psychologically becomes implicit in the plan because it is the mind that governs actions. Just as Parvati is transformed into Kali, he wants Bimala to metamorphose herself into his randomly manufactured conception of Kali that he visualizes for her—and then exploit her by relating the awakening of *Kundalini Shakti* with the emergence of liberating divine sexual desire inside her that often led to coitus. The point of the entire exercise is always to trap the woman into his clutches and not practice any nationalistic religion. Religious fantasy works through a process of conjunction in which experiences are modified at will—and in the case of Sandip it is for personal gain. He talks about Kali to flatter and motivates Bimala to imbibe the popular traits of the goddess but through a process of deduction and induction helps her go into delusions in which illusions and reality become blurred for her. Alfred Korzybski says that there is a tremendous difference between "thinking" in verbal terms and "contemplating", inwardly silent, on non-verbal levels. Sandip relies on this inwardly silent thinking that Bimala indulgences in alone. Where no words are used anticipated thoughts are made to birth in her. And they do in the novel as her actions prove. According to the *Samakhya* school of thought, it is *prakriti* and *purusha* that embody power and vitality respectively. Since the two are interdependent, their union is inevitable. It is such associations with Shiva and Kali that Sandip has in his mind when he tries to brain-wash Bimala, who catches the hints only too well being well versed with Hindu thought.

The mythological leads to worldly realizations and actions, provides justification for indulgences in the real world of mire which some spiritually inclined souls may describe as illusionary. Mother India, Radha, Kali and Durga are extra-absolute figures and they are understood not righteously but with selective deception for immoral ends by forcing praxis. The mythological contributes towards the communication with the self and affects our decision making in the very world in which we exist. Supra-sensations complicate existence and our actions whether right or wrong, moral or immoral are governed by them. The conscious and unconscious function in tandem and generate layers of meanings which control our destiny. The regenerative super-ego is suppressed continuously and social norms of morality are by-passed for pleasure and profit in the personal and public domain by Sandip and Bimala, both. The woman in love and over-powered by desire does not see reason independently, Bimala's logic is governed by Sandip's reason and cuddled by blind faith. The mythologies when interwoven together become a peculiar admixture of non-rational elements that condition the thinking of Bimala and encourage her into social damnation. In her fantasies, she consistently thinks in violation of the natural laws, at least, the rationale behind her actions is baffling. Her arbitrary constructs of the mind are pleated in misgivings that she has about her limited capacities and it is this cloudy and dim perspective that makes her knife-edged towards her husband. In *Ghare Baire*, it is through the divine camouflage worked in through Sandip's chicanery that the dark elements become deep-rooted and formidable, cause destruction and death. It is through the tragedy that Tagore tried to show the dodgy aspects of myths we live by unquestioningly and make the pedagogical aspects surface slowly. This happens because through language we are made to travel into the latent as perhaps Derrida might suggest. Tagore does not hesitate in making the profane implicit in the sacred myths and the pitfalls of the mysteriously divine we survive through. Even today there are men and women who believe that special powers have been granted to them by the divine, gods and goddesses, and it is under their spell that they act in defiance of reason, intuit—often to their own risk and those who believe in them.

Works Cited

Carroll, David. "Freud and the Myth of the Origin", *New Literary History,* Vol. 6, No. 3, Spring, 1975.

Chapman, Christopher. *Freud, Religion, and Anxiety.* Morrisville, NC: Lulu.com, 2007.

Heehs, Peter. "Myth, History, and Theory", *History and Theory,* Vol. 33, No. 1, February, 1994.

Lawson. "The Explanation of Myth and Myth as Explanation", *Journal of the American Academy of Religion*, Vol. 46, No. 4, December 1978.

Leeming, David A. "Myth and Therapy", *Journal of Religion and Health*, Vol. 40, No. 1, Spring, 2001.

Leeming, Margaret A., "Remarks on Myth, Interpretation, and Violence", *Journal of Religion and Health*, Vol. 41, No. 1, Spring 2002.

Levi-Stauss, Claude. *Myth and Meaning*. London: Routledge, 2001.

Moran, Richard. "Kant, Proust, and the Appeal of Beauty", *Critical Inquiry*, Vol. 38, No. 2, Winter 2012.

Spiro, Melford E. "Whatever Happened to the Id?", *American Anthropologist, New Series*, Vol. 81, No. 1, March 1979.

Tagore, Rabindranath. Trans. Sreejata Guha & Swagato Ganguly. *The Home and the World (Ghare Baire)*. New Delhi: Penguin Books, 2005.

8

Glimpses of Bengal in Rabindranath Tagore's Stories

Ajay B. Kukade

1913 was the landmark year for Indian literary scene when Rabindranath Tagore, the first Asian, was awarded Nobel Prize for literature. He was a man of true genius who wrote with utmost passion and with the child-like zeal. It is nearly impossible to talk about this great artist in a few words, or a paper. Tagore was a true multi-layered personality which is evident through his works as a novelist, poet, musician, short-story writer, painter, dramatist, activist, philosopher, musician, social reformer, a great academician, and above all a hardcore patriot! His works not only have enchanted the Bengalis but made the whole world dance to his tunes.

The Indian short-story in English has a century long history which dates way back into 1898 when Kamala Sathianadan's *Stories from Indian Christian Life* was published. Since then it has attained maturity in many different ways. The writers seem to be settled and explore the themes in more matured manner than ever. The result of which is that Indian works are being given due credit and importance. Experimentation has always been a highlight of Indian literature. Bengali and Marathi literature in particular have shown tremendous growth and have enchanted the readers for ages. Tagore clearly scores an advantage over the other writers as he wrote in both Bengali and English and translated himself the stories into English from Bengali. That has helped him to keep the soul of the stories intact. Moreover, his understanding of Bengali life has helped him immensely in producing powerful literary works. Having travelled worldwide gave him a chance to have a close look at the cultures of many countries and to compare it with Indian culture and also made stronger his belief in ancient Indian values and culture.

Tagore's short-stories are probably the most neglected of all his literary works. But if one goes through them thoroughly, it becomes crystal clear that his stories too are powerful and they belong to the league of its own! Tagore's short-story world is full of the portrayal of the protagonists chosen from cross-section of society. The stories take us into the boundless joys of a child's world, the sorrows and pathos of women, and the problems of working men. He has dealt an array of themes and depicted the characters with utmost care. India being a multi-lingual, multi-cultural country scores more as it has advantages of its own. The India—colonized and postcolonial —have shown tremendous maturity in its character. Though being ruled for more than a century and a half, India has maintained its essential cultural values throughout. The period in which Tagore wrote is considered as the Golden era of Indian literature as it witnessed the works of stalwarts like Mulk Raj Anand, Raja Rao, R.K. Narayan, Munshi Premchand. Works of these writers did establish Indian firmly on the world literary map.

The Tagore stories are presented in a no-nonsense attitude and focus upon the struggles of ordinary people. He gives full panoramic view of the then Bengal and its people and culture in most charismatic way. It is an accepted fact that no one else could have given the identity to Bengal the way Tagore has done that. The stories "The Kabuliwallah", "The Babus of Nayanjore", "The Postmaster" and "Subha" have the protagonists chosen from almost all walks of Bengali life. These stories are the case studies having the background both—rural and urban—and discuss the problems of the protagonists in most delicate manner.

Tagore's stories start abruptly and revolve round a trivial and ordinary looking theme. But as the story progresses one is given a chance to have an encounter with the most critical human problems. His stories take us into the world of unending problems of men and women, who struggle to meet both ends. Actually, his understanding of rural Bengali life comes from his own spending many years in calm and placid rural Bengal himself. Humayun Kabir writes:

> Many were surprised that the Maharshi should select his youngest son, already known as a Poet and dreamer, to be in-charge of the family properties. Tagore soon proved that his father had acted wisely in making a poet the manager of an estate. What is of interest to us is that made Tagore live for years in the village of Bengal. Much of this time he spent on a boat among the sandbanks of the Padma, and thus came into intimate contact with nature and man in rural Bengal. (*Rabindranath*, 10)

Tagore gave no place to bifurcation of ideals and culture in his life. A sense of the unity of life was his greatest strength. He gave importance to both—the poor and the rich—and gave way to their sufferings and problems. For Tagore short-story was a strong medium through which he discussed the human predicament effectively.

Tagore was a sensitive person for whom women held high esteem. He had keen observation of Bengali culture and as a tribute to women and their contribution to the society he wrote most of his stories with the women protagonists as the central characters. "The Postmaster" and "Subha" are the two stories dealing with women's problems. It presents the hardships and struggles of two young Bengali girls Ratan and Subha respectively. It also gives us a glimpse of the then Bengali life. In K.V. Dominic's words, "Tagore was a practitioner of psychological and social realism" (*Pathos*, 19). Through his stories Tagore also highlights the nature-man relationship. This human-nature relationship is another hallmark of his stories. "The Postmaster" is a classic example of Tagore's talent as a writer. The story is of a village girl brought up in the lap of nature. The simplicity and directness in her character are because of her being with nature all the time. This power-packed story deals with the bond between a postmaster and an orphan village girl. In fact, the bond is only a "one-sided traffic". The moment this postmaster enters the life of the girl, after joining his services in village Ulapur, Ratan's life changes drastically. Slowly but steadily, the girl realizes what brotherly love means. She starts taking care of the postmaster, her Dada, who in the end deserts her.

The story is full of gray shades and the setting is gloomy. The story evokes pathos, as in the end we feel for the girl who again will have to lead a "lonely" life which would be more difficult than ever for her! The complexities of relationship are the central feature of Tagore's stories. Sheer need of company forces the postmaster to be friends with Ratan, an orphan girl. Slowly, they both grow dependent on each other. Even when he yearns for a loving mate on a rainy afternoon:

> Oh, if only some kindred soul could hold near my heart! This was exactly, he went on to think, what the bird was trying to say, and it was the same feeling which the murmuring leaves were striving to express. (*Mashi,* 165)

After the thought flashes into his mind, he comes back to the world of reality and then calls Ratan to just console himself and to turn his thoughts to a different subject and says, "I was thinking of teaching you to read; and the rest of the afternoon he taught her the alphabet" (*Mashi,* 166). Their relationship grows naturally and at the end both of them are found tormented. When she asks him, "Dada, will you take me home with you?" (*Mashi,* 168), the postmaster laughs at this and says, "What an idea?" (*Mashi,* 168). This sharp reply shakes the girl throughout. For the whole night the postmaster's reply haunts her and makes her aware of the fact that she is an orphan girl! The girl faces the hour of truth when postmaster informs Ratan that he will ask his successor to look after her. She retaliates by saying, "No, no you need not tell anybody anything at all about me; I don't want to stay on here". For her he was the one who cares for her, but when the postmaster, who was not hard-hearted, tries to give her some money she says, "Oh, Dada, I pray you, don't give me anything, don't in any way trouble about me" (*Mashi,* 170). She feels humiliated at the hands of a man whom she loved and trusted much, as her love for her Dada was unconditional. Then her figure running about the post-office, hoping to see her Dada coming back, evokes sudden sympathy for the girl and also evokes anger over the harsh realities we have to face in life. Tagore's sympathy goes with the simple, troubled, and lonely girl whom the postmaster leaves behind without caring. The narration of the postmaster leaving the village in a boat lets us connect with Ratan immediately, who undoubtedly would find solace amidst the nature only!

Tagore's stories appear to be simple and having an uninteresting plot, but still they have a charm to carry with. He was a true humanist who craved for the equality and justice for all including children and women. The child in a family is often being treated as an inferior. He has used this theme in his story "Subha". In this story, he gives way to the life and troubles of dumb girl. The dumb girl Subhasini, the youngest daughter of Banikantha, leads a silent life. This silent sufferer finds solace amidst nature and befriends with two cows—Sarbashi and Panguli. Her own mother is ignorant to her and the belief that she is a curse to her father makes her more restless. She shares her feelings with the cows who for her are the best friends:

> Whenever she heard any words that hurt her, she would come to these dumb friends out of due time. It was as though they guessed her anguish of spirit from her quiet look of sadness. Coming close to her, they would rub their horns softly against her arms, and in dumb, puzzled fashion try to comfort her. (*Mashi*, 151)

It's a kind of slap on the face of whole human race where only the spoken words hold importance and a dumb one, though more capable than a normal human, has to lead a lonely and tortured life. In both the stories, a vital role is played by emotions. Ratan and Subha both are the victims of destiny and both feel handicapped and they are left at the mercy of the other human beings. Their loneliness is the cause of concern for the writer.

Tagore has developed both these stories in rural setting. His shades of being a painter and musician are clearly visible in these stories wherein he invests word-music and exhibits a canvas full of various colours. "The Postmaster" has a rural setting of a remote village Ulapur and its green slimy pond, and rainy season. It instantly creates picture of the same in the minds of the readers. In such setting, the story of two ordinary folks develops. Subha's house is on the bank of a river and she would go and sit there quietly for hours. There is a certain flow of a river throughout the story. In Mohinder Kaur's words,

> In story after story Tagore shows the different facets of life in Bengal and of life as such which peeps through the chinks of eternity. They are woven round their joys and sorrows of men, women and children enacting different roles in the mysterious drama of life.
>
> (*Critical Study*, 47)

On the other hand, in the stories "The Kabuliwallah" and "The Babus of Nayanjore" the setting is urban. Both the stories show the protagonists as the resident of Calcutta. "The Babus of Nayanjore" is a story of a man who lives in the dreamy world of his past glory. We are forced to pity Kailash Babu, the protagonist, once we are being made aware of his glorious past:

> .... They were noted for their princely extravagance. They would tear off the rough border of their Dacca muslin, because it rubbed against their skin. They could spend many thousands of rupees over the wedding of a kitten. On a certain grand occasion it is alleged that in order to turn night into day they lighted numberless lamps and showered silver threads from the sky to imitate sunlight. (*The Hungry Stones*, 175)

In fact, Kailash Babu had seen more than a man could see in his lifetime. He has had his share of glory. The flood had washed away all his splendors with it and to manage things he had to move to Calcutta. In Calcutta, he has to manage in a small house with only survivor along with him, his grand-daughter Kusum. His efforts to cling to his past glory are very amusing but at the same time are touching also. With the help of his servant, Ganesh he tries to impress his neighbours by telling them the lies in form of stories of his past. His true friends too show sympathy by accepting all his lies wholeheartedly. It is a story of a man who shifts from rural to urban area, having left no choice. Kailash Babu has no option but to hold fast to his past greatness, which makes him forget the bitter truth of his present poverty. His young educated neighbour tries to push him in tight corner, as is the ways of youth, and make fun of him. But his cruel joke hurts Kusum, the tender granddaughter of Kailash Babu. His heart fills with remorse and he, in all humility, comes to Kailash Babu with an offer to marry Kusum. The old man feels more joyous and he breaks out, "I am a poor man and could have never expected such great good fortune" (*The Hungry Stones,* 194). This was the first and the last time when Kailash Babu had ever confessed his poverty, which amaze the young man.

The story throws light on the pathetic conditions of the past glories of the landlords who used to live a very aristocratic and lavish life. But time changes and the extravagant life shifts to mere poverty, but the pride remains the same. This clash between the two persons from altogether different background is interesting. The actions of the young neighbour may anger us, but it was normal behaviour for the young man. Speaking about this Kabir says, "Men differ in appearance and build, they have different customs and traditions and even their emotional reactions differ because of differing backgrounds" (*Rabindranath,* 40).

"The Kabuliwallah" is arguably the best mythical story of Tagore which shows him at the height of his imaginative powers. It is a fine example of Tagore's artistic vision. The story is a milestone in his career as a short-story writer, which works on many different levels. In this story, Tagore weaves together several relationships that break the barriers of caste, creed and religion, in the background of Calcutta lanes. There are two different relationships explored in the story. One is the bond between two person with a huge age difference—Mini and Kabuliwallah, and the other is the bond between the narrator and the Kabuliwallah formed purely on the bases on one common factor of fatherhood. The character of Kabuliwallah is seems true to life. It evokes sudden sympathy for a man far away from his homeland, working hard to earn his livelihood for his family. It is a myth created by Tagore, which then acquires the stature of a legend. Myth has the power to hold societies together more strongly than languages. It provides insight into the mysteries of life, and to understand its intricacies we need to experience and appreciate it on its own. Rabindranath Tagore is probably the best myth user from Indian English literary field. According to K.R. Srinivasa Iyengar, "The myth-making power could be seen in 'The Kabuliwallah'. In this story the character is seized by inward vision and presented with total understanding and love" (*Rabindranath*, 72).

The story has a mix of both happy and sad moments set beautifully in the streets of Calcutta. A peddler working hard, leading a lonely life in a huge city away from his motherland and his family, meets Mini for the first time and instantly they become friends. The man finds a suitable substitute to his own child and Mini finds a suitable companion who would listen to her constant chatter patiently which for her was missing till then. For her, he becomes an embodiment of affection and fearlessness. Mini's mother having concern for her daughter tries to oppose this strange relationship, but the narrator neglects that:

> I tried to laugh her fear gently away; she would turn round seriously, and ask me solemn questions:
>
> Were children never kidnapped?
>
> Was it not true that there was slavery in Kabul?
>
> Was it so very absurd that this big man should be able to carry off a tiny child? (*The Hungry Stones*, 268)

Despite this the friendship grows. Tagore has taken due care in creating Kabuliwallah's and Mini's characters. Dr. Jaydeep Sarangi in his preface to K.V. Dominic's *Pathos in the Short Stories of Rabindranath Tagore* comments:

> "Kabuliwallah" is a study of the mind of Mini, a five-year-old Bengali girl who forms friendship with a middle-aged Afgan peddler Rahman. It also hints at the social hierarchy which persisted in Bengal during Tagore's time. (19)

The Kabuliwallah's joyous face after meeting Mini, his interactions with her, his grave face when he had to go to prison, everything seems to be familiar to us. How a father feels desperate to meet his child becomes obvious when after releasing from prison the Kabuliwallah straightway goes to the narrator's home to meet Mini. The narrator tries to avoid him as that was the day of Mini's marriage and he thought of Rahman, the Kabuliwallah meeting his daughter as a bad omen. But then the father in the narrator realizes the vows of another father after taking a look at a dirty piece of paper bearing the impression of a little hand:

> Tears came to my eyes. I forgot that he was a poor Kabuli fruit-seller, while I was—. But no, what was I more than he?
>
> He also was a father. (*The Hungry Stones,* 275)

The father in the narrator realizes that with the passage of time he can never experience the happy childhood of his daughter, which forces him to not only let the Kabuliwallah meet Mini, but to give him a currency-note! The story from happy trance moves into the never ending world of pathos where one father, the Kabuliwallah is suffering from the separation from his daughter and the other, the narrator was going to enter that state of mind. Tagore sums up the story in most touching words:

> Having made this present, I had to curtail some of the festivities. I could not have the electric lights I had intended, nor the military band, and the ladies of the house were despondent about it. But to me the wedding feast was all the brighter for the thought that in a distant land a long-lost father had met again his only child. (277)

The poet in Tagore never left him alone in other literary genres he explored. Even in his short-stories, also, the traces of Tagore, the poet pop up many a times. In K.R. Srinivasa Iyengar's words, "With Tagore's short stories the poetic flash is the main thing; it is the poet that sees the truth of things, the story-teller merely snapping the scene at the required angle"

(73-74). This reaction by Iyengar proves to be more apt when we go through lines from "The Kabuliwallah":

> The morning was bright. After the rains, there was a sense of ablution in the air, and the sun-rays looked like pure gold. So bright were they that they gave a beautiful radiance even to the sordid brick walls of our Calcutta lanes. Since early dawn to-day the wedding-pipes had been sounding, and at each beat my own heart throbbed. The wail of the tune, Bhairavi, seemed to intensify my pain at the approaching separation....
>
> (*The Hungry Stones*, 272)

No other writer, at least in India, could have made use of the poetic talent in short-stories too up to such extent. His mastery over all forms of art is deeply rooted in his constant communion with nature and with people. Humayun Kabir's remark over this quality of the great man speaks volume. He says, "Rabindranath Tagore loved man with all the fervour of his imagination and feeling and held that there is nothing in creation higher than the spirit of man" (29). This fellow-feeling of Tagore makes him a true genius India has ever produced.

Works Cited

Dominic, K.V. *Pathos in the Short Stories of Rabindranath Tagore.* Sarup Book Publishers Pvt. Limited, 2009.

Iyengar, K.R. Srinivas. *Rabindranath Tagore: A Critical Introduction.* Sterling Publishers, 1965.

Kabir, Humayun. *Rabindranath Tagore.* Pankaj Publications International, 1987.

Kaur, Mohinder. *Critical Study of Tagore's Short Stories.* S. Chand & Co., 1989.

Tagore, Rabindranath. *Mashi and Other Stories.* Kessinger Publishing, 2004.

———. *Hungry Stones and Other Stories.* Echo Library, 2006.

Venugopal, C.V. *The Indian Short Story in English (A Survey).* Prakash Book Depot, 1975.

9

Tagore: The Librettist of Orality

Saikat Banerjee

Rabindranath Tagore is chiefly known as a writer of lyric poetry but his remarkable versatility will be realized when one remembers that besides being a poet, he is a dramatist, a novelist, a literary critic, a renowned educationist, a religious teacher, a social reformer and a writer of children's books and poems and miscellaneous essays. The common thread that binds his versatility is his own personal aesthetic outlook and philosophical ideas.

Dr. Niharanjan Roy has beautifully used the metaphor of a forest for Rabindranath's life and works in his book *Artist in Life* said that "Rabindranath's life and art are so varied and extensive that it is not easy to grasp them, let alone pass judgement upon them. We may compare both with a huge forest, spreading and sprawling, where one can see tiny plants and winding creepers, towering and over shadowing trees, a forest full of sap, colour and beauty, sublime in its silence immensity. But once we are inside the forest all this majesty disappears, because then we can see only the plants and the creepers and the trees, separately. Whereas if we see it from outside from a distance, we do certainly feel the majesty but the charm and beauty of the separate trees and of their multitudinous foliage, their flowers and fruits, and their colours are lost. How then, do we find out way in this dense and vast forest of Tagore's vast creative output?" In 1913, Tagore was awarded the Nobel Prize for literature, the first Asian to do so.

Tagore's poetry has tended to overshadow his work as perhaps the outstanding dramaturge of modern India. Blending folk elements of the *Jatra* with classical Sanskrit drama, and aware of modern problems, his evolving idiom is a fascinating study, little known outside Bengal. *Jatra* (to go in procession) is a form of folk theatre popular in Bengal, where it originated, and in the eastern states of Orissa and Bihar as well as in Bangladesh. It is a very living and vivid form of music theatre and draws its plots from several sources such as Hindu mythology, popular legends, and even current events. There are several theories about the birth of *Jatra*. It seems that it has its roots in the 15th century *bhakti*-related dance processions, which culminated in the temple courtyards. It gained wide popularity in the 18th century. During the colonial period, in the 19th and early 20th centuries, it was used to convey political messages. *Jatra* is often performed outdoors on a square platform from which a gangway leads through the audience to the dressing room. The gangway also serves as an acting area when needed. The stage is usually empty. One chair may serve several purposes; it may be a throne, a mountain, a chariot, etc. The few props needed are brought and taken away by stage assistants.

This particular tradition had been successfully implemented by Tagore in his plays such as *The Cycle of Spring*, *Valmiki Pratibha*, *Saradotsava* and others. The oral tradition portrayed through these plays also seeks to articulate the ethical and spiritual values which had been considered as an inevitable part of the existential phenomenon of each individual other than its textual and staged form. As a librettist, Tagore tried to present a unique trio of classical, folk and Western strains of story-telling. His plays excavate the history which is engraved within the prolonged silence and his effort to break this particular silence includes the Western oral quagmire within the vital and perennial Indian oral tradition. This is, in fact, the subjugation of universality of orality and his initiative took this oldest tradition of story-telling to its apogee in the era of theatrical transition.

This paper seeks to have answers of some unheeded Tagorian inquiries and to establish a new paradigm of thinking about Indian oral tradition which is remarkably textualized and sensitized by Tagore.

At Jorasanko, the family-house of Rabindranath, plays were regularly staged in which the members of the Tagore family participated. The memory of these plays which he enjoyed very much during his childhood left a deep impression on his mind and in later years, he gave a thought to the writing of dramas along with his poetical and prose-writings. He wrote quite a number of dramas which mainly falls under the following categories:

(a) Musical dramas like *Valmiki Pratibha*, 1881 (*The Genius of Sage Valmiki*), *Prakitir Pratisodh* (*The Revenge of Nature*).

(b) Romantic dramas like *The King and the Queen* (*Raja O Rani*), *The Sacrifice* (*Visarjan*) and *Malini* (*The Gardener Woman*).

(c) Dramatic Lyrics like *Petition of the Queen Mother Gandhari* (*Gandharir Abedan*), *The Meeting of Karna and Kunti* (*Karna Kunti Sambad*), *Kach O Debjani* (*The Conversation between Kach and Debjani*).

(d) Farces or Humorous dramas like *The Committee of Confirmed Bachelors* (*Chirakumar Sabha*).

(e) Symbolic plays like *The Autumn Festival* (*Saradotsav*), *The Atonement* (*Prayaschitta*), *The King of the Dark Chamber* (*Raja*), *The Closed Palace* (*Achalayatan*), *The Post Office* (*Daak Ghar*), *Phalguni* (*The Cycle of Spring*), *The Open Stream* (*Muktadhara*), *The Red Oleander* (*Rakta Karabi*).

In *Phalguni* (*The Cycle of Spring*, 1916), we move from the sick bed to open air in the bosom of Nature, Tagore's unfailing standby. The theme of the play is renewal of life, and is perhaps not so dramatic but the songs with its beautiful lyrics make up for the absence of plot or action. The play matches the temperament of Rabindranath so much that he himself appeared in the role of the blind minstrel (*andha baul*).

The play opens with a prologue, which introduces a king who has fled away from his council-chamber to be in the company of a poet who promises to entertain him with a play of approaching spring:

> KING: Very well, Poet. Off with you. Make your stage preparations.
>
> POET: No, King. We are going to act this play without any special preparations. Truth looks tawdry when she is overdressed.
>
> KING: But, poet there must be some canvas for a background.
>
> POET: No. Our only background is the mind. On that we shall summon up a picture with the magic wand of music.
>
> KING: Are there any songs in the play?
>
> POET: Yes King. The door of each act will be opened by the key of song.
>
> KING: What is the subject of the songs?
>
> POET: The Disrobing of Winter.
>
> KING: But, Poet, we haven't read about that in any Mythology.
>
> POET: In the world—myth this song comes round in its turn. In the play of seasons, each year, the mask of the Old man, Winter, is pulled off, and the form of Spring is revealed in all its beauty. Thus we see that the old is ever new.
>
> KING: Well, Poet, so much for the songs: what about the remainder?
>
> POET: Oh, that is all about life.
>
> KING: Life? What is Life?
>
> POET: This is how it runs: A band of young companions have run off in pursuit of one Old Man. They have

taken a vow to catch him. They enter into a cave; they take hold of him, and then—

KING: Then, what? What did they see?

POET: Ah, That will be told in its own good time.

KING: But I haven't understood one thing. Your drama and your songs,—have they different subjects, or the same?

POET: The same, King. The play of Spring in nature is the counterpart of the play of Youth in our lives. It is simply from the lyrical drama of the World Poet that I have stolen this plot.

(*Collected Poems*, 352-53)

Thus, the prelude sets forth plainly the subject-matter of the drama and the dramatist takes a fling at the conventional playwright and stage-practitioner. The story is about the adventures of certain young men who are guided by a leader and one Chandra, in search of the Old Man whose one business is to kidnap men. The purpose of the play is to restore confidence in a king, who is afraid at the appearance of the young men who represents the "guiding impulse" in their life and the leader is assisted by one Chandra who is a personification of love. The leader on going inside the cave of the Old Man realises that he lives only in imagination. The young men alone exist and their leader when seen from behind actually appears to be old. The Old Man is when seen from behind actually appears to be old. The Old Man is winter when he is viewed in context to nature, which brings death to natural beauties. They are renewed or reborn in spring, so the decay that is caused in winter is more apparent than real. The old is always new and the play of spring in Nature is the counter-part of youth in our lives.

The play is not mere a fictional work of art coloured by beautiful imagery and made melodious with musical lyrics but is a serious work of art, which raises a number of problems. The real meaning underlying it is not merely an intellectual problem presented through allegory, neither any ethical problem revealed to us in a didactic fashion. The truth of the matter is that the inner meaning of Tagore cannot be grasped by the senses rather it has to be felt in the heart. This is the reason why he is so impatient with critic who finds it necessary to extricate meaning from his plays. He hints at this specifically in the following passage in the Prologue of the play:

> KING: Shall I be able to understand the sense of what you have written?
>
> POET: No, King. What a poet writes is not meant to have any sense.
>
> KING: What then?
>
> POET: To have the tune itself.
>
> KING: What do you mean? Is there no philosophy in it?
>
> POET: No none at all, thank goodness.
>
> KING: What does it say then?
>
> POET: King, it says "I exist." Don't you know the meaning of the first cry of the new-born child? The child, when it is born, hears at once the cries of the earth and water and sky, which surround him,—and they all cry to him, "We exist," and his tiny little heart responds, and cries out in its turn, "I exist." My poetry is like the cry of that new-born child. It is a response to the cry of the Universe.
>
> KING: Is it nothing more than that, Poet?
>
> POET: No, nothing more. There is life in my song, which cries, "In joy and sorrow, in work and in rest, in life and in death, in victory and in defeat, in this world and in the next, all hail to the "I exist."
>
> KING: Well, Poet, I can assure you, if your play hasn't got any philosophy in it, it won't pass muster in these days.
>
> POET: That's true, King. The newer people, of this modern age, are more eager to amass than to realize. They are, in their generation, wiser than the children of light.
>
> (*Collected Poems*, 350-51)

Youth is eternal and even victorious. It is always on the move, but it has more than mere movement. Thus, winter and spring, youth and age are only complementary parts of one and the same cosmic force which constitutes the universe, and the eternal law of getting and surrendering binds them all together in a harmonic chain. In the destruction of the present lies the promise of the future and in the eternal struggle for beauty and perfection lays the promise of fulfilment. The old order yields to the new.

Rabindranath Tagore is the notable instance of a dramatist who showed his touch band with the *Valmiki Pratibha*, his first play, composed and produced before he completed his twentieth year. The play deals with the life of Valmiki, who later turned into a sage and authored the great text *Ramanaya* of Hindu mythology. Since the dramatic action rests on the evolutionary potential of Valmiki, he is shown from the very outset as a person of an imposing stature and of a make-up different from that of his companions. Action proper starts as Valmiki sends his companions in search of a 'human sacrifice' to propitiate goddess Kali on the auspicious night of the new moon. A girl is being presented before him by his band of robbers at his behest. A sudden inexplicable feeling of pity for the victim aroused in Valmiki incapacitates him to execute the cruel act. This causes a new stirring in him as tears well up in his eyes and he feels his "heart of stone" melting. Pity, in Tagore's early plays, is an instrument of conversion, an effective solvent of hardened hearts and this solvent is very effectively used in *Valmiki Pratibha*. Valmiki's bidding to release the girl enrages his companions and he is left to lead a life of desolate existence. While wandering lonely in the forest he catches a glimpse of Goddess Saraswati. His ecstasy is short lived as the deity vanishes. Yearning to recapture the sight of the goddess he further ventures into the forest and notices a pair of fowlers who go ahead with the killing of the mating crane. The felling of the crane makes him break out in a metrical lament in Sanskrit, the language of the gods indicating his new acquired poetic skill. He is put to final test as Lakshmi, the Goddess of wealth, emerges to tempt him but Valmiki does not yield to her generous offers. So at last Goddess Saraswati reappears disclosing that she herself appeared as the helpless girl earlier to evoke the compassion in his hardened heart. She prophesies that Valmiki shall soften the hearts of millions as his heart has been during his own travail of self-realization.

In the musical play *Valmiki Pratibha*, the legend is handed freely for tracing the process of the conversion of a hard-hearted robber chief which in due course of time transforms him the status of a sage poet. Tagore described *Valmiki Pratibha* as “a little drama set to music”. Not intended to be read, “the musical text of the play” loses its significance...if it is not heard sung and seen acted.

A symbol, in the simplest terms defined by the *Oxford English Dictionary*, is something that stands for, represents or denotes something else. Not only the poets and the painters constantly use symbols, but music too becomes articulate and intelligible through their use. The symbol becomes important on its own account and our attention as representing or standing for something else is withdrawn. The poets and dramatists remind the readers and spectators of the hidden significance behind the external symbols. The drama, because it employs visible action, is very apt for symbolical treatment. The artist uses symbols which are definite and concrete and they are made to convey by indirect hints much more than they directly manifest. A symbolist’s work mainly will have two planes of meaning, the surface or direct meaning which is directly expressed and the subtle or overhanging meaning which is directly or overtly suggested.

Saradotsab (*The Autumn Festival*), the first of his symbolical plays, was written in 1908, and its English form, first appeared in *The Modern Review* of November 1919. This symbolical play centres on the Emperor Bijayaditya who takes a day off from his kingly affairs in order to participate in the celebration of the autumn festival in the union with all. The boys of the village have gathered round Thakurdada, the “grand-father”, as they call him, to celebrate the holiday. They sing:

> Let none go back home, brothers, this morning, let none go to work.
>
> Let us take the blue sky by storm and plunder space as we run.
>
> Laughter floats in the air like foam on the flood.
>
> Brothers, let us squander our morning in futile songs.
>
> (Ray, 119)

The king arrives in the guise of a Sanyasi which results in an intriguing situation. There is a variety of responses to this festival of nature right from complete irresponsiveness to an instinctive responsiveness to nature. The boys of the neighbourhood who are very happy and a wise old man "Thakurdada" are readily taken by the majesty of king in disguise. Amidst the merry making, a youth is engaged in the self-imposed task of paying off his master's debt to the miser Luckeswar, his creditor. Luckeswar is disturbed since the morning seeing the exuberant spirits of the boys and upset by the movement over the place where his treasure is hidden and is attracted too to the Sanyasi as well because he feels that it is the Sanyasi who can be of use to him in augmenting his wealth through his supernatural powers. On the other hand, King Sompal, a feudal chieftain of Emperor Bijayaditya, also drawn to Sanyasi who may help him in fulfilling his long-cherished desire to bring into subjection his overload, Bijayaditya. As a result of the operation of the diverse forces, things worsen and when the tension reaches its maximum, the minister of Emperor Bijayaditya along with other courtiers and a huge army presents himself before his sovereign and prays him to return to the capital when the kingly real identity is revealed. The complex knot of diverse forces is loosened. The rebellious Sompal now bows his head in and is chastened; Luckeswar is fully exposed. Upananada is freed from his indebtedness towards Luckeswar and is adopted by the Emperor.

Upananda may be taken to be the spirit of the autumn, who like the autumn itself, pays off the debt which he owes to the spring of joy by a sacrifice through sorrow, because he knows that it is sorrow alone that chastens humanity. The poet makes this idea very clear in the following conversation between the Sanyasi and Thakurdada:

> SANYASI: I know why this world is so beautiful—simply because it is ever paying back.
>
> Its debt. The rice-field has done its outmost to earn its fulfilment and the Betasini River is what it is because it keeps nothing back.
>
> THAKURDADA: I understand father. There is one who has given himself in creation in abundance of joy, and creation is every moment working to repay the gift and this perpetual sacrifice is blossoming everywhere in beauty and life.
>
> SANYASI: Wherever there is sluggishness, there accumulates debt and there it is ugly.
>
> THAKURDADA: Because where there is something lacking in the gift, the harmony is broken in the eternal rhythm of payment and re-payment. (Ray, 129)

To conclude it would be very apt to say that from the analysis of the above three plays Tagore has very aptly textualized the orality through his above-mentioned plays. Tagore through these plays has very successfully presented the Bengali folk traditions and orality considered to be a very pure form of natural art of the native common folk of Bengal.

Tagore's writings, particularly his plays, usher a way to re-think and reiterate the classical tradition of orality explicitly and overtly with a newness that expounds the beautification of such a tradition which has been treated as a form of art closest to the heart of the common people. To some extent, Tagore incorporated the emulative characteristic of Elizabethan tradition with folk theatre and such unique experiment was rarely found in Indian English Drama of that contemporary era. The implication of natural phenomena, use of soliloquies, vernacular language and the dynamic plot structure are incredibly presented through his plays. The musical insight correlating body and mind also vitalizes the Indian folk and oral tradition and Tagore undoubtedly gave a new shape to such spirit.

Works Cited

Ray, Mohit K. *The English Writings of Rabindranath Tagore*. Vol. 3. New Delhi: Atlantic Publishers and Distributors, 2007.

Tagore, R.N. *Collected Poems and Plays*. London: Macmillan and Co. Ltd., 1958.

10

Nautanki and Street Theatre: Community Folk Performance Traditions: A Study of Safdar Hashmi's Select Early Street Plays by Jana Natya Manch

Samina Khan

Nautanki is a highly popular folk operatic theatre performance tradition of South Asia, particularly in rural north India. Before the advent of Bollywood (Hindi film industry), *Nautanki* was the single most popular form of entertainment in the villages and towns of northern India. Rooted in the rural society of pre-modern India, this theatre vibrates with lively dancing, pulsating drumbeats, and full-throated singing. Mikhail Bakhtin's concept of performance as a carnival and Dwight Conquer good's notion of performance as an alternative to textocentrism facilitate to understand *Nautanki* as a community folk form as an expression of ordinary rural culture. It provides community members an opportunity to connect to their cultural heritage. It is also interesting to note how *Nautanki* creates participatory dialogues, builds community and opens possibilities for social change in rural India. Researchers suggest that *Nautanki* helps its audience to challenge various oppressive social traditions as dowry, child marriages among others and adopt certain pro-social thoughts and behaviours, including gender equality and better health practices. The present paper tries to analyse the position of *Nautanki* as a traditional form in a continuously changing global world. *Nautanki*, with its rich and varied folk dimensions, finds space in teleplays, cinema and political road shows.

Safdar Hashmi, Badal Sirkar, Habeeb Tanveer and Uttpal Dutt are some of the well-known playwrights who have made recognisable contribution in the field of the Street Theatre form in India. Safdar Hashmi's Jana Natya Manch (People's Theatre Front) was founded in 1973 by a group of Delhi's left wing theatre amateurs, who sought to take theatre to the people. It was inspired by the spirit of the Indian People's Theatre Association (IPTA). JANAM has played a significant role in popularising street theatre form to create social and political awareness. Safdar Hashmi gave voice to the marginalised and raised issues such as price rise, elections, communalism, economic policy, trade union rights, unemployment, globalisation, women's rights, education system, etc. Plays such as *Hatyara*, *Machine*, *Aurat*, *Raja Ka Baja*, *Apharan Bhaichaare Ka*, *Halla Bol*, *Samarth*, *Sangharsh Karega Jeetega*, *Andhera Aaftab Mangega*, *Jinhen Yaqeen Nahi Tha*, *Voh Bol Uthi*, *Yeh Dil Mange Motre*, *Guruji*, etc. fall among the early stage street plays performed by Jana Natya Manch. Habeeb Tanveer's early street play (1948) *Shantidut Kamgar* (*The Labourer, Messenger of Peace*) for IPTA was among Indian street theatre form's early experiments. JANAM is consciously political theatre, and sees itself as a part of, and contributing to the growing democratic movement in the country. It provides robust entertainment and promotes a democratic consciousness among the people. Hashmi's death triggered this theatre form resulting in the formation of several troupes in different parts of the country: Praja Natya Mandali in Andhra Pradesh, Nija Nataka Iyakkam in Madurai and Kala Kuzhu in Chennai. So far this group of self-trained actors have done over 8500 performances of nearly 70 odd street plays and 15 prosenium plays in about 140 cities in India.

JANAM's Street Theatre journey began in October 1978. On 15 October 1978, the first play *Machine*, a short, 13-

minute play with a cast of six, acted in a circle with the audience on all sides, with its lyrical, stylized dialogues depicted the exploitation of the industrial labours. Hashmi records how the idea of *Machine* emerged: "There is a chemical factory...called Herig-India. The workers there did not have a union. They had two very ordinary demands.... They wanted a place where they could park their bicycles and...a canteen where they could get a cup of tea.... The management was not willing to grant even these demands.... The workers went on strike and the guards opened fire, killing six workers. So, this old Communist leader told me about this incident...and he said, 'Why don't you write a play about it?'" (Hashmi, JANAM). The initial draft of *Machine* was written by Safdar Hashmi and Rakesh Saksena, and was finalised on the floor, where everyone present contributed. *Machine* is an abstract play, in a way. The machine, created very simply by human figures, is the symbolic representation of capitalism. The workers, the capitalist and the security officers are all parts of the machine; they are complementary parts of a system founded upon the exploitation of one by the other; their coexistence, then, is unequal. As the narrator puts it: "They stay together, they work together. Owner and worker, goon and victim. And more: mill and grain, thakur and dalit. Always together, forever together!" (*Machine*, JANAM). But of course the permanence of togetherness is illusory; an exploitative system breeds within it the seeds of its own destruction. The machine breaks down and comes to a grinding halt—the workers have revolted. Hashmi shares his experience after the performance, "After we sang the final song, the trade union delegates... lifted us on their shoulder. We became heroes.... The next day we performed at performed at the Boat Club for about 1,60,000 workers. So you see, our street theatre began very gloriously.... A lot of people tape-recorded the play.... A month after the rally we started getting reports from all around the country that people were performing *Machine*.... They had...reconstructed it in their own languages". The playwright has explained the success of *Machine*: first, because it is not just "interesting" but stylised, lyrical, near-poetic prose; second, because it captures in its abstractions a very real, living truth and trusts its audiences to make the connection between the abstraction and the reality; third, because abstraction and brevity lend it a certain simplicity, without rendering it simplistic. In the aftermath of the Emergency (1975-77), it became impossible to do large plays. As Safdar Hashmi told the theatre scholar Eugene van Erven in the summer of 1988:

> We discovered that the trade unions...were no longer in a position to bear the expenses of even 500 or 700 rupees for a performance...during the Emergency they had been destroyed. They needed our theatre in their reorganisation efforts but they had no funds. (*TDR*, 32-47)

This form of theatre has become a vital cultural tool for workers, revolutionaries, and social activists. Street Theatre addresses topical events and social phenomenon and takes them straight to people's places of work and residence.

An alfresco performance without the proper paying audience can be termed as the Street Theatre. One could witness the performance in any witnessed area, like bus stop, on the street in front of working place, behind any complex. Street is a place with different set of possibilities than the conventional theatre space. A group of people acting out a brief and terse play or skit for all those who wish to stop and consider. The aim is to reach to the people from all the echelons of the society, even those who could not afford to go to the theatres. Speaking more extensively, it communicates the current affairs and invokes the people to bring a change by exterminating the social evils. The theatre developed as an art form to underscore the feelings of the ordinary people resulting into a whole new theatre genre which was later characterised as "theatre by the people and theatre for one people" (www.indian_street_theatre.htm).

Thus, the focus is on the common people, their everyday customary life, predicaments and conundrums, making this particular genre of Indian *Natya* to stand apart in a multitude. It reaches out to people directly breaking all the barriers of stage. There have been discussions about the origin of the form. Some advocates of the Indian theatre hold the opinion that with the independence of our country this theatre form gained popularity representing economic and socio-political state of independent India, while the other thinkers argue that the Street Theatre is a form of communication deeply rooted in the Indian traditions. Arguably, the oldest form of theatre in existence, most mainstream entertainment, mediums can be traced back to origins in street performance, including religious passion plays. A website quoted Safdar Hashmi: “If street theatre has any definite tradition in India, it is the anti-imperialist tradition of our people forged during the freedom movement. In other parts of the world it is the people for a just social and economic order” (www.indian_street_theatre.htm).

Street Theatre necessitates simple costumes and props, generally there is no amplification of sound with actors depending on their natural vocal and physical ability. Badal Sirkar, the notable playwright expressed that the Street Theatre performance is all about the strength of the human body, the power to cast one’s voice in order to reach four thousand people without the aid of the amplifiers. Also, the plays performed are normally short and precise. Songs are included sometimes on catchy tunes which add an extra appeal to the performance. Executed in a circular area, *dholak* is used to draw the crowd. The Street Theatre exists in three basic forms: ‘Circle Shows’, ‘Walks-by Acts’, and ‘Café-busking’. While ‘Circle Shows’ attract incredibly massive crowd for it often includes magicians, acrobats, jugglers, ‘Walk-by Acts’, which are yet to get accolades in India, are performed specifically by a street performer giving a musical or any other entertaining atmosphere. Then there is ‘Café-busking’ done in cafes, pubs, bars and restaurants. Musicians are spotted in such performances who are mostly struggling artists in need of a renowned audience. The ‘Circle Shows’ are much popular in India. The script is narrated by a chorus or a by a single artist while others mime. Makeup is not applied, sometimes the faces are painted white and the eyes are highlighted with black colour. The movements are exaggerated making the play economic and simple.

The pleasure of *Nautanki* lies in the intense melodic exchanges between two or three performers; a chorus is also used sometimes. Traditional *Nautankis* usually start late at night, often around 10 p.m. or so, and go all night until sunrise the next morning (for a total of 8-10 hours in duration). There is no intermission in *Nautanki* performances. The performance is often punctuated with individual songs, dances, and skits, which serve as breaks and comic relief for audiences. Storylines of traditional *Nautankis* range from mythological and folk tales to stories of contemporary heroes. For instance, while *Nautanki* plays such as *Satya-Harishchandra* and *Bhakt Moradhwaj* are based on mythological themes, *Indal Maran* and *Puranmal* originated from folklores. In the first half of the 20th century, the contemporary sentiments against British rule and feudal landlords found expression in Nautankis such as *Sultana Daku, Jalianwala Bagh*, and *Amar Singh Rathore*. In the last four decades, new *Nautankis* are centred around contemporary social messages such as health, HIV/AIDS, women's empowerment, dowry, immigration, and family planning. They are of a much shorter duration—around two hours. This is to give audiences an opportunity to watch performances during a break in their daily routine.

Popular Traditional Nautanki Storylines

Syah-Posh (Paq Mohabbat): One of the most romantic *Nautankis*, depicting the true love between a handsome young merchant—Gabru, from Central Asia—and the daughter of the wazir (Prime Minister) of Rome (present-day Iraq), Jamal. One day when Gabru who was on a business trip to Iraq passes under Jamal's palace, he hears Jamal reading the Quran, but in the wrong way. He asks her to correct her reading. This upsets Jamal and she asks who he was. Gabru introduces himself and offers to teach Jamal the correct way of reading Quran. Thus, starts a conversation between them and they both fall in love with each other. Jamal accepts Gabru's offer and invites him to come and teach her Quran at the night time, but in secret, and warns him that if he is caught he would be put to death by his father, the wazir. Gabru accepts and starts coming to Jamal's palace every night. As fate would have it, he is caught one night by the Kotwal (who actually is the king of Iraq incognito) while trying to scale the wall leading to Jamal's palace. The Kotwal accuses him of trying to commit a theft and declares that he would be hanged the next day. What happens next is a very intense and engaging tale of love and righteousness which ends on a happy note for everyone.

Sultana Daku: This *Nautanki* was written in the early part of the 20th century and depicts the exploits of the notorious dacoit Sultana. Sultana was a Robinhood-like bandit who robbed the rich and helped the poor. He became a big symbol of local Indian resistance against British rule in northern India when he could not be caught by the British for many years. The *Nautanki* is a humorous tale of the cat and mouse chase between Sultana and the British superintendent of police, Freddie Young.

Indal Haran: A popular *Nautanki* which depicts the exploits of the famous 12th century warrior brothers Alha and Udal. These two brothers are considered divine human beings in central and northern India. This particular *Nautanki* is an amazingly engaging romantic and bravery tale which depicts how a princess from central Asia named Chitralekha falls in love with Indal, the son of Alha, and kidnaps him from the banks of Ganges during a festival. After facing many hardships, Udal (Indal's uncle) and Machala (Indal's mother) rescue him. Both Chitralekha and Machala have magical powers and use them for their purposes. The *Nautanki* ends on a happy note with the marriage of Indal and Chitralekha.

Amar Singh Rathore: This *Nautanki* is a stimulating tale based on the life of the famous 17th century Rajput warrior Amar Singh Rathore, and gives the message of communal harmony. The *Nautanki* depicts how some vested interests in Shah Jahan's court try their best to destroy the friendship and cooperation between the Rajputs and Mughals but their attempts are foiled.

Bhakt Puranmal: This *Nautanki* is based on the famous story of Puranmal, who was a very good looking prince of a kingdom situated in the areas around modern-day Punjab. Puranmal not only was handsome but also had high moral principles. After the death of Puranmal's mother, his father (who is approaching his old age) decides to many a young woman. Dissatisfied by her husband, the stepmother falls for Puranmal and invites him to make love to her. Puranmal politely says that he considers her as his mother. This upsets the stepmother greatly. After her repeated attempts to entice Puranmal fail, she gets very angry and threatens him. Puranmal does not give in to her demands and walks out. Deeply insulted, the stepmother goes to her husband and tells him that Puranmal tried to rape her and he should be put to death. The *Nautanki* goes on to follow a very touching and interesting storyline which is popular in every household in many parts of northern India.

The important place that theatre occupies in the cultural life of a nation cannot be denied. Tagore once said that a nation's culture can be judged by the standard of its theatre. Drama is education, entertainment and recreation. It is said that drama creates the conscience of the age; we cannot make people good by acts of parliament, nor is it possible by constitutional provisions to remove deep-seated social prejudices. Rather we influence social behaviour by creating public opinion. Street Theatre form is socially, politically and artistically motivated, and with its cultural and political dimensions, opened possibilities of direct confrontation of energy as well as artistry. One of the blatant instances of the increased distance between the people and political action is the growth in the role of media which tends to brush aside local issues and issues of the powerless. The marginalised are unable to articulate their concerns. It is here that Street Theatre assumes its crucial role. No art can be truly popular if it is not controlled by the people. It is the people who will sustain resistance art. Bertolt Brecht wrote, in the context of imminence of fascism in Europe, "there is only one ally against the growth of barbarism: the people on whom it imposes these sufferings" (Drain, 188).

Literature written to be heard (oral) and viewed (visual) is different from that to be read only. It makes this art form close to life and experience. Street Theatre form is an art that makes us sensitive about society and imparts awareness about democratic values of just existence. Its tradition of orality and visuality make it a cultural embassador and an expression of real "Indianness" as an identity of its own space in word literature. In an interview to Anjum Katyal, Moloyashree Hashmi said, "Drama has to be created and crafted, even on the streets" (*Seagull Theatre Quarterly*, 57-71). Street plays (*Nukkad Natak*) retaining all traditional and original aesthetic features, evolving and adopting modern forms of political road shows, folk form, radio and television shows, legal literacy missions, cultural and NGO organizations, University Drama Clubs, theatre festivals and government propagandas, are examples of robust and rough theatricality. *Nautanki* and Street Theatre face numerous challenges including competition from an expanding media, changing audience preferences, and non-professionalism among its ranks. However, it seems that community folk performance traditions will continue to hold their place in the changing media atmosphere as they are more immediate and connect to their audience in an intimate manner. Consistent threats of terrorism and growing insecurities, fear, mutual distrust and communal violence seem to affect all such creative community practices. Creative literature, art forms, social activism and intellectual scholarship still combine to reclaim the dignity of such forms by reshaping and remodelling Street Theatre forms as an instrument for social change, peaceful coexistence and communal harmony in India. If drama is to be one of the most powerful manifestations of the human mind, there must be maturity of mind and greatness of soul as without these we cannot win and hold the affection of people across distances of time and space.

Works Cited

Drain, Richard. *Twentieth Century Theatre: A Sourcebook*. London: Routledge, 1995.

Hashmi, Moloyashree. *Seagull Theatre Quarterly*, No. 16, Dec. 1997.

Hashmi, Safdar. *Right to Perform: Selected Writings of Safdar Hashmi*. New Delhi: Sahmat, 1989.

Van Erven, Eugene. "Plays, Applause and Bullets: Safdar Hashmi's Street Theatre", *TDR* (T124): 32-47, 1989.

www.indian_street_theatre.htm

11

The Heroic Monomyth: A Study of *Duggar* Folk Hero Bawa Jitto

Vandhana Sharma

Folk has its origin from the soil and is ostensibly rooted in human mind. Folk imagination encompasses entire native perception and visualization of a particular race in different parts of the world. As a literary genre, folk imagination is inborn in a race and is derived from its roots, its tradition and is carried further from generation to generation with myth and culture intertwined in it. A close analytical investigation of folk literature gives an insight in to an unadulterated record of the first reaction of man to natural and social environment in all its primeval intensity besides providing a glimpse in to certain truths of history and other formal archives of humanity.

The tradition of prowess on the battlefield and the spirit of sacrifice to rejuvenate the society is the leit motif of Dogri folk heroic literature. To name a few, *Bawa Jitto, Daata Ranpat, Mian Dido, Raja Bahu Rull* and *Vazir Zorawar* are the most revered and popular dogra folk heroes who have been immortalised in the *Duggar*[1] sacred geography as their heroic deeds have been immortalised in the *Duggar* folk ballads called *Karaks*[2] *and Bars.*[3] Among the these ballads, the *Karak of Bawa Jitto* is one of the most popular ballads consisting of 374 lines which has been published by the Academy of Art, Culture and Languages, Jammu and Kashmir.

The legend of Bawa Jitto has been explored by various writers and scholars of Jammu and Kashmir. Amongst numerous literary pieces on the life of this dogra folk hero, who has figured in the oral tradition of the region, one of the most prominent and pioneering works is the dogri play *Bawa Jitto* written by Padmashree Ramnath Shastri which has been translated into English by me. In this play, Ramnath Shastri has skilfully interwoven the *karaks* and the dialogues as an attempt to preserve the *duggar* folk tradition. The *karaks* in the play are sung by a choral character called *devotee*[4] and like its counterpart in Elizabethan drama can be viewed as "author's vehicle for commentary on the play, as well as for exposition of its subject, time and setting, and the description of events happening offstage" (Abrams, 50).

The play is based on the life of a peasant who lived in the fifteenth century in a village by the name Ghaar in the lap of the Trikuta hills, the abode of goddess Vaishno Devi in the State of Jammu and Kashmir. Jitto's father Rupa was of lineage of Siddh who migrated from Kashmir and settled in Ghaar village centuries earlier. Siddh had only one son by the name Tirath Ram who had two sons, Janardhan and Nitu. Both the sons of Tirath Ram were given equal share of land. Nitu's son Achuhu had only one son, Rupa, who in turn also had only one son, Jitto. Jitto's family was financially stable and prosperous. Janardhan's branch of family was relatively huge with more shareholders in the ancestral land. This was the root cause of jealousy and rivalry between the two branches of Tirath Ram's progeny. Jitto's mother was Jojalan. She was a simple rustic woman ignorant of property manipulations. Her sister was Jojan who too was married in the Malkhotra family of Ghaar. This made the two families close to each other. Jitto's father Rupa was a devotee of Goddess Vaishno and was a frequent visitor to the shrine of the Goddess. Satisfied with his small family he devoted himself to the service and worship of the Supreme Goddess. Theirs was an illustrious family of Ghaar. People of Ghaar used to seek their advice and valued their opinion on various matters. Being a religious-minded family, they were well wishers of everyone and prayed to the Goddess for the welfare of all.

Raja Mandalik[5] was one of the most revered and popular deities in Northern India in the fifteenth century. Jitto's family developed reverence for the deity and became his devotees. They established a place of worship for Raja Mandalik in the village and started treating people who were affected by any illness or were victims of black magic. More and more people started thronging this place as it provided them relief from their miseries. Jitto was married to Maya but she did not survive after child-birth. The death of his parents followed by that of his spouse dejected Jitto and he involved himself more and more in the worship of Raja Mandalik besides bringing up his motherless daughter Gauri. He sought his aunt's help to bring up his daughter, Gauri. To the delight of Jitto's kin, his devotion to Raja Mandalik was perceived as a sign of his renunciation and his kin started grabbing his land. Jitto, although aware of all this remained impervious to his kin's ill intensions, Motherless Gauri was growing up developing a strong bond with her father. During a festive occasion in the village, she went to bathe in the river with her friends. On returning home, she fell ill. Medicines and therapies failed to cure her illness. Jitto took her to the sacred place of Raja Mandalik and thereunder the spell of the deity he found the image of his aunt Jojan which meant that Jojan was a witch who had attacked Gauri with her black magic. When Jojan came to know about it she hatched various manipulations to defend herself because in those times if a woman was proved a witch, she was annihilated with her head tonsured and face painted black. Jojan started conspiring against Jitto and her seven sons even went to the extent of attempting to kill Jitto.

Disillusioned with the agnatic rivalry, Jitto planned to leave his village Ghaar. Small kingdoms existed even in the hilly areas of Jammu and Kashmir in those times. Jitto wanted to go away from his kith and kin. So he decided to settle in the plains of Jammu region. Jitto along with Gauri came to a village by the name Pinjor where his old friend, Rullo lived. Rullo extended generous hospitality to Jitto and helped him in every possible way. Rullo took Jitto to the mansion of Mehta Bir Singh who was the *zamindar* of that region. Jitto pleaded to

Mehta to grant him some land for cultivation so that he could sustain himself and his daughter. He was given a barren forest area by Mehta on the condition that he would give a fourth share of the yield to Mehta. Jitto had befriended Iso Megh during his short stay in the village. He made Iso his partner and both the partners toiled to clear the forest and made it arable. Their hard work bore fruit and the yield was miraculous. When Mehta Bir Singh saw the quality and quantity of crop his intentions took an evil turn, however, driven by avarice, Mehta asked his men to fill up the sacks. Jitto made several pleas to Mehta and even reminded him of the deed but all that was in vain. On finding himself helpless in front of tyrant and callous Mehta, Jitto stood on the heap of grains and thrust a dagger in his chest.

The sacrificial act of Jitto shocked Mehta Bir Singh, as he was frightened about its repercussions. His men consoled him and hid Jitto's corpse in the dense forest so as to avoid any revolution in the village. Poor Gauri was inconsolable at the death of her father. With the help of Iso, she found the corpse of her father and decided to give up her life at the pyre of her father. A wave of grief and shock spread across the village and people assembled to witness a young girl of eight committing *sati*. In those times, *sati* was thought to be an incarnation of the Goddess. This was the first instance of a young girl committing *sati*. People started worshipping Gauri as an incarnation of Goddess.

Bawa Jitto and Bua Gauri sacrificed their lives in the year 1482 and were immortalized in the annals of history. Professor Shiv Nirmohi in his paper titled "Duggar Da Shaheed Devta: Bawa Jitto" describes Bawa Jitto as "a shaheed devta". According to him, deification of a martyr has been a tradition in *duggar* and a person sacrificing his life for his rights is deified and is called a martyr deity in *duggar*.

In this paper, I have attempted the hero's journey in *Bawa Jitto* as the migration of Jitto from Ghaar to Kanachak follows the pattern of a monomyth quest as propounded by Joseph Campbell in his empirical study on the "monomyth". The heroic journey is performed through the path of mythological adventure and Joseph Campbell held that during his journey, the hero undergoes various phases when he leaves his place and proceeds on his mythological path, meets helpers, faces tests and finally returns as a hero. Campbell calls these phases, "separation, initiation and return which might be named the nuclear unit of monomyth" (*The Hero*, 30). Campbell and other scholars such as Eric Neumann, describe narratives of Buddha, Moses and Christ in terms of the monomyth and Campbell argues that classic myths from many cultures follow this basic pattern. This paper analyses the herculean struggle of Bawa Jitto against the *jagirdaar's* oppression in the pattern of the monomyth.

Bawa Jitto's migration from his native place Ghaar pinjor to Kanachak follows "the standard path of the mythological adventure of the hero" (Campbell, 30). The *karak* in the play aptly describes the beauty of Bawa's native place and the central conflict in the play which initiates Jitto's separation from his land:

> In the lap of the hills of Trikuta nestles a village Ghaar
>
> Replete with rippling musical rivulets embellished with swaying pines.
>
> Here an ever-burning flame consecrated to Jitto was lit
>
> Here dwelt Jitto and his innocent daughter
>
> Sustained himself by tilling his land with the sweat of his brow
>
> Yet the envious consumed by his success made difficult his existence
>
> Aunt Jojan, an avowed witch kindled malevolence against him
>
> The virtual sorceress goaded her sons against the virtuous Jitto.
>
> O my Ram, What a pity! (*Bawa Jitto*, 12)

Campbell describes the hero of the monomyth as a "personage of exceptional gifts" who is honoured by his society, frequently unrecognised or disdained" (37). As reflected in the *karak*, Jitto is a man of action who toils to sustain his living with exceptional honesty. Moreover, being devotee of the divine Goddess he holds a revered place in the village irrespective of the fact that village society is afraid of the evil doers and dare not stand against them. Hence, irrespective of their inward support for Jitto his goodness is unrecognised with the apparent victory of wrong doers and he is forced to leave his native place after the unfair decision of the village Panchayat. His speech in the village assembly is an expression of his distressed soul:

> Revered Sarpanch, Today's assembly was called by me. That's why I accept the decision of the Panchayat in humility. I've decided that I'll give all my land to aunt Jojan and leave this village Ghaar. I'm not at all pained to give my fields to my cousins; I'm distressed, however, to realize that the soil of Ghaar has lost the fragrance of self-esteem. Our moral cowardice has emasculated us We cannot distinguish between good and bad, white and black. Undue advantage to the wicked is germinating in this soil and the innocents of this land will be forced to taste its bitter fruits in future....
>
> (*Bawa Jitto*, 26)

The first unit of the monomyth manifests in Jitto's separation or departure from his native land which signifies that destiny has summoned him and "transferred his spiritual centre of gravity from within the pale of his society to a zone unknown" (Campbell, 58) and he follows the "the Call to Adventure", the first subsection of the first stage. Jitto's adventure nevertheless is not out of his own volition or as a mere blunder but out of the "symbolical deficiency" in the society in which he finds himself. Jitto's aunt and the village Panchayat represent inclination of the society towards wicked ways of life be it the evil intentions of Jojan or unjust verdict of Sarpanch.

The "Departure" of Jitto leads to "Initiation" which deals with the adventures he faces after his separation from his native place. In "The Road of Trials" the hero undergoes the succession of trials, tests and ordeals and Jitto overcomes all barriers because of his unflinching faith in the divine Goddess.

Campbell calls it "The Meeting with the Goddess" which is often represented by the power of love which is all-powerful, all-encompassing and unconditional that a fortunate infant may experience with his or her mother, Jitto gets the power of divine love from his daughter Gauri whom he considers an incarnation of the divine Goddess herself. While leaving his native land and while consoling Gauri, who is tormented by the feeling of leaving her village, her house and above all the remembrances of her dead mother, he submits himself to the supreme Goddess and declares "We are firm believers in hard work. Moreover, you are with me and I feel as if Goddess Vaishno is around me" (28).

Jitto's arrival in Kanachak where he is given shelter by a friend Rullo and is granted a piece of land by the landlord set the ground for a series of tasks and ordeals that he undergoes in the mythological journey. According to Campbell in "The Road of Trials", "the hero is covertly aided by the advice, amulets, and secret agents of the supernatural helper whom he met before his entrance into this region." Rullo and Iso are such secret agents of supernatural help who provide physical as well as moral support to Jitto during his struggle to convert a barren piece of land into a fertile terrain. Jitto's path is perilous but the rich harvest and the golden crop is the fruit of the benign power of the Goddess and the aid of Iso, thereby, leading to his discovery that there is a benign power everywhere supporting him in his superhuman passage" (Campbell, 97).

Jitto's confrontation with Mehta Bir Singh, who holds ultimate power and authority in Kanachak is his "Atonement with the father". In many myths or stories this is the father or father figure who has life or death power. This is the central point of journey. All the previous steps have been moving into this place, all that follows move out from here. Although this step is most frequently symbolized by an encounter with a male entity, it does not have to be a male, just someone or thing with incredible power. According to Campbell, "Atonement consists in no more than the abandonment of that self-generated double monster—the dragon thought to be God (superego) and the dragon thought to be Sin (repressed id). But this requires an abandonment of the attachment of ego itself, and that is what is difficult" (130). Just as Christ had to suffer for the sins of the humanity, Jitto thrusts a dagger in chest to shake the edifice of feudalism which has created a wide chasm between the peasant and the landlord. *Jagirdars* possessed supreme dictatorial power over landless peasants in feudalism and Jitto encounters him in his fight for the justice and righteousness.

Jitto's final act conveys his "abandonment of the attachment to ego". His final words "I now intermix the yield of my land with my own flesh and blood" (64) is his offering to the mankind like Lord Jesus's offering of bread and wine in Lord's Supper (Eucharist). This is what is known in the heroic monomyth as the "Apotheosis" and Jitto's sacrifice reaffirms his final "Return", the third step of heroic monomyth. Just as Christ returns to the ordinary world after his resurrection; Jitto's returned as a martyr deity to redeem the mankind. His temple has been erected in Jhiri, Kanachak which is thronged by devotees every year particularly at the annual congregation in November.

In the Foreword to *Bawa Jitto,* Prof. G.K Das aptly comments, "There is something intriguingly atavistic about Bawa's action for which there can be no simple explanation in terms of behavioural psychology or cultural anthropology". He further says that Jitto's action has the power to regenerate the society similar to the practices of animal/human sacrifice for regeneration of life and crop and of James Frazer's accounts of older community life and of fertility gods who were consigned to death for new and better yield (*Bawa Jitto,* viii). Jitto's "perilous journey was a labor not of attainment but of reattainment, not discovery but rediscovery" (Campbell, 39). Jitto as *duggar* folk hero "is symbolical of that divine creative and redemptive image which is hidden within us all, only waiting to be known and rendered into life" (Campbell, 39). Ostensibly, his action leads to his mastery of two worlds which in turn leads to his freedom from fear of death, the final stage of the monomyth where he is able to give life to others through his own death.

Notes

1. Another word for the land of Dogras. Dogras are inhabitants of Jammu province, southern regions of Punjab, Himachal Pradesh and some parts of Pakistan like Sialkot. Before partition 22 ranges of Dogras existed which were ruled by Dogra rulers. Duggar has its own culture, folklore and language. The political divisions after partition brought immense demarcations in the land of Dogras. Jammu is now predominantly considered the land of Dogras.
2. Karaks are folk ballads in dogri which are mainly narratives of lives of those who have died before time, by accident or self-sacrifice or because of injustice and of supernatural powers that get attached to them after such death. Some karaks are in praise of local deities or 'Puranic' gods and goddesses. Karak is derived from the 'Vedic karika'. Dogra psyche is characterised by its propensity to idolise common people for their virtue and valor. There are several instances of ordinary human beings raised to the pedestal of local deities because of extraordinary circumstances or self-imposed death. Each village deity has a karak which is sung at the annual festival at the shrines of village deities. The aim of singing karak is to propitiate the deites.
3. Bars are another form of folk ballads in dogri like karak which is meant to be sung and in which death acts as a catalyst. The only difference is that they aim at commemorating incidents of valour. Both Bars and Karaks have pre-dominance of 'Karuna Rasa' but Bar shows 'Vir Rasa' in the first halves.
4. Devotee: A folk singer who sings the glory of folk heroes and deities.
5. Legend has it that a deity of that name came to Jammu and Kashmir during the reign of King Bajdev (1164-1215) from Rajasthan. During an invasion in Rajasthan people sought refuge in hilly areas. It is believed that they brought their deity with them and established temples in different areas of J&K. Since then Raja Mandalik is regarded as a supreme visitor deity of J&K and is worshipped in a number of Hindu ceremonies.

Works Cited

Campbell, Joseph. *The Hero with a Thousand Faces*. London: Princeton University Press, 1956.

Datta, Amaresh. *Encyclopaedia of Indian Literature*. Sahitya Akademi, 1987.

Meyer Howard Abrams, Geoffrey Galt Harpham. *A Glossary of Literary Terms*. Tenth Edition. USA: Wadsworth Cengage Learning, 2012.

Shastri, Ram Nath. *Bawa Jitto*. Trans. Vandhana Sharma. Jammu: Saksham Books International, 2011.

12

Dogri Folk Narrative Songs (*Lok Gathas*): Their Socio-Cultural Context

Mrinalini Atrey

Oral expression and transmission has been the cornerstone of sustaining, perpetuating and disseminating information in many cultures throughout the world. This is especially true in many African, Middle Eastern and Asiatic societies that view oral transmission as an avenue to preserve the history, traditions, genealogical and cultural legacies of their communities. This practice of maintaining and transmitting traditional cultural practices by word of mouth and by custom and practice rather than by printed documents is referred to as Oral Traditions. Oral tradition now holds a special place among sources especially for the history of pre-literate societies. It exists in form of ballads, folk songs, folktales, legends and myths, etc.

Like other parts of the country, Jammu region is also fortunate in having rich heritage of oral tradition in form of folk songs, folktales, folk ballads so on and so forth.[1] These oral traditions are available in local dialects of Dogri, Gojri, Pahari, Bhaderwahi, Kishtwari, Poonchi, etc. Herein except Dogri, other dialects have their own exclusivity due to a limited spread area. Gojri is spoken by Gujjars, the major nomadic tribe of the region, Pahari is a dialect of people living in higher reaches of Jammu hills whereas Bhaderwahi is spoken only in Bhaderwah area of the region, Kishtwari in Kishtwar and Poonchi in Poonch region. In comparison to these, Dogri has more spread area. This has been due the extension of Dogra culture and its dialect from the nucleus centres of Basholi, Jasrota and Bhillawar to other areas of the region throughout the historical period. Moreover since last two hundred years, especially from the time of Maharaja Ranbir Singh (1857-85 A.D.), efforts were made for the promotion and development of Dogri as a result of which Dogri has got enriched and achieved the status of a language. In 2003, it got recognised as one of the major languages of India by its incorporation in the Eighth Schedule of Indian Constitution.

The present paper tends to explore the possibility of understanding the socio-cultural traditions in the region with the help of Dogri *Lok Gathas*. It also aims to discuss various generic forms of Dogri *Lok Gathas* the purpose of composition of the ballads, the singing community connected.

Lok gatha is combination of two words, *lok* and *gatha* wherein former means folk and latter refers to a narrative therefore it means a narrative of the folk. It is usually a long narrative song which is performed to the accompaniment of music. It is organised into paragraphs and some of them run into several hundreds of pages and their performance is spread over several days like epics but they do not fall in the genre of epics. Moreover, the number of such narratives is also quiet less. At the same time being oral in tradition probably they appear to have undergone many changes, though not in subject matter, before being documented in view of the fact that the narrative of the folk language is rustic rather than being refined. Yet it is verbose and story is loaded with miracles. The narrative is performed to the accompaniment of music which is set on long note and high volume. Unlike the folktale there is absence of moral lesson. In the *lok gatha,* the protagonist is usually a deity, folk hero, or a martyr who has sacrificed his life for a common cause. The *gatha* narrates the life story and main events connected with these heroes.

This generic form of *lok gathas* is available in the oral traditions of other regions of India as well. We find it in Hindi, Punjabi, Bengali, Rajasthani, Marathi languages so on and so forth. All these *lok gathas* have been placed in the folk ballad genre as ballad also in general means a narrative set to music. However, when we compare it with European counterpart then technically they do not confirm to it. These narratives cannot be placed in genre of folk ballads. However, to use ballad for the same requires a bigger debate not only at pan-Indian level but also at international level with regard to *lok gathas*. Therefore, to avoid any confusion the author would restrict herself to using the term *lok gatha* as a folk narrative song rather than folk ballad.

In Dogri language also many variants of *lok gathas* are available. However, the scholars do not agree to all the variants. This is probably due to the fact that being oral in tradition, the documentation process is still going on and with the coming to light of new forms the controversy with regard to its generic forms starts. Initially, only two major forms, *karaks* and *bars* were recognised as forms of *lok gatha*. This is also due to the fact these two forms were documented in large number in the beginning. However, over a period of time many more narrative songs have come to light which can be placed in the genre of *lok gathas*. The different forms are as follows:

Generic Forms of the Dogri *Lok Gathas*

(1) *Karaks Gathas:* Religious Narratives

Karaks are the narratives with religious theme. The word *karak* has been derived from Sanskrit word *Karika* which means *Shalok* or special song. They are primarily the narratives connected with Brahmanical gods and folk deities of the region set in local conditions. *Karaks* form two sub-groups among themselves as (a) the *gathas* dealing with Brahmanical gods and goddesses called as *Puranic* and (b) *gathas* of folk deities and family deities. Narratives of the Brahmanical gods largely centre around the stories of Shiva-Parvati, their marriage and magic rituals associated with lord *Shiva*.[2] *Gathas* of folk deities includes *gathas* of family deities (*Kul Devtas* and *Kul Devis*), *Naga deities* (Serpent deities), and village deities (*Gram devtas* and *devis*) who over a period of time have achieved the status of folk deities like Raja Mandleek, Kali Beer and Narsingh. On the other hand, narratives connected with the family deities includes those of *Bawa Jitto*, *Bawa Ranpat*, *Bua Kauri* and *Bua Banga*. *Karaks* are usually performed at the time of festivals held in honour of the deities especially at annual congregations (*Mela*) at their shrines. The purpose of the *karaks* is to invoke the deity to get favours in form of agricultural prosperity, wealth, progeny and protection from natural calamities. These *karaks* are sung by traditional folk singers called *Gardis* and *Jogis*. They are the people belonging to lower strata of the society, namely the Megh or Dum sub-caste in Jammu region.

(2) ***Yogi Gathas*: Yogic Narratives**

They are also sacred in nature as they contain stories of various people who came under the influence of *Nath Panthis* and became *Yogis* (master of supreme *Yoga*). *Nath Panth* is a spiritual heterodox tradition within the Hindu cult. These *Yogis* came from all walks of life—rulers, royal persons and common folk people like Brithri, Raja Gopichand, Baba Pir Charangnath and Raja Hodi who followed the path of renunciation. Their *karaks* are also sung on special occasion at their shrines by their disciples.

(3) ***Baran Gathas*: Narratives of Heroism**

The second form of *gatha* prevalent in the region is *Baran*. *Bar* is corruption of Hindi term *Vir*, which means brave or chivalrous. Since these narratives deal with the theme of prowess and adventure, they are called *Baran* or narratives of heroism. These narratives, extol the bravery of warriors who at some point of historical period showed their military prowess and chivalry. However, these *gathas* have been documented only from 17th century onwards. *Gathas* prior to it, if they existed, have been lost to posterity. The available heroic ballads include tales of warriors like Mian Dido, Raja Ranjit Dev, Baj Singh, etc. Mian Dido was a Dogra chief who did not accept Sikh suzerainty (Raja Ranjit Singh of Punjab) unlike Gulab Singh (another chief who later became Maharaja Gulab Singh) and wanted to expel Sikh power from the region. He put up a brave front but ultimately was killed in the Trikuta hills. Raja Ranjit Dev was ruled over Jammu Principality from 1728-80 and is considered most enlightened ruler who put a ban on *sati* (immolation of wife on the death of her husband). Baj Singh was the Army general of Maharaja Pratap Singh (1885-1925) who quelled the revolts in Gilgit and Chitral (in Ladakh).

Bars were sung during the battles and in the courts of the Dogra rulers to inspire and infuse a sense of bravery among the soldiers. They were sung by the traditional singers called *Dareas* who were followers of Islam, but Dogra lords always asked the company of these bards especially during battles. With their thundering voice and rhythm they always inspired the soldiers on the battlefield (Jerath, 61-62). These bards created the *gathas* instantaneously and sung the praises of their lords. They used a stringed instrument for rhythm popularly called *Chakara*.

(4) *Pranya Gathas*: Love Narratives

They include the *gathas* of Kunju-Chanchlo, Sunni-Bhukhu, Mira-Julahi Phulmu-Ranjhu, Pirthi Sing, Inder Dei, Mian Te Maine, Nand Lal, Hemraj, and Channa Plasar.[3] Kunju-Chanchlo is the love story of a Soldier (Kunju) killed in the battlefield and his beloved (Chanchlo). Sunni-Bhukhu were the lovers who belonged to Gaddi tribe and died on receiving wrong news about each other's death. Chann Plasar is the story of two lovers from different castes. The boy (Chann) was from Brahmin (Priestly Caste) and his beloved was from Harijan community (untouchables). When there was an opposition from the society, boy became Harijan for his love. Raja Hosn is a story of prince who had won his bride in the swayamvara and when bride's brother refused to acknowledge the marriage, he had to fight a hard battle with bride's family.[4] Mira-Julahi is again a tragic love story of a lady and her warrior. Asoka Jerath, an eminent folklore collector also refers to love narratives of Phulmu-Ranjhu, Pirthi Sing, Inder Dei, Mian Te Maine, Nand Lal, Hemraj, etc. (Jerath, 62-64). Siva Nirmohi another folklore collector has also referred to these love narratives (Nirmohi, 155-62). He opines that the *gatha* of Kunju-Chanchlo and Sunni-Bhukhu have got transformed into folk songs (Nirmohi, 162-63). It is true not only in case of love ballads but also in other forms of *gathas* that have been shortened into folk songs. As a result many of scholars have refused to accept them as *gathas*.

(5) **Seasonal Narratives**

(a) **Chettri or Dholru Gathas.** Dholru *gathas* fall into the group of seasonal narratives as they are sung in particular seasons of the year. They are sung in the Hindu months of *Phagun* (eleventh month of Hindu calendar, from middle of February to Middle of March) and *Chetr* (twelfth month of Hindu calendar from middle of March to middle of April) (Goswami, 6). Therefore, they are known as *Chettri* ballads as well. Their theme revolves around the birth of Lord Ram, his marriage with Sita and also his exile set in the local conditions.[5] They are sung by the traditional folk singers called *Dholru* singers. The *Dholru* singers of Ramnagar, Basholi, Duggi Dhar, Bhaddu, and Bhillawar are well known for their excellent singing.

(b) **Bar Saware.** They fall in the group of seasonal narratives. They are sung in the Hindu months of *Assu* (sixth month of Hindu calendar, from middle of September to middle of October) and *Ketah* (seventh month of Hindu calendar from middle of October to middle of November). Herein the *gatha* titled *Sarban Geet* (*Shravan*) is especially sung which tells the story of an obedient son called Sharvan Kumar whose parents were blind. When he was incidentally killed by King Dasrath of Ayodhaya (of Ramayan fame), his parents cursed the king Dasrath that he would also die, longing for his son. The story does not belong to Jammu region but has come from outside and got set in local tradition.

Bar Saware are sung by traditional bards to the accompaniment of local musical instrument called *Dhaka*.

Unlike *karaks* and *bars*, these ballads were usually a source of entertainment for the village folk. *Chettri* singers are also known to have knowledge about astrology, rains and agricultural operations which they shared with village folk. Therefore, they were highly respected in village community.

(6) *Gusten Gathas*: Ritualistic Narratives

Masade and Gujri fall in the genre of ritualistic narratives. The *Masades* are sung during the performance of rituals like *Gusten*. Therefore, they are also called as *Gusten Gatha*. *Gusten* are the rituals performed when the first offering of the new harvest is made to the family deity to invoke the blessings of the deity for prosperity. As such they are sung in the month of *Katah* (seventh month of Hindu calendar, from middle of October to middle of November) and *Magr* (Eighth month of Hindu calendar, from middle of November to middle of December), when the new crop is ready (Goswami, 7). They are also sung in the months of *Magh*, *Phagun* and *Chetr* when winter harvest is ready and is to offered to the deity (Goswami, 7).

They are performed by the traditional bards called *Gurahiya*. However, it is pertinent to mention here that the meaning of the words in the documented *Masades* is not clear. Scholars working on their documentation also showed their helplessness with regard to the meaning of the words. One view is that this tradition of *Gurahias* is dying away as most of the exponents have died and those who have acquired this singing skill have forgotten the exact meanings of the words.

(7) Anjaliyas

This form of narrative has been highlighted only by Om Goswami in Duggar Lok Gatha. Herein he has put the gathas narrating the stories of Pandava brothers of Mahabharat fame and Shiva-Parvati marriage.

(8) Chijji

Chijj is a special type of *gatha* which means high volume noise. They are called so because they are sung in high pitch with fast playing of the musical instruments. They include devotional songs (*Bhajans*) of Mother Goddess, Durga and also some of the popular Bars like that of Bir Jodh, Chaudhari Kima, Prithvi Raj Chauhan (Goswami, 8). They are sung for the entertainment of the common folk and therefore appear to be of popular nature. Though earlier it was the traditional singers who performed in a group of three or four people, it has now been taken over by professional singers. Nowadays, people invite these singers to sing *Chijj Bhajans* at their homes on auspicious occasions.

Composition of the *Lok Gathas*

Although the composition of the *lok gatha* generally involves both individual and community effort, yet in case of dogri *lok gatha*, it is appears to be largely the result of the effort of the community of the folk singers. Traditional bards *dareas gardis, jogis, guriyas,* and *dholru* singers not only performed these *lok gathas* but also composed them. *Dareas* would compose *bars* in the battlefield itself. Moreover, with regard to *karaks* and *barans,* they could not be sung by all the folk singers but only by *gardis* and *dareas.* So the bards were not only composing and performing but also acted as the custodians of the same.

Socio-cultural Context of the *Lok Gathas*

As these narratives form an essential part of the living heritage of the region, the subject matter contained within the narrative can use to understand the socio-cultural aspect of the regional society. Therefore, the study of the *lok gathas* is significant not only from literary point of view but also from socio-cultural aspect as it is the narrative of the folk and gives us an insight into the beliefs, rituals and traditions of the people in the region. This is especially in case of *gathas* of the folk deities, *karaks*. They can provide us information about the classes on which we hardly have any source material. They can supply us evidence on society in making that is the transitional phase from pastoral life to settle agricultural as evident in ballads connected with Martyr Deities.[6] The accounts of peasant resistance and other variety of social conflict in the society also get reflected in the narratives. This becomes clear from the following discussion on the *karaks,* a major form of Dogri folk narrative songs.

(a) References to Extinct Tribes: The importance of the *gathas* lie in the fact that they provide us with a lot of information on the various tribes and communities that dwelt in the region in the earlier period, for which we have no data available. This is especially in case of the Naga and Yaksha tribes who once inhabited this region but now they cannot be located in the present population. Naga tribe is believed to have been dominant tribe in the region at some stage of historical period. This becomes evident not only from the existence of numerous shrines of Naga deities in the region but also from presence of numerous narratives connected with them. These *gathas* provide us with lot of information on the Nagas and their tribal character.

Likewise, the existence of Yaksha tribe is evident from the narratives, especially from that of Vasuki Naga devta and Bhair Naga *devta.*[7] This information, when corroborated with evidence of shrine of Yaksha deity in the Hiranagar *tehsil* help us to confirm it.[8] This also leads us to think that the village names such as Jakh Badh, Jakh Tala, Jakh-a-Jadha may have been corrupt form of Yaksha and these villages may have been associated with Yaksha tribe.

(b) References to Migrations of Many Tribes. The *gathas* connected with exotic deities such as that of Brihatri, Raja Mandleek, and Kalibeer tell us that these deities came from outside with migrating tribes and got assimilated into the local deity cult. Their narratives can be used to gather useful information about the migration of the various tribes into the region as we know that deities do not travel by themselves but they migrate with tribes and social groups. For example, the *gatha* of Brihatri exists not only in Dogri dialect (Jammu) but also in Kulai (Himachal Pradesh) and Bhojpuri (Banaras) dialects. As such a comparative analysis of these *gathas* can help us to study the path of migration of both the deity and the tribe, which brought it.

(c) **References to Worshipping Modes.** These *lok gathas* also throw light on the religious beliefs of the people in the region. *Karaks*, the religious narratives, as already pointed out, are devoted to the local deities—*Kula Devtas* and *Kula Devis*. It shows that the worship of local deities has been the dominant religious practice of the people in the region and it continues to be so. No ritual or religious ceremony is considered complete without reverence to these deities. In fact, the every ritual starts with initial offering being made to the *Kul Devtas* and *Kul Devis*. Brahmanical gods are placed second in importance to them in spite of the fact that most of the region has now been brahmanised. This shows harmonious co-existence of little tradition with greater tradition and little tradition maintaining its identity.

(d) **References to Customs and Rituals.** These folk narratives also give us information about rituals connected with birth of a child. The marriage customs and rituals existing in the region also get reflected in the *gathas*. The narratives connected with female deities shows that girls were usually married before puberty, whereas boys were married at a little advanced age. For example, the *gatha* of Bua Makhna and Bua Bukhi—two *sati* deities of the region—tell us that they were married off before attaining puberty.[9] Similarly much can be gleaned about marriage rituals from the narratives especially those dealing with marriage of Shiva-Parvati. In fact, this *gatha* exists in Dogri and Bhaderwahi dialect (spoken in Jammu and Bhaderwah district of Jammu region). A comparative study of both the *lok gathas* in these dialects also shows a lot of regional variation in customs and rituals in the above-mentioned sub-regions of Jammu.

(e) **References to Position of Women in Regional Society.** Female deities are specially revered in the region in form of *kula* deities. They have been categorized into local goddesses, Silabantis (who performed *sati*) and village deities. The various narratives about these female deities in their narratives give us a glimpse of the social status of the women in the region. As discussed earlier, the girls in the region were married at an early age and probably they did not have an access to any kind of formal education. Moreover, the overall picture of status of women in the region as evident through *lok gathas* is not encouraging. They appear to be a suppressed lot who suffered at the hands of the society in one way or the other. She was victim of dowry system and we find many instances where she killed herself or was killed due to the atrocities of the in-laws and consequently out of fear, the family started worshipping the daughter-in-law to escape her wrath. A pertinent example is that of Bua Bhuki and Bua Makhana. Bua Bhuki was forced by her in-laws to do hard labour because of which she fell seriously ill. However, no doctor was called in and even her brothers refused to take care of her. As a result she died and her in-laws started worshipping her out of fear.[10] Likewise Bua Makhana killed herself by drowning in the village pond. As the story goes, she had recently lost her brother. One day she wanted to go to the local festival of Rade. When she sought the permission of her mother-in-law, the lady insulted her so badly that Makhna got perturbed and killed herself by drowning.[11] *Gatha* of Bua Amro is a story of yet another lady who was tortured and killed by her mother in-law.[12]

We also come to know about the prevalence of *sati* custom among the women of the region through the *lok gathas*. Women in the region are known to have committed *sati* not only on the death of their husbands but also when she lost her father or son. *Gatha* of Bua Kodi (daughter of Bawa Jitto) tells us that she died along with her father.[13] Datti Chargu committed *sati* on the funeral pyre of her son who had died of snakebite. Her only son Radhe was bitten by a snake and became seriously ill. She took him to the nearest Naga shrine and pleaded for his life but he died and she also committed *sati*.[14] It is said that since this incident people in the village have stopped worshipping Naga deity and they also do not celebrate *Naga Panchami* (local festival connected with snake worship). The *gatha* of Bua Laddo is a story of a lady who became *sati* on the death of her fiancé Bhalla who was killed when he was proceeding to her (bride) place.[15]

However, in spite of the fact that women suffered in the society, the *lok gathas* also tell us the stories of enlightened women who not only fought for their own rights but for social justice as well. The narrative of Bua Banga carries the story of such an enlightened lady who revolted against the imposition of the new excessive taxes by the feudal lord of the area. She organized the people of her area and asked them not to pay undue taxes. When the soldiers of the feudal lord came to arrest her, she committed *sati* along with her infant child.[16] Similarly, Dabbojwali Dati also took a brave stand against the atrocities of the feudal lord and when she was unable to withstand it further, she performed *sati* to protect her womanhood.[17]

(f) **References to Feudalistic Features.** Prevalence of feudalistic practices in the region is also evident through the *lok gathas*. We come to know about the kind of relationship existing between the feudal lord and the peasant and the picture is not very encouraging. The feudal lords were usually harsh in their treatment of the peasants. They afflicted atrocities on the peasants not only in the process of tax collection but also indulged in excessive taxation for one reason or the other. There was no limit to the tax, which was levied, most of times it was excessive amount that the peasant could not pay. As discussed above the *gatha* of Bua Banga and Dabbojwali Dati give us an insight into how excessive taxation was levied by the feudal lords. Similarly, Data Koda resented the excessive tax being levied by the local feudal lord for the purpose of building a new palace for his newly wedded wife. As a result the soldiers of the feudal lord took away his cattle. When he failed to get justice, he killed himself in front of palace of the feudal lord.[18] The peasant also felt helpless when the feudal lord forcibly took away good harvest. The story of Bawa Jitto is pertinent example in this regard as also that of Baba Ballo of Mathwar. The ballad of Bawa Jitto shows how the feudal lord wanted to carry away his grain and when the poor peasant was unable to stop him from doing so, he killed himself on the heap of his grain.[19] The feudal lords also used to forcibly carry away the cattle of the poor peasants. Datta Sukho lost his life while rescuing the cattle belonging to a poor shepherd of a low caste from a *zamindar*.[20] Another important aspect of the society of the region, which gets highlighted through the narratives, is the practice of cattle raids and boundary disputes. The narratives show that there used to be violent conflicts and murders for the cattle among the commoners as well. Many incidents are referred in the *gathas,* when the cattle strayed into the neighbouring field and destroyed the crop, leading to conflicts. Data Rangu now revered, as a martyr deity was a shepherd belonging to Jat class of peasants. One day his cattle intruded into the farms belonging to peasant of Majbe caste and destroyed the crop. This infuriated the Majbe farmers who got together and killed Rangu. When his mother heard of the incident and the death of her son she also committed *sati.* Consequently, the village people fearing retribution from their heinous crime got a shrine built in their honour and started worshipping them.[21] Likewise Data Hallo was a Jat farmer whose cattle was stolen by another Jat peasant and taken away to his village. This led to a violent conflict between two parties wherein Data Hallo was seriously injured and lost his life. The village folk started worshipping him as a brave warrior and a protector.[22]

The occurrence of boundary and land disputes also becomes evident from the study of the subject matter in the narratives especially from that of Data Ranpat and Data Bihran. The ballad of Data Ranpat tells us that he was killed while attempting to settle a land dispute between two clans of *Charak Rajputs* of *Birpur* village.[23] Similarly, Datta Bihran was also killed over a land dispute. According to *gatha*, he was Jat peasant and belonged to Tilakpur village. There was a conflict between him and Brahman of Gaud sub-caste. In the conflict, he was killed and later on people responsible for his death got a shrine built at Assad village.[24]

The boundary disputes and cattle conflicts also reflect that the society of the time was in transitional phase moving from pastoral way of life to settled agriculture society. Therefore, the narratives depicting cattle raids and boundary disputes can be a source to study the change from pastoral society to agricultural one in the absence of conventional sources.

(g) References to Human Sacrifice, Magic and Witchcraft. Practice of human sacrifice was also prevalent here, though it does not seem to be widespread. The *gatha* of Baba Thalu and Raj Bahu Rahuul are examples of this practice. Baba Thalu was a child of five years who was stolen away from his parents and sacrificed by the feudal lord of Methab Garh (near Lakhanapur principality) to firm the foundations of new fort being constructed.[25] Raj Bahu Rahuul on the other hand was the daughter-in-law of the king of Kangra and she sacrificed her in-laws family for the purpose of building a canal.[26] Such narratives not only tell us about the prevalence of human sacrifice in the society but also give an insight into the superstitions existing therein.

The *Yogi* narratives such as those connected with Brihatri contain lot of information regarding magic practices and superstitions existing here. There is a narrative called Siva Jharia, which talks of various magic and witchcraft practices of the region exhibited through Siva as the main protagonist. There is no reference to the ballad in any of the brahmanical literature which shows that the practices referred in it are the local in origin, which have now been associated with Siva.

(h) References to Praha Pratha among Brahmans. Brahman as a learned person has always been looked upon with respect and simple folk usually looked to him for guidance and protection. In Jammu region also, the Brahmans seem to have lived up to their duty. Many of the ballads refer to the practice of *Praha Pratha*. It was a kind of passive resistance or self-torture sometimes culminating in self-immolation and self-killing. A Brahman would practice it to take up stand against the injustice of the rulers and would sacrifice himself if he were unable to receive justice from him. Therefore, he acted as a check on the misdeeds of the ruler. Moreover, it was also practiced against individual wrongdoer as well who created problem in the society. Bawa Fittu, Bawa Kahan and Bawa Jitto are the examples of those few who sacrificed their life through *Praha Pratha*. Bawa Fittu killed himself when he failed to persuade the in-laws of a girl of his village who was maltreated by them for want of dowry.[27] Bawa Kahn was a *Brahman* who took to money lending as a profession. He starved himself to death in front of the house of a feudal lord. According to the ballad, the sons of the said feudal lord had taken credit from him and which they had refused to return it. When his appeal was not heard, he sat on *Praha* and gave his life.[28]

Conclusion

Dogri *lok gathas*, in nutshell, are an important aspect of our intangible heritage. An attempt should be made to document all its generic forms lest they are lost to posterity forever. They are significant not only from literary point of view but also as major source to understand the socio-cultural processes of the regional society.

Notes

1. Jammu region is a geographical entity which has been identified as a tract lying between River Jhelum and River Ravi, that is, between Plains of Punjab and the ascending hills of Pir Panjal. The region is further divided into sub-regions of The Eastern Plains, the Eastern Hills, the Western Plains and the Western Hill. Presently, the region forms a part of the state of Jammu and Kashmir, the northern most state of India. However, some part of it including Bhimbar, Khari-Kharyali and Mirpur now form a part of Pakistan.
2. Parvati, the consort of Lord Shiva, is considered as daughter of the land and Shiva is considered as the son-in-law of the region. Their marriage is said to have been performed at Sudh-Mahadev. Most of the local god and goddesses are now considered as incarnation of Lord Shiva and Parvati.
3. Ashok Jerath, *Dogra Legends of Art and Culture*, Indus Publishing, p. 65.
4. In ancient India, *Swayamvara* was a practice of choosing a husband, from among a list of suitors, by a girl of a marriageable age. *Swayam* in Sanskrit means self and *Vara* means choice or desire also synonymous with bridegroom.
5. Lord Ram, the incarnation of Lord Vishnu (of the Trinity Gods—Brahma, Vishnu and Mahesh in Hinduism), ruler of Ayodhya, hero of *Ramayan* fame.

6. The ballads connected with Naga deities such as those of *Baba Surgal, Baba Bhair, Baba Basak, Baba Kaillu, Baba Balikaran* and so on.
7. "Eighty-four sons, grandsons Raja called Looking for Bhair! Find he could not! Trembling wazir Yaksh! Lie did he tell! "This excerpt is from the Ballad of Baba Bhair devta. See Nilamber Dev Sharma and Khari singh Madhukar (Ed.) *Dogri Lok Geet,* Vol. II, Jammu & Kashmir Academy of Art, Culture and Languages, Jammu, 1990, pp. 14-18.
8. This is the only Yaksh Shrine to be found in the region.
9. Ballads documented in Siva Nirmohi, *Duggar ki Lok Gathye*, Radhakrishanand and Company, Jammu, 1982. pp. 104-05.
10. Her shrine is at Madun village in Kathua district. For ballad see Om Goswami (Ed.) *Dogri Lok Gathye,* Jammu & Kashmir Academy of Art, Culture and Languages, Jammu, 1990, pp. 104-07.
11. Siva Nirmohi, *Duggar ki Lok Gathye*, Radhakrishanand and Company, Jammu, 1982. p. 104.
12. Her shrine is situated on Jammu-Gajansu road. See also Mrinalini Atrey, *Deity, Cult, Rituals and Oral Traditions in Jammu*, Saskham Books International, Jammu 2008, p. 39.
13. Bua Kodi became *Sati* at the tender age of eight years along with her Father Baba Jitto. She enjoys the status of folk deity in the region and her shrine is spread at various places in the area. For ballad details see the ballad of Bawa Jitto in Nilamber Dev Sharma and Khari singh Madhukar (Ed.) *Dogri Lok Geet,* Vol. II, Jammu & Kashmir Academy of Art, Culture and Languages, Jammu, 1990, pp. 50-66.
14. Her shrine is at Ghamyal village in Hiranagar tehsil of Kathua district.
15. Shrine at Prawaha village in Nagbani area on Jammu-Akhnur highway.
16. Her shrine is at Thera Galwalin Bhillwar area. Complete Ballad given in Om Goswami (ed.) *Dogri Lok Gathye,* Jammu & Kashmir Academy of Art, Culture and Languages, Jammu, 1990, pp. 96-97.
17. Her shrine is at Dabboj village in Sambha district. See also Mrinalini Atrey, *Deity, Cult, Rituals and Oral Traditions in Jammu*, Saskham Books International, Jammu 2008, p. 42.
18. His shrine is at Sundrikot villagein Bhillawar tehsil.

19. Major shrines at Kanachak, Jhiri and Addhar Jitto. For ballad see ballad of Baba Jitto in Nilamber Dev Sharma and Khari Singh Madhukar (Ed.) *Dogri Lok Geet,* Vol. II, Jammu & Kashmir Academy of Art, Culture and Languages, Jammu, 1990, pp. 50-66.
20. His shrine is at Akalpur village in Jammu tehsil. For the ballad see Om Goswami (Ed.) *Dogri Lok Gathye,* Jammu & Kashmir Academy of Art, Culture and Languages, Jammu, 1990, pp. 174-76.
21. His shrine is at Tikri Dayala village in Marh block of Jammu tehsil.
22. Shrine at village Layalyal in Marh block and enjoys the status of village Deity.
23. His shrine is at Birpur village. For the ballad see in Nilamber Dev Sharma and Khari Singh Madhukar (Ed.) *Dogri Lok Geet,* Vol. II, Jammu & Kashmir Academy of Art, Culture and Languages, Jammu, 1990, pp. 38-47.
24. His shrine is at village Assadchak in Marh block of Jammu. For ballad see Om Goswami (Ed.) *Dogri Lok Gathye,* Jammu & Kashmir Academy of Art, Culture and Languages, Jammu, 1990, pp. 177-79.
25. His Shrine is at Mehtabpur in Kathua district. For ballad see Om Goswami (ed.) *Dogri Lok Gathye,* Jammu & Kashmir Academy of Art, Culture and Languages, Jammu, 1990, pp. 151-55.
26. Her ballad is popular in Jammu region, though it seems to have originally belonged to Kangra region. However, she is considered as Kula deity in Jammu region as well.
27. He is the Folk Deity of Majalta area.
28. His shrine is located in Ramgarh area of Akhnur tehsil where he is the Kula Deity of Ramgarhia Rajput community.

Works Cited

Atrey, Mrinalini (2008). *Deity, Cult, Rituals and Oral Traditions in Jammu,* Saskham Books International, Jammu, 2008.

Gadgal, Surinder. *Marh block ke Shaheed Devtas.* Jammu: Dogri Sanstha, 1980.

Goswami, Om (ed.) *Dogri Lok Gathye.* Jammu: Jammu & Kashmir Academy of Art, Culture and Languages, 1990.

Jerath, Asoka Dogra. *Legends of Dogra Art and Culture*, Indus Publishing, New Delhi, 1998.

Nirmohi, Siva. *Duggar ki Lok Gathye*. Jammu: Radhakrishan and and Company, 1982.

Sharma, Nilamber Dev and Madhukar, Khari Singh (Eds.). *Dogri Lok Geet*, Vol. II: Jammu: Jammu & Kashmir Academy of Art, Culture and Languages, 1990.

The Census Report of India, 1911.

13

The Jatayu Myth in Gujarati Poem "Jatayu"

Indira, N.

Proof of the universal and enduring appeal of the great myths is their constant reuse and reinterpretation by creative writers of all times and countries. A myth is an attempt to explain something—a natural phenomenon or a particular belief, custom, or practice of a society. Myth also explains how something came to exist. Like the Western myths, there are an equal number of popular myths in India too. In Gujarati literature, the word used for myth is "purakalpan". It has been defined as the creation of not one individual but of a race and has been passed on from one generation to the next. Myth has been used by Gujarati writers in two ways: one is to take the ancient myth and use it in contemporary literature while the second is to totally change the ancient myth even in its structure and use it in a new form. The contemporary poet and critic Sitanshu Yashashchandra uses myth in the latter form. In his collection of poems "Odysseusnu Halesu" he uses a Western (Greek) myth while in "Jatayu" he uses an Indian myth.

The two epics *Ramayana* and *Mahabharata*, with dates varying thousands of years, continue to inspire writers even today. Whether it is in thematic concerns, character portrayal, allegorical representations or symbolic interpretations, writers of all the languages in India have been inspired by these epics. "At all times in India there has been under the higher mythology of gods and great demons a lower mythology of spiritualized matter less remote than the gods of sun, storm, etc. and less remote even than the recognised spirits inhabiting yet not confined to such matter...this lower mythology has various aspects that blend it with the higher..." (Hopkins, 3). One could look at the higher mythology of Gods and Goddesses and *Devas* and other Heavenly beings as well as the lower mythology of semi-human creatures as well as flora and fauna. Jatayu is one such creature who figures in the *Ramayana* at a critical moment in the story. He is the son of Aruṇa and nephew of Garuda. A demi-god who has the form of a vulture, he was an old friend of Dasharath. He tried to rescue Sita from Ravana when Ravana was on his way to Lanka after kidnapping Sita. Jatayu fought valiantly with Ravana, but as Jatayu was very old Ravana soon got the better of him. As Rama and Lakshmana chanced upon the stricken and dying Jatayu in their search for Sita, Jatayu informs them of the fight between him and Ravana and the direction in which Ravana had gone (i.e. south).

Jatayu and his brother Sampati, when young, used to compete as to who could fly higher. On one such instance Jatayu flew so high that he was about to get seared by the sun's flames. Sampati saved his brother by spreading his own wings and thus shielding Jatayu from the hot flames. In the process, Sampati himself got injured and lost his wings. As a result, Sampati lived wingless for the rest of his life. While Jatayu was wounded and lying on the ground when Lord Rama arrived, Lord Rama sensed the end result and decided that Jatayu get *moksha*. Lord Rama hit an arrow in the ground so as to call all seven sacred rivers, called *teertha*. Six rivers' waters arrived, one river water failing to obey Lord Rama's call. Since Lord Rama was himself an incarnation of Lord Vishnu, He forced the Gaya teertha to arrive at the spot. Finally Jatayu was given the waters of seven rivers and he attained *moksha*. Today, the six river waters are seen together in one pond, whilst the seventh is a few feet away as a punishment. It mixes with the remaining six waters in an invisible manner. This is the story of Jatayu in the *Ramayana*.

Jatayu has always been seen as representative of goodness, devotion, courage to face dangers, ability to adhere to truth even in the face of seemingly insurmountable evil and violence. Even as an old bird, he holds on to dear life so that he is able to convey the direction in which the abducted Sita was carried away and finally in the spirit of the true *bhakta* attains *moksha* by dying in the presence of his Lord and master.

In 20th century Gujarati literature, with terms like modernism and post-modernism being the order of the day, realism and surrealism play a major role. Of the poets of this period, Shri Sitanshu Yashashchandra Mehta deserves special mention as his writings gave a new turn to Gujarati poetry. He began his poetic journey with two collections "Odysseusnu Halesu" and "Jatayu". This writing is characterised by a tone of revolt and a feeling of ruin and destruction. In his writings, there is also a novel use of language which has been described as 'automatic writing'. In "Jatayu", the poet has used the myth of the mythological bird in a genre that is called 'khand-kavya' in Gujarati and Hindi as well as in Marathi. Among the well-known Hindi 'khandakavyas', we can list *Noorjahan* by Gurubhakt Singh, *Haldighat* by Shyamcharan Pandey. In Gujarati, the form developed best in the hands of Kant—two important works being 'Atignan' and 'Vasant-vijay'. In this form, an event or character from the epics is dealt with as a separate, independent story. It has been called a 'narrative lyric' and a 'dramatic lyric'. It has been suggested that in this form, the struggle within the mind of one character is dealt with. It is not the external happenings that this form is connected. Unity of impression is stressed upon. The nearest English genre seems to be the ballad, a suggestion made by some well-known Gujarati critics. Again, that it does not exist even in other Indian languages makes the form unique to Gujarati literature. This paper attempts to analyse the use of the Jatayu myth in the poem of the same name.

In "Jatayu", which is a seven-stanza poem, the story has been shifted to the present day. Jatayu's battling with Ravana as he abducts Sita and moves in the direction of Lanka is portrayed as contemporary man's battle with evil/untruth for the protection of good/truth. The *Ramayana* has down the ages been interpreted as a constant battle between the bi-polarities of truth-untruth, *dharma-adharma*, Heavenly beings and those of the nether-worlds, culture and barbarism, etc. In continuation of this polarity, the poet chooses a locale for the poem which is in contrast to the two well-known cities of Ayodhya and Lanka.

The poem begins with:

> Nagar Ayodhya uttare, ne dakkhan nagari lanka,
> Vacche sadasadjjyot vihonu van pathrayu rank. (96)
>
> Ayodhya city in the North, and in the South Lanka,
> And between them the never-ending forest.
>
> (Translation mine)

The place is characterised by darkness all around, a place between the two cites, a place in time between life and death, a place chosen for the heroic deed of an old helpless Jatayu. The poet then goes on to describe the flora and fauna of the place. In a lyrical language, the poet describes the activities of the birds and animals there: "Chare, phare, rati kare, garbhane dhare, avatare, mare" (96) meaning "Graze, wander, make love, carry offspring, are born and die". So uncomplicated is life there that just looking into the crystal-clear water seems to quench their thirst. The first stanza ends with:

> Jem aavya tem jeevya kare kaain vadhu na jaane rank:
> Kyaan upar ayodhya uttare, kyaan door dakhane lanka. (96)

Translated as

> They take life as it comes, no nothing else these poor/simple:
>
> Where above in the North Ayodhya, and where in distant South Lanka.

In the second verse, he continues describing the fauna, and the birds of prey, and the last word is "Jatayu"—the protagonist is introduced in a matter-of-fact manner, with no poetic frills attached. Probably, it is this direct approach that raises the poem to an aesthetically high level. Among birds which can fly high, "are lifted high by the winds", among the vultures is one vulture who looks left and right but seems to make no distinction between the two directions and that vulture: Jatayu:

> Eva gidonni vacche ek giidh ek giidh che: naam jatayu. (97)

Translated as

> In the midst of such vultures is one vulture: named Jatayu.

In the third verse, the poet describes Jatayu in the days of his youth when among the common birds there was something uncommon about him. With an individualistic streak in him, he loved to fly high. He is different, because he wants to fly high—above the height of all other birds. Crossing the known into the realm of the unknown, and hence into the forbidden and the dangerous, is another characteristic. In the fourth stanza, he describes the youthful activities of the bird while also drawing attention to the boundaries of the forest which determine the limits of the range available to the creatures of the forest: "Vanna vaasi vanna cheda" (98) translated as "Edge of the forest, creatures of the forest". In the fifth stanza, the poet describes an event which takes place in the old age of the bird when there is a transgression of the limits drawn and in the sixth the results of that. The seventh stanza which is the concluding stanza ends with a total breakdown of faith in the mind of the protagonist when he questions: "Aa ansamjhu van vacche shu maru marvanu che aam?" (99) translated as "Do I have to die like this in the midst of this confusing forest?"

Like Kant of a century ago, Sitanshu Yashashchandra has been able to link a very personal experience with an impersonal concept like the myth. The inevitability of life as experienced by the Existentialists of the 20th century is a part of the poet's experience too. Sartre and Camus have had a great effect on the poet who questions many accepted ideas and attitudes of contemporary society. Hence, the poem ends with Jatayu's vain attempts to convey to Raghava the important details about Sita's abduction where Rama is "the master of time" while Jatayu is "mortal and will not live long".

He wonders how far Ayodhya is from this forest and whether he has to die like this in the forest that is incomprehensible to him. "Nathi Dashanan Dakshine ane Uttarma Nathi Raam" (99) translated as "There is no ten-headed in the South nor Rama in the North". The poet ends the poem on a note of total negation, of the absence of either good or bad, of *paap* and *punya*, of hope, of redemption or punishment, of Heaven or Hell. The narrator/commentator is able to link each verse with the previous one while at the same time allowing each stanza to stand independently.

The well-known Gujarati poet-critic Umashankar Joshi has analysed "Jatayu" by making contextual comparisons of the poem to the compositions of some of great poets of the 19th and 20th centuries. Drawing on his breadth and depth of reading, the critic writes that the poet is able to portray modern man in his description of the protagonist as well of the milieu. We see this in his contrasting *dharma* and *adharma*, in the darkness of the forest a reference to the darkness within the womb (with its propensity for creation of life), the innate desire of the bird to fly high which is akin to man's ambitions and his efforts to attain them, the habit of looking at the boundaries of the forest, the decision to wage a war even if it proves to be futile. The poet's description of the flora and fauna, especially in listing shows traces of an earlier style of poetry in Gujarat. A note of parody too creeps in occasionally. Though seemingly similar in characteristics, each animal has its unique feature like the parrot searching for chillies and butterflies in search of nectar. And then the vultures and among the vultures—Jatayu. From the physical description, he moves onto the metaphysical state of the bird. The desire to fly is conveyed through the kinetic sensation as in spite of its body-weight Jatayu always desired to fly high. Contemporary man's quest for success is obviously being suggested here.

From the third verse, the protagonist holds centre-stage. The poet describes how Jatayu is different from other vultures in wanting to fly sky-high without being deterred by his weight. The first and last lines of the third stanza reiterate his desire to fly high with the commentator's "He had the habit of flying very high" having the unemotional balance of a third-person narrator while the father's "He had the habit of flying very high" has an emotional relationship and sorrow associated with it. "Flying high" becomes a metaphor for man's ambitions, his attempts to reach peaks and the existential angst which often results from it. The contrast between the ambitious young bird who could have been burnt by the rays of the sun but is protected by his brother Sampati and the aged Jatayu who finds it difficult to fly can be compared to the protagonist of *The Old Man and the Sea* who wages a futile battle against the elements at sea. Jatayu is in a vertical direction as he attempts to fly high but remains linked to the forest and the horizons as the boundary in a horizontal dimension. In bi-polar indications, the poet excels as in 'small eyes' both the limited vision and the concentrated vision are indicated. With words like "forbidden", "limits", etc. restricting the movement of this aged bird, the poet suggests man's life today which is claustrophobic with "dos and don'ts". His final danger occurs when he crosses the boundaries of the forest, like the Biblical "eating of the forbidden fruit", the original sin. Man's neglect of rules leads to the condition of lawlessness. In describing the bird as "hungry", the poet is obviously referring to much more than physical hunger: indicating the vacuum in which man lives.

The poet uses the medium of myth to portray the condition of modern man. The loneliness of Jatayu in spite of the various animals and birds in the forest is symptomatic of the condition of modern man. The vacuum of contemporary society is hinted at.

Beginning with faith in the existence of good and bad as represented by Ayodhya and Lanka, the poem ends with a total loss of faith as there is neither Ayodhya nor Lanka, neither good nor bad, but thinking makes it so!

Works Cited

Hopkins, E. Washburn. *Epic Mythology Varanasi*: Indological Book House,1968.

Joshi, Umashankar. *Pratibha ane Pratibhav*. Ahmedabad: Gangotri Trust Prakashan, 1981.

Shukla, Jaydev. *Khandakavya.* Ahmedabad: Chandramauli Prakashan, 1986.

Upadhyaya, Darshan. *Sitanshu Yashashchandra*: Kavyasarjan Vishesh Ahmedabad: Divine Publication, 2010.

14

Naturally Supernatural—The Role of Animals and Nature Spirits in the Myth and Folklore of The Lepchas

Catherina Moss

> ...We the Beloved Children of Mother Nature and God,
> When the bamboos originated in this world,
> When the first bamboo shoots originated in this world,
> When the broom grasses originated in this world,
> The Lepchas, likewise, originated in this world,
> Better you understand,
> The Lepchas, bamboos and broom grasses are alike!
>
> (Lepcha, 21)

Folklore offers a wide exploration of the supernatural in various forms, often dealing with fantastical subjects yet forming an integral part of the culture of almost every community or tribe. In the world of folklore, nature leaves an indelible mark on the world of man which is inextricably linked not only with the world of nature but that of the Gods, the spirit world and the greater universe.

My paper is a case study of folklore of the Lepcha community in India with special emphasis on the relation of the community to the land, its creatures and the supernatural realm. In addition, it also incorporates the tenets of ecocriticism within a broad structural framework to examine the role of animal and nature spirits in Lepcha myth and folklore. It also offers a comparative angle with folklore from various other tribes and communities.

Research on folktales, myth and orality are indebted to Vladimir Propp's seminal work *Morphology of the Folktale* where he proposes that all wondertales can be reduced to one formula based on the action and not the characters which are interchangeable. In fact, even Levi Strauss who vehemently opposed his ideas along with many others like Aarne and Max Muller, says, "Whatever our ignorance of the language and culture of the people where it originated, a myth is still felt as a myth by any reader anywhere in the world" (*Theory and History*, 33).

This implies a uniting factor among various races and tribes as most folktales do not have a specific author. Rather than focus on differences, our collective imagination showcases the points of similarity which make us human. Keeping in mind Max Muller's concept of slow transmission of culture in this context, it seems to account for variations in the same tale among various races and communities. For instance, in the Lepcha folktale "The Stairway to Heaven", the once united tribes such as Lepchas, Bhutias and Limboos constructed a stairway to heaven which was destroyed by the artisans at the foot of the structure due to a miscommunication which is reminiscent of the biblical story of "The Tower of Babel". Other examples of stories from other communities with various versions are those of night calls of one's name and were-tigers which find parallels in were-wolf folklore in the West.

Although Alan Dundes acknowledges Propp's work which helped to "open up an understanding of any number of cultural and aesthetic forms" (Ahmitt, 21), in an age of increasing cultural diversity, Levi Strauss believes that the folktale cannot be reduced to a mere formula as folktales of every race "are based on a morphological system of their own" (*Theory and History*, 79). This emphasizes the uniqueness of each race and tribe and allows for the hybridization or reinterpretation of tales. Although Stocks finds it strange to believe that "Lepchas hardly have any original material of their own" (Beauvior, 341) given the insularity of the tribe, it once again points towards the polygenesis (*Theory and History*, 28) of the Lepcha folktales which though influenced by the culture of India and Tibet, are unique nonetheless.

The Lepchas occupy various regions such as Sikkim, Kurseong, Silguri, Kalimpong, Darjeeling, Eastern Nepal and Southwest Bhutan. They are primarily clan based and given the various influences by outsiders and the different regions occupied by them, there is no strict uniformity in their folktales some of which may differ from clan to clan. They call themselves Rong which translates as "Mother's loved ones, children of the snowy peaks, children of God." The Lepcha creation myth has some similarities with the biblical stories of Adam and Eve who disobeyed the Creator and were banished from paradise. It is as follows:

> Itboo-Moo, the Mother creator created the mountains along with lakes and rivers as their complements. She also made the first man and woman, Fudongthing and Nazong Nyu, who were forbidden to live together. Their disobedience led to the birth of several monster/demon children (whom they abandoned) and their banishment from the sacred realm. Later Itboo-Moo came to bless her children as she was pleased with them. However, they hid their two eldest. The children subsequently disappeared and were transformed into guardian spirits by the Mother creator.

Unlike the biblical creation myth, however, the Lepchas attribute creation to a female creator who is devotedly worshipped and given offerings in much the same manner as female deities Vaishno Mata and Pingala—Mata about whom there are numerous karakas in Dogri folk literature.

Tushar. K. Niyogi's comment in *Folktales and Myths of Riang and Tripuri Community* can be extended to the Lepcha community as well where "the ecological system dominates over both the sacred and the profane, terrestrial and transcendental activities of the community..." (*Folktales and Myths*, 21). This is illustrated in the following Lepcha folktales about the origin of agriculture, music and dance.

Accordng to Gorer, “the people of Mayel consist of seven brothers each with their own name and each patron of some sort of grain. These seven brothers are the ancestors and guardians of the Lepchas. They were created by Itboo-Moo who placed rice, millet and maize in their charge when she made these crops.... In the country of Mayel, crops grow a hundred times as big as in the world of man. These crops are always ripe for harvesting. The migratory birds are called Mayel-fo, birds of Mayel, and they are sent out by the people of Mayel to the Lepchas to indicate the seasons and the times when the various agricultural acts should be performed” (*The Lepchas*, 236).

The Lepchas, who have a rich heritage of dance and music also believe that Narok Rum, the God of music decended from Rum Lyang to join the Lepchas in celebration after they defeated the demon, Lasso Mung Puno. He was so impressed by them that he gave them his crown of music which was decorated with beautiful feathers and blessed them with the power to excel in music and dance much of which is based on the sounds and movements of nature and animals. It also includes references to folklore, and reflects the Lepchas’ pride in their land and culture.

According to the Lepchas, the land is a record of the life of the tribe, not owned but divinely given. It shapes their world view. Geoffrey Gorer says, “...for the Lepcha not a single feature is the same.... Every piece of land is meaningful for them.... The Lepchas do not see the landscape; they see the records of their lives, and of the lives of their ancestors, and of the lives to come of their children” (*The Lepchas*, 81).

Propp also states that the wondertale “derives from reality” and is a reflection of “primitive thought” (*Theory and History*, 24). This is often animistic and anthropomorphic in nature. In this sense, I believe that it seeks to unite a race’s roots with its reality; the past with the present and that the tales which survive are those which balance reality and creativity. For instance, the story of Thekung Thek and Khye Bumsa explains events leading to the coronation of the first Chogul and the supposed blood pact signed between the

Lepchas and the Bhutias which was used by Bhutan to justify its usurpation of Lepcha lands.

Folklore often attempts to make sense of events in reality which are often inexplicable and offer themselves for reinterpretation in creative ways which reflect the needs and attitude of society towards various issues such as the need to preserve the environment and cultural identity as well as develop respect for nature and various life forms. Bansari Mitra in *The Renovation of Folktales by Five Modern Bengali Writers* says that Tagore's: *Raj Kahani*..."[teaches humans that they] should be kind to animals. The planet belongs to all. [And that if] a child is so naughty, that he tortures animals needlessly, he shall be punished accordingly. He would be reduced to their size so that he would be even more helpless and terrified...." (*The Renovation of Folktales*, 58). Lepchas, who also respect nature and the supernatural, according to Gorer, [avoid the abodes of malevolent supernaturals] "because the devil might be annoyed at the intrusion on his privacy and would show his resentment by inflicting illness on the intruders. Similarly, the supernatural would resent any injury done to his house such as cutting down his tree or chipping off parts of his stone, and would punish the rash man by paining him in that portion of his body which corresponded to that portion of the house which had been destroyed..." (*The Lepchas*, 77). Similarly, in *The Weretiger and Stories of the Supernatural* edited by Bose, Shaiontoni, Arundhuti Dasgupta, Bunny Gupta and Nilanjana Gupta, the Santhals "hold sacred the spirits of trees and earth, of air and water" (*The Weretiger*, 65). (Bongas) as are the Naga gods who reside in various water bodies and the sacred trees like Tulasi and Peepal which are revered by many Dogra Brahmin families.

It is also seen that elements of nature which are often the abode of tree, mountain and water spirits are a conduit to the realm of the uncanny which according to Todorov as quoted in Lucie Armitt's *Theorising the Fantastic* is "associated with supernatural devices" and "may readily be accounted for by the laws of reason, but...are, in one way or another, incredible, extraordinary, shocking, singular, disturbing or unexpected" (*Theorising the Fantastic*, 30).

Again Gorer states, "Nearly every family line or ptso originated from the union of a particular lake and a particular mountain.... To these maternal lakes...offerings must be made by all the descendants, or the inhabiting supernatural will withdraw her favour..." (*The Lepchas*, 78-79).

There is a need to placate angry demons and deities and invoke their protection against natural calamites such as landslides and earthquakes. Thus, the Lepchas whose livelihood depends entirely on the mercies and whims of Mother Nature, offer sacrifices to the Gods of hunting, agriculture and various other deities. They also worship mountains such as Mt. Kanchenjanga, lakes and various other natural elements which are witnesses to all important events of Lepcha life such as naming ceremonies, marriages and funerals. Festivals such as Chu Rum Faat and Lyang Rum Faat are conducted to worship the mountains and the land respectively.

Similarly, tribes in the Sundarbans worship Bon Bibi who protects them from tigers and storms while in the Himalayas as quoted from *The Weretiger and Stories of the Supernatural*, "it is believed that demons lurk in the forests.... It is necessary...to propitiate them and call upon the Buddha for protection..." (Bose, 30).

In many cases, myths and folktales are also used to explain the topographical features of the land. A brave captain in *The Dragon of Rabdentse* slays an evil dragon by cutting it in half. The front piece of the dragon disappeared while the latter half transformed into a rock statue in the water which can still be seen today. Another story about the race between the rivers Teesta and Rangeet with the help of animal guides explains the reason why the two rivers follow different paths and then unite in North Bengal.

Lepchas exhibit an essentially animistic view towards animals. Bears, tigers, lions, monkeys, storks, frogs, geese, dogs, birds, etc. feature frequently Lepcha folktales. As quoted in Greg Garrard's *Ecocritcism*, Steve Baker in his work *Picturing the Beast* (1993) states, "...culture shapes our reading of animals just as much as animals shape our reading of culture..." while John Berger in his essay "Why Look at Animals?" (1980) says, "When we look at animals they return our gaze, and in that moment we are aware of both likeness and difference" (*Ecocriticism*, 139-41).

Gorer states, "According to Lamaist beliefs everything in the world...possesses a soul; for the soul is the animating principle of all life, without whose intermediary nothing could move or grow.... The souls of animals (with the exception of leeches and mosquitoes which are believed to be emanations of a devil and therefore soul-less) are far more important; it is a major sin to destroy an animal for it is possible that its soul may be that of an ex-human being; and pious people will erect prayer-flags for animals killed through accident or in the course of modern life..." (*The Lepchas*, 191). Some Lepchas also believe that a person has an 'apil' or essence of life. Many give odd or vulgar names to their children until they are older in order to protect their 'apil' from demons.

Virginia Anderson is quoted in *Postcolonial Ecocriticism: Literature, Animals and Environment* by Graham Huggen, and Helen Tiffin, "Aware of the power of animal spirits, native hunters treated their prey with respect and performed rituals defined by reciprocity. Although not quite a relationship of equals, the connection between (Red) Indians and prey was not essentially hierarchical" (*Postcolonial Ecocriticism*, 10). The same ideas apply in the case of the Lepchas who maintain the balance of the ecosystem by not taking more than what is required from the land and releasing animals like fish from traps if they are too young or in excess.

As in "...Nagaland [as quoted in *The Weretiger and Stories of the Supernatural*]" many believe that Jungle spirits exist to protect animals from hunters..." (Bose, 39). Lepchas, according to Gorer, also believe that "on the road to Mayel are three guardian spirits called Sok-po, who are brothers; the eldest is called Mayel Yook rum/Pong rum when hunters sacrifice to him; his younger brothers Mik-tik and Tom-tik...are the special guardians of the ibex and musk deer which come from Mayel, which is the reason why these animals are so difficult to kill" (*The Lepchas*, 236).

As in the folklore of many other communities, animals in Lepcha folklore are often invested with speech and supernatural powers in the roles of helper, teacher and trickster. For instance in the story which tells of the origin of chi, the original yeast was stolen by a trickster cockroach from Anyu Matli Mu, the God of wine, who put the curse of quarrelsomeness on it. The Buth when ingested by the black cobra, bee and some birds caused them to develop venom, poisonous stings and turn carnivorous. The Kugreafo bird taught the Lepchas to trap the demon Lasso Mung Puno and was therefore adorned with white, crown-like feathers on its head while animal guides, Tutfo (mountain bird), and Paribu (snake) directed the rivers Rangeet and Teesta in their respective paths towards their meeting place.

Lepcha folktales also reveal the keen observation of natural phenomenon by a community whose culture is greatly influenced by nature and the supernatural. A tiger, bee and toad fight with the guards of a God in order to make him send rain to the parched earth. This explains why the croak of a frog signals the onset of rain. In another story, a foreign princess who married a Lepcha king asks the river Teesta to carry a message to her mother to send her a sign indicating the right time to plant the crops. Her mother sends a bird and today the Lepchas begin sowing cucumbers when they glimpse the arrival of this migratory bird.

In some stories, shape-shifting into another species is also observed. For instance, while being pursued by a Bothing or priest, the demon Lasso Mung Puno transforms into twelve different animals which form a part of the twelve year cycle in the Lepcha calendar which is reminiscent of the Chinese calendar.

According to Bansari Mitra, "The closeness of humans to wild beasts must have led to these legends springing up about them" (*The Renovation*, 13). It may indicate the unspoken but ever prevalent human desire to identify oneself with and imbibe the raw, physical strength, mysterious and often superhuman like sensory and extra-sensory abilities of animals.

The Lepcha interaction with nature is intimate and intense. Their folktales reflect a close synchronization with changes in natural cycles and are a representation of their relationship to the land and their culture as well as their respect for the spirit world. It is thus apt to conclude with the words of Wendell Berry as quoted in Greg Garrard's *Ecocriticism*, "A human community, too must collect leaves and stories, and turn them to account. It must build soil, and build that memory of itself...that will be its culture. These two kinds of accumulation, of local soil and local culture, are intimately related (115). After all, in the case of the Lepchas it's not just natural, its super-natural.

Works Cited

Armitt, Lucie. "Tzvetan Todorov Walks the Tightrope" in *Theorising the Fantastic*. London: Arnold, 1996.

Bose, Shaiontoni. Arundhuti Dasgupta, Bunny Gupta and Nilanjana Gupta, *The Weretiger and Stories of the Supernatural*. New Delhi: Penguin Books, 2002.

Garrard, Greg. *Ecocriticism*. London and New York: Routledge. 2007.

Gorer, Geoffrey. *The Lepchas of Sikkim*. New Delhi: Gyan Publishing House, 1996.

Huggen, Graham and Helen Tiffin, *Postcolonial Ecocriticism: Literature, Animals and Environment* .New York: Routledge, 2010.

Lepcha, Lyangsong Tamsung. *The Indigenous Lepchas and their Songs*. Kalimpong: The Indigenous Lepcha Tribal Association Headquarters. 2010.

Mitra, Bansari. "The Function of Some Minor Characters in *Thakurmar Jhuli*". *The Renovation of Folktales by Five Modern Bengali Writers*. Kolkata: Archaeological Survey of India, 2002.

Niyogi, Tushar K. *Folktales and Myths of Riang and Tripuri Communities*. Kolkata: Archaeological Survey of India, 1983.

Propp, Vladimir. *Theory and History of Folklore*. Minneapolis: University of Minnesota Press, 1984.

Stocks, C. de Beauvoir. "Folktales and Customs of the Lepchas of Sikkim," *Journal and Proceedings of the Asiatic Society of Bengal* (New Series) XXI, No. 4 (1925).

http://aachulay.blogspot.in/

http://aachulay.blogspot.in/

http://www.lepcha.info/

15

Deification and Divestment: Perspectives on Female Divinization in Mrinal Pande's Works

Shashi Khurana

This paper seeks to examine the cult of female divinization in its prevalent and popular form practised by men and women alike and how it has been perceived through the narratives in Mrinal Pande's short story "Girls" and the novella *Devi: Tales of the Goddess in Our Time*. The texts will be read in the light of literature of quest which seeks to explore, write and redefine ways in which women are appropriated. Women and men inherit patriarchal hierarchies and identities unquestioningly, socialised into various theological literatures which by and large support the status quo. However, there are, from time to time voices of dissent which create space for alternative identities, review old ways of thinking and visualise if not wholly experience new patterns of social relations and spiritual insights.

The paper will be structured in three parts. The first part will deal with theoretical aspects of literature of quest and its importance in the writings of women and what it brings forth for readers of women's writings since women's writing provides a critical place for creating and subverting myths. The second part will critically analyse the story and the novella as gynocritic texts which look askance at mainstream regional traditions ensconced in mythologies which remain alive through oral renderings in the form of *kathas* and *kirtans*, ceremonious rituals, creating self-defining belief systems. Such forms of religious-cultural practices have distinct class/caste and gender dimensions which are subjected to critique also along class/caste and gender sensitive positions. The third part of the paper will assess the significance of this literature from a theoretical perspective and some critical responses to the work.

The sources used for the paper are both primary and secondary. Oral responses from some readers who have engaged with at least one text collectively will also be cited, bringing into the paper the way pedagogy generates criticism in the space of a classroom.

Literature of Quest and Women's Experience

Feminist critical writing has legitimised women's experience as a valid hermeneutical key giving rise to and shaping the body of what may simply be described as Literature of Quest. This literature seeks answers and discovers inalienable identities of women protagonists, narrators sometimes as a personal triumph, sometimes as a spiritual triumph but seldom as a social triumph, given the patriarchal structures of existence:

> It is my contention that there are significant differences between masculine and feminine experience and that the feminine experience reveals in more emphatic fashion certain aspects of the human situation which are present but less obvious in the experience of men. Contemporary theological doctrines of love have, I believe, been constructed primarily upon the basis of masculine experience and thus view the human condition from a male standpoint. Consequently these doctrines do not provide an adequate interpretation of the situation of women.
>
> (Saving, 25-42)

Both Carol Christ and J. Plaskow take up Saving's contention that theology is "mutilated" because it fails to incorporate the experiences and insights of women. The incorporation of women's views is essential to save theology from becoming a dangerous and damaging force besides becoming irrelevant. Women's literature, thus, acquired a privileged medium of access to women's experience. Christ puts forward an expanded exploration of four significant moments in the spiritual quest, termed nothingness, awakening, insight and new naming. Nothingness conceptualises women's experience of mainstream cultural invisibility and lack of self-worth. Women's educational and occupational disadvantages are coupled with the unease they feel about their bodies. Thus, "women need a literature that names their pain and allows them to use the emptiness of their lives as an occasion for insight rather than as one more indication of their worthlessness" (Carol Christ, 1979). The strength gained in confronting nothingness leads to an awakening, i.e. responding to the "powers of being" in themselves, in other women and in the material forces of the natural world. The awakening brings about the insight into connectedness with nature, with other women and the sense of the power of being in her own body as she unites with other creative forces to produce life. The sources of power of being may be identified with a devotion to the goddess. The new insight as part of the quest would require a new naming. The process involves resisting "false naming" (Mary Daly) and to shape the world anew. Christ suggests that insight should be employed "to resist dualism through a re-evaluation of the negative poles of the Western binary system." Caution is suggested in advocating the abolition of difference by enforcing "a new monism". What is of importance is to end the definition of existence in hierarchical or oppositional categories.

Women in a Land of Goddess Worship

Women in India are often described as having two sharply contrasting aspects. In a region known for its goddesses with multiple visages, identities and functions, the first visage is that of the serene, primordial mother Great Goddess (*Devi*), Primal Energy (*Shakti*), and Nature (*Prakriti*), a gentle boon-giver who also slays demons. The other is the clouded face of the domestic handmaiden trailing behind men in life expectancy, nutrition, health, education, pay and other rights on the subcontinent. How did this dualistic picture emerge and become acceptable? Ancient and classical texts reveal that the earliest interface between Aryan and local Dravidian-aboriginal cultures created a set of values which spread across the subcontinent. This was the high honour given to female chastity, stipulated by men, as it challenged women's natural intelligence as revealed archaic texts and there were numerous ambiguities as the texts were composed by multiple male authors separated by centuries. Moreover, the genres of hymnal, epic poetry and *shastra* (scripture, religious manual) facilitated several typologies of women as divine, heroic, maternal, saintly, victimised, lustful or manipulative.

Sita Anantha Raman's research shows that divine maternal appears early (ca. 3000 BCE) in pre-Aryan artefacts of the Indus Civilization, and it also appears in the Sanskrit scriptural Vedas (1600-300 BCE). In the early first millennium BCE, society also began to accord high respect to male and female celibate hermits or *sanyasins* as they were called. The views and questions of women sages Gargi and Maitreyi were carefully recorded in the *Brihad Aranyaka Upanishad*. Unlike the *Vedas*, the popular epics *Mahabharata* and *Ramayana* contain socially pertinent messages on the honour given to faithful wives. Thus, while Indians celebrate the *Mahabharata* heroine Savitri for outwitting Death, the annual fast by Indian wives is a reminder that their chastity ensures the husband's longevity. Similarly, the *Ramayana* makes it clear that male strictures on female sexuality were paramount, so that even the innocent Sita was punished for residing as a hostage in Ravana's forests. This schizophrenia about women became more rigid in the classical era (250 BCE-500 CE) when India witnessed waves of immigrants and conquerors. The resultant "mix" of different ethnic groups and intergroup relations led to greater controls over female sexuality. New texts by "elite" men reined in mortal women's sexuality but exalted the feminine divine as Devi. As local cults to divine female guardians were subsumed into the traditions of *Devi* worship, ordinary women were kept in their domestic place by authors of *Manusmriti*, which was cited as sacrosanct law code by most upper caste Hindus.

The long experience of gender inequality on the subcontinent makes it an important social issue. Despite the persistence of local pockets of aboriginal and Dravidian matrilineal societies, and enclaves of Buddhist, Jaina and Hindu nuns, the many layers of mainstream patriarchal society were cemented by adopting Sanskritic values. These occurred centuries before Islam and European Christianity infused their own patriarchal features into Indian society. However, women did rebel quietly through non-conformism and more sharply through religious and protest literature.

Mrinal Pande's point of view underlying the short-story "Girls" does not mince words in its critique of religious ceremonies which highlight the ambivalent social attitude to women. The girl child narrator of the story questions the most obvious contradictions which are internalised and perpetuated through generations. The story opens in an atmosphere of stifling activity in a household which is full of anxiety over the gender of the unborn child. "Ma" who is the focus of all eyes is portrayed as completely dispossessed of any identity; her body and mind are preoccupied with becoming the urgent bearer of male progeny, which becomes the centre around which the story revolves. The prescribed movements in a woman's life from natal home to marital, back to natal home and the return to marital home capture assumptions and expectations underlying patrilocal marriages. The strong belief in superstition reflects the diffidence and uncertainty which characterise the life of the disempowered woman. The narrator sums up such a woman, "To Ma, everything in life is problem. As far as she is concerned, whether we are at home or at school, ill or just playing around, we are a problem." The portrait is of a woman experiencing nothingness. She seems to be caught in a web not of her own weaving, groping for a niche made possible by giving birth to a son: "I hope it's a boy this time. It will relieve me of the nuisance of going through another pregnancy" ("Girls", 22). The child narrator overhears this and re-imagines the stereotypical exchange between the women of her household over the issue of the irrational obsession with sons. The imagined is translated into reality on arrival at Naani's house, where maama's son is the centre of attention and adoration. The story continues to build the fixation for sons through image and action while also building the reaction to it. "Even though I pinched Maama's son, he kept following me around like an idiot. He was very fair, chubby and supposed to be cute. He was also tall for his age, and though only five years old could easilypass for seven" (23). The narrator's attitude to the boy is in sharp contrast to that shown by all the adult characters in the story. The anger displayed towards the narrator over her "naughtiness" reflects a suppressed resentment over her being born an unwanted girl, as the third daughter in Ma's household. The narrator learns more and more about women's subservience to sons from snippets of conversation among them. The old lady from the neighbourhood: "This time Lali will definitely have a boy. Just look at her complexion—when she was expecting the girls it was pink, but now it has a tinge of yellow. I am sure it will be a boy this time" (23). In sharp contrast is the imagined world of the narrator. The story juxtaposes the ideologically subservient world of adult women with the horror stories told by the narrator to her smaller cousins who "followed me all over the house like mice following the Pied Piper" (26). The contrasts are consciously created. They are the contrasts between adults and children, between two generations, between dependency and freedom of thought, between acceptance and critique. The contrasts contain an anticipation of the climactic moment in the story. The poignant moments are direct comments on the psychological impact of overt gender bias in real life. "For a long time I sit outside the house watching the birds flying and wishing that I had been born a bird. 'Do mother birds too think their girl birds are inferior?' Then I hear a voice calling, 'Where has she gone?' and I know someone is searching for me. I wish, I wish that somewhere, anywhere, I could find that magic betel nut which would make me invisible as soon as I put it in my mouth. What wonderful fun that would be!" (27). The social world is tilted heavily against the third girl child!

The final conflict between convention and modernity, the old and the young, the irrational and the rational and the need to confront the issue of son preference in real life along with deifying girls through gendered rituals is also the story's resolution and awakening of the reader. The story generates new insight into the hypocrisy of social attitudes towards girls. The new naming addresses the rejection of customs which are cushioned in layers of violence which threatens the lives of women and girls. "I start moving back towards the wall and screaming, 'I don't want all this halwa-puri, tikka or money. I don't want to be a goddess.' I scream so loudly that the pigeons pecking at the scattered grain in the courtyard take off in a flurry, as if a bullet had been fired somewhere put" (28-29).

Mrinal Pande's novella weaves the *Shakti* mythology through the contemporary into the home and hearth sustained and perpetuated by women. What evolves is a cocoon-like genre which resonates with humour, critique and a quiet understanding of the ways of women. The novella is clearly intended to belong to literature of women and if men don't take much note, the novella stands confidently and breezily on its own, much like any of the *Devis* who are invoked, evaded and sung about. Like the songs, the narrative reaches out by addressing an ever-ready listener.

> Sunahu tat yeh akath kahani
> Samujhat banat, na jai bakhani.
> 'Listen, my dear,
> To these indescribable tales'
> Hard to follow, and still harder to narrate. (Preface)

The Goddess tales are hardly ever the same, they are re-told with some variation or the other and they are tales of a wide gamut of emotions, aspirations, dissatisfaction, desire, struggle and revenge.

> Sunahu tat yeh akath kahani....
> Indescribable tales that travel in small groups.

The focus of the narrative shifts to another corpus of tales. "Tales of women behind closed doors, women weeping quietly, women walking down endless roads and forests, women laughing out loud. Women whom the Goddess' spirit has entered. To recount their tales is to move into mysterious grey cremation grounds littered with the half-burnt bones of generations. It means stepping into the timeless kingdom of Mahakali and the Nine *Durgas*, there to tick like mad clocks, striking minutes and hours off time" (*Devi Tales*, xx).

Tales of Goddesses are the tales of women who have invented and created alter egos both in form and spirit. Their names recall the regions where they sprung up and their actions are neither inimitable nor divine, but decisive and regenerative. The writer uses a child's perspective to respond to the predominant and integral presence of goddesses in the daily lives of women. Though the Goddesses are surrounded by a sense of well-being and supremacy, there is a distinct absence of religiosity. On one level, the work reads like a compilation of kathas, re-told with an appeal to the wondering mind of a child. "Shailputri, she who is the defiant daughter of the mountain, Brahmacharini, the loner, who has chosen to be a celibate, Chandraghanta, she who wears the moon round her neck, Kooshmanda, she who is thc warmth of the ova within the womb, Skandmata, the mother of skanda, the warrior, Katyayani, who has slain fearsome demons like Katyayan, Kalratri, who is the dark destructive Goddess of the final night of Navratri, Mahagauri, the fairest of them all, and ultimately, Siddhidatri, the giver of the ultimate boon.

> When being consumed by fires; when in the midst of a battle among enemies, facing a tough, hard and lonely journey, scared and confused, we turn to Thee, to remove the impediments and set us free to move.... (*Durga-Saptashati*)

On another level, the novella uses the tales to tell other tales in a way that mythology is made as real as contemporaneity and the contemporary is mired in a crassness which glorifies mythology. "All we know is that the Goddess-tales lean towards human tales. They soak each other up" (*Devi Tales,* xix).

The telling of Goddess tales acquires the importance of an agenda designed to recapture the images and niches of a pantheon of female *Shakti.* The pantheon which seems to have become severed from its moorings in the snow-clad abode and subjected to ritualised periodicity.

> Strange tales are being used like tools to hammer and carve the Goddesses into mothers of men. Grimly, steadily, almost ritually, these tales are replacing the real legends. Loudspeakers play raucous modern songs sung by the sons of Mata a benign mother of men, enthroned in the house, steady as a rock. Day and night, television and films writing away the life from sublime stories to fashion serials around this Mother Goddess, as testaments to the transferring powers of men and money. Here Goddesses are presented through word and image as overdressed, bejewelled and fawning mothers, givers of wealth and gentle imposers of discipline. Those unpredictable outbursts of temper, that fury off wild hair, those rolling eyes, the lolling tongue and other manifestations of an inescapably complex presence, are all being erased from Goddess-lore. One hears songs that ask the Mata to come to Bharat and slay the infidels, to present worshippers with houses with marble floors, to help the daughters-in-law bear only sons, to help businesses prosper and daughters get married early to suitable boys. We the tellers of tales are sardonic witnesses to this sly coming together, in the name of the Mother, of the land-grabbing urban householder, the corrupt rural farmer, the oily politician and his supporters in the gutter press. They wait to find a gap in the tales, then rush in to substitute the fake for the authentic.
>
> (*Devi Tales*, xxii)

The Preface to the novella projects the degeneration of a distinct mytho-fictional genre sustained by women through oral narratives. The mission for the writer is to recoup what has been appropriated by growing patriarchies. To retrieve what is defiled and to reveal the defiling nature of contemporary reality, Mrinal Pande structures the text around alternating sub-texts of journalistic commentary, feminist critique and a refreshingly relevant devi story which seems to scroll out, "Our times. December 19, 1994: A somewhat cold day in the capital of India. There is smoke from woodfires, smoke from hundreds of chimneys that belong to illegal factories in and around the city. It's a Monday, and the world seems to be in a state of turmoil. In New Delhi, the Congress Party is crumbling; in the Chechen Republic, Russian planes and tanks are raining death and destruction on the people of Grozny. In Karachi, militant Sunnis are gunning for Shias, and in Europe, Serbs and Bosnian Muslims have set out to destroy each other to the last speck of life" (*Devi Tales*, 2).

One piece of casual, journalistic reporting is divided from another and together the reports create an ideological canvas on which the goddesses keep appearing in their human, sub-human and superhuman forms slugging at the old and new ironies of survival, and cycles of life to which women are central. The autobiographical and biographical reminiscences bring into the novella the female world of three generations. "Mother told us how one of her naughty cousins had urinated on one of the memorials, upon being dared to do so by other children.... Another aunt capped this with the story about the *Lati Yogini* (the mute one). She was the one who had chopped off her tongue as a sacrifice to Kali. 'Not a thread of clothing did she have on her, not a thread, remember? And how she pulled on the hashish in her clay pipe and made the flame leap up three spans high, like a man. She slept near the embers from dying pyres in the Someshwar cremation grounds, totally unafraid of the terrible ghosts and demons that lurked there. In fact, some said they heard her converse and laugh with unseen companions. Only men would dare go see her, only men!' the aunt said and the women rolled their eyes like mad cows" (*Devi Tales*, 27).

Insanity, renunciation, suicide and slaughter underscored with intuitive and logical understanding were inevitable experiences of women in the hills and while the theatre of the natural and the supernatural kept growing out of each other, the plains became pitted with "black holes" throwing up innumerable tales like the tale of Vijaya.

> The same Vijaya was gone. She had killed herself suddenly, for no apparent reason.... Presumably she had been hinting at her dark anger with words and gestures we couldn't quite put a meaning to. The exact pathology of her fury was something that would always elude our sensible worlds, although our cookies too were frequently crumbling, and our pots of milk boiling and boiling over till nothing was left, except a charred skin that crumbled on touch. Black is a terribly persistent colour. It dots the landscape even after the body is gone (*Devi Tales*, 25).

The case of Vijaya's suicide is a symptom of domestic rot and alienation for women whose status within patriarchal marriages remains unchanged or perhaps they have not learnt to propitiate Saraswati, as suggested by the Tales.

> "No one shall die for me, as I shall die for none."
>
> Understandably, such a Goddess could be venerated by the simple-minded and earthy householders, but not loved and fussed over by them like her regal sister Laxmi, or even feared and held in awe like Shakti. Saraswati remains the unblemished ascetic goddess, to whom no temples are built and who offers nothing except knowledge, no institution, no protection, no riches.... There was no statue of Saraswati in our family puja room, but a picture wherein she sat upon a swan.... No special fasts or rituals were observed for her, nor did she pop up in Grandmother's tales with the frequency of her sisters Laxmi and Parvati. (*Devi Tales*, 60-61)

The tale of Laxmi mirrors the gradual divestment of the essence of the goddess as Chanchala—the ever mobile one—who stays only with those who can retain her. Reduced to the conventional, subservient wife, she has become the contemporary symbol of unscrupulous materialsm and stark hunger. The story of Revati the Prostitute is the story many a woman who allows "men to do 'it'" so that they can send money home their families of fatherless children and ageing parents. "Revati's mother has told the villagers that her daughter works in Calcutta as a maidservant. The villagers nod knowingly. Most young girls in the village have been 'sent' to Calcutta as maids. They all remit money home regularly. The boys, however, once they've left for the city, are seldom seen again" (*Devi Tales,* 72). Women are the agents for preserving the family 'laxmi' giving birth to sons.

The declining sex ratio, growing son preference, dowry deaths and so-called suicides of women of all ages in the land of goddess worship is the irony captured in the novella. The irony cuts through 'modern-day society' in which men have appropriated goddesses to conform to their perception of a religio-social order. In her novella, Mrinal Pande skilfully and artistically parallels mythology with reality, putting a womanly signature to a new form of writing or a new naming of women's imagination and social reality. How can the past not be visited time and again, consciously or unconsciously? "At the age of seventy-four when Badi Amma lay dying, she too had inexplicably asked for fragrant flowers to be heaped around her: *mogra, sone, juhi, champa, chameli, parijata*. 'They remind me of the smell from the Devi's temple we used to visit in the hills,' she said to one in particular" (*Devi Tales,* 184).

Works Cited

Anantha Raman, *Sita*: *Women in India. A Social and Cultural History*. Vol. 1, ABC-CL IO, LLC. 2009.

Christ, Carol and Plaskow, Judith. *Woman Spirit Rising: A Feminist Reader in Religion*. San Francisco: Harper and Row. 1979.

Pande, Mrinal. *Devi Tales of the Goddess in Our Time*: New Delhi: Penguin. 1996.

Pande, Mrinal. *The inner Courtyard: Stories by Indian Women*, ed. Lakshmi Holmstrom. New Delhi: Rupa and Co. 1990.

References and page nos. in "Girls" have been sourced from *Fluency in English*-1. Delhi: MaCmillan, 2005.

Saving, Valerie. "The Human Situation: A Feminine View" in C. Christ and J. Plaskow (eds.), *Woman Spirit Rising: A Feminist Reading in Religion*. San Francisco: Harper and Row, 1979.

16

Revisionist Myth-Making: Acts and Enactments of Feminist Anti-Authoritarianism and Resistance

K.S. Vaishali

The myths, fears and idols of patriarchies are recast and revised in many ingenious ways by contemporary feminist writers. Reinstating the marginalised in the face of the dominant often entails a complex process of epistemological deconstruction. In the words of Adrienne Rich, "The revisionary task of reminiscence and retrieval involves re-inscription, a process in which old narratives, stories, scripts, mythologies become transvalued, represented in different terms" (Yorke, 1). Mahasweta Devi's poweful, haunting portrayals of the exploitation and oppression of the gendered subaltern in her short-stories have been seen as rich sites of feminist discourse. Positioned at the intersection of vital contemporary questions of politics, gender, class and caste, she is a significant figure in the field of socially committed literature. She employs fascinating revisionist strategies to recast some of the well-known Hindu mythological female figures such as Draupadi and Jashoda to foreground the subalternisation of women from lower class in the Hindu patriarchy. Often this task of "Re-vision" is one of violent, Promethean transgression for the feminist writer because it entails making of new subjectivities for women canonised within the Hindu patriarchal value system as beau ideals of Indian womanhood and creates alternative fields of signification within which women may identify themselves. As manifestoes of the hopes, desires and resistances of marginalised people, the feminist revisionist short-stories of Mahasweta Devi adumbrate the genesis of an authentic female voice and decode the hitherto subliminal, camouflaged messages of female anger, protest and rebellion.

Mythology does not seem like a hospitable terrain for women writers. When we think of women of Greek mythology such as Helen, Clytemnestra, Circe, Pandora, Medea, we find that these characters neatly fit into the reductionistic stereotypes of women as 'angels' or 'monsters'. Therefore, a feminist writer who reclaims and re-examines some of these mythological heroines as instances of devaluation of women within an androcentric mythopoeic imagination decontructs the myth as a cultural signifier. She sensitises the readers to an important dimension of myths as "quintessentially intimate material, the stuff of dream life, forbidden desire, inexplicable motivation—everything in the psyche that to rational consciousness is unreal, crazed or abominable" (Ostricker, 314).

In this context, I would like to begin with examples from the literary works of the Canadian writer Margaret Atwood, a feminist revisionist mythmaker par excellence. Atwood's classic feminist dytopian novel *The Handmaid's Tale*, is an example of a mythopoeic, dystopian vision that depicts a creation myth in a future world of darkness and silence. In a futuristic terrorist biblical patriarchate of Gilead, all women are only reproducers and non-reproducers. They are "ambulatory chalices" who belong to their male commanders to whom they owe their reproductive services. By presenting haunting images of suppression, subjugation and fear, Atwood explores the terror aroused in men by women's sexual autonomy in contemporary United States. In another poem entitled "Helen does Countertop Dancing," Margaret Atwood trenchantly recasts the mythical beauty, Helen of Troy, who metamorphoses into a contemporary young American woman, a striptease dancer in a night club who lays bare the grim sexist reality of female sexual objectification and commodification.

Through the monologue of Helen, Atwood re-envisions the episode in the mythological story where the beautiful queen of Sparta, the wife of king Menelaus has been used by her insensitive husband as a naked trophy. Menelaus decides to show off his wife's voluptuous body to the princes and kings who visit him in Sparta where the Trojan prince Paris Alexandros is also present. At her husband's behest, Helen dances nude before the royal guests and the mordant irony in Atwood's poem is poignantly discernible:

Helen of Troy does Countertop Dancing
The world is full of women
Who's tell me I should be ashamed of myself
if they had the chance. Quit Dancing.
Get some self respect
and a day job.
Right. And minimum wage,
and varicose veins, just standing
in one place for eight hours
behind a glass counter
bundled up to the neck, instead of
naked as a meat sandwich.
Selling gloves, or something
Instead of what do I sell.
You have to have talent
to peddle a thing so nebulous
and without material form.
Exploited, they'd say. Yes, any way
you cut it, but I've a choice
of how, and I'll take the money.

I do give value.
Like Preachers, I sell vision.
like perfume ads, desire
or its fascimile. Like jokes
or war, it's all in the timing
I sell men back their worst suspicions.
that everything's for sale.
and piecemeal. They gaze at me and see
a chain-saw murder just before it happens,

when thigh, ass, inkblot, crevice, tit and nipple
are still connected.
Such hatred leaps in them,
me beery worshippers! That, or a bleary
hopeless love. Seeing rows of heads
and upturned eyes, imploring
but ready to snap at my ankles,
I understand floods and earthquakes and the urge
to step on ants. I keep the beat,
and dance for them because
they can't. The music smells like foxes,
crisp as heated metal
searing the nostrils
or humid as August, hazy and langorous
as a looted city the day after,
when all the rape's been done
already and the killing,
and the suvivors wander around
looking for garbage
to eat and there's only a bleak exhaustion.

Speaking of which, it's the smiling
tires me the most
This and the pretence
the I can't hear them.
And I can't, because I'm after all,
a foreigner to them.
The speech here is all warty gutturals,
obvious as a slab of ham,
but I come from the province of the Gods
where meanings are lilting and oblique.
I don't let on to everyone,
but I lean close and I'll whisper:
My mother was raped by a holy swan
You believe that? you can take me out to dinner.
That's what we tell all the husbands
There sure are a lot of dangerous birds around.
Not that anyone here
but would understand

The rest of them would like to watch me
and feel nothing. Reduce me to components
as in a clock factory or abattoir.
Crush out the mystery.
Wall me up alive
in my own body.
They'd like to see through me
but nothing is more opaque
than absolute transparency.
Look—my feet don't hit the marble!
Like breath or a balloon, I'm rising,
I hover six inches in the air
in my blazing swan egg of light.
You think I'm not a Goddess?
Try me.
This is a torch song.
Torch me and you'll burn.

Atwood's Helen bestows a contemporary dimension to the sordid exploitative realities of prostitution, rape and reification of the female body. The "Circe/Mud Poems" from Atwood's poetry collection *You are Happy* (1974) is another example where we see a radical reworking of Greek myths from a feminist angle. Here Atwood rewrites the myth of Circe in Homer's *Odyssey*. In Homer's epic, Circe is depicted as a beautiful enchantress, luring men by her mellifluous voice and later transforming them into pigs. But Atwood's Circe is also a contemporary woman addressing contemporary man. Atwood's Circe tells Odysseus the story of the mud woman which she had heard from another traveller passing through her island. The traveller and his friend had carved a female torso out of mud and had named her the "mud woman". The woman herself began at the neck and ended at the knees and elbows. They stuck to the essential parts. Every sunny day, they would row across to the island where she was and make love to her. The traveller narrating his story to Circe, tells her that his love for the 'mud woman' was perfect, he could say anything to her and into her he spilled his entire life. But she had been swept away in a sudden flood. He had confessed that no woman since then had equalled her. To her horror, Circe realises that Odysseus too would want her to be a 'mud woman'. Atwood's Circe tells Odysseus that she cannot be a passive receptacle of his desires like a 'mud woman'. Circe's narration of the story of the 'mud woman' is a travesty of the creation myth in the Bible. In the words of Simone de Beauvoir, "Eve was not fashioned at the same time as man, she was not fabricated from a different substance, nor of the same clay as was used to model Adam: she was taken from the flank of the first male. Not even her birth was independent. She was destined by Him for man: it was to rescue Adam from loneliness that He gave her to him, in her mate was her origin and purpose. She was his complement in the order of the inessential. Thus she appeared in the guise of the previleged prey" (*The Second Sex*, 173). Mythic revisionism here becomes an act of rewriting female subjectivity.

Likewise, Mahasweta Devi also bestows a contemporary dimension to the story of another mythological heroine Draupadi, subverts and rewrites the episode in the epic *Mahabharata* where Draupadi is saved from the humiliation of disrobement by the divine intervention of Lord Krishna. In Devi's story, Dopdi Mehjen, a Santal woman who is gang-raped by the police men, emerges as a powerful agent after rape by refusing to put on clothes and hide her nakedness in defiance. Nowhere does Mahasweta Devi romanticise Draupadi. There is relentless subversive irony in Devi's portrayal. In her introduction to the English translation of Devi's story, Spivak points out Draupadi's legitimised pluralisation as a wife of five husbands. Further Spivak alludes to the strange civil status of Draupadi in a polyandrous marriage. Therefore, circumscribed within the inexorable logic of scriptural texts, a woman like Draupadi who has many husbands could be designated as a prostitute and consequently there is nothing improper in bringing her clothes or unclothed into the assembly. But Draupadi is saved by the divine intervention of Lord Krishna. In Devi's story, Dopdi is a Santal tribal woman, wanted by the police for the vital information that she can provide about the hide outs of the naxal rebels who are carrying out their guerilla operations in the Jharkhani forests. The police capture her and she is gang raped by them. But after this Draupadi insists on remaining naked. To quote Gayathri Spivak again, "It would be a mistake to read the modern story as a refutation of the ancient. Dopdi is Draupadi. She is also what Draupadi—written into the patriarchal and authoritative sacred text as proof of male power—could not be. Dopdi is at once a palimpsest and a contradiction.... It is when she crosses the sexual differential into the field of what could only happen to a woman that she emerges as the most powerful 'subject', who, still using the language of sexual honour, can derisively call herself 'the object of your search', whom the author can describe as a terrifying superobject—'an unarmed target'" (*Breast Stories,* 10-11).

Draupadi says to Senanayak "You asked them to make me up, don't you want to see how they made me?" Draupadi's black body comes even closer. Draupadi shakes with an indomitable laughter that Senanayak simply cannot understand. Her ravaged lips bleed as she begins laughing. Draupadi wipes the blood on her palm and says in a voice that is terrifying, sky splitting and sharp as her ululation, 'What's the use of clothes? You can strip me, but how can you clothe me again? Are you a man?....' 'There isn't a man here that I should be ashamed. I will not let you put my cloth on me. What more can you do? come on, kounter me'. Draupadi pushes Senanayak with her two mangled breasts, and for the first time Senanayak is afraid to stand before an unarmed target, terribly afraid" (*Breast Stories,* 10-11).

In Mahasweta Devi's reworking of the myth of the divine mother Jashoda in her short-story "Breast-Giver", the subversive vein of irony is unmistakable. "Jashoda is fully an Indian woman, whose unreasonable, unreasoning and unintelligent devotion to her husband and love for her children, whose unnatural renunciation and forgiveness, have been kept alive in the popular consciousness by all Indian women from Sati-Savitri-Sita through Nirupa Roy and Chand Osmani" (*Breast Stories,* 10-11). The story "Sthanadayini" is about a poor woman Jashoda, the wife of Kangalicharan who becomes a wet nurse in order to maintain her karge family when her husband Kangali is crippled. A mother of 20 children and suckling scores of sons born in her master Haldar's household, Jashoda is a milk mother for so many children. But she is abandoned by all her sons and the sons of the Haldar household who were nursed by her when she develops breast cancer. Finally, a delirious Jashoda, in the advanced stages of breast cancer is shifted to the hospital and dies alone. Lying in a state of excruciating pain, Jashoda says spiritlessly, "If you suckle you're a mother, all lies! Nepal and Gopal don't look at me, and the Master's boys don't spare a peek to ask how I'm doing. The sores on her breast kept mocking her with a hundred mouths, a hundred eyes" (*Breast Stories*, 10-11).

Further, the story concludes: "Jashoda was God manifest, others do and did whatever she thought. Jashoda's death was also the death of God. When a mortal plays God here below, she is forsaken by all and she must always die alone" (*Breast Stories*, 10-11).

Mahasweta Devi's subversive representations of the subaltern are radical departures from the female identity fashioned and inscribed by patriarchy and male authority. In her oppositional reading of the original classical myth or what has been termed by Walter Benjamin as "reading against the grain", the feminist writer will not passively acknowledge the myth nor does she simply retell the myth. Instead she relives the myth, entering into it to explore a moment or character, perhaps opening up an under-developed element in the myth.

In order to decode the colonising, sexist practices embedded in the patriarchal culture, many feminist writers have instituted a trenchant enquiry into a whole range of myths, conventions and linguistic codes perpetuated by cultural practices. Myths and mythologies drawn from miscellaneous sources are also reworked from a feminist perspective. The diasporic lesbian feminist writer Suniti Namjoshi's *Feminist Fables* is a fascinating example. Fable is a moralistic medium, it has a didactic form. But more often than it preaches something, it actually questions something. It can be a satirical form. For Suniti Namjoshi, "The power of a myth is that it mutates—in the hand of a different poet, it is retold in a different form. Take the myth of Narcissus: for one poet it could be about romanticism of falling in love with beauty, for another it could be Echo and her fate and her voicelessness. Since myths never mean one thing, all poets mutate them. *Feminist Fables* sought to question social assumptions and subvert the male dominated literary tradition" (Vijayashree, 175). Namjoshi's reworking of the Medusa myth in her fable is perhaps inspired by Helen Cixous's celebrated essay *The Laugh of the Medusa*. Namjoshi's other representations of the racial minority lesbian, creative body as sites of both otherness and empowerment like the blue donkey and Bhadravathi, the lesbian cow are finest instances of ingenious myth-making. By inhabiting the subject positions of a diasporic Indian lesbian woman, by operating from multiple liminalities, she engages in a political act, thus opening up spaces in which she inscribes her resistance to stable genres and essentialised traditions. To be a lesbian, a woman of colour and a migrant is perhaps to be minoritised many times over. Patriarchal discourses have traditionally constructed lesbians as monsters and grotesque aberrations. A lesbian is a disrupter of heterosexist gender dualism. She is threatening because she challenges the hegemony of the 'normal' and 'ideal' in relation to the nature of society, family, man-woman relationships and the universality of heterosexuality. Namjoshi's unconventional fables allow for new resonances. In their feminist revisionist representations of sinister female mythical figures such as Medusa, Circe and Scylla, Namjoshi and Atwood re-examine the most ancient and universal of myths re-articulated by Simone de Beauvoir in *The Second Sex*: woman as sorceress, an enchantress, casting a spell over men and women as a formidable enigmatic 'other'.

Re-instating the marginalised in the face of the dominant is not a facile trick that can be deftly performed by a prestidigitator. It involves a painful process of epistemological deconstruction that decodes the epistemic violence perpetuated by dominant signifying practices and representational strategies. In departments of literature, it can be witnessed as canon-wars and major revisions of curricular frameworks to make them more inclusive of writings by women and minorities. Feminist politics has erased the disciplinary boundary between the political and the aesthetic and brought the concept of mythopoeic imaginary into the discursive domain. It is nothing less than a means of redefining female subjectivity by re-negotiating the distribution of power and the legitimacy of existing centres of power in the socio-cultural imaginary and thereby making the earth a less uninhabitable, violent and expropriatory place.

Works Cited

Atwood, Margaret. *Morning in the Burned House.* New York: Knopf, 1996.

———. *The Handmaid's Tale.* New York: Fawcett Crest, 1986.

———. *You are Happy.* Toronto: OUP, 1974.

Cixous, Helen. *The Laugh of the Medusa.* trans. Keith Kohen and Paula Cohen. *Signs*, 1, No. 4 Summer, 1976.

De Beauvoir, Simone. *The Second Sex* trans. H.M Parshley London: Picador, 1988.

Devi, Mahasweta. *Breast Stories.* trans. Gayatri Chakravorty Spivak. Calcutta: Sea Gull, 1997.

Namjoshi, Suniti. *Feminist Fables.* Great Britain: Sheba Feminist Publishers, 1981.

Ostricker, Alicia "The Thieves of Language: Women Poets and Revisionist Mythmaking" in Elaine Showalter (Ed.) *The New Feminist Criticism: Essays on Women, Literature and Theory.* London: Virago Press, 1986.

Vijayashree, C. *Suniti Namjoshi: The Artful Transgressor.* Delhi: Rawat Publishers, 2001.

Yorke, Liz. *Impertinent Voices: Subversive Strategies in Contemporary Women's Poetry.* New York: Routledge, 1991.

17

Tradition of Myth in Chitra Banerjee's *The Mistress of Spices* and *The Palace of Illusions*

Geetanjali Multani

Myths have always held great fascination for all since times immemorial. Earlier these tales were considered to be simple stories written or transmitted orally among people of simple origin and intellect. However, in the twentieth century a study of myths as a repository of the Collective Human Experience was initiated by Carl Jung. Studies have revealed that myths are not always culture specific, but many a times they reveal a dynamic set of images, symbols, narrative patterns, even characters and themes that have an affinity and similarity despite being distanced from each other geographically, historically and socially. This has led to an interesting interpretation of the universality of myths despite their diversity. Thus, myths are by nature "Collective" and "Communal". This led Carl Jung to develop his theory of racial memory and archetypes, expanding Sigmund Freud's theories of the personal unconscious, asserting that beneath this is a primeval collective unconscious shared in the psychic inheritance of all members of the human family. And these become manifest through archetypes. Jung defines archetypes as primordial forms that belong to the realm of the activities of the instincts and in that sense they represent inherited forms of "psychic behaviour"...older than historical man,...have been ingrained in him from earliest times, and eternally living. Jung further elaborated that myths are the means by which archetypes, essentially unconscious forms, become manifest and articulate to the conscious mind. Myths are in fact projections of innate psychic phenomena. They are what Jung characterizes as depersonalized dreams. This explains a revival of interest in mythologies as a storehouse of man's universal, collective experience of existence that lies embedded in the unconscious, a study of which can unfold many mysteries of our world in terms of mind and matter. Jung detected an intimate relationship between dreams, myths and art in that all three serve as media through which archetypes become accessible to consciousness. The great artist as Jung observes possesses the "primordial vision" that enables him or her to transmit experiences of the "inner world" through art.... It is only logical that the artist will resort to mythology in order to give his experience its most fitting expression.

In this paper, I seek to study the polemics in Chitra Banerjee's rendering of the tradition of myth in two of her famous novels, *The Mistress of Spices* and *The Palace of Illusions*. The subtle use of myth is woven into the very fabric of her novels through which it is possible to discover a kind of Transcendental Reality that is universal. However, the use of mythical tradition is completely different in both these novels. *The Mistress of Spices* is set in the present times in America thus resonating the modern experience and through that the eternal experience of woman transcending time and space. But in *The Palace of Illusions* the writer takes us back to the times of the great Indian epic *The Mahabharata* and makes us conscious of the fact that myths are not just, as is very wrongly believed primitive fiction, illusions, tales of opinions based on false reasoning but are actually a repository of the Human Collective Unconscious.

Mistress of Spices is written in a unique style that blends fantasy and reality; the past and the present. As Divakaruni reveals in one of her interviews that it was her near death hospital experience in which she was hovering between life and death that triggered her focus on boundaries and she says that it seemed to me in some wordless way that the art of dissolving boundaries is what living is all about. I ached to give this discovery a voice and a form. But I didn't know how until Tilo, my heroine...came to me...I dipped into the language and imagery of my childhood, the tales I grew up on and altered them with slang from Oakland's inner city streets. And I wrote in a spirit of play collapsing the divisions between the realistic world of twentieth century America and the timeless one of myth and magic in an attempt to create a modern fable. Thus, *Mistress of Spices* unfolds the mythical saga of Tilottma as Divakaruni documents Tilottma's journey through the realms of the timeless and the time bound; the fantastic and the real, passing through the different phases of life that reflect her stages of rebirth or transformation unfolding a woman's archetypal journey and her search for her true identity and salvation. This interplay between the fantastic and the real as a means towards the realization of her identity that reflects a woman's existential quest forms the bases of Divakaruni's novel. For me Tilo became the quintessential dissolver of boundaries moving between different ages and worlds and the communities that people them, passing through trial by water, then a trial by fire and finally trial of earth-burial to emerge transformed each time with a new name and a new identity... [while revising] I was surprised to find how much I identified with her. But looking back I see that it is not so surprising after all. I too have lived in diametrically opposed worlds of India and America. I too have taken on a new identity in a new land. And I too, in my quiet way have visited that emptiness, at once vast and minute, that simmers between life and death.

Thus, Divakaruni's personal experience assumes archetypal proportions through a blend of fantasy and reality as she unfolds the fable of Tilottma. The novel opens on a note of stark reality in one of the poverty-stricken villages of India, where an unwelcome girl child is born. And ironically she is named Nayan Tara, star of the eye, by her parents whose faces were heavy with fallen hope at another girl child. But as she grows up she reveals supernatural powers, for which she is revered and feared by both her family and villagers. This is her victory which is nonetheless tinged with a "deep wordless sorrow" (*Mistress of Spices,* 9). As her fame spreads; she is abducted by the pirates who bring ruin and destruction to her family and village. Ultimately, she overthrows the chief pirate to become the queen of the pirates. She wields absolute power. But an emptiness always gnaws at her soul, "I want...but what I longed for I didn't know, except that it wasn't this" (*Mistress of Spices,* 21). She wanders aimlessly in the vast expanse of sea water. The walls of reality in the novel start to dissolve as the pirate queen passes through a trial by water. Assisted by the mythical sea serpents and the sea she reaches the island of magic and fantasy for which she had been yearning for so long. Even her kidnapping by the pirates is enshrouded in mystery and magic. Nayan Tara reveals that it was the power of her thought that lured the pirates to her village and they became mere agents in delivering her to the island of the First Mother, a place of completely mythical and magical proportions.

She reaches this place completely bereft of her earlier identity. Even her clothes are torn off by the salty sea water. From Nayan Tara she becomes the disciple of the First Mother who can be seen as the archetypal image of the wise old man who guides the protagonist towards her true destiny. Here on this magical island that exists in a timeless world; she is initiated into the art of ancient spices. Once fully initiated, the now immortal Tilottma is ready to enter the real world of present-day America with a new identity, new knowledge and a new mission of curing other people's maladies with her knowledge of the magical powers of spices. This knowledge and initiation comes at a price. To serve the spices and the First Mother she must leave her own form of youth and beauty and live in the body of an old woman in Oakland as the mistress of spices. These spices will obey her as long as she keeps her promise of not revealing her true identity, never using these powers for herself and not having any physical or emotional bond with her customers. Her re-entry into the real world of present-day America is through a trial by fire. She transcends time and space and like the mythical Shampati "bird of myth and memory" or Phoenix-like, her earlier identity is consumed in fire and she is born to a new identity as an old woman ready to live her new existence in Oakland, California. The name that she has chosen for herself is significant as Tilottma was the name of an apsara, the chief dancer at Indra's palace who fell in love with an ordinary mortal and was punished as her beautiful body became bent and twisted by a cruel disease.

America has always been seen as a land of boundless opportunities, a place where human beings, have a chance of actually fulfilling their mythic yearning for a return to paradise...in the bright new world of the American Continent. So the myth of the American dream entices the immigrant Asians who come to this land of "Edenic dream" for the fulfilment of man's eternal quest for fame, money and prosperity. But the all too familiar immigrant tales of shattered dreams, pain and struggle is what greets them in America. And it is Tilo who brings solace, comfort, warmth, security, confidence back into their lives with her secret knowledge of the magic of spices which she administers to cure and heal people who visit her store. There is Lalita who is trapped in an unhappy married life with a man chosen by her parents. She does not want to hurt her parents and quietly accepts abuse and neglect. Then there is Jagjit, the shy, frightened boy transformed to Jag by the endless hostility he has to bear for his accent and his turban. He hits the road with a yearning for power. But he promises Tilo to start a new life over. And Haroun, the cab-driver who fled Dal lake, where generations of his family had rowed Shikaras for tourists. He lands in America an illegal immigrant but he looks forward to riches and happiness in this land. The three generations of the Banerjee family are in a war over values, only to realise the love and understanding can overcome every barrier. Thus, through these tales is unfolded the archetypal image of the "Good Mother". True to her nature the Good Mother is appropriately associated with the life principal, warmth, nourishment, protection, growth and abundance. So this sensitive mistress reaches out and touches the lives of many people who come to her store. But ironically she herself remains lonely and alienated because of her sacred vow that prevents her from maintaining any association with her customers. She has to hide herself behind a persona of old age and ugliness. Her true self remains hidden. But when a lonely American ventures into her store, he arouses in her a forbidden desire and finally makes her to shed her mask and confront her Anima, what Carl Jung characterizes as the image of the opposite sex that [a person] carries in both his personal and collective unconscious, in other words, the psychological characteristics of the opposite sex in each of us are generally unconscious revealing themselves only in dreams or in projections on someone in our environment...we tend to be attracted to the members of opposite sex who mirror the characteristics of our own inner selves. So Raven or the lonely American is the one who is able to recognize Tilo as his soul mate. He is a native Indian American, uprooted from his culture and wandering aimlessly seeking power through money to fill a void in his life. He is able to recognize his soul mate, Tilo through his dream of a black and beautiful bird. Whenever he dreams of this black Raven he feels bliss. A similar feeling he experiences when he meets Tilo. That is why despite Tilo's persona of ugliness he is able to recognize her inner beauty. The bird becomes the symbol of "earthly paradise" where Raven wants to go along with Tilo. The raven in Native American myth is often depicted as the creator of the world who stole the sun, the moon, fresh water and fire and brought it from the world of spirits to this world.

Tilo, despite her emotional and spiritual attraction towards Raven cannot disclose her true identity and break her sacred vow to the First Mother and the spices to follow the dictates of her heart. She is in a dilemma as voices from the past intersperse her consciousness reminding her of her vow. Thus, within the text of the novel is woven the archetypal dilemma of a woman torn between duty and dictates of her heart. She oscillates between the two. Like the lady of Shallot she ultimately breaks the spell, crosses the boundary of her store and experiences the touch with the real world, is ready to be punished for her transgression. She is reminded of a tale from her forgotten childhood, of Lord Shiva who consumed the dreadful poison churned by the gods and demons to save the world and she thinks, "Even for a god it must have been painful but the world was saved" (*Mistress of Spices,* 298). And it is then that her epiphanic moment dawns, "I Tilo am no goddess but an ordinary woman only...this truth I have tried to escape all my life. And though once I thought I could save this world, I see now that I have brought brief happiness in a few lives" (*Mistress of Spices,* 298). This is the moment she has made a choice, and is ready to face the wrath of the Great Mother. She has no illusions about her fate. Not only will she lose her immortality but she would also be imprisoned in the body of an old woman forever. She would lose her soul-mate Raven and would thus have to lead a painful and lonely existence. But she has no regrets. She is all prepared to atone for her transgressions. But the First Mother forgives her. The First Mother is indeed the archetypal image of the wise old man who guides Tilo towards her final destiny of leading an ordinary life of a mortal with the person she loves. Tilo is indeed forgiven but not before she passes the trial of earth-burial. She is buried in the debris of her store in an earth quake. Finally rescued by Raven, they are on the verge of leaving Oakland, a site of complete disaster because of the powerful earthquake that strikes the city, in pursuit of their "earthly paradise", until Tilo stops midway as she realizes that there is no earthly paradise, only a state of mind that can experience contentment and bliss by relieving the sufferings and pain of others by bringing light and joy in their lives, "there is no earthly paradise. Except what we make back there, in the soot in the rubble...in the guns and needle..., the young men and women lying down to dreams of wealth and power and waking in cells. Yes, in the hate in the fear." This is not Tilo the immortal mistress of spices curing the maladies of people without the human touch. Tilo is now relieved of her beautiful, terrible burden, ready to lead an ordinary life with the person who is brave enough to share her dreams and be by her side always. And so, this time she has metamorphosed into a new being. Her new name, her new identity completes the quest of this woman whose name is now, Maya. This name becomes all the more meaningful as she says, "...it can mean many things. Illusions, spell, enchantment, the power that keeps this imperfect world going day after day" (*Mistress of Spices*, 298).

Coming to *The Palace of Illusions*, Chitra Banerjee revives the rich, magical experience of the great Indian epic *The Mahabharata*. And so takes us back in time that is half history, half myth and completely fantastical. In her rendering of the great epic, Chitra Banerjee has chosen Draupadi, the wife of the five mighty Pandavas to unfold the great saga. The mythical tale of epical magnitude is disclosed through the eyes and heart of this powerful yet enchanting female voice. She resonates the aspirations and anguish; the agony and ecstasy of every female in a timeless world. As the writer reveals, "But always listening to the stories of *The Mahabharata* as a young girl.... I was left unsatisfied with the portrayal of women. And I thought if ever I wrote a book, I would place the women in the forefront of the action.... I would have one of them tell the story herself with all her joys and doubts; her struggles and her triumphs, the unique female way in which she sees her world and her place in it. And who could be better suited for this than Panchaali? It is her life, her voice, her questions, her vision that I invite you into in the Palace of Illusions" (*Palace of Illusions*, 1)". The entire story as narrated by Draupadi is unfolded in four parts.

The first part dealing with her birth and childhood is the stage of innocence, simplicity but more important, impatient waiting to grow up and fulfil her destiny of changing the course of history. The novel opens with a mention of her father's palace that doesn't meet her approval for she doesn't like its cold lonely walls. She would have a palace full of beautiful flowers and water flowing. She is very fond of listening to Dai Ma's vibrant, colourful stories. Her favourite being the story of her birth: How king Drupad driven by his desire to seek revenge from Drona performed a fire ceremony in which he prayed for a son, who would avenge his humiliation. And then after thirty days, from the fire emerged a boy. But what was surprising and unexpected was the emergence of a girl who was as dark as the boy was fair, as hasty as he was calm. And despite king Drupad's indifference towards the girl, the boy held on to his sister's hand and didn't let it go. The bond of love that was established at this time binds them together throughout their lives. Like any sister she is caring, protective, concerned towards her brother whom she addresses as Dhir. But as Dhir has to go for his princely duties, it is Lord Krishna whose occasional presence in the palace brings sunshine in Draupadi's life. He is her mentor, who infuses her with confidence; quenches her thirst for knowledge which he brings from around the world. So during her childhood Dhir, Dai Ma and Krishna are her source of love and friendship. Draupdi wondered how long she had to wait before her destiny of changing the course of history would be fulfilled. And the time did come and culminated in the lavish *swayambar* that her father, Krishna and Dhir arranged for her. Her father for political gains and Krishna for leading her towards her destiny. It is Arjun the great archer that they want her to marry. But she has already given her heart to Karan. Krishna rebukes her and tells her that he would be there on the crucial day to keep her from choosing wrongly. Finally, the day of *swayambar* comes. Who doesn't know the story of Panchaali insulting Karan, calling him a chariot driver's son, a lowly born. But Chitra Banerjee's Draupdi rejects Karan not because of pride or vanity but for her brother's love. When her brother's life and reputation is at stake, she doesn't hesitate even for a moment, even if that means sacrificing her utmost desire. When Karan challenges Dhir after he is stopped by Dhir from contesting, Draupadi intervenes for she knows that Dhir is no match for Karan. She will not marry a lowly born. Karan withdraws like a wounded lion. And along comes Arjun in the guise of a Brahmin, for he is in hiding in exile. He wins Panchaali's hand and takes her along with him towards an unknown destiny. This princess follows him bare-footed, her feet bleeding determined and dedicated to be a good wife; is happy that Dhir, Dai Ma and Krishna are happy. Vainly, she imagines the palace of her dreams that her husband would make for her. Here we see a princess, a doted sister, a carefree girl who forsakes all luxuries of her palace and enters a tiny hut along with four other men, who she immediately recognises as the Pandav brothers. Her entry into this meagre hut marks her initiation into womanhood and a ghastly realization that the mother of these five men has asked them to share whatever they have got. How can she be the wife of five men? But Kunti's order cannot be revoked. Not only are Panchaali's romantic illusions of love and marriage dashed to ground but her reverence for Kunti, the great noble queen is also shattered. Thus, ensues the power-politics between mother-in-law and daughter-in-law. Draupadi gradually wields more control over her husbands than Kunti. This is reflected in the trip undertaken by the Pandavs along with their wife to Duryodhan palace, despite Kunti's resentment. This trip marks Draupadi's initiation into the next important stage of her life. But before that so much has happened. The exile of Pandavas is over. Once again cheated of their rights, they are given the barren land of Kandav, which they to convert into a rich and prosperous land. Draupadi gets her dream palace made by none other than Maya, the maker of the palaces of gods. This is her very own Palace of Illusions, a name appropriately chosen by her. Her palace abounds with flowers, fountains, springs and waterfalls. She is delirious with happiness. Life moves smoothly for her until she decides to invite the Kauravs to her palace. This she does despite Maya's warning, "live in the palace. Enjoy. But don't invite anyone to come and see" (*Mistress of Spices*, 298). But how can a woman's heart resist the temptation to show off. Duryodhan like a greedy child wants the palace. He invites the Pandavs to his own palace in Hastinapur.

The famous game of dice, where Yudhister lost everything to Duryhodhan; his kingdom, his brothers, their belongings, their palace or rather Draupadi's palace and yes, Panchali too. Chitra Banerjee depicts this scene through the prism of Draupadi's complex feelings that collide all at once to project the helplessness, agony, anger, shame, anguish that she experiences at that time, as she is dragged by her hair through the corridors before a shocked gathering including her protectors—the five mighty, powerful men that ever lived in the tide of times; Bhisham Pitama, her secret admirer, Karan. Seeing them she was anxious not desperate. She became desperate only when they failed her in her most desperate hour of need. As she closed her eyes in helplessness Lord Krishna picture flashed across her mind. She overcame her vulnerability as Krishna's voice resonates in her mind, "No one can shame you if you don't allow it" (*Palace of Illusions*, 305). The miracle of these words saves her." "They and not I should be ashamed for shattering the bounds of decency" (*Palace of Illusions*, 305). She opens her eyes and sees Dushasan on the floor unconscious. She is saved, but she has learned so much in a span of a few minutes. Her husbands of whose love and protections she was so sure of failed her. For them notions of honour and loyalty were more important. They would avenge her later only when it would get them heroic fame. A woman doesn't think that way she would have thrown herself to save them without caring for anything else. She also learns a lesson from Karan, that the desire for revenge is stronger than the longing to be loved. Now she too loses herself in this violent emotion of revenge and curses the entire Kaurav Clan, declaring that she would not comb her hair until the day she bathes it in Kaurave's blood. Ironically, she is tainted by the same affliction which she could never understand in her father; unquenchable thirst for revenge.

She is deified, rises up as a goddess of revenge and retribution which she does get but after fifteen years of exile. By that time she is old, wrinkled with matted hair almost like a witch. And when the time comes for her to take revenge through the war, for which she had been thirsting for so passionately she realizes the futility of war even before it starts. Demons of doubt engulf her as she encounters an ordinary soldier's wife who recognises her by her uncombed hair and frightened runs away from Panchaali—the wronged one or is it as Draupadi realizes the other way round. For her petty, selfishness she is going to bring calamity to an entire kingdom. For the wives of the common soldiers she was a witch who would transform them into widows. It is now that all her illusions are shattered, the illusion of the palace comes crumbling down, and it is erased from her mind and consciousness. Its physical presence was lost in the game of dice. It's false presence in her consciousness is cleansed now.

The last stage of Draupadi's life is when she renounces the world along with her husbands to the snowy summits of Himalayas leaving her husbands far behind she falls down the icy cold mountains when cold and death grips her. Her eyes close she is delivered of numbness and cold as she experiences the warmth of her soul mate around her, who is none other than lord Krishna.

The transformation of Draupadi from a young innocent girl with hope and dreams in her eyes to her image of a witch and her final salvation resonates a woman's journey from the stage of innocence to experience and finally enlightenment.

So Chitra Banerjee's use of myth in both the novels moves on two different planes. In one there is a poetical blend of fantasy and reality and in the other there is a direct rendering of the great epic *The Mahabharata* from a woman's perspective. *Mistress of Spices* reflects the mythical journey of an ordinary woman from extraordinary to ordinary life. And *The Palace of Illusions* echoes the aspirations and the anguish of every female in a timeless world.

Works Cited

Annis, Practt, Barbara. White, Loewenstein, Andrea. *Archetypal Patterns in Women's Fiction*. Bloomington: Indiana University Press, 1981.

Divakaruni, Chitra Banerjee. *The Mistress of Spices*. London: Black Swan, 1997.

Divakaruni, Chitra Banerjee. *The Palace of Illusions: A Novel*. London: Picador, 2008.

Guerin Wilfred L., Labor, Earle. ed. *A Handbook of Critical Approaches to Literature*. 5th edition. New York: Oxford University Press, 2005.

Vickery, John B. ed. *Myth and Literature: Contemporary Theory and Practice*. Lincoln: University of Nebraska Press, 1966.

18

Contextualising Myth for Re-Presentation of History and Politics: A Reading of Shashi Tharoor's *The Great Indian Novel*

Prakash Chandra Pradhan

I: Myth as Re-presentation

The success of narrative technique of Salman Rushdie's *Midnight's Children* in the international level has influenced numerous Indian writers to shape the Indian English fiction in a new direction in relation to treatment of history, politics, culture and myth. In recent times, some of the Indian novelists in English such as Salman Rushdie, Amitav Ghosh, Shashi Tharoor, Vikram Seth, etc. have discussed the contemporary political history of India. In this context, Madhusudan Rao makes pertinent comment: "History is a matter of the soul's search for finding for one's roots in its essential human significance. In such an imaginative capturing of its essence, history is richly humanized" (*Salman Rushdie's Fiction: A Study,* 155). The post-Rushdie fiction has represented the recent Indian history, more specifically India's freedom struggle movement, the trauma of Partition, post-independence political history and the national Emergency. Though treatment of history is not new in Indian English fiction, what is distinctive about it in this period is that these novelists adopt innovative methods in narrative technique, representation of character and theme, construction of plot, linguistic improvisation such as hybridization, chutnification of language, intertextuality and magic realism. In the context of the process of fiction writing in this post-modern period, Balaswamy makes the following appropriate remark:

> Among the processes of disintegration, dissolution and explosions in this genre, one perceptible development over the recent decades has been the gradual demise of literary realism and the conscious use of the non-realistic modes such as allegory, myth, archetype, etc. Referred to, for the sake of convenience, as the mode of fabulation, it has given rise to the writing of what is paradoxically called "Fables of fact".
>
> (*Indian Literature Today*, 228)

The present paper is an attempt to show how Shashi Tharoor contextualises the myths of the *Mahabharata* to re-present the recent Indian history in *The Great Indian Novel.* Re-presentation of myth, orality and folklore for a discussion of contemporary reality helps us for a deeper understanding of the world-order, human relationships and interrelationships of man, nature and universe/cosmos. That is why the writers in recent times are more inclined to represent myths and folklores of their cultures in their creative writing to re-interpret life and society in the contemporary perspective. Discussing the relevance of myth, P. Lal comments:

> Myth feeds or nourishes the pagan outlook; myth holds communities and races more strongly than language, territory and government; myth provides insights into the mysteries of life and death with a poetic richness that has startling truth and immediacy. There is no secular substitute for myth. (Naik, 15)

R.N. Tagore believes that

> Man must realize the wholeness of his existence, his place in the infinite: he must know that as he may strive he can never create the honey he needs within the cells of his hive, for the perennial supply of his life blood is outside their walls...in our self-expression we try to startle and not to attract; in art we strive for originality

> and lose sight of truth which is old and yet even new, in literature we miss the complete view of man which is simple and yet great.... Man appears instead as a psychological problem." (Naik, 15-16)

Tagore, therefore, views that we miss the "complete view of man if we forget the meaning of myth" (Naik 16). In the recent Indian fiction in English, myth has often been recontextualised in the representation of contemporary reality: its history, politics and culture for our better understanding. In this paper we discuss how Shashi Tharoor has recontextualised the myths of the *Mahabharata* to discuss the contemporary reality in a playful style as well as humorous and sarcastic tone.

II: Mythic Structure in *The Great Indian Novel*

In the novel, Tharoor presents the characters of the epic like men and women as portrayed in a burlesque. Bhisma has been presented as Gangaji who takes us back to Gandhiji because of his adherence to determined actions in his life. Among other things, the "obsession with celibacy" is a common truth with both of them. The blind Dhritrashtra is Jawaharlal Nehru in the novel. Queen Gandhari, mother of Kauravas, gives birth to Priya Duryodhani, who is capable of indulging in evil actions of the hundred Kaurava sons. The other parallels with certain twists can be thought of as follows: Pandu as Subhash Bose, Vdur as Sardar Patel, Drona as Jaya Prakash Narayana, Yudhisthira as Morarji Desai, Amba-Shikandi as Godse, Karna as Muhammed Ali Jinnah, Bhima as the Army, Arjuna as Press and Shishupal as Lal Bahadur Shastri. Draupadi Mokrasi represents "Democracy"; Kaurava Party is presented as the powerful Congress Party. Priya Duryodhani represents Indira Gandhi, and Lord Krishna has been caricatured as a local MLA of the Kaurava Party, and Secretary for a remote taluk in Kerala. Tharoor has been meticulous enough in drawing parallels between the *Mahabharata* and the political history of the 20th century India relating to freedom struggle, post-independence problematic leading to the Emergency Rule of Indira Gandhi, collapse of Janata Party Govt., and the restoration of Indira regime after the collapse. Tharoor's Gangaji is Gandhi, a man of knowledge because of his understanding of "the great works of the past and the present, reading Vedas and Tolstoy with equal involvement, studying the innumerable laws of Manu and the eccentric philosophy of Ruskin" (*The Great Indian Novel,* 25). In the *Mahabharata,* Bhisma is a man of wisdom with vast knowledge on politics, administration, Vedas and a soldier-general *par excellence.*

Ved Vyas, the old sage of the epic, is the old politician of the novel. Tharoor converts the ancient epic into a modern novel. In the epic, the age of Ved Vyas is not known, whereas the octogenerarian in the novel is 88 years old. He narrates his story in the novel: "This is my story; the story of Ved Vyas, eighty-eight years old and full of irrelevancies, but it could become nothing less than *The Great Indian Novel*" (Tharoor, 18). Tharoor starts the novel with an argument that India is not an underdeveloped country: "They tell me that India is an underdeveloped country...stuff and non-sense, of course I tell them that I have no knowledge of history.... India is not an underdeveloped country but a highly developed one in an advanced state of decay" (Tharoor, 17). In rather a playful tone Tharoor referring to the pre-historical, mythical episode of Parasara and Matsyagandhi Satyavathi, demystifies it by arranging an ordinary natural union between two human beings, a Brahmin and a fisherwoman in an island at a place with "a thick copse of trees" and "a mist around the island" (Tharoor, 19). Superimposing modern Indian politics and recent events of Indian political history on the mythic structure, he has been able to recontextualise mythology to re-present the contemporary Indian reality. He has therefore tried to delineate the relevance of ancient India's epic in the post-colonial/post-modern context. For example, the novel begins with the princely state of Hastinapur and its annexation to the British Empire. Thereafter the narrative turns to describe the freedom struggle through such incidents as Jallianwala Bagh massacre (Bibigarh Massacre/Hastinapur Massacre), movements of peasants and industrial workers (Motihari peasants of Bihar and Budge Budge industrial workers in

Bengal), Ganhiji's Dandi March (Gangaji's Great Mango March), partition of India, the excesses of the Emergency Rule, post-Emergency chaos/disorder, installation and collapse of Janata Party Govt. and restoration of Indira regime, and Ved Vyas's dream episode of Yudhisthir's path of salvation and awakening to the reality of contemporary India of "computers and corruption".

The first ten books deal with the history of Indian freedom struggle re-enacting the drama of the *Mahabharata*, and twisting the episodes corelating the myths to the events of pre-independence struggle. Book 11 deals with the partition of India and Indian independence corelating the episode of "the bed of arrows of Bhisma" with Gangaji's death by Amba-Shikhandi-Godse. Books from 12 to 18 deal with the post-independence situations of the country leading to Emergency rule of Priya Duryodhani (Indira Gandhi) and Janata Party rule headed by Yadhisthira (Morarji Desai) and its collapse, and subsequently the dream of Ved Vyas regarding Yudhisthir's path of salvation and his encounter with Dharma, his father. It is also important to note the narrator's predicament regarding the critical socio-political condition of the country at the end of the novel:

> I woke up, Ganapathi, to today's India. To our land of computers and corruption, of myths and politicians and box-wallahs with moulded plastic briefcases. To an India beset with uncertainties, muddling chaotically through to the twenty-first century. (Tharoor, 418)

Ved Vyas thinks that the story has been told by him by a "mistaken perspective". He should therefore start telling the story afresh to Ganapathi when the novel ends.

III: Pre-colonial Contextualization

The novel begins with the comments of Ved Vyas, the narrator that India is not an underdeveloped country:

> I tell them they have no knowledge of history and even less of their own heritage. I tell them that if they would only read the *Mahabharata* and the *Ramayana*, study the golden Ages of the Mauryas and the Guptas and

> even of those Muslim chaps the Mughals, they would realize that India is not an underdeveloped country but a highly developed one in an advanced state of decay. (Tharoor, 17)

Veda Vyas further tells them that "every thing in India is over-developed, particularly the social structure, the bureaucracy, the political process, the Financial system, the university network" (Tharoor, 17). The narrator realizes that he shall not enter the twenty-first century with them. The 88 years old Ved Vyas tells his story to Ganapathi, who would write the details which "could become nothing less than the Great Indian Novel" (Tharoor, 18). In a satirical tinge, the narrator tells that he is "a bastard, but a bastard in a fine tradition, the offspring of a fisherwoman seduced by a travelling sage" (Tharoor, 19). Referring to the Brahmins, he says: "India is littered with the progeny of these twice-born traveling salesmen of salvation, and I am proved to be one of them" (Tharoor, 19). The first book ends with the birth of Dhritarashtra, Pandu and Vidur, who will shape the destiny of India in the next few years: "From Ambika emerged Dhritarashtra, blind, heir to the Hastinapur throne, from Ambalika, Pandu, the pale his brother, from the servant girl, Vidur, the wise, one day counseller to kings. Of all these I remained the unacknowledged father. Yes, Ganapathi, this is confession time" (Tharoor, 32). In course of time the children grew in the palace and became well-educated to prepare themselves for the challenges they must face in future. Gangaji took care of them. His renunciation of sex and marriage, his idealistic life and his principles of truth and non-violence spread all over India. Ved Vyas comments in this context: "That is where Ganga spoke for the genius of a nation; we Indians have a great talent for deriving positives from negatives. Non-violence, non-co-operation, non-alignment, all means more, much more, than the concepts they narrate" (Tharoor, 48). Leaving the palace, Gangaji would now lead a simple, ascetic life in an ashram with his followers of all castes, both high and low.

Re-enacting the myths of the *Mahabharata* in relation to Hastinapur, the union of the sage Parashara, and Satyavati, the fisherwoman, the vow of Bhisma, the marriage of Santanu and Satyavati, the births of Dhritarashtra, Pandu and Vidur through the union of Ved Vyas with Ambika, Ambalika and the maid, after the death of Santanu's son Chitraganda and Vichitravirya, the narrative now focuses on the political history of India during the British rule when Mahatma Gandhi (Gangaji) would fight with the British administration for getting the freedom of the nation. Getting an invitation from Raj Kumar, a peasant, Gangaji would visit the latter's district, Motihari, where he would be moved to see the suffering of the Indian folk beyond measure during the days of colonialism:

> Ganga saw the situation with eyes that, for all his idealism had too long been accustomed to the palace of Hastinapur. He saw men whose fatigue burrowed into their eyes and made hollows of their cheeks. He saw women dressed day after day in the same dirty sari because they did not possess a second one to change into while they washed the first. He saw children without food, books or toys, snot-nosed little creatures whose distended bellies mocked the emptiness within. And he went to the planters' club and saw the English and Scots in their dinner-jackets and ball room gowns, their laughter tinkling through the notes of the club piano as waiters bearing over laden trays circled their flower-bedecked tables. (Tharoor, 50)

Here Tharoor brings out a contrast between the two worlds—the life of poverty and suffering of the native Indians and the luxurious life of the British rulers in India. Gangaji's inquiries into the injustice done to Motihari peasants were obstructed by the orders of the authorities. He, however, faced the challenge without submitting. Gangaji, therefore, argues before the judge:

> As a law-abiding citizen...my first instinct, upon receiving an instruction from the authorities to cease my activities would normally have been to obey. However, this instinct clashed with a higher instinct, to respect my

> obligation to the people of Motihari whom I am here to serve. Between obedience to the law and obedience to my conscience I can choose only the latter. I am perfectly prepared however, to face the consequences of my choice and to submit without protest to any punishment you may impose. (Tharoor, 53)

It was a great surprise that the Lieutenant-Governor instructed to drop all charges against Gangaji, and he was appointed to the inquiry committee which unanimously recommended for the abolition of the system which lay at the root of the injustice. Such protests continued in different towns and villages of India by his followers. However, Gangaji and his followers were to be imprisoned occasionally and released from prisons thereafter. In this perspective the following comments of the narrator are noteworthy:

> Ganga took the issue of freedom to the people as one of the simple right and wrong—law versus conscience—and gave them a method to which the British had no response. By abstaining from violence he wrested the moral advantage. By breaking the law non-violently he showed up the injustice of the law. By accepting the punishments the law imposed on him he confronted the colonialists with their own brutalization. And when faced with some transcendent injustice whether in jail or outside, some wrong that his normal methods could not right, he did not abandon non-violence but directed it against himself. (Tharoor, 55)

Being furious at Gangaji's policies of protest against peasant exploitation at Motihari, Sir Richard and Heaslop planned annexation of Hastinapur in the line of Lord Dalhousie's Doctrine of Lapse. After the announcement of Annexation of Hastinapur, Gangaji, the ex-Regent was to address a meeting of people at Bibigarh Gardens. Sir Richard asked Heaslop to call the Cantonment under Colonel Rudyard to control the situation. As a result the army fired guns at the peaceful crowd of Hastinapur at Bibigarh:

> The soldiers fired just 1000 bullets that day, Ganapathi. It was so mechanical, so precise; they used up only the

> rounds they were allocated, nothing was thrown away no additional supplies sent for. Just 1600 bullets into the unarmed throng, and when they had finished, on, perhaps ten minutes later 379 people lay dead, Ganapathi, and 1,137 lay injured, many grotesquely maimed. When Rudyard was given the figures later he expressed satisfaction with his men. "Only 84 bullets wasted," he said. "Not bad." (Tharoor, 81)

After the Annexation of Hastinapur and Bibigarh massacre, Ved Vyas's family entered the Indian politics in the pre-independence period. Both Dhritrashtra and Pandu spearheaded movements. Though Vidur resigned from ICS by this time he was persuaded to remain in the Govt. so that he could help them in their struggle. The British exploitation on our people reached its peak. The workers were not given proper wages and bonus. The industries were owned by the English people. The peasants were to work as landless laboures. The children remained unclad. Poverty, ignorance and starvation perpetuated in our land. In this perspective the narrator indulges in his emotions while depicting the suffering of the folk:

> Not of the Indian weavers whose thumbs the British had cut off in order to protect the machines of Lancashire; not of the Indian peasants whose lands had been signed over to Zamindars who would guarantee the colonists the social peace they needed to run the country; and not of the destitution and hunger to which these policies reduced Indians. Indulge an old man's rage, Ganapathi, and write this down: the British killed the Indian Artisan, they created the 'landless labourer', they exported our full employment and they invented our poverty. (Tharoor, 95)

The mill workers agitated and struck work over the wages issue in Budge Budge town of Bengal at the call of Gangaji. However, the Scottish mill owners including Montague did not concede. Gangaji, therefore, fasted unto death till the demand of 35% wages was agreed upon by the mill owners. Finally, the mill owners were to agree on the workers' demand, and therefore Gangaji could prove the strength of 'fasting' as a weapon to defeat the power of Empire. This strong determination of Gangaji to sacrifice his life for a genuine cause set the tone of the national movement as this sacrifice led to other sacrifices that cost the British rulers India's freedom. Ved Vyas is, however, critical of the contemporary fasts, observed by the politicians, which are merely symbolic:

> What could be more absurd than the widely practiced 'relay fast' of today's politicians, where different people take in turns to miss their meals in public? Since no one starves for long enough to create any problems for himself or others, the entire point of Gangaji's original idea is lost. All we are left with is the drama without the sacrifice-and isn't that a metaphor for Indian politics today? (Tharoor, 106)

Gangaji's method of protest was based on peace, non-violence and non-cooperation that inspired a lot of people and students throughout the nation to fight for freedom. Though the Kaurava Party had been in existence for the last thirty years when Gangaji joined politics, the move for Indian self-rule did not progress much. Gangaji's strategies were often resisted from within the Party, for example, Pandu did not appreciate his 'Great Mango March'. There was also misunderstanding between Dhritrashtra and Pandu for leadership of the Kaurava Party. Gangaji, the Mahaguru, is not only the runner of the party affairs any more after the famous Mango March. The British also incited the division between the Hindus and the Muslims. Though India was not homogenous even during those days, they were living together in all their diversities. However, the British Empire deliberately infused the poison of hatred between these two communities so that they would rule them by drawing a division between them. Mohammad Ali Karna, the Muslim leader in the Kaurava Party openly opposed the style of the Mahaguru for achieving independence. There was also rivalry between Dhritrashtra and Karna for power. After getting his education in London, Karna joined the Kaurava Party while a practicing lawyer in Bombay. Karna's arrogance in the party meeting aroused curiosity among the leaders:

> We cannot hope to rule ourselves by leading mobs of people who are ignorant of the desideratum of self-rule. Populism and demagoguery do not move parliaments, my friends. Breaking the law will not help us to make the law one day. I do not subscribe to the current fashion for the masses so opportunistically advanced by a family of disinherited princes. In no country of the world do the "masses" rule: every nation is run by its leaders, whose learning and intelligence are the best guarantee of its success..... (Tharoor, 138)

However, Karna's vision and ideas are not approved on the pretext of being a driver's son. It is relevant to reflect upon the remarks of the narrator in this context:

> That is how things often work in our country, Ganapathi. If a man cannot overcome on merit, you can always expose him by uprooting his family tree. Family trees are versatile plants, Ganapathi; in our country incompetence and mediocrity also flourish under the shade of their leafy branches. (Tharoor, 139)

Karna was to depart the Kaurava Party on a variety of causes such as the co-equal roles of Dhritrashtra and Pandu, religion and his arrogance. Even there was dissension in the Kaurava Party with Panduites. When Pandu dissented, and stood for Presidency of the Kaurava Party, the Mahaguru advised Dhritrashtra to refrain from the race, and think of the future leader of the Indian Govt. After being elected as the President, Pandu expressed his "unbound reverence for the Party's mentor and spiritual guide" (Tharoor, 171). However, he did not have any respect for Gangaji's political methods. There was misunderstanding between Pandu and Gangaji in course of time for which Pandu was to resign because of no-confidence of the Working Committee. The narrator sarcastically comments on the discriminatory attitude of the Mahaguru:

> The moral pressure (and mind you, the Mahaguru never thought of it as anything else,—the moral pressure he

> placed on Pandu to bring about my pale son's capitulation was merely the political equivalent of the flattened tyres of Raja Salva early in our story. No violence done, no blood spilled—but oh, Ganapathi, what hurt and humiliation, what sadness and suffering can be caused in the defence of Truth! (Tharoor, 175)

During Pandu's self-exile, the difference between Dhritrashtra and Karna increased; Jaya Prakash Drona taught the Pandavas and Aswathaman in the palace. Gangaji started a new civil disobedience movement, namely "Quit India". A number of followers including Gangaji were imprisoned. By this time Pandu struggled hard in Berlin and Singapore. Karna was preparing for a showdown with the Kaurava Party and Amba was planning her revenge on Gangaji as she failed to procure any hired assassin to kill him: "Amba would have her revenge at last. But it would not be as Amba, the betrayed beauty of Bhumipur..." (Tharoor, 209). To move with her mission, she would be a man at last, and therefore she would tell the doctor: "Take from me these milkless breasts, doctor, seal this unseeded womb. Make me a man, doctor. A man made like all other men" (Tharoor, 209).

After World War II, when the Labour Party came to power in England, it wanted the end of Empire in India. However, Karna, the leader of the Muslim groups would not satisfy himself to die a minister in India. He rather needed a country to lead. He, therefore, wanted Karnistan to be carved out of India. The Mahaguru was disturbed to think of the division of the motherland. Though Gangaji refused to reconcile to the new reality, he could not direct history for shaping the country: "History was catching up with itself, and it was running out of breath" (Tharoor, 211). There was widespread communal frenzy and spilling of blood between the Hindus and Muslims. Lord Drewpad was appointed new Viceroy to give in the power to the Indians for self-governance. However, Karna was adamant for partition of the country. The Mahaguru suggested Dhritrashtra to give up Premiership in favour of Karna so that the country could avoid a split, though he would not agree to this. Breaking the country means breaking the heart of the

Mahaguru. For his selfish motive Dhritrashtra would rather mobilize the Working Committee of the Kaurava Party to take a hurried resolution for the partition of the country even if it meant breaking the heart of the Mahaguru. It is startlingly painful to note the grim situation of the country:

> The killing, the violence, the carnage, the sheer mindlessness of the destruction, burned out something within me. I could not understand, Ganapathi, even I could not understand what makes a man strike with a cleaver at the head of someone he has never seen, a son and husband and father whose sole crime that he worships a different God. You tell me Ganapathi. What makes a man set fire to the homes and animals and sometimes the babies of people by whose side he has lived for generations? What makes a man tear open the modesty of a girl he has never noticed, spread her legs apart with a knife to her throat.... (Tharoor, 227)

However, Dhritrashtra was fortunate/misfortunate enough not to see these inhuman actions. He remained busy in meetings/conferences to involve himself in the process of the end of Empire. These circumstances gave him a chance to develop a relationship with Georgina, Lady Drewpad. India at last conquered Great Britain, India became free. Now Amba came to Gangaji for revenge: "What a wreck you are, Bhisma.... What a life you've led...you have lived long enough.... You don't still want to live, do you? (Tharoor, 232). Then she spat out three bullets in quick succession. Sara-behn, sitting close to him, screamed to see that the Great Bhisma was no more. The era of Bhisma was gone to pave for a new beginning.

History has its own designs; it cannot be shaped according to human wishes: "It is the fate of the wise to understand the process of history and yet never to shape it" (Tharoor, 163). A story never ends because there is always a new start of the story when it ends. In this perspective, it is significant to note the philosophical comments of Ved Vyas, the narrator: "There is, in short, no end to the story of life. There are merely pauses. The end is the arbitrary invention of the teller, but there can be no finality about his choice. Today's end is, after all only tomorrow's beginning" (Tharoor, 163). The story, therefore, does not end with death, "the great symbol of finality". Knowledge is also transient. It changes with the passage of time whereas wisdom is eternal though it proves to be irrelevant in the flux of time:

> A philosopher is a lover of wisdom, Ganapathi. Not of knowledge, which for all its great uses ultimately suffers from the crippling defect of ephemerality. All knowledge is transient, linked to the world around it and subject to change as the world changes. Whereas wisdom, true wisdom is eternal, immutable. To be philosophical, one must love wisdom for its own sake, accept its permanent validity and yet its perpetual irrelevance. It is the fate of the wise to understand the process of history and yet never to shape it. (Tharoor, 163)

The inevitability, therefore, happens. It is beyond human control. Ved Vyas is but a pawn in the chess game of History. He is to tell the story only rather than shaping its direction. He thus confides his own limitations and predicaments in his story telling: "It is my truth, Ganapathi, just as the crusade to drive out the British reflected Gangaji's truth, and the fight to be rid of both the British and the Hindu was Karna's truth. Which philosopher would dare to establish a hierarchy among such verities?" (Tharoor, 164).

India got her freedom. Gangaji died. The British Empire came to an end. But Dhritarastra became the Prime Minister of India, and Karna ruled the Partitioned Karmistan. Draupadi Mokrasi, the illegitimate child of Dhritarastra and Georgina would be brought up in India to emerge as the symbol of Democracy in the India to be ruled by Priya Duryodhanai. Jaya Prakash Drona, Aswathamam, Yudhisthira, Bhima, Arjuna, Nakul and Sahadev, Vidur and Ekalavya would play their roles in a post-independent India to perpetuate her story. It is very important to note that Tharoor has very skillfully portrayed the great story of India by employing his criss-cross method by interrelating the myths, historical events and political realities in his fictional imagination. He has created the characters and situations in such a way that his characters/situations seem to be simultaneously mythical, historical, political, realistic and fictional. Superimposing the mythic structure on the historical-political reality of 20th century India, he has effectively touched our psychic imagination to understand the Indian realities quite perceptively. In recontextualising, *the Mahabharata* myths in the contemporary perspective, Tharoor has been able to put forth his vision through his power and imagination. As a result his characters seem to be down-to-earth, life-like and real.

IV. Post-Independence Scenario

Flux is the way of life. Change is a constant process. Even history is in constant process of evolution. All institutions, the world, the universe and all human life regularly/irregularly change. Each moment, everything in the universe is constantly created and recreated and going through the unending process of birth and rebirth. India has therefore been "born and reborn scores of time, and it will be reborn again. India is forever, and India is forever being made," India, being independent in 1947, is undergoing a cathartic process of regeneration, another stage in this endless cycle" (Tharoor, 245). The trauma of partition is a part of this process because the events in this world are not predicted. They rather come suddenly and unexpectedly. We are subject to the dramas of crises and emergencies. We are, therefore, in a "state of continual disturbance, all stumbling and tripping and running and floating along from crisis to crisis" (Tharoor, 245). In this process, human beings are "building a life, a character, a tradition that emerges from and sustains us in each succeeding crisis. This is our dharma" (Tharoor, 245). It is however interesting to note that the forces of destiny remain unperturbed through these unpredictable incidents and painful process of renewal:

> They are never thwarted by the jolting and jarring of history's chariots. The vehicles of human politics seem to run off course, but the site of the accident turns out to have been the intended destination. The hopes and plans of millions seem to have been betrayed, but the calamity turns out to have been ordained all along. That is how a

> nation's regeneration proceeds Ganapathi, with several bangs to every whimper." (Tharoor, 245)

Tharoor pleads that this constant rebirth is never a simple matter of the future shipping bodily from the open womb of history. Instead, there is rage, and violence, and a struggle to emerge or to remain, until circumstances bloodily push tomorrow through the parted heaving legs of today" (Tharoor, 245). India's story therefore proceeds through a complex interrelationships: Gangaji died, his assassin, Shikandi, was hanged, Karnistan was carved out of India, Dhritrashstra became the Prime Minister of a country full of chaos and disorders; and Draupadi Mokrasi was born out of this chaos and grew up with her struggle "into an admirable, beautiful complicated, desirable" woman. Drona was to settle scores with Heaslop, the Pandavas were to face the conspiracy of Priya Duryodhani, Vyabhichar Singh, the Maharaja of Miamir was to lose his throne, Karna, the Prime Minister of Karnistan was to incite communalism in India and many a thing evolved in succeeding days to come:

> The India of those early years of Independence was in a state of continuous ferment. It was constantly being rethought, reformed, reshaped. Everything was open to discussion: the country's borders, its internal organization, its official languages, the permissible limits of its politics, its orientation to the outside world. (Tharoor, 246)

Vidur's efforts made Miamir a part of India rather than that of Karnistan. Drona resigned from the Council of ministers and preferred to do some constructive work along with the five Pandavas and his son Aswathaman. Drona asked the Pandavas if they would accompany him in his mission:

> Look...I'm not sure I want to inflict my plans on you. For Aswathaman of course, it's a different matter—he's my son. But the rest of you, princes of Hastinapur wandering with me seeking social change in the villages—I don't think it's going to work. For one thing, you've never wandered around before. Aswathaman and I have. (Tharoor, 265)

Leaving Kunti alone, the five brothers accompanied their Guru, in his mission. In the meanwhile, Kanika Menon, the High Commissioner in America suggests Dhritrashtra to eliminate his rivals whenever they come on his way. In the fitness of things, he should therefore eliminate Drona and his five nephews on his way. Priya Duryodhani learnt all these crooked methods and suggestions while she was listening to her father talking to Kanika, and she would follow these methods in her life: "She was glad her idealistic father had some less idealistic friends. Dhritrashtra might forget Kanika's advice, but Priya Duryodhani would remember every word of the acerbic High Commissioner's brutal counsel. And she would not hesitate to act on it" (Tharoor, 273). She would therefore engage the hired assassins to kill the five brothers to which Vidur would intervene secretly and diplomatically to their rescue. In the meanwhile, the death of Karna would shake Kunti severely for her unacknowledged son:

> Far away, in a non-descript hotel room in charmless Varanavanta, Kunti Devi Yadav, relict of the much lamented Pandu, heard the news on a tinny radio and wept. She wept for the son she had never known, and for the fate that had deprived her of that knowledge. She wept, too, for lost innocence and acquired guilt: the innocence she had surrendered in the arms of Hyperion Helios, and the dreadful guilt that only a mother who has survived a child can know. A mother who, in this case, was obliged to mourn her son alone, and in silence. (Tharoor, 278)

The Pandavas, after a diplomatic rescue operation by Vidur for them, traveled southwards seeking their security in constant movement, and performed a lot of good deeds in the different parts of the country. In Delhi blind Dhritshastra ruled with Priya Duryodhani by his side to take the country with industrial flavour rather than on prosperity of a socialistic pattern. Factories were established, and India became the 7th largest industrial nation. Big dams were constructed that rendered many people homeless. In spite of this fact, 80 per cent rural folk continued to live without electricity and clean drinking water. The new rulers also neglected the rural education as had been the case with the British Rulers. Subsidised institutions of science, technology and medicine gave the best possible education to the selected few to serve in the best institutes of America, London and Arab countries, while the rural people continued to suffer due to poverty, ignorance and disease. This was the miserable condition of Indian poverty when the Pandava brothers were having numerous ordeals in their adventurous expedition of India. Undergoing a lot of sufferings, they would come to normal life when Arjun would win Draupadi Mokrasi in the competition meant for it. Subsequently, all the five would marry her. In course of time Arjun would undertake his exile under the circumstances which would give him a chance to befriend Krishna, the MLA of Gokarnam and local secretary of Kaurava Party of a taluk in Kerala. In the meanwhile Dhritrashtra would die, Sisupal would be Premier for a short period. There would be Indo-Karnistan war and India would come out victorious. Consequently, Priya Duryodhani would occupy the post of Prime Minister. After one year of Prime Ministership in 1967 of Priya Duryodhani, the country would go for the fourth general election in which though the Kaurava party retained power because there was no alternative, the party lost so many seats all over the country to a number of political parties. In the post-election meeting of the Kaurava Party Working Committee, Yudhistir bluntly argued that the loss of seats of the party was due to lack of strong leadership. However, Duryodhani argued that people wanted a change in the election, and she represented that change. She further emphasized that the Kaurava Party could not do without her. Yudhishtir, however, strongly protested with a challenge: "I'm willing to put that to the test" (Tharoor, 340). At this critical juncture, Ved Vyas, the senior politician intervened to calm them down. Yudhisthir furthered the argument by pleading that the spirit of Democracy demands that the leader of the party should be elected. Vyasji, however, effected a temporary reconciliation between them by suggesting the creation of the post of Deputy Prime Minister. The views of the narrator are worth mentioning in this context: "Once again, Ganapathi, I had acted for the greater national interest. But this time it was only to delay the inevitable course of history, not to facilitate" (Tharoor, 341). However, Duryodhani's rule did not change the misfortunes of the people—their ignorance, poverty and disease. Their suffering multiplied during her regime:

> Nothing changed in the daily lives of ordinary Indians, who still tilled and toiled to scratch an existence from the country's exhausted soil or sought pitiable betterment in the foetid city slums. The majority of our people remained illiterate; an overlapping majority remained below a poverty-line drawn lower and lower by Duryodhani's experts; and an overwhelming majority resigned themselves to being overwhelmed—by their fate, by the heartless ineptness of the one in whom they had placed their trust. (Tharoor, 356)

Due to her misgovernace, chaos and disorder prevailed in every sphere of life. The socio-economic situations deteriorated to such an extent that there was no escape. Duryodhani was unable to cope with the situation without a perspective in her vision. She would, therefore, use the excesses of the state machinery to govern in totalitarian pattern:

> ...while the poor remained as poor as they had ever been, while striking trade unionists were beaten and arrested, while peasant demonstrations were assaulted and broken, all this while more and more laws went on to the statute books empowering Priya Duryodhani to prohibit, proscribe, profane, prolate, prosecute all the freedoms the national movement had fought to attain during all those years of my Kaurava life. (Tharoor, 357)

Failing to cope with such reality, Ved Vyas dreams of *Agni,* the mythic fire that blessed Arjun to have the power to create at this critical juncture of nation. Arjun would have to ignite the Fire to multiply in due course being metamorphosed by the power of Drona's ideology and Krishna's guidance. Duryodhani's style of functioning disappointed Yudhisthir resulting in his resignation from the cabinet. Even he was cornered in the Party's Working Committee meeting on the policies and programmes of the Party. He would, therefore, resign from the Committee. The party's official candidate for Presidency was not supported by the Prime Minister. She would, support Eklabya rather than the official candidate Vyasji. After the defeat of the official candidate, the party would split into Kaurav Party® and Kaurava Party (o), and Duryodhni became the supreme leader of her splintered party, Kaurava Party®. Though she had no sincerity to remove poverty, she woud now indulge in a gimmick "Remove Poverty". The "Gelabi Desh war" helped her to raise her stature as "Ma Duryodhani", "Duryodhani Amma". The people of India, after East Karnistan's liberation from the domination of West Karnistan, "saw in her the embodiment of the female principle of Shakti, the power and the strength of a national mother Goddess" (Tharoor, 355).

Certain developments during the totalitarian governance deeply hurt Drona. He found that the suffering of the people increased day by day. In order to bring an end to her autocratic functioning, he spearheaded a national movement protesting against her mis-governance. By this popular uprising, a provincial court convicted her guilty of a corrupt electoral practice for making a campaign speech along with President, Eklabya. Though she should have resigned, she would rather promulgate "Internal Siege" at the advice of the Bengali Lawyer Shakuni Shankar Dey. The Prime Minister could assume absolute powers, and ruled like a Goddess. Critics protested, and, therefore, the uprising leaders were imprisoned. She justified her stand accompanying a 20 point socio-economic programme to the promulgation of Emergency Rule. The Prime Minister ordered the censor of the press, banned public debates, and placed restrictions on reporting the speeches of the Opposition leaders. Ved Vyas, the senior leader would have to do something; otherwise the country was leading towards a collapse. One day Arjun would, therefore, persuade him with his infinite sadness: "You've got to be wrong, or the whole world wouldn't make sense any more" (Tharoor, 374). These careful words shattered the equilibrium of Ved Vyas for which he thought of Draupadi, the symbol of Indian Democracy, who was stripped of her clothes by

Duryodhani's agents of misgovernance. She along with her minions robbed "the nation of the values and institutions "the freedom fighters cherished. The Siege had been a license for her to demolish everything that had been nurtured through the years. However, at the peak of these crises Priya Duryodhani declared the elections in which she would be defeated along with her party. She was also imprisoned for her electoral malpractice/misgovernance Yudhisthir became the Prime Minister, but the internal squabbles within the Janata Party brought premature death of his government: "The Indian people gave themselves the privilege of replacing a determined tyrant with an indeterminate collection of tyros" (Tharoor, 402). Yudhisthir and his colleagues lost the opportunity of protecting the Indian Democracy. As a result there would be the collapse of the Government, and Duryodhani came to power again: "Dharma had turned full circle. "This is the story of "betrayed expectations."

V: Tharoor's Vision in *The Great Indian Novel*

In the battle of Kurukshetra none was a victor in true sense of the term. That is because in the battlefield victory is only a misnomer in the perspective of waste and horror that war causes. Referring to the situation of the aftermath of the battle of the *Mahabharata*, Ved Vyas comments:

> The story of the Mahabharata...does not end on the field of battle. What happens afterwards is tragedy, suffering, futility, death. Which underlies the only moral of that battle, and that epic: that there are no real victors. Everyone loses at the end. (Tharoor, 391)

Elaborating further Ved Vyas explains Ganapathi how that was a battle between cousins to deceive each other for a win: "They were killing each other's flesh and blood, shooting arrows into their own gurus, lying and deceiving their elders in order to win. There was good and bad, dishonour and treachery, betrayal and death, on both sides". Contextualising the *Mahabharata* myth, Ved Vyas therefore comments: "This election is not Kurukshetra, life is Kurukshetra. History is Kurukshetra. The struggle between dharma and adharma is a struggle our nation, and each of us in it, engages in on every single day of our existence. That struggle, that battle, took place before this election; it will continue after it" (Tharoor, 391). In a playful, humorous as well as sarcastic tone, Ved Vyas further tells Ganapathi how the functioning of Democracy in Contemporary India is not proper:

> Democracy, Ganapathi, is perhaps the most arrogant of all forms of government, because only democrats presume to represent an entire people: monarchs and oligarchs have no such pretensions. But democracies that turn authoritarian go a step beyond arrogance; they claim to represent a people subjugating themselves. India was now the laboratory of this strange political experiment. Our people would be the first in the world to vote on their own subjugation. (Tharoor, 391)

Shashi Tharoor therefore sees the relevance of the myth of the *Mahabharata* in the context of recent Indian history and politics. These myths have been represented in *The Great Indian Novel* as modes of consciousness to understand the Indian realities which are as problematic today as it had been in the mythic times. Shashi Tharoor's perceptions of contemporary realities of India—her history and politics—in terms of the myths of the *Mahabharata* are commendable as far as a deeper understanding of Indian nation is concerned. The war-like situations of the *Mahabharata* still continue in our country in different forms, and will also continue in the internal squabble among the politicians who rather fight for their own interests leading the country to disastrous situations as are the cases illustrated by Tharoor in the context of Emergency Rule (Indira Gandhi-Priya Duryodhani's style of functioning) and post-Emergency muddles continued by the Janata Party Government (Yudhistir-Mararaji administration).

Works Cited

Abrams, M.H. *A Glossary of Literary Terms*, 6th Ed. Bangalore: Prism Book Edition, 1993.

Balaswamy, P. "The Presence of the Past: Shashi Tharoor's *The Great Indian Novel* as Histriographic Metafication." *Indian Literature Today*. Vol. II. Ed. R.K. Dhawan. New Delhi: Prestige, 1998.

Bell, Michael. "Anthropology and/as Myth in Modern Criticism." *Literary Theory and Criticism: An Oxford Guide*, Ed., Patricia Waugh. Oxford: Oxford University Press, 2006.

Belliappa, K.C. "Problematising Indian History in English." *The Journal of Indian Writing in English*. Ed. G.S. Balarama Gupta, 2002.

Chandra, Bipin. *India's Struggle for Independence*. New Delhi: Penguin, 1989.

Chowdhury, Kanishka. "Revisioning History: Shashi Tharoor's *The Great Indian Novel*." *Twane Companion to Contemporary World Literature* Vol. 1. Ed. Pamela A. Genoa. New York: Twayne Publishers, 2003.

Dasan, A.S. "Questing for Truth: History-Fiction Interface in the Recent Indian English Fiction." *Kakatiya Journal of English Studies*. Vol. 29/2010.

Frye, Northrope. "Myth, Fiction, and Displacement." *Literary Criticism: A Reading*, Ed. B. Das and J Mohanty. Calcutta: Oxford University Press, 1985. Print.

Gandhi, M.K. *An Autobiography or The Story of My Experiments with Truth*. Ahmedabad: Navajivan Mudranalaya, 1927.

Kirpal, Viney. *Introduction. The Post modern Indian English Novel: A Study of the 1980's and 1990's*. Ed. Viney Kirpal. New Delhi: Allied Publishers, 1996.

Lal, P. "Mod. Bharata." *Littcrit* 16. 12 Jan. Dec. 1990.

———. "Myth and the Indian Writer in English: A Note." *Aspects of Indian Writing in English*, Ed. M.K. Naik. New Delhi: Macmillan, 1979.

Mukherjee, Meenakshi. *The Twice Born Fiction: Themes and the Indian Novel in English*. New Delhi. Arnold-Heinman. Publishers, 1974.

Pandit, M.L. "Sub version of Faith as Fiction Salman Rushdie's *The Satanic Verses* and Shashi Tharoor's *The Great Indian Novel*." *New Commonwealth Writing: A Critical Response*. New Delhi: Prestige, 1996.

Pathak, R.S. Pathak. "Introduction." *Recent Indian Fiction*. New Delhi: Prestige, 1994.

Rajagopalachary, M. "Re-presentation of History in the Recent Indian Fiction in English: An Overview" *Kakatiya Journal of English Studies*. Vol. 29/2010.

Rao, M. Mudhusudhan. *Salman Rushdie's Fiction: A Study*. New Delhi. Sterling, 1992.

Rao, T. Viswanadha. "Myth and History in Shashi Tharoor's *The Great Indian Novel*". *Kakatiya Journal of English Studies*. Vol. 29/2010.

Rushdie, Salman. *Midnight's Children*. London: Vintage, 1995.

Tharoor, Shashi. *The Great Indian Novel*. New Delhi: Penguin India, 1989.

———. "Timeless Epic". *The Hindu Literary Review*. Jan, 2005.

19

The Past in the Present: Myth and Folklore in Girish Karnad's *Yayati* and *Hayavadana*

Geetanjali A. Rana

Girish Raghunath Karnad is a man of many talents. Not only is he one of the outstanding Indian English dramatist, he is also active in the world of Indian cinema, working as an actor, director, producer and screen writer for more than four decades Karnad has been composing plays, often using history and mythology to tackle contemporary issues. Kirtinath Kurtkoti, in his "Introduction" to *Hayavadna*, has remarked, "He has the genius and the power to transform any situation into an aesthetic experience, the quality of which, to use Joyce's vocabulary, would be 'static' rather than 'Kinetic'." Karnad along with other playwrights like Vijay Tendular and Rakesh Mohan revived the trend of theatre. They have been trying to uphold rich cultural heritage of India by using myths, legends, histories and traditional stories in their plays. Karnad has made an effort to fight the legacy of colonialism by upholding Indian values and its cultural ethos. The themes do have contemporary significance but the focus is on the presentation of complex cultural fabric of India.

Girish Karnad as a dramatist uses deftly the historical personnel and the folk motifs for the narratives of his dramatic art. In some of his plays, he uses the motifs of history for universalizing the humanitarian notes and folklore for unveiling the real intents of human mind. Karnad employs mythical, historical and folk themes as the skeleton for his plays but they are identified with the contemporary scene. He has done a great service to introduce the folk tradition into his drama and thus expand the very horizon of the Indian stage. Karnad is very fond of going back to standard Hindu myths or folk myths for treatment in his plays and for reinterpreting them in light of contemporary events or situations. Myths have been a very important phenomenon in world literature and they are the eternal source of inspiration for the creative writers. Mark Schorer, in *William Blake: The Politics of Vision,* points out that, "Myth is fundamental, the dramatic representation of our deepest instinctual life, of a primary awareness of man in the universe, capable of many configurations, upon which all particular opinions and attitudes depend" (29). Myth has always had a very significant position in human psychology and society from its beginnings as primitive religious narrative to its recent adaptation as an aid in the exploration of the unconscious mind.

In many interviews, Karnad has honestly confessed that he does not like to take up the contemporary themes and treat them realistically but prefers to go back to myths and history and invest them with contemporary relevance. Girish Karnad derives resources of the myths and folkloristic devices from the epics of India. India is a fertile land of rich, varied and endless mythologies. Even the smallest village of the nation has one or the other myth to offer. In a way, myths are the part and parcel of Indian way of life. *A Handbook of Critical Approaches to Literature* explains, "Myths are by nature collective and communal; they bind a tribe or a nation together in common psychological and spiritual activities" (Guerin, 184). These are reflected in various shades of colours in the everyday life of the people of the nation.

It would not be an exaggeration to say that the Indian life and Indian culture are based on the solid foundation of her myths. Vedic mythology, religious mythology, mythologies of great kings, warriors, saints, rishies, rulers, etc. are spread everywhere. Through generations different stories in Indian mythology have been passed from generation to generation either by the world of mouth or through carefully stored scriptures. The stores of Indian mythology vary from simple maxim conveying tales of *Panchtantra* and *Jataktales* to subtle life paradigm defining stories from the *Bhagvad Gita,* the *Ramayana* and the *Mahabharata.* Karnad fully agrees that Indian myths are the embodiment of the basic and general ideas that govern the mindset of Hindus. He exploits them in his plays to gain a fresh and newer vision and to arrive at a reinterpretation of life situations. Karnad's immense interest in past which is loaded with mythology is there because it remains an integral part of the living culture of India. In his well-known plays like *Yayati* (1961) and *Hayavadana* (1971), we find the predominance of mythical element and structure.

His first play *Yayati* is based on *Adiparva*, the first book of *Mahabharata*. It interprets an ancient myth in the modern context. In the Puranic lore, Yayati marries Devyani, the daughter of the sage Shukracharya and later takes Sharmistha, the daughter of the king of Asuras as his wife. His marriage to Sharmistha infuriates Devyani, who in her anger and jealousy goads her father to bring curse of senility decrepitude upon Yayati. Yayati, who is cursed to old age for his moral transgress, wishes to exchange his old age for money, land and even a part of his kingdom. None, including his three elder sons, accepts the offer, when Puru, his youngest son, with a great sense of filial obligations and respect for his father, offers his youth for his old age and takes the curse on himself. But the old age bring no knowledge, no self-realization, only the senseless of a punishment meted out for an act in which he had not even participated. The original story in *Mahabharata* tells us that the more Yayati indulged, the thirstier he grew. At last he realizes that no object of desire can satisfy the desire of man and he finally asks Puru to take back his youth and Yayati then retires to the forest to perform penance. In due course of time, he attains perfect state of Brahman.

Karnad's *Yayati* re-tells the age-old story of the King Yayati and invests new meaning and significance for contemporary life and reality by exploring the king's motivations. Karnad in his play makes King Yayati confront the horrifying consequences of not being able to relinquish desire and through other characters, he highlights the issue of class/caste and gender coiled within a web of desire. Karnad invented the character of Chitralekha, Puru's newly wedded wife, who is unable to bear her husband's old age. She wishes to offer herself to Yayati but then commits suicide out of shame. Yayati is horrified to see the disastrous result of his action. He finally takes back the curse from his son.

Thus, Karnad's first play *Yayati* explores the complexities of responsibilities and expectation within the Indian family. Drawing on a myth from the *Mahabharata,* Karnad expresses in it a personal dilemma between his family's demands and his own wish for freedom. As Karnad has mentioned in his "Introduction" to *Three Plays,* "But looking back, I am amazed at how precisely the myths reflected my anxieties at the moment, any resentment with all those who seemed to demand that I sacrifice my future" (3). Moreover, Karnad interprets the ancient theme in modern context. Like King Yayati, the modern man today is groping in the darkness of material and sexual pleasures. He finds himself in a world in which the old spiritual values have been entirely swept away and new spiritual ones are yet to be discovered.

Karnad's next play *Hayavadana* reveals the conflicts brewing in human mind. It is a play on the theme from *Kathasritsagar,* an ancient collection of Sanskrit stories. The story of *Hayavadana* comes partly from Thomas Mann's story entitled *Transported Heads,* which in turn is based on one of the versions of the story in *Vetal Panchavimshati. Hayavadana* is a bold and successful experiment on folk theme. Karnad uses the conventions and motifs of folktales and folk theatre. Masks, curtains, dolls and the story within story have been safely employed to create a bizarre world.

Hayavadana is a based on the myths revolving around Vakratunda and Hayagriva. Vakratunda is the first of the twelve names of Lord Ganesha. If the trunk and broken tusk are on the right side, he is Vakratunda and if on the left side he's Siddhivinayka. In the mythic story, Lord Ganesha is given a new life after a head of an elephant is planted on him and he rises as Vakratunda, with human body and animal's head. Thus, he becomes the embodiment and symbol of incompleteness. Yet, he is the primal God who unfailingly offers his blessings to all of his devotees with completeness in all their endeavours. O.P. Budhia in *Girish Karnad: History and Folklore*, has commented, "The text which begins with the prayer of Ganesha O Elephant-headed Herambha becomes symbolic of two things: the great tradition of Indian drama and the question of incompleteness of the benign Lord Ganesha, himself a symbol of in completeness, is the destroyer of incompleteness" (52). But according Karnad, God cannot be challenged by man and he points out in his "Introduction" to *Three Plays*:

> It seemed unfair, however, to challenge the thesis of the riddle by using a god. God after all, is beyond human logic, indeed beyond human comprehension indeed. The dialectic had to grow out of grosser ground, and I sensed a third being hovering in the space between the divine and the human, a horse-headed, man. (14)

Literal meaning of *Hayavadana* is 'Horse-faced' which comes from 'Haya' meening 'horse' and 'Vadana' meaning 'face'. Man's search for completeness and the body-mind dichotomy and man-woman relationship happen to be the philosophical concerns in the play. The dichotomy between mind and body is presented through two characters Devdatta and Kapila, who are a pair of binary opposites. Whereas Devdatta is a man of intellect, Kapila is a man of the body. Devdatta is un-rivalled in intelligence and is the only son of a revered Brahmin. Kapila is a brawny man and a son of iron-smith. Though, characteristically, they are poles apart, yet they are close and complementary to each other. As the play progresses, Devdatta falls in love with Padmini, daughter of a leading merchant and Kapila finally succeeds in bringing the lovers together into matrimonial bond. After marriage Devdatta and Kapila live like friends and brothers for some time. As days go by, Devdatta develops subtle kind of jealousy for Kapila as he notices Kapila's attraction for Padmini. Even Padmini cannot help appreciating the handsomeness of a man other than her husband. One day on their way to Ujjain fair, all three of them stop at Kali temple. Devdatta severs his head as an offering to goddess Kali which he had promised to the goddess long time back. Kapila unable to bear the sorrow too cuts off his head. Later, due to heavenly intervention of goddess Kali, Padmini is asked to put back the severed heads on the respective bodies. But in her excitement, Padmini, mixes them up so that Devdatta's head goes to Kapila's body and vice-versa.

Now that Devdatta and Kapila are revived, the situation becomes comic and absurd at the same time. After the exchange of heads a new confusion of identities is created. A theoretical question about whether a man is his body or his mind is posed here. Thus, the dichotomy between the mind and body is created. Devdatta in the body of Kapila unlocks the syllogistic reasoning of the supremacy of head over human body:

> Of all the human limbs the top most in position as well as in importance is the head. I have Devdatta's head and it follows that I am Devdatta. According to the sacred texts.... (37)

Final solution is offered by the Rishi: "As the heavenly Kalpa Vriksha is supreme among trees, so is the head among human limbs. Therefore, the man with Devdatta's head is indeed Devdatta and he is the rightful husband of Padmini" (40). The central message of the play seems to be that man searches for completeness but unfortunately it is not possible. The arbitrary completeness that Devdatta and Kapila achieve does not remain for long as everything is subject to the effect of time. So, the quest for completeness remains only a wishful desire rather than a permanent possibility. Though Karnad has based his play on mock heroic Sanskrit tale, yet the theme is modern. There is an irresistible urge for completeness and search for identity. The main characters in the play, *Hayavadana*, Devdatta, Kapila and Padmini and fractured personalities suffering from want of wholeness. Padmini torn between the two is also a shifted personality. Hayavadana in the sub-plot who combines the human and animal elements in him, is also incomplete. Hayavadna too goes to the same goddess Kali and wins a boon from her that he should become complete. Logic takes over. The head is the person. Hayavadna becomes a complete horse. In the sub-plot, he is completely transformed into a horse. His search for completeness ends comically. Hence, in a world of absurdity of human condition the attainment of completeness is a distant mirage. Thus, the characters in these re-written myths are placed in existential situation employing problems of selfhood, search for identity, isolation and frustration. Girish Karnad, thus, seen, has taken the plunge into the unfathomable depths of age-old Indian mythologies to look for the subject matter of this plays and has successfully and artistically converted them into the worlds which fits into the present framework to reflect the present-day social dilemmas and problems. Karnad fully agrees that Indian myths are the embodiment of the basic and general ideas that govern the mindset of Hindus. He exploits them in his plays to gain a fresh and newer vision and to arrive at a reinterpretation of life situations.

Girish Karnad's contemporary playwright, Vijay Tendulkar puts its aptly, "Karnad was groomed in mythology". Dr. Iros Vaja has said, "Karnad has found myths a powerful vehicle to carry the complex ideas of the modern times. Besides, the use of myths enables him to link the continuity of emotions from the beginning of the civilization to the present age. Thirdly, he is able to interpret the past in terms of the present and vice versa". Karnad's plays testify to a larger cultural matrix of a myths modes, oral folk forms, and narrative conventions than any other plays written and preformed in recent times. His re-writing of myths and folk-tales instills unique emotional and intellectual angles to the given protototypes. Baskaran and Meeran, in their essay on "Myth and Folklore in Girish Karnad's *Hayavadana*" have commented, "In-depth knowledge and thorough consciousness of the primitive phase of meta physical thoughts in the myths enables Karnad to render his dramas as great literary products of art" (245).

The playwright's immense interest in past which is loaded with mythology is there because it remains an integral part of the living culture of India. There Indian myths are not themselves literature but they are indubitably a perennial source of information and inspiration to Karnad. As he himself observes in his "Introduction" to *Three Plays* that in India "the past is never totally lost; it coexist with the rest as a parallel flow" (12).

Works Cited

Baskaran, G. *Girish Karnad and Mahesh Dattani: Methods and Motives*. Jaipur: Yking Books, 2012.

Budholia, Om Prakash. *Girish Karnad: History and Folklore*. Delhi: B.R. Publishing Corporation, 2011.

Guerin, Wilfred L. et al. *A Handbook of Critical Approaches to Literature*. 5th Edition. New Delhi: OUP, 2010.

Karnad, Girish, *Hayavadana*. New Delhi: OUP, 1975.

Karnad, Girish, *Three Plays*. New Delhi: OUP, 1994.

Karnad, Girish, *Yayati*. New Delhi: OUP, 2008.

Schorer, Mark. *William Blake: The Politics of Vision*. New York: Holt, 1946.

Vaja, Dr. Iros. *Myths in Girish Karnad's Plays*. Jaipur: Paradise Publishers, 2010.

20

Destabilizing Fixities: Intermingling of History, Myth and Realism in *Ghasiram Kotwal*

Anita Bhela

The colonial period in Indian history contributed to a break with the Indian performing traditions and in the year 1945 Kamaladevi Chattopadhyay commented that "it is a strange as well as a tragic fact that the general national awakening in India, resulting among other things, in a tremendous revival in fine arts and various aesthetical pursuits, should have completely by passed the drama and the stage" (*Modern Indian Theatre,* 451). The modern proscenium theatre arose in the mid-nineteenth century under the direct influence of British theatrical tradition. Kamaladevi was of the view that dance-drama through which most Indian festivals are celebrated to be "the most poignant and impressive medium for conveying religious as well as philosophic ideas through an extraordinary technique evolved out of the collaboration of dance, song, and an elaborately perfected gesture" (*Modern Indian Theatre,* 452). But at the same time she felt that "however marvelous and perfect the traditional theatre might be, it can no more serve as a spontaneous and natural medium through which the mind of the people is to manifest itself" (*Modern Indian Theatre,* 452). She desired that "the traditional theatre should be revived and preserved as the rich heritage on which to build the new theatre of today and the structure of tomorrow" (*Modern Indian Theatre,* 452). She wanted theatre to act as a medium of expression for new "vivified impulses and emotions" not in "any single type or form" (*Modern Indian Theatre,* 455), but in a variety of shapes. One playwright who achieved what Kamaladevi Chattopadhyay had visualized for Indian Theatre was Vijay Tendulkar and in 1970 he was honored with the Kamaladevi Chattopadhyay award for drama, and the Sangeet Natak Akademi award for playwriting.

Indian theatrical traditions are of an infinite variety and vary not only from region to region but also from village to village. Traditional theatre performing styles generally include song, music and dance in distinctive combinations to dramatize/narrate/enact stories of the epics or traditional popular religious stories. Performance space, costumes, headgear, masks, narrative styles and musical instruments used in these performances are unique and peculiar to each region of India. Traditional stories have been told and retold in countless ways but audiences are still eager to hear them. In fact, these stories and storytelling forms are so much a part of the cultural tradition of India that they are now being transmuted, transcribed or subverted by modern writers to convey new meanings in new (con) texts. In the year 1972, Tendulkar wrote *Ghashiram Kotwal,* a political satire whose presentation style was a unique amalgamation of traditional Marathi folk music and drama styles and contemporary theatre techniques. It broke new ground for Indian theatre and being experimental not only in form but also in theme, it took some time before the new form could take hold of the audiences. Pandit Bhaskar Chandravarkar, the music composer of the Pune production of the play by the Puppets, Pune, states that "after the first show *Ghashiram* left an impact of something unexpected. People were somewhat confused on its form and wondered what it was. They started understanding the strong political outlook of the play only after about the 10th show" (*Ghashiram Kotwal* video recording). While many appreciated the play, a section of the people did not approve of it at all. One section felt that it was slanderous against the Brahmin community and the other section felt it distorted history and defamed Nana Phadnavis—

the 18th century statesman. After this criticism, a movement to stop the play began. A few prominent political parties also joined the stir and Vijay Tendulkar faced the threat most. He was even physically man handled. However, Pandit Bhaskar Chandravarkar sees the controversy surrounding the play as a success of the play in one sense, for the play deals with fascists and their muscle strength. The controversy surrounding the play was of course also a testimony to its "newness".

In an effort to liberate Indian Theatre from its colonial moorings, proponents of the new theatre began a return to the "roots" movement. Suresh Awasthi, coined the term "theatre of roots" and stated that this return was "a part of the great cultural renaissance generated during the post-independence period" due to which there "occurred a most meaningful encounter with tradition in various fields of creative activity. The return to and discovery of tradition was inspired by a search for roots and a quest for identity" (*Modern Indian Theatre*, 295). He viewed it as a "part of the whole process of decolonization of our lifestyle, values, social institutions, creative forms and cultural modes" (*Modern Indian Theatre*, 295). As a result of a meaningful interaction with tradition, Indian theatre was put back on the track of the great *Natyasastra* tradition (*Modern Indian Theatre*, 296):

> Setting in the Western conventional sense of an aggregate of scenic means, using a variety of materials and devices, is unknown to traditional Indian theatre. Rather, the setting is contained in the text and incorporated in the actor's body through highly stylized make-up, costume and symbolic hand-gestures...the various elements of performance such as music, movements, gestures, all have an independent status and retain their character. They do not become just an appendage to the dramatic dialogue intended to heighten emotional mood and create an atmosphere as is their objective in the realistic, illusionistic theatre. (http://www.4to40.com/music/article_print.aspp=Performance_Tradition_Aesthetics_and_Practice&k=Make-up_ And_Scenic_Design)

In *Ghashiram Kotwal*, Vijay Tendulkar through a judicious and innovative amalgamation of a wide variety of traditional Indian theatrical performing styles presents a scathing satire on the intricacies of power politics. Subverting the mythic narrative pattern of the eternal conflict between good and evil and the assured victory of good over evil, he presents a conflict in which evil confronts evil and the greater evil wins. Intermingling history and myth Tendulkar's play ostensibly makes a break with the realism of colonial theatre and returns to the "roots", but the return paradoxically is only in the use of the traditional fantastical theatrical performing styles, while the play itself aims at destabilizing fixities through the portrayal of an uncanny, horrific and gruesome reality. As a result of the mixing of the brute realism of the story with the fantastic in the narrative style of presentation, "magic realism" of a special kind takes effect in the play. The use of the fantastic entertains but also masks the stark realism portrayed and makes it less shocking than it would be if presented in its nakedness. To shake people out of their habitual perceptions of their surroundings, Tendulkar initiates a cultural transmutation of tradition and adapts it to suit the needs of the times. In the play, Tendulkar successfully interweaves the fantastic and the real to put across powerfully and effectively a harsh critique of the socio-political forces operating within society.

Tendulkar's return to the roots in *Ghashiram Kotwal* is a return to the classical performing traditions of India but the purpose and aim, as stated earlier, is very different. The aim is not religious but social and the story is a subversion of mythic patterns and mythic stories. Mircea Eliade in *Images and Symbols: Studies in Religious Symbolism* states that "today we are well on the way to an understanding...of one thing of which the nineteenth century had not even a presentiment—that the symbol, the myth and the image are of the very substance of the spiritual life, that they may become disguised, mutilated or degraded, but are never extirpated" (Eliade, 11). And speaking of the survival of "the great myths throughout the nineteenth century" he says "they were humbled, minimised, condemned to incessant change of form, and yet survived that hibernation, thanks chiefly to literature" (Eliade, 11). Thus, according to Mircea Eliade our connection with the mythic past is kept alive sometimes even in a subverted form through literary works and one such work is *Ghashiram Kotwal*. In order to truly understand and appreciate the play, knowledge of the Indian religious epics, concept of *dharma*, good and evil is essential.

Ghashiram creatively uses traditional forms to present a contemporary theme. The play is a strong and direct portrayal of "overlapping orbits of power struggle, criminal tendencies and sex". Bhaskar Chandravarkar states that it is believed that one learns from the past. But it is questionable whether one really learns anything from history. If not so, then why are some mistakes repeated every now and then? In "Geronition" T.S. Eliot expresses a similar idea and states how history deceives, is tragic and repeats itself:

> Think now
> History has many cunning passages, contrived corridors
> And issues, deceives with whispering ambitions,
> Guides us by vanities. Think now
> she gives when our attention is distracted
> And what she gives, gives with such supple confusions
> that the giving famishes the craving. Gives too late
> What's not believed in, or if still believed,
> In memory only, reconsidered passion. Gives too soon
> into weak hands, what's thought can be dispensed with
> till the refusal propagates a fear? Think
> neither fear nor courage saves us. (Eliot, 34-44)

And in "Sweeney among the Nightingales" he shows how the history of sex and violence is continually re-enacted and that the present can be just as sordid as the past:

> The nightingales are singing near
> The Convent of the Sacred Heart,
> And sang within the bloody wood
> When Agamemnon cried aloud,
> And let their liquid droppings fall
> To stain the stiff dishonoured shroud. (Eliot, 35-40)

The contemporary relevance of the play cannot be overemphasized. Ghashirams crop up again and again and history is continually swept by violence and sex. Speaking of his play, Tendulkar stated: "It is a story, in prose, verse, music and dance set in a historical era. Ghasirams are creations of socio-political forces which know no barriers of time and place. Although based on a historical legend, I have no intention of commentary on the morals, or lack of them, of the Peshwas, Nana Phadnavis or Ghasiram. The moral of the story, if there is any, may be looked for elsewhere" (*Ghasiram Kotwal,* iv). Innumerable number of Ghashirams are created by those in power and destroyed or killed when they get out of hand as when the monster in *Frankenstein* gets out of hand its creator desires to destroy it. Although *Ghashiram* is not based on true history, it does convey a historical truth that we come across time and again. Pandit Bhaskar states that in the 21st century, a manifestation of this truth was Saddam Hussein and he feels that Tendulkar's achievement is that he wrote a play about Saddam 35 years before he emerged. The play's political theme created awareness about those in power and power politics and made people think and ponder over these issues.

The Indian epics, the *Mahabharata* and the *Ramayana*, focus on *dharma*, but not by "stringing together lists of 'shoulds' and 'shouldn'ts' but chiefly through narrative and sometimes didactic passages. The word *dharma* is ubiquitous in them, and their chief characters openly question its meaning in their eventful lives" (Lipner, 125). The pursuit of *artha* and *kama* regulated by *dharma* is of great importance to Hindus. In *The Bhagvad Gita,* Lord Krishna says that he reincarnates himself in various *yugas* to restore *dharma* in the world. The epics, the *Ramayana* and the *Mahabharata* are part of the living traditions of India and not "relics of the past, of interest only to classicists and literati". In fact, "the chief episodes of the *Ramayana* and the *Mahabharata* are the sap of the Hindus and nourish its growth" (Lipner, 136) and "the interest in the public enacting or reciting of sacred texts is ethical not literary. The style of presentation is traditional, innovation being permitted only minimally and within an established framework

(Lipner, 141). The religious enactments of the epic stories "sacralise space and time", and draw "the audience into the religious event they celebrate; they instruct and inform, renew and perpetuate a cultural identity and bestow the fruit of participation" (Lipner, 142).

Tendulkar in search for appropriate narrative forms borrowed the expressive means of various epic narrative styles but adapted them to suit his purpose. Tendulkar also exploited the moral ethical codes embedded in the mind of the audiences through repeated listening and relistening to epic stories by subverting those ethical codes in order to shock his audiences—who see the reverse of what they had been expecting. His play does not end with the satisfaction of seeing the victory of good and defeat of evil or the establishment of some eternal moral ethical norms and codes. Through a compounding of traditional elements, Tendulkar portrays harsh realism. Eliot in "Four Quartets" states that "humankind cannot bear very much reality" (Burnt Norton, 1) and Tendulkar using elements from the Indian performing style traditions masks the realism to make it palatable. Though portraying realism, the style is non-realistic. The events are shown to be happening but in a surreal world—the stylized chorus, song, music, dance and miming endow the play with a kind of magic realism. The narrative structure itself consists of detached, highly dramatized scenes. Tendulkar changed the traditional features of the genre to meet changing expectations and a desire to express a different kind of reality.

The element of folk music is a vital vehicle of the play's theme. Music is not an accompaniment but integrated into the theme of the play. In fact, "*Ghashiram* set new yardsticks for evocative and dramatic music". To convey unconventional ideas, it is at times necessary to break the conventional framework. To convey its message the play uses a most popular Marathi art form called "Tamasha". The word is derived from Arabic 'fun', playful entertainment. The folk form is popular and renowned for its adaptability and openness. In fact, *Tamasha* evolved as a "composite, borrowing elements from *Dasavatar, Gondhal, Kirtan* and

Vaghyamurali (worshipers of the folk God *Kandoba*). Yet the concoction became a unique blend with comedy, eroticism and music as integral parts" (Kumar, 407). It is interesting to observe that the *Tamasha* form was first introduced during the period of Peshwas (Kumar, 420). *Tamasha* during the Peshwas was started with prayers to Lord Ganesh or other gods and goddesses. "After the prayers, Radha-Krishna love songs were sung by *Goulan*, i.e. by the other women singers. After that different style of *Lavanis* were sung to entertain the Peshwas" (*Ghasiram Kotwal*, 42). The *Tamasha* artists were given "priority to entertain Peshwas rather than common people and they were treated as *Asthana Kalakars* (who were appointed in palaces by kings)" (*Ghasiram Kotwal*, 42). After the downfall of the Peshwas, *Tamasha* artists lost the patronage and subsequently *Tamasha* artists became wanderers, moving from one place to another. Later, *Tamasha* emerged as a folk art form that subverts established ideologies of social power by presenting them in an inverted and dangerously funny manner, "as a reprieve for people to vent their suppressed anger against hegemonic hierarchies" (Lal, 407). Tendulkar used the popular folk art form but adapted it creatively to suit his theme. As mentioned earlier, *Tamasha* is an assimilation of various traditional art forms, one of which is *Dasavatar* (Ten *Avatars*). The Konkani, Marathi *Dasavatar* is derived from *Yakshagana* and is a religious art form. It brings to life the story of any one of Vishnu's ten *avatars*. *Dasavatar* plays "combine pageant, and entertainment, exhibiting generic mixtures" (Lal, 220). The structure of *Dasavatar* retains some features of Sanskrit theatre and consists of two parts "Purvaranga" (prologue) and "Uttaranga" (the later performance). The performance takes place at night and continues on to the wee hours of the morning. The performance space is "any temporary open stage where the *sutradhara* sits in front of a small orchestra with musicians playing harmonium, drums and cymbals. The troupe worships its deities and masks before the beginning" (*Ghasiram Kotwal*, 220). The play opens with *Ganesh Vandana*, a song in praise of Lord Ganesh, the symbol and giver of success and Saraswati, the Goddess of Learning, both impersonated by actors and a priest performs *puja*. Tendulkar follows the pattern closely. The play begins with an invocation to Lord Ganesh and Saraswati and a priest performs *puja*. But to this duo Tendulkar adds a third deity Lakshmi. This is significant for Lakshmi is the Goddess of wealth and prosperity and it is wealth that Nana and Ghashiram worship. They believe that with wealth and power anything is possible. Ghashiram lives in the world of illusion and believes that one day he will find a husband for his daughter, whom he has used to become Kotwal. He says "It's easy to find a bridegroom when one has money, jewels, and respect!" (*Ghasiram Kotwal*, 398).

Throughout the play a mingling of the sacred and the profane takes place, not only in terms of the obvious ironical co-relationships but also hidden and not so obvious ones. In the *Dasavatar* stories, a superhuman benevolent God destroys a demon to free the earth from his atrocities. In this play, Nana is the mock-heroic *avatar* of God who kills the demon Ghasya and frees the people of Poona from his atrocities. Addressing the citizens of Poona, Nana says: "The citizens of Poona. A threat to the great city of Poona has been ended today (the crowd cheers). A disease has been controlled. The demon Ghasya Kotwal, who plagued all of us, has met his death" (*Ghashiram Kotwal*, 415). He absolves himself of all responsibility for Ghasya's death and attributes everything to fate and the will of the Gods. The irony is that the public, the general citizen, is beguiled and cannot see the truth. The real demons like Nana who play God are not recognized and go scot free.

The *Dasavatar* plays are performed at night and *Ovi* a song by Haridas ends the show at dawn. In *Ghashiram Kotwal*, the lecherous and morally degraded Brahmins spend their nights, not listening to *Dasavatar* stories, but at *Bavannakhani* with women of ill-repute, women like Gulabi. And to show the moral degradation of the Brahmins, Tendulkar mingles *kirtan* and *Lavni* music. Traditionally, dawn is the harbinger of light and appropriate time for religious prayers but ironically, dawn in the play brings to light the most gruesome scenes: Nana leering and entrapping Gauri;

Ghashiram committing atrocities; and Ghashiram being murdered. Devoid of spirituality and their true vocation in life, the protectors and propagators of religion become predators, making a travesty of religion and putting its teaching to their own use to dupe and befool others. Nana often quotes/misquotes the *Gita*. An ironical comparison with the theme of *Dasavatar* cannot be ruled out. While in *Dasavatar* stories, a superhuman, benevolent god destroys a demon to free the earth from atrocities, we have the cunning and authoritarian figure of Nana assuming the role of Vishnu's *avatar*—Krishna to subvert the religious doctrine of the *Gita*. Nana creates demons like Ghasya himself and then destroys them when they get out of hand.

Ghashiram and Nana are consciously immoral. The play presents society as a sordid jungle, where no norms of morality exist and each individual is being consumed by the other. The success of the power games played by people like Nana is extremely depressing as also the degradation of people like Ghashiram, who can pawn their own daughter to rise in life. The play subverts the traditional idea of mythical stories that good conquers evil and is always victorious by presenting the success of evil men like Nana. The play does not shy from revealing the dark but bitter truths of life, but makes them bearable both visually and psychologically by interweaving music and dance in the theme. Tendulkar's play combines "tradition, continuity and change" and shows us that "one can have roots, and roots can grow into flowering trees. And on these trees are birds ready to spread their wings and fly" and they symbolize "the completeness of life and its representative called theatre" (Dattani, 472).

Works Cited

Awasthi, Suresh, "In Defense of the Theatre of Roots" in *Modern Indian Theatre* ed. Nandi Bhatia, OUP, 2009.

Chattopadhyay, Kamaladevi. "Towards a National Theatre" in *Modern Indian Theatre* ed. Nandi Bhatia, OUP, 2009.

Dattani, Mahesh. "Contemporary Indian Theatre and Its Relevance" in *Modern Indian Theatre* ed. Nandi Bhatia, OUP, 2009.

Eliade, Mircea. *Images and Symbols Studies in Religious Symbolism.* Trans. Philip Mairet Kansas City, KS: Sheed Andrews and McMeel, 1961. *Questia.* Web. 17 May 2012.

Eliot, Thomas Stearns. *Poems.* From New York: A.A. Knopf, 1920; Bartleby.com, 2011. <www.bartleby.com/199/>

Kumar, Pradeep. "Tamasha Folk theatre of Maharashtra" Diss. University of Hyderabad, 1996. <http://dspace.vidyanidhi.org.in:8080/dspace/bitstream/2009/1298/1/UOH-1996-355-Prelim.pdf>

Lal, Anand. ed. *Theatres of India: A Concise Companion.* OUP, 2009.

Lipner, J. *Hindus: Their Religious Beliefs and Practices.* London and New York: Routledge, 1994, rpt. 1999.

Tendulkar, Vijay. *Ghashiram Kotwal* in *Collected Plays in Translation.* Trans. Jayant Karve and Eleanor Zelliot. New Delhi: OUP, 2003.

Tendulkar, Vijay. *Ghasiram Kotwal*, English trans. Calcutta: Seagull Books, 1986.

Video recording

Ghashiram Kotwal. Alurkar Music House, Produced by Puppets, Pune, Music Pandit Bhaskar Chandravarkar.

21

The Stories of R.K. Narayan: A Return to Myth, Orality and Folklore

Pulakesh Ghosh

Wole Soyinka in his *Myth, Literature and the African World* observes that man exists in a comprehensive world of myth, history and mores, and myths arise from man's attempt to externalize and communicate his inner intuitions. Although R.K. Narayan was not a religious man in the orthodox sense, as a writer he has his roots in Indian myths and lores. S. Krishnan has traced this back to his childhood memory of oral narration, "undoubtedly absorbed from his grandmother and other old relatives" (*Encyclopaedia,* 1080). R.K. Narayan opulently used folklore, myth and the Indian narrative technique in his novels. Narayan identifies three major narrative devices in the ancient texts: (i) A poetic setting, (ii) A dramatic, dialogue based question-and-answer format, (iii) A layered narrative structure with time shifts. His Sahitya Akademi Awarded novel *The Guide* is mainly based on a Puranic myth of the goddess Ganga descending to earth as the result of the penance of Bhagiratha. The shifts in time scale in the narration recreate in the novel the mould of Hindu epics and *puranas.* In his novel *The Maneater of Malgudi,* Narayan draws upon the paradigm of a mythic ritual—the fall of a demon being synchronized with the celebration of a divine marriage. By using the myth of a demon, Narayan tells an almost unbelievable story with the perfect ease of an oral narrator facing high believing listeners, and he can do so because "he works on the readers (Indian) prior knowledge of, and sharing in, the mythology he invokes" (Kundu, 33). The daily life of the Indians, the traditions of the land and the superstitions and values of Indian life gain a form in some of the stories of his short-story collections. It is worthwhile to explore to what effective use Narayan could put folklore within the tighter form of the short-story. The paper tries to map out the elements of folklore, myth and the oral story telling tradition of India in Narayan's short-stories and the stories retold from Indian epics and legends and examine how they contribute functionally to the structure and the texture of his stories.

Folklore and fairytales draw freely on the imagination and depend for their effect on the wonderful, the impossible, the never-never-land. The backdrop of Narayan's novels and short-stories is Malgudi. His creation of the fictional town, Malgudi, has become a part of modern Indian folklore. In his "Author's Introduction" to *Malgudi Days,* Narayan says, "Where is Malgudi? All I can say is that it is imaginary and not to be found in any map.... If I explain that Malgudi is a small town in South India I shall only be expressing a half-truth, for the characteristics of Malgudi seem to me universal" (viii). He further says, "I can detect Malgudi characters even in New York: for instance, West Twenty-third Street, where I have lived for months at a time off and on since 1959, possesses every element of Malgudi, [...]. Malgudi has been only a concept but has proved good enough for my purposes. I can't make it more concrete however much I might be interrogated" (*Malgudi Days,* viii-ix). Actually, Malgudi is a locale of the mind in the fictional universe of R.K. Narayan.

The age-old story telling tradition of India used the element of fantasy, the device which allowed the writer to have superb flights of imagination. Narayan used fantasy in his short-stories to expose the Indian reality, the superstitious beliefs and attitudes as well as the fine simple feelings of people living in Indian villages. Some short-stories of Narayan, mainly animal stories with the Talkative Man as the narrator, create an atmosphere of fantasy. In his *An Astrologer's Day and Other Stories* and *Lawley Road and Other Stories*, there are about nine stories narrated by "The Talkative Man." All the stories except "A Career" deal with themes and situations unfamiliar, strange, far-fetched and even fantastic. In "The Tiger's Claw", the Talkative Man tells a story about a fantastic incident he happened to face in a station room in the village Koppal. He fell asleep and dreamt, but as the chair barricading the door came hurtling through and fell on him, he opened his eyes and saw at the door a tiger pushing himself in:

> It was a muddled moment for me: not being sure whether the dream was continuing or whether I was awake. (*Malgudi Days,* 41)

In the struggle with the tiger, "I cut out, let me confess, three claws, before I had done with him. I had become bloodthirsty as he" (*Malgudi Days,* 43). In stories like "The Tiger's Claw" the Talkative Man tends to create a world of mystery and wonder created by fantasy, which consists of things wonderful, unheard of and unimaginable. It is pertinent to observe here that Wole Soyinka, in his discussion of the relationship of myth and literature in Africa, dismisses the idea of "fantasy" which he holds to be an individual experience; instead he stresses the concept of a collective inner world and a "primal reality" (*Myth,* 33). The inner world or "inner reality", to use a phrase of Soyinka, is a world made up of deities, demons, beasts, lores, myths, rituals, and its own systems of belief and justice. The nature of "an inner world in a cohesive society is the essentialisation of a rational world-view, one which is elicited from the reality of social and natural experience and from the integrated reality of racial myths into a living morality" (*Myth,* 34). It is to this "cohesive archetypal motifs of a primal inner world" (*Myth,* 34) that Narayan turns for artistic inspiration and thematic-narratorial devices.

In Narayan's short-stories, we perceive the atmosphere of oral story-telling tradition of India. In *The Talkative Man* stories, the Talkative Man starts a story like an ancient village story-teller with audience around him: "I was once camping in Koppal, the most obscure of all the villages that lie scattered about the Mempi region. You might wonder what I was doing in that desolate corner of the earth. I will tell you (*Malgudi*

Days, 39). The Talkative Man can tell a story and entertain his audience very engagingly with all its drama, suspense and excitement like an ancient story-teller. Narayan's "Under the Banyan Tree" is a story on a story-teller who poses to be in time of the tradition of oral narration. Nambi the story-teller of the village Somal in the story could make up a story, in his head. On the nights he had a story to tell. He lit a small lamp and placed it in a niche in the trunk of the Banyan tree. He never repeated the same story, and the village folk considered him a sort of miracle. But the time came when he saw himself failure to complete a story: "And then...and then...what happened?" The final realization of the story-teller is a kind of observatory comment on his own situation: "...Nambi is a dotard.... But what is the use of the jasmine when it has lost its scent? What is the lamp for when all the oil is gone? Goddess be thanked.... These are my last words on this earth; and this is my greatest story" (*Under the Banyan Tree,* 191). Narayan's own comment about the story and its ending in his "Introduction" to *Under the Banyan Tree and Other Stories* (1985) is noteworthy: it is the "story of an old story-teller who concludes his career by taking a vow of silence for the rest of his life, realizing that a story-teller must have the sense to know when to stop, and not wait for others to tell him" (*Under the Banyan Tree,* 191). We can say that Narayan assumes to be the story-teller here as these are the words of his last story in the last published collection of short stories, *Under the Banyan Tree and Other Stories.*

Narayan's the Talkative Man in stories like "Old Man of the Temple", "A Career" and "The Roman Image", etc. is none but the modern impersonation of the "narrator" technique of ancient Indian tradition. "A Career" begins thus:

The Talkative Man said:

> Years and years ago I had a ship. It was in those days when Lawley Extension was not what it is now. (*Under the Banyan Tree,* 43)

His generic name confers upon him the stamp of a universal type:

> .... The fact that Narayan gives him only a generic rather than a specific name suggests that he conceives him mainly as a typical character. In him, Narayan has created and immortalized universal type, familiar particularly to any unhurried and leisurely society, rural and suburban, in which there are people eager to listen to tales and anecdotes and therefore there are tellers of tales. In such a world and such a set up the kind of stories the Talkative Man tells can be told and listened to. He could be regarded as a South-Indian version of a universal type. Both the narrator and his listeners belong to a long established oral tradition of story-telling, which is still alive in our country. (Jayantha, 174)

In this perspective, C.V. Venugopal goes a step farther to find a prototype for the Talkative Man in the Bodhi Sattva of the *Jataka Tales*. Like Valmiki who is a narrator of the *Ramayana* and one of the characters in the narrative, the Talkative Man is a participant in the action of the story in the puranic tradition. Myth-making is evidently a universal feature of the human mind and it is story-generating function of the mind:

> We can add that myth-making is evidently a primal and universal function of the human mind as it seeks a more-or-less unified vision of the cosmic order, the social order, and the meaning of the individual's life. Both for society at large and for the individual, this story-generating function seems irrepressible. The individual finds meaning in his life by making of his life a story set within a larger social and cosmic story. (Cupitt, 29)

Narayan draws on the ancient myths, fables and rituals, and revitalizes them to underscore their contemporary significance. Narayan's short-story "The Snake Song" deals with the old myth of snake's love of music. In the story, the Talkative Man-cum-musician refused to give either food or a coin to a "sadhu". Even he denied him of his music, and then the "sadhu" cursed him:

> I am going. But remember, this is your last day of music. Tomorrow you may exchange your flute for handful of dried dates. (*Malgudi Days*, 64)

When he began the snake song in "Punnaga Varali", he saw a black cobra between the door and himself. It had opened its immensehood and was swaying ecstatically. But the moment the songs ceased, the cobra turned and threw a glance at him, and moved forward. As he felt that he was going to drop dead in a few seconds, he flung down the flute, got up and prostrated before it. Next day his master advised him to throw away the flute because he may get the snake in again if he plays. He wept at the thought of this renunciation and lamented for his roughness with the "sadhu". So, the story also throws light on the mythical belief about the curse of "sadhus". Here we find the reflection of the Hindu view of *karma*, the past action determining the present fortune or misfortune. Narayan himself stated that with "the impact of modern literature we began to look at the gods, demons, sages and kings of our mythology and epics not as some remote concoctions but as types and symbols, possessing psychological validity even when viewed against the contemporary background" (Narayan, 21).

The simplicity and vigour, the clear-cut characters and homely similes, the insistence on the essential human values, which contribute to the uniqueness of the folktale tradition are conspicuously copious in the short-stories of Narayan. To make a vow is a very common folk tradition among Indian people and Narayan gives it a subtle humorous treatment. "Nitya", the first story in *Under the Banyan Tree and Other Stories* is a story about a vow to God in a distant hill that Nitya's head would be shaved clean and his hair offered with due rites if his life was spared. Nitya has grown up; now he is a college boy, and his parents reach the temple with Nitya. But he agrees to give only four inches of his hair. When nobody agreed to his proposal, Nitya grew angry and declined to give an inch. Through the character of Nitya, the new generation representative, Narayan throws some satirical questions against the so-called religious vow-making. In the story "A

Snake in the Grass", a snake has reportedly got into the compound. People were to find it out with every available knife and crowbar and began to hack the garden. A beggar approached and took stock of the sentiment by saying that it was not snake but God Subramanya who has come to visit them. Mother was in hearty agreement: "You are right. I forgot all about the promised Abhishekam. This is a reminder" (*Under the Banyan Tree*, 94). Narayan is, at his humorous best, in his fusion of satire and humour. In stories such as "Attila", he makes full use of the humorist exaggeration. In the story a dog was named Attila and he was named after the "Scourge of Europe." In the story "Lawley Road" of *Lawley Road and Other Stories,* the council suddenly decides to "Nationalize" the names of all streets and parks, in honour of the birth of Independence. They find no difficulty in renaming the Coronation Park—"whose coronation God only knew"—as Hamara Hindustan Park. As a result of what the foolish council did, letters went where they were not wanted, people were not able to say where they lived or direct others to a place. So, in the short-stories of Narayan, we see that satire serves the didactic purpose of folktales and puranic stories.

Thc allcgorical garb of *Panchatantra* stories—of observing the human world through the animal one—has a strong impress on some great short-story writers in English. Narayan's short-stories like "Chippy" included in *Under the Banyan Tree and Other Stories* is a significant story in this respect. The beginning of the story has the traditional ambience of oral story-telling, as if the story-teller is sitting before his audience and starting a story to tell, as if it is a live presentation: "I cannot give a very clear account of Chippy's early life. All that I am in a position to say is that he was born in London,..." (*Under the Banyan Tree,* 77). It is an animal story. Chippy is the name of a pet-dog. He used to enjoy all the cares and caresses of his master. He felt jealous of the new entrant, another dog, in the house, who was sharing the privilege that was solely his due. He left his master's house in despair and fortunately discovered a lane that could satisfy his hunger pleasantly. He decided to spend the rest of his life there. But after two weeks or so, he hungered for his master's company. He came back. His master, Swami, dragged him to the garden and washed him rubbing a bit of soap on his back. Swami informed him, "I am sure you will be miserable to hear this: your little friend is gone.... Don't worry. I'll get you another companion soon" (*Under the Banyan Tree*, 81). What an irony! Chippy is shown to have possessed some characteristics of the human world. Chippy felt a prick of jealousy when a newcomer intrudes into his world of love and warmth. Just as Swami could not sense the gestures or language of Chippy, we fail to read the heart of our fellow beings. "Chippy" is a story in which the human world is observed through the animal one and it falls in the allegorical garb of *Panchatantra* stories.

Narayan retold the two great Indian epics, *The Ramayana* and *The Mahabharata,* as well as well-known incidents from Hindu mythology and folklore in *Gods, Demons, and Others.* If Narayan himself said, "After all, for any short-story writer, the prototype still inevitably remains to be our own epics and mythological stories" (Narayan, 13). Narayan was quoted by S. Krishnan in the "Introduction" to *The Indian Epics Retold* as saying: "I was impelled to retell *The Ramayana* and *The Mahabharata* because that was the great climate in which our culture developed. They are symbolic and philosophical. Even as stories they are so good. Marvellous. I couldn't help writing them. It was part of a writer's discipline". They are not translations, but the response of a highly creative artist to those cultural manifestations that have shaped the national psyche.

Narayan's introduction to *Gods, Demons, and Others*, titled "The World of the Storyteller", is a long and reminiscential essay evoking the homely joys of the rural people who flocked to the story-teller, a most learned man, and derived pleasure and peace from his retelling of stories of gods and goddesses, kings and queens, demons and beasts. For *Gods, Demons, and Others*, and *The Mahabharata*, Narayan went to the original Sanskrit versions. Being ignorant of that language himself, he studied them with a pundit. For *Gods, Demons, and Others*, he chose the stories he wanted to retell from his earlier recollections, and had the pundit read out the original Sanskrit and explain it to him. Narayan said in "The World of the Storyteller", "My method has been to allow the original episodes to make their impact on my mind, as a writer, and rewrite them in my own terms, from recollection" (Narayan, 388). This method is the fundamental feature of orality tradition, telling a story from memory. Again, in keeping with the traditional method, as Narayan said in the same essay, "I have retained the narrator in the background, who occasionally comes forward with an explanation or an introduction" (Narayan, 388). A story like "Draupadi" in *Gods, Demons and Others* begins thus: "The story-teller was in a loquacious mood. He sat me on his mat as usual, brought me a plateful of sweets, and said, 'I collected these at weddings I attended today, quite a lot of them...'" (Narayan, 529). This is how the story-teller is going to start the story of Draupadi and her marriage with five Pandavas. In his *Gods, Demons and Others*, Narayan makes a serious use of ancient Hindu mythology, religion or epics, and his intention behind grouping gods and demons together in the same collection may be traced back to Indian mythology and lores. According to *New Larousse Encyclopaedia of Mythology*, "The Indian conception of demons is special to them, and moreover has many different aspects. To start with, the line separating demons from gods is not very clear. Generally, "Devas" are translated as "gods" and "Asuras" as "demons", but in point of fact both are essentially beings gifted with a remarkable and mysterious power which is manifested simultaneously by moral and physical attributes. For instance, Varuna who enjoys a remarkable moral prestige is ranked as "asura" while Indra, unquestionably less refined, is a "deva". Surya, the sun, is called "the asura-chaplain of the Devas" (Guirand, 334). Later in *Atharva Veda* the word "asura" is applied only to demons, and henceforth that is the generally received meaning. Though the *Devas* and the *Asuras* are often seen at war with each other they come, according to the Satapatha Brahmana, from a common ancestor, *Prajapati*. The only difference, though a major one, was that the *Devas* chose truth and the *Asuras* chose falsehood. "the *Asuras* at first by their lies won riches, but in the end found destruction" (Guirand, 334).

Although Narayan says, "I'd be quite happy if no more is claimed from me than being just a story-teller. Only the story matters, that is all. If readers read more significance into my stories than was meant originally, then that's the reader's understanding of things" (Krishnan, 1082), he hastens to add, "But if a story is in tune completely with the truth of life, truth as I perceive it, then it will be automatically significant." In his article, "Gods, Demons and Modern Times," Narayan emphasizes the contemporary relevance of ancient Hindu literary works. "It is inevitable", he says, "that a writer, though he may be a 20th century product, should see the world and its affairs through the concepts of these myths (Hindu myths) and read their symbolism in modern terms" (*The Literary Criterion,* 50). Referring to Sanskrit literature Narayan observes, "...traditional literature, style and material inevitably become a background for one's own efforts, even if one generally writes of a modern society with recognizable characters and characteristics" (*The Literary Criterion,* 47). He has always said that having firm roots in one's family and one's religion is an imperative for proper self-development. Narayan's retold stories, though generally puranic, deviate from the puranic norm in being less religious, less scholarly, more informal in tone, structure and texture. His puranic or mythological retold stories are more than being mere retold stories as Narayan has made them transcreated stories to suit modern sensibility. In his short-stories and the stories on the Indian epics and legends, Narayan has drawn sustenance from tradition and he has modified it with his individual talent bringing to bear on it the modern perception of life.

Works Cited

Cupitt, Don. *The World to Come.* London: SCM Press, 1982.

Guirand, F. *New Larousse Encyclopaedia of Mythology.* Tr. Richard Aldington and Delano Ames. N.Y.: The Hamlyn Publishing Group, 1959.

Jayantha, R.A. "The Talkative Man Stories of R.K. Narayan: A Study." *R.K. Narayan: An Anthology of Recent Criticism.* Ed. C.N. Srinath. Delhi: Pencraft International, 2005.

Krishnan, S. *Encyclopaedia of Postcolonial Literature in English.* N.Y.: Routledge, 1993.

Kundu, Rama. "R.K. Narayan: A Return to Ritual and Folklore." *New Insights into the Novels of R.K. Narayan.* Ed. M.K. Bhatnagar. New Delhi: Atlantic Publishers & Distributers, 2002.

Mishra, Ganeswar. *How Indian is the Indian Novel in English.* Bhubaneswar: Utkal University, 1990.

Narayan, R.K., *A Writer's Nightmare: Selected Essays 1958-1988.* New Delhi: Penguin Books, 1988.

——. *An Astrologer's Day.* Madras: Indian Thought Publications, 1947.

——. "Gods, Demons and Modern Times." *The Literary Criterion.* X, Winter, 1972.

——. *Lawley Road and Other Stories.* Madras: Indian Thought Publications, 1956.

——. *Malgudi Days.* Madras: Indian Thought Publications, 1943.

——. *The Indian Epics Retold.* New Delhi: Penguin Books, 2000.

——. *Under the Banyan Tree and Other Stories.* Madras: Indian Thought Publications, 1985.

——. "View of an Indian Novelist." *Indian and Foreign Review.* Vol. 16, May 15, 1970.

——. "English in India: The Process of Transmutation." *Aspects of Indian Writing in English.* Ed. M.K. Naik. New Delhi: Macmillan, 1979.

——. *The Maneater of Malgudi* (1961). New Delhi: Penguin Books, 1983.

Ram, Atma. *Perspectives on R.K. Narayan.* Ghaziabad: Vimal Prakashan, 1981.

Ray, Mohit. K. "Re-Orienting the Oriental Story-Telling Tradition: A Study of the Stories of Manoj Das." *Studies in English and Comparative Literature.* Eds. Gortschacher, Wolfgang & Holger Klein, Tubingen, Austria, Stouffenburg Verlag Brigitte Narr Gmb H, 2004.

Soyinka, W. *Myth, Literature and the African World.* Cambridge: Cambridge University Press, 1976.

Venugopal, C.V. *The Indian Short Story in English.* Bareilly: Prakash Book Depot, 1970.

22

The American Hero's Passage to India: Geography, Frontier Myths, and Planetary Perspectives

Alan Johnson

Introduction

Preamble

The mountains in Katra are similar to those around my home institution in Idaho, in the western United States. Idaho State University, where I teach, is located in a hilly region of the U.S. called the "intermountain west" that, although it cannot compare in religious and ancient legacy to the sacred Katra area, holds a special place in American popular history. In what follows, I will describe some national and folk heroes in the United States and suggest some ways of explaining their popularity. I will make three primary points: First, geography is an inseparable part of any mythic of folktale. Second, we need to recognize the intercultural and global interconnections among such stories so that they can speak to us in meaningful, moral ways. Finally, history and folktale overlap in fascinating ways, and it is important for us to evaluate how this overlap helps define our present. In the United States, many groups have their own folk heroes. Only by examining how these stories compete with or complement one another can we begin to recognize how we are all implicated in narrating our world.

American Vistas

The explorers Lewis and Clark, sent by President Jefferson two centuries ago to find a passage to the Pacific, passed through Idaho and have been deified by writers, filmmakers, and artists ever since. Part of Jefferson's eagerness to find a route through what was then considered wild Native American territory was to increase trade, including the trade routes to India that Columbus had failed to discover. But Jefferson also famously wanted the explorers to find the bones of extinct species of animals such as mammoth, as a way of demonstrating that the New World was as biologically important as Europe. Specifically, in his *Notes on the State of Virginia*, Jefferson wanted to counter the famous French scientist's belief that "nature is less active, less energetic on one side of the globe than she is on the other" (Jefferson, 111). Jefferson was so passionate about this that he shipped a load of mammoth bones to Paris as evidence that America bigger and better, at least in the realm of nature. And the notes and collections of Lewis and Clark's expedition provided ample evidence of the continent's rich biodiversity.

In ushering in the white settlement of this part of the continent, Jefferson's explorers instantly entered the quasi-historical, quasi-imaginary realm of national legend, and their expedition became what Henry Nash Smith sixty years ago called "the enactment of a myth that embodied the future". Walt Whitman, in poems like "Enfans d'Adam", celebrated this journey as a myth of newness and regeneration, with new Americans "coming westward from the vales of Kashmere,/ From Asia". In the 1869 poem "Passage to India", which Whitman wrote on the opening of the Suez Canal, Whitman extends his vision of America's connection to other lands by celebrating the cultural richness of India as a means of generating a similarly mythic and geographically imposing new nation. Whitman was no imperialist, but he was quintessentially American in his geographical and futuristic outlook. Like many nineteenth-century Americans, Whitman believed that the young nation needed to produce comparably young heroes who could do two things at once: Stand outside history (like Native Americans) in order to break free of Europe, and, at the same time, start a new history. Whitman tries to imagine this by linking the United States to India, whose deep culture and geography could never, he believed, be subsumed into European history. Historical figures like Lewis and Clark; their indispensable 15-year-old female Native American interpreter Sacagawea, of the Lemhi Shoshone nation (located in Idaho, the state I live in); the Apache warrior-rebel Geronimo; and fictional creations like James Fennimore Cooper's *Natty Bumpo* and Mark Twain's *Huckleberry Finn*—all emblematize the American nation's need for original mythic icons that are free of old paradigms yet still walk an epic national stage in the way that Odysseus and King Ashoka did.

What is notable about the American national desire for such iconic figures is the vast geographical as well as temporal spans they inhabit. Perhaps this is what all nations require, though America's case is somewhat unique given its history of white settlement, slavery, and Native American displacement. The national mythic story of America—and this is true for Canada, as well—is paradoxical, for it draws on the rich stories of the very people, Native Americans, whom the nation romanticizes but also destroys. America also draws on European folktales and, as with President Jefferson and Mark Twain, creates its own rebellious heroes who, in the words of Huckleberry Finn, "light out for the territories", that is, head into the frontier. This talk therefore compares and contrasts America's conception of mythic frontier landscape with other mythic stories by using examples from a range of American, Indian, and African narratives, including recent novels. I do so to argue that only a truly global perspective of myth and folklore can help us make sense of our rapidly changing world, one in which old stories are re-told, new ones emerge, and some are revised to suit modern sentiments.

American Mythic Constructs and Ideals

In his famous 1893 essay "The Significance of the Frontier in American History", Frederick Jackson Turner differentiates the American frontier from the European, a frontier that is "a fortified boundary line running through dense populations. The most significant thing about the American frontier is that it lies at the hither edge of free land. In the census reports it is treated as the margin of that settlement which has a density of two or more to the square mile. The terms is an elastic one, and for our purposes does not need sharp definition. We shall consider the whole frontier belt including the Indian country and the outer margin of the 'settled area.'"[1] The American cultural historian Richard Slotkin observes that Turner celebrates farmers as being at the forefront of American development, as opposed to historian and future President Theodore Roosevelt's preference for what Slotkin calls "the literary mythology of the Frontier, especially [James Fennimore] Cooper's *Leatherstocking Tales*" (*The Last of the Mohicans,* 33). Specifically, Roosevelt favored Cooper's much-copied heroic figure "the man who knows Indians", who forges the way toward the industrialized and civilized present (33, 35). This was, in fact, the popular conception white Americans held, one that was celebrated in the era's cheap dime novels. Turner, by contrast, viewed the present as a corruption of a pure past. Rather than refute Turner's exaltation of rural husbandry as opposed to industry, Roosevelt embraced Turner's thesis as one that supplemented his own man-of-action in the wilderness who is intrinsically democratic and who therefore lays the groundwork for the modern nation (Slotkin, 34).

Elements of these ideas are not new, of course. Homer's Odysseus, for example, is famously a warrior but also the king of an island that sustains itself by harvesting the land. He is certainly the wily man of action, but the success of his ultimate vengeance over the corrupt men who have tried to usurp his rule depends, after all, on a loyal cowherd and swineherd. The *Odyssey* is interspersed with scenes of peaceful eating and story-telling, and it concludes with Athena, who has helped Odysseus throughout his journey home, ordering peace. Seeing Odysseus and his men about to slaughter the suitors' army, Athena "cried out/in a piercing voice that stopped all fighters cold,/Hold back, you men of Ithaca, back from brutal war!.../--

shed no more blood—make peace at once!" The men's weapons fall to "the ground", as if to enjoin the Ithacans to return to the plow. The work of the swineherd and cowherd is vindicated. In a sense, Homer's epic long ago conjoined the ideals of Roosevelt's warrior and Turner's farmer.

The American heroic ideal differs in important ways, however, from that found in ancient epics or in other national folktales. For one thing, the American frontier image spans a continent. It assumes a limitless expanse before the individual, a concept that historically was conceived first as territory and then as knowledge, both usually in acquisitive form. This is perhaps why Americans think in large terms, are prone to suburban sprawl, and jealously guard their personal space. Another distinction is that the American settler mythos is always forward-looking, less historically grounded than that of other nations. It relies on a masculine story that seems to follow what Slotkin calls a plot of violent confrontation, redemption and regeneration (12). For white settler America, at least, it is hard to conceive of a folklore that is separable from the idea of the nation-state. Part of this has to do with the country's immigrant make-up: it has inherited tales from every continent. Slotkin thus distinguishes America's mythic movement as one that impatiently turns certain historical events into linear mythic tales, and that celebrates the white adventurer who knows and interprets Native Americans but who nevertheless turns that knowledge against them, thereby clearing a path for commercial settlement (16). In Slotkin's view, therefore, the American frontier myth attaches to both actual and symbolic forms of violence (13). These themes, moreover, are consciously reiterated for every generation. In modern political terms, American society, as political theorist Paul Schumaker observes, self-consciously emphasizes individual independence and self-governance, which political scientist Rogers M. Smith sees as belonging to "narratives of peoplehood", which stories are told to inspire and unite a diverse population, perhaps in the way Sudipto Kaviraj has described as "fuzzy communities" (Schumaker, 192; Kaviraj, 20). In America, the desire for community therefore competes with the cult of individualism, as is evident in the country's stories (Dundes, 197).

Of course, the broader American mythos is not only made up of the white settler outlook, as Slotkin and other scholars observe. Native Americans, African Americans, and other minorities contribute to the mythic landscape in crucial ways, as we will see. Here, however, it is worth noting the late American folklorist Alan Dundes's view that myth is not the same as folklore. Dundes understands myths to be "'sacred narratives explaining how the world and mankind came to be in their present form' that are told as true and set in the postcreation era", whereas folktales are "narratives understood to be fictional" (*The Meaning of Folklore,* 326). Coming from outside the field of folkloristics, but having taught some notable myths and folktales, Dundes's distinction makes sense to me. Perhaps the more important point here is the debate between those who believe myth conveys universal, archetypal symbols and those who choose to emphasize the human, changeable component of mythic constructs—in sum, the debate between structuralists and comparativists, as Dundes views it. European scholarship would seem to have been dominated by structuralist views, from Freud's notion of universal human aggression as an engine of history to Claude Lévi-Strauss's somewhat Jungian understanding of paradigms of human thinking (*The Meaning of Folklore*, 193). One's views on this matter are of course entwined in one's views of nationhood, as the American example illustrates. Although I cannot pretend to bring a folkloric understanding to this debate, I can try to suggest how these outlooks may apply to some notable American cultural symbols. I therefore turn to some specific narratives that seem to be expressive of American mythologies in all their complexity. In the case of the United States, it is impossible, as I have indicated, to separate the dominant American mythos from the American nation, since they originate at about the same time.

Narrative is, as we know, indispensible to cultural self-perceptions. It is also, as philosopher Alisdair MacIntyre has argued, indispensible to a moral world view. Since we are, as

MacIntyre rightly says, "story-telling animals," mythic tales are "at the heart of things". The nature of story-telling requires a coherent tale that is not only recountable, but accountable to its audience. As MacIntyre puts it, "To be the subject of a narrative" is "to be accountable for the actions and experiences which compose a narratable life" (MacIntyre, 173-76). This, in turn, requires that the listeners or readers of this tale be accountable participants in it, for both the story-teller and the listener/reader, to continue MacIntyre's insight, are necessary in order to make sense of a complex world and in order to create a whole, unified, and coherent community. It follows that those who imagine themselves to be "detachable from [their] social and historical roles."

We thus return to the importance of history, but history as narrative rather than ideology. Here MacIntyre's views align with Slotkin's, for both perceive how traditional narratives necessarily encompass "continuities of conflict", a "living tradition" whose continual re-telling and re-negotiation enable people to live a moral life. In this sense, myths and folktales equip us with the intellectual and moral capacity to "grasp...those future possibilities which the past has made available to the present" ("Narratives", 1-39). The correlative to this point is that a loss of such living traditions may lead to a loss of communal or national direction. Nobel Prize-winning novelist Toni Morrison has helped turn our critical attention to this living tradition in demonstrating how the American ideals of "autonomy, authority, newness and difference, [and] absolute power"—the very attributes exhibited by Cooper's *Deerslayer* hero Hawkeye—are "made possible by, [and] shaped by" the presence of black Americans, or what she calls "Africanism" (Morrison, 44). Given the comparative silence on this presence, Morrison advocates a re-telling of historical remembrance that she terms, in the words of her character Sethe in the novel *Beloved*, "rememory". Morrison means this to be both verb and noun, an active re-enactment of past memory as it shapes the present (Morison, 47). The same is true of Native Americans, whose presence and stories are interwoven in the American mythos in complex and often contradictory ways. What is clear is that these various strands of American story-telling cannot be separated from one another. (Yet another strand of stories is that of more recent American immigrants, though I do not have space here to consider those.) In what follows, I compare and contrast such historical myth-making and Native American myths to reflect something of the contradictions that, as Michael Elliott argues, abound in any understanding of U.S. self-fashioning (Morison, 10-11).

Stories: Heroes, Tricksters, Mountains

A favorite popular group of settler tales in North America features Paul Bunyan, a logger, or lumberjack, who roams the forests with his giant blue ox, Babe. American schoolchildren read about Bunyan's unusual birth, which required five—rather than one—stork to carry the giant infant to his parents' home. His laughter and clapping were so powerful that they broke every window in the house. At just seven months old, he sawed the legs off his parents' bed in the middle of the night. He was also responsible for the Grand Canyon: as an adult, he and his blue ox dug out the canyon when he dragged his axe behind him. He also created the great mountain called Mount Hood by piling rocks atop his giant campfire to put it out, and dug out the Great Lakes in order to create a place for his ox to drink. Like all such tales, Paul Bunyan's origins are mixed. He may have been conceived by French-Canadian loggers in the early nineteenth century, with the name Bunyan possibly rooted in the French "Bonyenne", a colloquial French-Canadian term of surprise similar to "My Goodness!" On the other hand, Bunyan is the surname of a favorite seventeenth-century Christian author among North America's English settlers, John Bunyan, of *Piligrim's Progress* fame. Americans embellished the tale by saying that two legendary historical figures, the outdoorsman Daniel Boone (on whom novelists James Fennimore Cooper based his character Hawkeye) and Davy Crocket (also a frontiersman who died in the iconic Texas siege of the Alamo), had befriended Bunyan and gifted him the giant ox. Today, several towns feature Paul Bunyan exhibits and even giant, touristy statues. Bunyan is a classic

American legendary figure who incorporates the values modern Americans idealize: He is innocent, free, and larger than life, and he works hard, welcomes challenges, invokes humor and, perhaps most importantly, is intimately connected to the landscape. Perhaps his height affords him a vantage point that we all dream of, the ability to have a bird's-eye view of the land we inhabit. Although Bunyan is selfless and cares for those around him, his vocation of tree-cutter means that he is in the service of larger, more industrial forces about which he is seems unaware. Perhaps most importantly, he has no sacred ideals as such.

Native American lore expresses personal attributes that contrast with Bunyan's. Their folk characters usually convey the following: a sacred awareness of the land; quietness (as opposed to white American volubility); patience (versus modern American impatience) and an elastic sense of time; the sharing of one's belongings with all other tribal members (i.e. mutualism); an "open work ethic"; a holistic approach to life, at once physical, spiritual and communal; and, perhaps given their long experience with oppression, wariness about non-tribal members' intentions.[2] Rather than being occupying a large space, as does Bunyan, Indian folk characters are skilled at changing shape, running stealthily, and evading capture. But as in many traditions, the figure of the trickster such as the Coyote Trickster, works to subvert social norms and cross cultural boundaries. Folklorist S.E. Schlosser defines this well: "A Trickster is a mischievous or roguish figure in myth or folklore who typically makes up for physical weakness with cunning and subversive humor. The Trickster alternates between cleverness and stupidity, kindness and cruelty, deceiver and deceived, breaker of taboos and creator of culture."[3] Native American tales of the Coyote trickster celebrate these features. He is a figure who is simultaneously sacred and profane, foolish and wise. Perhaps most interesting is the Native American trickster's ability to adapt to the times, so that his duality and mischief target European American settlers and antagonists such as General George Armstrong Custer.

The Custer Myth is important to both Anglo-American and Native American cultures, so it is worth taking a moment to consider its implications for myth and folklore. Custer's "Last Stand" in 1876 became for whites of the period a symbol of selfless bravery by an American Army officer at a time when the nation was still in the process of healing following the violent American Civil War. A hero of Lincoln's northern army during that war, Custer turns his attention to the west, where the so-called "Indian problem" seems intractable to the United States Government. For Native Americans, of course, Custer symbolized the opposite: a hated representative of enemy forces. Interestingly, even today these two myths collide in the media, although Custer's reputation has suffered of late. How might the trickster figure play a role in the story of this mythic encounter? Robin Derosa, drawing in part on the critical insights of African American scholar Henry Louis Gates, Jr., advocates a "trickster criticism" that is aware of its own shortcomings even as it strives to interpret the texts at hand ("Critical Tricksters", 182). In Derosa's sense, we would look at both sides of the Custer Myth, both written histories and transcribed Native testimonies, not in order to arrive at a definitive version but, rather, to highlight the inevitable contestation at the heart of story-telling. In other words, mythic tales are performative, not static, and scholars need to take this into account—even to the extent, Stromberg argues, of producing self-consciously contingent criticism. Perhaps most importantly, the American Indian trickster, like other forms of this narrative device, has (in Gerald Vizenor's words) "no histories and "no political or economic signification" (13)—quite distinct from the Anglo-American view of Custer.

We can see elements of this in the Native American version of the Paul Bunyan story. A relatively recent story told among the Anishinabe people of Minnesota, for example, describes how their trickster hero Wenabozho fights Paul Bunyan to stop the white lumberjack from cutting down every tree in their area. Wenabozho defeats the unbeatable Bunyan, who is forced to leave. The story also operates a natural-origin myth, for it explains why the forests have remained untouched in recent memory (Lawrence, 130). To return to the formation of the Grand Canyon, a legend among the Hualapai people of Arizona similarly counters the Paul Bunyan-creation story. The Hualapai hero Pack-i-tha-a-wi created the canyon after a great flood. Using a large stone knife and heavy wooden club, he dug into the ground beneath the flood until he had formed a trough through which the water could rush to the sea. Another Native people of this region, the Hopi, believe that their ancestors climbed out of the earth from the underworld through the Grand Canyon, symbolizing a womb-like entry into the surface world. This is why some Hopi believe it is wrong to try to re-enter the canyon: to do so is to flirt with death.[4] These tales are clearly more mythic and less folkloric, and emphasize the creation of a people-centered, as opposed to individual-centered, world.

Even when Native American stories incorporate historical figures such as U.S. Army General and Civil War hero Custer, they are comparatively more mythic than Anglo accounts, and are woven into the ancestral history of the people. That is to say, in the imaginary of many Native peoples, especially the Lakota Sioux, Custer's death in 1876 at the hands of Sioux warriors on the American plains is woven into a collective and sacred memory that, through oral story-telling, has withstood non-Indian efforts to erase it. The essentials of the event are this: General Custer, a flamboyant war hero and self-promoter, was leading his men into the territory of the Sioux people, in what is now the state of Montana. Previous army victories over Indians had led Custer to believe that he would have an easy time of it. To his great and fatal surprise, the Sioux had great numbers of warriors on the ready, and used ingenious tactics to annihilate Custer and his men. The event continues to be known popularly as "Custer's Last Stand".

For Native Americans, not surprisingly, Custer holds none of the mythic attributes we find in a folk figure like Bunyan. He is, instead, a man who is emblematic of a white settler society that steals Native land. Michael Elliott has discussed the ways in which the Custer myth has been contested ever since the battle occurred, and how the Native American viewpoint has not only survived, but emerged as an influential symbol of Toni Morrison concept of "re-memory", of the necessary re-telling, and subsequent re-formation, of historical consciousness. Yet the Native American viewpoint has, as Elliott shows, become part of a "political[ly] emotional" point of reference in the consciousness of nationalism ("Indian", 1010). A telling point in this regard is the 1991 re-naming of the event site from "Custer Battlefield" to "Little Bighorn Battlefield". They Lakota Sioux people work for the National Park Service as guides, and a new memorial signifying a Native perspective opened in 2003. The fact remains, then, that both Native peoples and the U.S. Government treat the site as sacred ground.

The modern Native American writer Sherman Alexie has dealt with this fact in both serious and humorous ways such as in the great 1998 film he wrote (and which Native Americans directed and acted in) titled *Smoke Signals*. Early in the film, young Native American boys playing basketball sing:

> Oh, I took the ball to the hoop and what did I see?/
>
> General George Armstrong Custer was a-guarding me, a-guarding me. (Elliott, 994)

The words and context point to a living trickster tradition that uses humor to comment on a complex and difficult world. Vine Deloria, Jr. was a Lakota scholar who wrote about this in his well-known 1969 book *Custer Died for Your Sins*, a title taken from an ironic Native American slogan. Deloria recounts the joke Native peoples tell about Custer: He was, they say, well-dressed for battle, because when they found his body, he had on an Arrow shirt. And Native Americans joke about one another. The Sioux, who defeated Custer, still "tease other tribes...for not having been at the [battle]" (Deloria, 150-52).

Where settler and Native American stories do coincide is in their general understanding that geography is destiny, that living off the land, and an appropriate respect for the land, are critical to humanity. More importantly, all parties in the contest over land recognize that without stories, there can be no real connection to the environment one inhabits. Consider the iconic, table-topped mountain in the western U.S. state of

Wyoming called Devil's Tower, which some people know from its prominence in the 1977 Steven Spielberg science fiction film *Close Encounters of the Third Kind*. In the film, the protagonist, played by Richard Dreyfus, has persistent visions of the mountain, so much so that his family believes he is mentally disturbed. The truth, as we learn, is that aliens are communicating with him, and with another character, subliminally, instructing them to go to the mountain so that the aliens can peacefully land their spacecraft and meet with representative humans. In choosing this famous mountain for the alien landing, the film re-fashions the mountain's past association with the Frontier myth, which was also part of Hollywood mythologizing. Native peoples, notably the Lakota Sioux, Kiowa and Cheyenne, have always viewed the mountain as sacred land—which may partly explain why Spielberg chose it for his film. Rising to 1500 vertical meters straight from the plains, and distinguished by grooves along the full length of its cylindrical sides, the mountain catches one's eye from many miles away. The mountain has also been a favorite of climbers for over a century, and this has led to friction between Native peoples in the area and climbing enthusiasts. Recently, climbers went to court to contest tribal claims to all rights to the mountain, including the right to prohibit any climbing in the sacred month of June. As Lakota scholar Deloria puts it, "It's not that Indians should have exclusive rights" to the mountain. Instead, "[i]t's that the location is sacred enough so that it should have time of its own." Devil's Tower is, in other words, animated by a spiritual presence that requires a measure of peace and quiet, away from human interference—a concept that tends to confuse non-Native Americans.[5]

To better understand this outlook, it is worth recounting a popular Native American story about the mountain's origin. The story goes that long ago, two young Native children are lost in the prairie, the plains of North America. After a time of play, the children discover that they have lost their sense of direction. After several days of surviving off the land, they are chased by a giant grizzly bear called Mato. Just as the bear is about to catch and eat them, they pray to their Creator,

Wakan Tanka, to save them. All at once the ground shakes and rises, and they along with it. In a few moments, they find themselves perched on a flat-topped mountain, with the giant bear below them. The bear, unable to reach the boys, is infuriated and claws at the mountain for a long time, creating its distinctive groove marks. Hence, the Native American name Matho Thipila, or Bear's House. This also explains the English name, which an American army officer misinterpreted in 1875, just one year before the Custer battle, to mean "Bad God's Tower", which later shifted to "Devil's Tower". The conflict between Native American myth and modern recreation symbolizes the continuing power of such sacred stories and the cultural tension that can result in our modern world. The Native American novelist M. Scott Momaday, whose Kiowa tribe inhabits this region, conveys his own awe at this landscape in a book of great poetry that describes his people's modern predicament. "There was a house made of dawn", he writes in his 1968 novel *House Made of Dawn*. "It was made of pollen and of rain, and the land was very old and everlasting. There were many colors on the hills, and the plain was bright with different-colored clays and sands. Red and blue and spotted horses grazed in the plain.... The land was still and strong" (1). And in *The Way to Rainy Mountain*, he describes hearing the creation story of Devil's Tower from his grandmother. In an interview, Momaday says, "I certainly can point to an understanding of the relationship between man and the landscape.... I grew up with that, and that's such an important equation in the Indian world. That has been of great value to me all my life."[6]

Another major dimension of America's folktale tradition comes from the African-American community, particularly through music, notably folk ballads and slave songs. For example, the famous "John Henry" song tells the story of an American folk hero in typically exaggerated fashion. John Henry is a "steel-driver", a man who must use a hammer and chisel to cut through rock in the order to form railway tunnels. In the legendary song and story, John Henry's famed ability as the best steel-driver in the land leads to a wager that his hammer and chisel cannot out-perform the new invention of the steam-powered drill. He wins the contest, of course, but dies immediately afterward, still gripping his tools. John Henry is thus in the direct tradition of Paul Bunyan and other larger-than-life heroes, in this case one whose human spirit is a kind of last stand against modern machinery. Significantly, John Henry is a former slave who epitomizes black strength and the ordinary working man, and who defeats in competition the white owner of the machine. But his death also allegorizes the inevitable triumph of the machine, and it is the contestation of machine against nature, the perceived threat of mechanization against an innocent and pastoral world that Leo Marx has called the "machine in the garden", a tension that has defined, and continues to define, American conceptions of environment and technology. The continued popularity of the John Henry ballad attests to this tension and to the values American society idealizes. Perhaps the lines from the song are self-explanatory in this regard. When John Henry's foreman describes the new steam drill to him, Henry replies, in the famous lines from the song: "A man ain't nothing but a man/ But before I let that steel beat me down/ I will die with this hammer in my hand." When he dies, the lines intone: "Oh they took John Henry to the graveyard/ And they buried him in the sand/ And every locomotive come rolling by/ Said, 'There lies a steel driving man, Lord,/ John Henry was a steel driving man'" (Bicknell, 173-80). But according to Alan Dundes, John Henry's image proves to be less about the machine-versus-man ideal or even about a former slave's revenge against white power. One reason for its continuing appeal to dominant society, Dundes points out, is that Henry poses no threat to this dominance: his hand clutching a hammer could never form a fist, and his death preserves, as if in a museum, the image of a good man devoted not of freedom, but to labor and his white employer's business (Bicknell, 281). How one interprets the ballad, then, depends upon one's current position in society, a position that changes from place to place and over time. We interpret stories according to our prejudices.

I conclude with yet another folk story originating in the Dutch settler community of New York, the famous "Rip Van Winkle". As you may recall, the story Washington Irving offered in his famous version, published in 1819, describes how the young man Rip, who lives among the Adirondack mountains of New York in the 1760s, escapes his nagging wife and small children by wandering off into the hills with his dog. A man calls out to him—a man dressed in old Dutch clothing who needs Rip's help to carry a barrel of ale further up the hill. They eventually arrive at a natural hollow, where Rip discovers the source of the thunder-like sounds he had heard earlier: a group men dressed just like Rip's strange companion are playing a game of nine-pins, an early form of bowling. No one says a word, but all drink from the barrel of ale, including Rip, who falls into a deep sleep. When he awakens, he finds his gun has rusted, he has a long gray beard, and his dog is missing. When he returns to his village, no one seems to recognize him, and he finally discovers that his wife has passed away and many of his friends have died in some kind of war. Rip declares his loyalty to King George III, whose portrait had been painted on a pub sign, and which Rip does not realize has been replaced by a portrait of George Washington. After meeting another man named Rip Van Winkle and speaking to others, he learns that he has been away for twenty years, during which the Americans have defeated British forces to found a new nation. The mysterious men he met in the mountains, we are told, are the ghosts of seventeenth-century explorer and navigator Henry Hudson's Dutch crew. Rip reunites with his daughter, who takes him in, and soon the other men in the village envy his twenty-year absence as Rip resumes his idle habits—this time drinking and chatting at the George Washington pub.

Irving's story may owe elements to the German folktale of Peter Klaus, a Jewish story about a man named Honi M'agel, an ancient Christian story about a group of worshippers who escape Roman persecution by sleeping for 200 years, a story that the Quran also re-tells. Indeed, Irving, who wrote a biography of Prophet Muhammad, may have discovered his source here.[7] Whatever his inspiration, Irving's story echoes some common story-telling themes: the oppressed person's, or group's dream of escaping difficulties; the lure of untouched nature for the townsperson; and, most importantly in this story, the recognition that political change does not always result in change for the common person. The story's irony, after all, is that Rip completely misses the most eventful time in United States history, and that there is a new King George named Washington. Rip's escapist dream also echoes a slave story about escaping slaves who magically walk back to Africa on the bottom of the sea or who fly there,[8] just as the theme of change resembles Native American tales of changes wrought by nature or, more recently, European settlers. A literary critic might see in Irving's story an allegory of interpretation: Rip cannot see the difference between the image of King George and George Washington, resulting in his momentary misinterpretation of his fellow villagers' lives. This begs the question: If daily life remains the same—that is, if the semantics of everyday existence do not noticeably change—how does the change in a single sign, a single component, alter this semantics? Perhaps Irving's contemporary readers read into this a caution against complaisance and apathy; or they may have detected a wry acknowledgement of the limited power of politics far away from the centers of power. What remains, of course, is a story, one whose meanings shift with time.

Conclusion

In conclusion, I think it is fitting to return to Whitman's poetic invocation of the Lewis and Clark transcontinental journey, "Passage to India". Since that expedition in the first decade of the nineteenth century, certain American politicians had formed the doctrine of Manifest Destiny, by which they meant that European-Americans had a divine right to establish dominion over the breadth of the continent. Whitman, perhaps the closest America has to a national poet, and whose writing seems to me to resemble Tagore's, views territorial expansion not as conquest, but as an opportunity for countries to connect with one another to produce "one great bond" in "peace, and piety".[9] Among the images of landscape in Whitman's poem, that of mountains seems most pronounced. He describes, for instance, the western range of the Rocky Mountains, the Wasatch range: "I see...the Wasatch mountain and the/ Eagle's Nest, I pass the/ Promontory, I ascend the Nevadas,/ I scan the nobel Elk mountain wind/ around its base...." He wants to link these to "the gardens of Asia" and to Bengal's "flowing literatures, tremendous epics" and "religions". In fact, the image of this passage to India becomes a metaphor for the soul's journey across time and space, its "Passage to more than India!" Like the twentieth-century Greek poet Constantine Cavafy's great poem "Ithaca", the epic journey of people across vast seas and landscapes is every individual's life journey. Invoking the island home of Odysseus, Cavafy writes" "As you set sail for Ithaka/ hope the voyage is a long one,/ full of adventure, full of discovery". Towards the poem's, we have: "Ithaka gave you the marvelous journey./ Without her you would not have set out."[10] The land, then, prompts our voyages, and its natural monuments—the Columbia River for Native Americans and for Lewis and Clark, Devil's Tower for the Kiowa people, the mountains of New York for Rip Van Winkle—mark the way, just as the mountains of Jammu mark the way for pilgrims—and, I might add, for scholarly conferences. Our gathering here also reminds us that we do not journey alone. Just as Lewis and Clark could not have made their journey to the Pacific Ocean without the help of no less than twenty-four separate Native American nations, so do we travel with companions, both living and past, which include the stories we tell each other to make sense of our journey. For Cavafy, Homer is a constant companion; for many in Bengal, it is Tagore. For many of us here, no doubt, stories from across the globe inform our understanding of what it means to be human. As the character in Amitav Ghosh's novel *The Shadow Lines* puts it, "[S]tories are all there are to live in, it [is] just a question of which one[s] we choose" (179).

Notes

1. Turner, "The Significance of the Frontier in American History," originally presented 1893; accessed at: us.history.wisc.edu/hist102/pdocs/turner_frontier.pdf
2. From <http://nwindian.evergreen.edu/curriculum/Values Behaviors.pdf>; accessed 12 March 2012.
3. Cited in *ibid*. Note, too, the following description: "In the antics of the Coyote Trickster, people sometimes learn more about their own weaknesses and foolishness. This figure teaches through his mistakes and by being a bad example for the Indians. Through Coyote's actions, the Native Americans learn to laugh at themselves and their occasional acts of self-deceit. Jill Stefko has this to say about the Coyote Trickster: 'He is often fooled and astonished by the outcome of his own pranks. He survives this, then goes onto not learning by his mistakes and makes bigger ones. He denotes both folly and wisdom and the balance of the two. Wisdom is hidden in the foolery. He may have lost the skirmish, but remains unbeaten. Coyote is keeper of magic, teacher and creator...Trickster[s] of Native American tales often gets duped, but he always rebounds and, at some point, even teaches himself lessons he learns from." However, because he is a Trickster figure, he is not all bad. He brought fire to the Native Americans, but can also cause floods. Coyote is a very chaotic neutral figure, more seen as a force of nature (or maybe a deity) than a particular, mortal person or figure. Coyote is sometimes seen to be a shapeshifter or an opportunist. He is also seen to be cunning and stealthy. "He can represent white and dark magic, creativity, illumination, experience, and new life" (Stefko). Tricksters dissolve boundaries and break taboos. They delight in the ambiguous and in confusion." http://eng254project.webs.com/coyoteasatrickster.htm. 3/12/12
4. <http://grand-canyon-vacation-information.com/grand-canyon-mystery.html>; accessed 11 March 2012.
5. Deloria online quote reference: http://www.sacredland.org/devils-tower/
6. Momaday, Interview 28 June 1996, Academy of Achievement, Sun Valley, ID; accessed: http://www.achievement.org/autodoc/printmember/mom0int-1
7. Wikipedia entry, accessed March 2012.

8. Regarding such stories, see (March 2012): <http://themoonlitroad.com/coastal-georgia-slavery-ibo-landing/>.
9. "Passage to India," accessed March 2012 at: <www.daypoems.net>.
10. Constantin Cavafy, "Ithaka," accessed March 2012 at: http://www.ithaka.org/poem>.

Works Cited

Bicknell, Jeanette. "Reflections on 'John Henry': Ethical Issues in Singing Performance," *The Journal of Aesthetics and Art Criticism* 67: 2, Spring, 2009.

Bronner, Simon J. *The Meaning of Folklore*. Ed. Bronner. Logan, UT: Utah State University Press, 2007.

Deloria, Jr. *Custer Died for Your Sins: An Indian Manifesto*. New York: Avon, 1970.

Derosa, Robin. "Critical Tricksters: Race, Theory, and Old Indian Legends," Ed. Ernest Stromberg *American Indian Rhetorics of Survivance*. Univ. of Pittsburgh Press, 2006.

Dundes, Alan. *The Meaning of Folklore*. Utah: Utah State University Press, 2007.

Elliott, "Indian Patriots on Last Stand Hill," *American Quarterly* 58: 4. Dec. 2006.

Freud, Sigmund. *Civilization and Its Discontents*. New York: Norton and Co., 1961.

Ghosh. *The Shadow Lines*. New York: Penguin, 1988.

Jefferson. *Notes on the State of Virginia: With Related Documents*. Ed. David Waldstreicher. New York: Bedford/St. Martin's, 2002.

Lawrence, W. Gross, "Cultural Sovereignty and Native American Hermeneutics in the Interpretation of Sacred Stories of the Anishinaabe," *Wicazo Sa Review* 18:2. 2003.

MacIntyre, "Narratives of the Good Life Guided by Living Traditions," Ed. Paul Schumaker, *The Political Theory Reader*. Malden, MA: Wiley-Blackwell, 2010.

Marx, Leo. *The Machine in the Garden*. OUP. 1964.

Momaday. *House Made of Dawn*. New York: Harper Perennial, 2010.

Morrison. *Beloved*. New York: Everyman's Library, 2006.

Morrison. *Playing in the Dark: Whiteness and the Literary Imagination*. New York: Vintage, 1992.

Sudipto, Kaviraj. "The Imaginary Institution of India," Ed. P. Chatterjee and G. Pandey. *Subaltern Studies* VII. Delhi: OUP, 1992.

Vizenor. "A Postmodern Introduction," *Narrative Chance: Postmodern Discourse on Native American Indian Literatures*. Norman, OK: Univ. of Oklahoma Press, 1993.

23

When N'api Dances Day: Myth, Orality and Process in Pikuni (Blackfeet) Trickster Narratives

Jay Hansford C. Vest

In offering this paper, it is my intent to address the trickster in a tribal Native American-Indian context specifically drawing upon the Pikuni or Blackfeet tribe of Montana and Alberta. The trickster is a primal foundation that expresses irony within the oral traditions of Native America. Often associated with an immoral mischief-maker, the trickster takes on several forms within these indigenous traditions. These forms include the rabbit-hare throughout much of the eastern woodlands and southeast; iktomi, the spider, in the plains Dakota traditions; coyote as trickster is found widely throughout the west; raven is the figure associated with this tradition in the northwest coast area; sacred clowns manifest this character among the pueblo Indians of the southwest; and "old man" serves as trickster throughout much of the subarctic region, far northeast and northwest plains. In all cases, he is a liminal figure who lives by his desires particularly when seeking food and sex. Often manifest within his desire-fullness, he manages to transpose his actions into unconscious acts of creation thereby serving the heroic benefit to his respective people. In this manner, the trickster is an ironically transformative figure. As creator, he generates innovation by intentionally serving his base desires; unlike an almighty god, he expresses no cosmogonic master plan but imbues life with an ironic chaos as a means to creation. In his wanton gluttony and self-serving behavior, he is a slave of his desires; he is caught in a quagmire of immoral mischief where he is fool or anti-hero in reference to normative social mores and morality. Even when his actions produce good, it is done so by accident and he is at best an ironic cultural hero in such cases.

Trickster narratives are a special form of myth in the sense that mythology within an oral tradition is an expression of the sacred word revealing metaphorical truths that speak beyond the simple location of our abstract modern ideologies. In this case, myth is a much deeper narrative form born in orality beyond the abstract influence of literacy. Problematically, post-Platonic notions of myth have been decreed illusionary suggesting a void of wisdom and infused with lies and falsehood; this conception is itself deluded and misbegotten in the vortex of literacy and the birth of Plato's philosophy (Eric, 1-19).

As a means of introducing this topic of the trickster in Pikuni (Blackfeet) mythology, there are three themes that I wish to discuss in the context of traditional indigenous communities. Herein, I am referring to myth, orality and process as a trio of epistemological function in any given indigenous based society. The knowing distinction manifest in the transformation of a society from *oralcy* to literacy is critical as a means to discovering intrinsic insights into a people's indigenous ethos (*The Technologizing*). Hence, I speak of an oral paradigm characteristic of a pre-literate reality free of secondary rationalizations and bound in an organic world of ecological interaction. In contradistinction with *oralcy*, there is the birth of modernism featuring an all consuming ideological orientation born in the advent of literacy; hence, literate societies are subject to their ideological abstractions and divorced of the essential organic understanding of the world about us (Abram). It is in the literate paradigm that societies fall into the illusion of metanarratives—the notion of universal absolute truth claims—and terminal creeds that ideationally have no organic context and are thereby lacking in a natural referent. In my opinion, such divergent epistemologies serve to therefore threaten our very organic existence and pose a grave danger to our planetary ecosystems. These ideological abstractions bear the risk of losing touch with organic reality and threaten our very nature of existence; hence, in offering these examples of an organic paradigm, I hope to trigger some small insight and methodological means into the discovery and ability to recover residual orality in our contemporary literary bound world. To this extent, I suggest "process" refer to an ecological based epistemology born of *oralcy*. Accordingly, I will attempt to elaborate upon the character and meaning of—myth, orality, and process—as they serve to orient the reader to a traditional oral-based paradigm necessary for discerning insights into the primal trickster narratives to be examined in this paper.

Turning first to a deeper reading of myth, we can acknowledge that "mythology is not a lie, mythology is poetry, it is metaphorical. It has been well said that mythology is the penultimate truth—penultimate because the ultimate cannot be put into words" (Campbell, 163). Affirming this perspective, Thoreau called myth "an approach to that universal language which men have sought in vain". Indeed, he continues: "This fond reiteration of the oldest expressions of truth...is the most impressive proof of a common humanity.... To some extent mythology is only the most ancient history and biography. So far from being false or fabulous in the common sense, it contains only enduring and essential truth, the I and you, the here and there, the now and then, being omitted. Either time or rare wisdom writes it.... In the myth as a superhuman intelligence uses the unconscious thoughts and dreams of men as its hieroglyphics to address men unborn. In the history of the human mind, these glowing and ruddy fables precede the noonday thoughts of men as Aurora the Sun's rays" (Thoreau, 52-53).

Manifesting its Greek etymological origins, myth expresses the sacred in words. Furthermore, myth is an expression of time beyond human knowing, and hence the events and realities manifest therein are altogether different from the facts that concern everyday life. In myth, cosmological and chaotic events and concomitant values are expressed in the now; they are "time outside of time", wherein time as a mundane event is suspended in favor of the eternal verities of creation happening with each narrative recital. Mythic time, therefore, reveals creation as an ongoing, continuing cycle where the forces of nature are realities of this eternal process. "The recitation of a myth defining creation, for example, is not experienced in terms of an event of linear past, but rather of happening of eternal reality, true and real now and forever, a time on the 'knife edge between the past and the future'" (Brown, 84-85). Myth, then, informs us of truth; not in the linear context of fact-based history or science, but in the events of ever-active creation, occurring and recurring in the cycles of days or seasons and in death and rebirth. Myths respond to creation in the immediacy of process; informing of creation as it is "ever happening and observable through all the forms and forces of creation" (Brown, 86).

Myth, moreover as mystical knowledge is the literature of the spirit; it occupies the same zone as dream, a zone that Campbell call "the Wisdom Body". This insight stands in stark contrast to the Cartesian mode to think of consciousness as being particular to the head. Campbell's notion of "the Wisdom Body" embraces consciousness in the body as born of nature; he explains: "when you go to sleep, it's the body that's talking. What the body is moved by are energies that it does not control. These are the energies that control the body. They come in from the great biological ground" (Campbell, 94). Myths are thus metaphorical of the spiritual potentiality in the human body, a potentiality that is itself born of nature and which observes that the same powers that animate human life also animate the life of the world (Campbell, 22). Upon recognizing this wisdom, it is conceivable that we might understand Thoreau's maxim, "in wildness is the preservation of the world"; moreover, given that myth is the penultimate truth which is born of the body as acted upon by nature, then truly it is a perennial philosophy of wildness beyond human desire and intentionality.

It has been said that the function of myth is to put humanity in accord with nature; indeed, myths have to do with creating relationships. Mythic narratives abound with human visitors learning from the nature; according to Turner, "such narratives express the interconnectedness and interdependence of all life" (Turner, 11). In this context, the living myth manifests the interlocking cycles of nature—inclusive of mineral, energy, flora and fauna. Embracing without distinction both the numinous and the phenomenal, myths center us upon the timeless realities amid which we live.

Turning to orality, we would do well to consider the comments of Jesuit priest Paul Le Jeune, who in 1636 declared, "Metaphor is largely in use among these peoples; unless you accustom yourself to it, you will understand nothing" (Thwaites). Speaking from his experience with the Algonquian peoples, Le Jeune is referring to the Native disposition to allegorical expression and manifest natural referents. This is a figurative system associated with oral discourse acknowledging reason in the presence of the object as opposed to a stipulative symbolism, which reasons in the absence of the object. We can observe examples of this practice in the Pikuni (Blackfeet) language used for the naming of themselves in confederated tribes. In the pre-conquest origin, three tribes composed the Nitsitapi confederacy—the Siksika, the Kainaa, and the Pikuni. In the primal understanding of these names, the metaphorical configuration that Le Jeune references is aptly expressed. The term "Siksika" refers to the blackfoot or hoof of the bison, hence the English translation of Blackfoot. Kainaa or many chiefs, references the organic nature of the bison herd where the bulls and their harems constitute the animals' social organization in exemplifying herd reproduction and fecundity. In the third tribal confederate, Pikuni, there is reference to bison and its annual cycle. Translated as scabby round robe, Pikuni, denotes the spring molt where, following winter, the bison shed their hair and begin anew their annual life cycle. Together these tribes constitute a linguistic and social fellowship of "real people", the Nitsitapi, where all member tribes speak the same language. In an earlier expression sometimes used to denote the confederacy, the term "Saagitapi", prairie people, was used, thereby completing the figurative symbol that is the people of the bison.

In large measure, I have sought to elaborate and affirm this metaphorical character of oral-based societies in an earlier essay concerning Seneca (Iroquois), narrative traditions but widely perceptible in all oral-centered societies (Hansford, 41-62). It is in this context that Campbell affirms the sense that mythology concerns the mystical dimension, for without this you have ideology (Campbell, 31, 126). As a mode of transformation, myths inveigh an alternate consciousness that is owed to our oral past or what may be called an oral paradigm. Conversely in suggesting "myth" to be a precursor to modern science, Plato and his successors imposed a unilineal shift from myth to philosophy in ancient Greece, which in time has given way to the structuralist such as Levi-Straus who is committed to an ethnocentric binarism (Goody, 8). As s signpost of moderninsm and its notions of progress, this view juxtaposes the primitive with the advanced while favoring the latter.

Following the standardized research at first, anthropologist Jack Goody has concluded that the features closely linked with writing, specifically alphabetic systems, reflecting a stipulative symbolism served in a restrictive sense as an instrument of analytic procedures and a function of writing. He concluded, moreover, "it was the setting down of speech that enabled man clearly to separate words, to manipulate their order and to develop syllogistic forms of reasoning..." (Goody, 11). As a result, it is concluded that logic in its development is a function of writing. This thesis, however, demands that logic is solely derivative of writing, and as such, it is a point of contention that would omit an oral logic.

In the deeper analysis, oral societies have demonstrated an abundance of abstract thought, however, its form is not exponential or secondary, but instead, reliant upon an abundance of concrete procedures and mnemonic referents. Among natives, moreover, abstraction is embedded in daily life and connected to the array of succeeding natural referents.

There is something of this order, which is behind the notion that among natives, religion is a way of life and, therefore, it is not something practiced in the lenses of stipulative symbolism.

It is, moreover, "the nature of oral tradition", according to Goody, to hold a "capacity to swallow up the individual achievement and to incorporate it in a body of transmitted customs that can be considered as the approximate equivalent to what Tylor called 'culture' and Durkheim 'society'" (Goody, 7). In this manner, Goody concluded that literacy or the written mode is responsible for formalization that directs the rules of logic. He adds, however, "Philosophic discourse is a formalisation of just the kind one would expect of literacy. 'Traditional' societies are marked not so much by the absence of the proper tools for constructive rumination (Goody, 44). What is at issue, however, is the modality of logic. Writing, moreover, creates a different kind of critical discourse. It is thus a discourse that is charged with *simple location* favoring conceptual abstraction to the point of the impoverishment of reality.

Affirming the highly metaphorical character of native world views, Ruth Underhill has suggested that these traditions constitute a "magic language" fluid with striking natural metaphors (Ruth, 16). The languages, moreover, carry both a metaphoric and a mnemonic value association with the local natural idioms (Cruikshank, 2). Largely, these metaphorical expressions are concrete and attached to the natural forms and forces or nature persons characteristic of American-Indian religious cosmologies (Briton, 10). In these accounts, the recurring narrative theme is one of connection between people, nature and place. These connections are explored through kinship in association with a sense of place. This kinship ethos is much more than a mere narrative structure;[1] it is a defining truth. Nature, moreover, is referent truth and as such, it should not be confused with an ideological ethos and the modern meta-narrative characteristic of the modern-postmodern debate.

Conversely, literalism in the interpretation of myth gives way to the fallacy of mis-placed concreteness, so that subsequent modern-oriented readers will perpetuate the fallacy and amplify it among unwitting future generations. As a result, traditional mythology becomes lost in a series of quantum abstractions devoid of its original meaning and referents. Committed to an "allegory of simulation", according to Jean Baudrillard, such texts are given to a lack of referential being, or substance, and they become "hyperreal", or "models of a real without origin or reality" (Baudrillard, 1).

Often future generations are compelled from an ethnocentric loyalty to accept and follow the interpolative simulation, passing it along into the realm of hyper-reality. In this mode of hyper-reality, Baudrillard notes, "the whole system becomes weightless, it is no longer itself anything but a gigantic simulacrum—not unreal, but a simulacrum, that is to say never exchanged for the real, but exchanged for itself, in an uninterrupted circuit without reference or circumstance" (Baudrillard, 5-6). This condition is the quantum abstraction born of the *Fallacy of Misplaced Concreteness*, which voids the organic truth and imbues itself with endless fantasy compounded in the abstract qua abstract venue of literacy and belief in meta-narrative truth. In the course of quantum abstraction, then, ethnicity is no claim to authenticity. Reason is given to concur with Goody that literate procedures, herein affirmed as modernity, inhibit the study and affirmation of the pre-literate, Primal, modes of thought and worldview (Goody, 53).

While the post-modern is an essential means to check the modern, it cannot stand as an end unto itself. There exists, moreover, the fallacy of the meta-narrative critique and the illusion that is hyper-reality. Given that a meta-narrative is an absolute, universal truth claim and that post-modernism denies all meta-narratives, then it betrays itself within a meta-narrative syllogism. While this observation may trouble the naive, there is a response that we may consider before dismissing this significant critical mode. If, on the one hand, post-modern criticism exhibits, moreover, a logical contradiction, then on the other hand, logic is itself born of the literacy based meta-narrative, therefore, a category mistake ensues denying all analysis. As a means of further responding to this dilemma, we must consider *oralcy*.

As noted before, literacy inhibits the study of *oralcy*. As with a view to accounting procedures, literacy begins with categorization employing lists and tables. These techniques, according to Goody, serve to simplify reality; as a result, there is a compulsion to mistake metaphor for mechanicism (Goody, 73). We have observed this in Whitehead's notion of *simple location* where metaphorical meaning is nominalized in the time and space of literalism. As noted, this confusion leads to the *Fallacy of Misplaced Concreteness* where abstractions are given a false ontological status in the course of history creating through *simulation* and endless *simulacra* a *hyper-reality* devoid of organic referent. Characteristic of this problem, Goody warns, "the formalisation of writing flouts the flexibility of speech, and it does so in a manner that is both distorting and generative" (Goody, 112). By this last remark, I conclude that the endless cycles of simulation and simulacra that Baudrillard described is inferred and this practice is the work of quantum abstraction creating a hyper-reality that results in the impoverishment of reality.

Perhaps the venue of this quantum abstraction is linked to the origin of literate philosophy. In, for example, the intellectual accomplishments of the ancient Greeks, Plato offers a reprise to the question of literacy and its impact is a curious legend involving the Egyptian King Thamus. In the legend, the God Thoth with the gift of writing approaches Thamus for the Egyptian people. Thoth has promised that writing will make people wiser and improve their memory, but after considering this promise, Thamus concludes otherwise, musing:

> If men learn this, it will implant forgetfulness in their souls; they will cease to exercise memory because they rely on that which is written, calling things to remembrance no longer from within themselves, but by means of external marks. (Phaedrus, 275a)

Addressing this point, Abrams concludes that according to the king—"spoken teachings, once written down, easily find their way into the hands of those who will misunderstand those teachings while nevertheless thinking that they understand them. Thus, the written letters bring not wisdom but only "the conceit of wisdom", making men seem to know much when in fact they know little" (Phaedrus, 275b). Plato's Socrates concurs with this assessment and in recording it in his dialogues, it is clear that Plato intended his readers to take the criticisms of literacy seriously (Phaedrus, 277e).

In so doing, Plato appears to have anticipated the fallacy of Rene Descartes' well-known separation of mind from matter, which disassociates our experiences with the natural world and commits its followers to an ideological hyper-reality. It is within this ideological hyper-reality that both the modern and the post-modern are contained. Despite its contentions that it has gone beyond epochal criticisms, the post-modern has remained a slave of this ideological hyper-reality. It has, however, discerned and supplied important transformational tools such as an identification of the meta-narratives of hyper-reality, in challenging modernity as born of literacy.

Turning to an organic sense of process, we may examine the Pikuni (Blackfeet) notion of the trickster—N'api or Old Man. In doing so, we must be prepared to see more than an historical figure in simple location but something more of an organic metaphorical status of being. Associated with the Sun (*Natos*), *N'api* is a compound expression of "the word *Ni'nah*, man, and the particle *a'pi* that expresses a color, and which is never used by itself, but always in combination with some other word." George Bird Grinnell explains further that *a'pi* really conveys the tint of early morning light—the dawn—which is an off-color white with a faint yellow cast: thus, *N'api* seems to mean man-yellowish-white or dawn-light-color-man. Grinnell further suggests that the idea of light as the Creator would be absurd to the Blackfeet of today: "The statement that Old Man was merely light personified would be beyond his comprehension, and if he did understand what was meant, he would laugh at it, and aver that N'api was a real man, a flesh and blood person like himself" (Grinnell, 255-57). James Willard Schultz concurs with Grinnell declaring that the meaning of *N'api* is "dawn, or the first faint, white light that gives birth to the day." Thus, he concluded: "the original religion of the Blackfeet was the worship of light personified" (Schultz, 97). Further demonstrating the personhood of *N'api*, anthropologist John Ewers points to his role as trickster explaining: "It is significant that they looked upon Old Man [*N'api*] not only as the Creator but as a humorous little fellow who went around trying to play tricks on people and animals whose tricks sometimes backfired. Many *N'api* stories are not only funny, but also obscene (Ewers, 145). Similarly, Clark Wissler and D.C. Duvall record *N'api's* role as "the blunder, the immoral mischief maker, as well as Creator" (*Mythology*, 53).

The personification of light and *N'api* is an anthropomorphosed "non-human person", therefore sharing the attributes of personhood. In consequence, this example is an ontological acknowledgment of the native metaphysic of nature that Brown identified (Brown, 37, 60, 70). A central point here is that light is the most important thing in life. In this context, the beginning of the day is analogous to the beginning of the world, and since light comes before the sun—creates it or brings it forth, so to speak—then it is the antecedent of the sun as the Creator. Dawn light has thus assumed the form of Dawn Bringer constituting an archetypal image within Native American mythology (Campbell, 134-35).

This mythical figure suggests more than a mere ontological first man in the Western reading of *Genesis*. Moreover, this trickster/creator manifests an oral investiture in Nature that anthropologist Irving Hallowell characterized as an "Other-than-Human Person" and who are morally considered beings (Irving, 141-78). In this case, an ecological process that is the personification of dawn. Furthermore, the process of dawn-bringing is one of creation and as such it has the standing personhood—other-than-human, no less—among the Pikuni (Blackfeet) in having organically avoided the simple location of Western anthropocentricism. Hence, the Dawnbringer—*N'api* or Old Man—is an ecological process associated with the dawn light and deemed creator in its role of bringing light into the world. The Dawn Bringer motif is apparently an "elementary idea" within American-Indian mythology conveying ecological process through the organic dream-based paradigm heretofore examined in the mythic discourse above. As I've pointed out earlier, traditional mythic narratives have an eternal luminosity revealing the pen-ultimate truth. Although they may in various ways continue to speak today, their message is born of the wild manifest nature and the harmonious balance which a people realize through their oral traditions. Unfortunately, there are many problems inherent in the development and rise of literacy that challenge access to the transcendent but essential organic wisdom that such narratives contain. In this context, the classicist C. Kerényi has written: "True mythology has become so completely alien to us that, before tasting of it, we would do well to pause and consider—not only the uses and dangers of mythology...but also our possible attitude towards it. We have lost our immediate feeling for the great realities of the spirit—and to this world all true mythology belongs—lost it precisely because of our all-too-willing helpful, and efficient science" (*Science*, 1).

Explaining the lack of causality in a traditional myth, Kerényi reflects upon their role as precedent to an ideal and the "guarantee of the continuance of that ideal" (6). It is in this context that we may acknowledge "the universals of human experience..." in mythology are manifesting wildness rather than the ideological rationalizations characteristic to allegory or pseudo-myth. "Metaphor", then according to Lakoff and Johnson, "is one of our most important tools for trying to comprehend partially what cannot be comprehended totally: our feelings, aesthetic experiences, moral practices, and spiritual awareness" (*Metaphors*, 193). Thus, we realize in metaphor "the masks of god" that eternal transcendent truth that is beyond words and which mythos—words—manifest as the penultimate truth.

Largely overlooked by the literary critics, we may also recognize in these native mythological accounts a quality that I will call the force of narrative. Acknowledging that myths are born of the nature, then their force of narrative is the accord achieved with nature; this accord is manifest in cultural identity both individuality and collectively. Furthermore, a cultural identity stands in stark contrast from a contrived or stereotypical identity. Throughout Native America, the people will declare their creation occurred in their present environment; notwithstanding, while these claims appear to fly in the face of scientific study they are not necessarily desperate. Moreover, they are different ways of establishing relationships. On the one hand, anthropology seeks to determine a sequence of historical facts, while on the other mythology is about relationships and an organic union with one's environment. In the traditional native context where all forms of nature are respected for their inherent power or life force, identity is formulated about these powerful metaphors of the ultimate power. This process is achieved through dream and vision in giving birth to mythologems and ritual communion. For example, Campbell writes: "That dream and vision have been, everywhere and forever, the chief creative and shaping powers of myth is generally recognized today by the leading students of mythic lore;...the keystone of the dream, [is] the point of which it ascends into the unknown. ...we may expect to find in dreams everything that has ever been of significance in the life of humanity" (Campbell, 4). Accordingly, the life of the individual is caught up in the ecological forces of place; associations here expand ordinary temporality into time immemorial.

It has been well said that mythology as a phenomenon "in profundity, permanence, and universality is comparable only with Nature herself" (Kerényi, 1). As Campbell has informed us, myths: "may be recognized in themselves as *natural* phenomena, opening backyard to mystery—like trees, like hills, or like mountain streams—antecedent (like the wood of trees) to the "meanings" that have given them and the uses to which they have been put.

What is the "meaning" of a tree? Of a butterfly? Of the song of a rushing stream? Such wonders simply *are*. They are antecedent to meaning, though "meanings" may be read into them....

Mythology as a production of nature, serving, on one hand, the biological function of fostering a wholesome maturation of the psyche, and, on the other hand, the metaphysical, or mystagogic function of the Buddha-thing, "thus come", *tathagata*, opening backward to mystery" (Campbell, 1).

Despite these powerful conceptual ideas—Campbell's Wisdom Body and Kerényi's *begründen*, there is a tendency among scholars and laymen alike to overlook the power of place and the essential role of wildness in continually informing and maintaining myth-based cultural traditions. This problem is most pronounced in the dilemma surrounding Native American sacred geography, for as the traditional landscapes are domesticated developed and transformed so too are the dreams and visions empowering the traditional myths and potential visions; ultimately lacking *begründen* in the manner of Western rationalism. Brown has implicitly affirmed this notion of *begründen* in Native American traditions stating: "Where Indians are still able to live in an area of as-yet-unspoiled nature, potentially they have access to a vast array of transcendent [mythic] values." Without wildness, itself the Wisdom Body, there remains merely vacuum-tube like abstraction. Hence, if trickster narratives are a form of myth, they must contain essential "Wisdom Body referents or nature begründen" as suggested by Kerényi above.

In turning to the trickster, however, I wish to acknowledge first their ironic character and concomitant moral inflection before considering this underlying organic wisdom. Interpreting trickster myths is an act of reading irony into the expression of normative behavior. Acknowledging the immoral character of the trickster, the Franciscan priests of early seventeenth century California imposed a ban on the telling of such stories among the Indians at the Mission of San Juan Capistrano. Responding with incomprehension, the natives questioned the priests declaring: "How can our children grow up to be good people when you deny them our stories." Imbedded within the trickster tradition, there is a clear understanding of reverse psychology that motivates the telling of the immoral acts and mischief born of the anti-hero or fool that manifest themselves in trickster behavior. Contextually then the trickster is a reverse barometer of the good; in his repeated failures with the concomitant negative consequences, there is an ironic insight into right behavior that serves the moral imagination. Hence, a child is given to ponder and reflect upon the trickster's immoral mischief as it leads to adverse consequences; in so doing, he or she is given to an intrinsic realization that such base desire-full behavior is accompanied with negative results. Accordingly, the trickster's anti-social and immoral behavior reveal a reverse measure of the good that its normative opposition defines the good. Ironically, the trickster is, therefore, a moral agent oppositional to the norm; this gives insight into the good through his wrong doings and thereby teaches a reasoning process that reveals in juxtaposition normative behavior. Thus, the trickster is irony.

The moral insights derived from the trickster are gain through an intrinsic intellectualization that generates an original epistemological grasp of morality; hence, the student of the trickster is given the opportunity to realize the good through ironic deduction that includes a personally reasoned insight versus a command centered dictate or normative dogma given without explanation. It is from this context that the natives of San Juan Capistrano questioned the reason of the Franciscan Priests who acting in their rote centered simple location oriented normalcy served to defeat the idea of an intrinsic moral insight. In contradistinction to the idea of a dedicated good dictated in moral mandate, the act of doing good is best realized when one truly understands the underlying reason or reasons central to doing the good. Moreover, the good is best engaged when it is understood why one must do the good; this benevolent understanding is not well obtained from a command-centered logic but from a meditated insight of reason wherein the moral agent truly understands the virtue of doing the good. Hence, morality derived from the intrinsic insight of the trickster's extreme irony when serving his base desires serves to enlighten the individual and make him or her aware of myriad of negative consequences that ensue when engaging that self same desire-fullness of trickster like behavior. The good is thus intrinsically internalized and understood within so that agent can act in moral intentionality. Such is the moral genius of indigenous trickster centered orality.

It is at this point where we may turn to selected Pikuni (Blackfeet) trickster narratives, which may give discovery to my thesis heretofore articulated. In the scope and context of this presentation, moreover, there are four Pikuni (Blackfeet) trickster narratives that I wish to present and assess through the foregoing approach that I have outlined above. It is my suggestion that trickster narratives contain key moral and ecological referent knowledge that is essential to the good as defined in a traditional society. Accordingly, I will present the four narratives and subsequently assess them collectively for their moral insights and mythological significance in revealing an all important nature *begründen* or ecological referent values.

A—N'api (Old Man) and the Roasted Prairie Squirrels

> Old Man came to a place, where many ground squirrels were seated around a fire, playing a game. They would bury one of their number in the ashes, until he squealed, when they pulled him out. Old Man said that he would like to learn the game. The squirrels explained that it was very easy, and invited him to take part. He asked them to bury him first, but, as soon as he was covered over, he yelled, and they quickly pulled him out. Old Man then said that it was the squirrels' turn, but since there were so many of them, it would save time to bury them all at once. They agreed, so he covered them all over with hot ashes, excepting one mother squirrel, who was afraid. He warned her to run away, so that there might be other squirrels, but left the others in the ashes, until they were well roasted. He ate so many of the roasted squirrels that he fell asleep, when a lynx came along and ate up the others. Old Man followed the lynx, until he came upon him fast asleep. He was so angry, that he seized him by the ears and shortened his head by

hammering it against a stone. He pulled out his long tail and, breaking it in two, stuck the brush part on his rump, making a bob-tail. He stretched his legs and body, making them long and slender, and then cast him upon the ground saying, "You bob-cats will always look like this, and you will always be so short-winded, that you will never be able to run far."

Old Man having been burned by the fire called upon the wind to blow. The cool air made him feel better, so he continued calling upon it to blow harder and harder, until there came such a fierce wind that he was blown away. Every tree that he caught hold of was torn up by the roots, and he could not stop himself, until he lay hold of a birch tree. When the wind went down and he was rested, he denounced the birch saying, "Why have you such strong roots, that you cannot be pulled up like other trees? I was having a good time being blown around by the wind, until you spoiled my fun." He was so angry that he drew his stone knife and gashed the birch all over.

This is the reason why the bark of a birch tree always has such a nicked appearance.

(McClintock, 338-40)

B—N'api (Old Man) and the Mouse Dance

Old Man found a large elk-skull lying upon the ground. He looked inside and saw some mice having a dance. The Chief Mouse always started the dance by singing Ka-wa-skiau ap-a-nok-se = "Mice-winking-their-eyes." Then all stood up and joined in the singing, taking hold of each other's paws and dancing in a circle. Old Man asked if he could join them. The Chief Mouse replied, that his body was too large to get inside the skull, but he might stick his head in and keep shaking it up and down, which would be almost the same thing as dancing. He told him, however, that the dance would last all night, and advised him not to fall asleep. In spite of the warning Old Man soon fell asleep, and the mice ate off all his hair. When he awoke in the morning, the mice had gone, and he was unable to pull his head from the skull. He could not see, because the skull covered his eyes. Losing his way, he walked over a steep hank into a river. He swam down stream with the elk-antlers sticking out of the water, until he drew near an Indian camp, where his appearance caused great excitement.

When Old Man heard the people shouting, "Here comes an elk", he made a noise like an elk, and kept on swimming. The Indians roped him with lariats, and pulled him ashore, but they did not discover that it was Old Man; until an old woman broke open the skull with a stone-hammer.

(*Ibid.*, 341-42)

C—N'api (Old Man) and the Rock

While Old Man was travelling with a Fox, they came to a large rock, where they stopped to rest. It was a very hot day and Old Man was very tired of carrying his robe. As they were leaving, he said, "Poor Rock! You have been living here uncovered so many years, that you are turning black. I am so sorry for you that I will give you my robe for a cover." He and the Fox then continued their journey. A big black cloud soon came up, and he decided to send the Fox back for the robe. But the Rock refused to give it up saying, "Whenever anything is given to me, I never part with it." Old Man asked the Fox to try to borrow the robe, but it was in vain. Old Man then ran back himself and said, "Rock you have stood here many years without a cover and now you have become too particular." He angrily pulled the robe from the Rock, and continued his journey with the Fox. They had not gone far, when they heard a mighty roar, and saw the Rock coming after them. Although they ran their fastest, the Rock gained on them so rapidly that Old Man called upon the night hawks for help. To rescue him they kept swooping down upon the Rock and each time a piece fell, until finally it broke into pieces.

The remains of the Rock can he seen today scattered over the plains.

(*Ibid.*, 342-43)

D—N'api (Old Man) and the Magical Leggings

Old Man came to the lodge of a man who owned a wonderful pair of leggings. Wherever he went they set fire to the grass. If he wished to kill buffalo, he had only to walk around them when they would be caught in a circle of fire. Old Man wanted these leggings very much. He said that he had come a long journey to get them, but the owner refused to give them up. Old Man then decided to remain all night in the lodge. When the owner and his wife were sound asleep, Old Man stole the leggings. After running a long distance he became tired and lay down to sleep in a thicket with the leggings under his head. But, when he awoke in the morning he found, to his surprise, that he was back again in the lodge. When the owner asked him how it happened that he had his leggings under his head, Old Man told him a lie, saying, "I had nothing else, so I used them for a pillow."

On the following night, Old Man made another attempt to carry off the leggings, but morning found him back again in the lodge where the leggings belonged. The owner then told Old Man that, if he wanted the leggings so badly he would give them to him. He warned him, however, not to make use of them more than three times. Old Man was so proud of the fire-leggings that he put them on to show off in every camp he entered and paid no heed to the warning of the owner. He used them three times successfully, but the fourth time he put them on he set fire to the grass, wherever he stepped. The grass burned so fiercely that Old Man became frightened and started to run. The fire followed him, wherever he went, burning his clothes and his hair, until he was compelled to jump into a river. But the magical leggings were burned up (*Ibid.*, 347-48). In the end the Old Man was reminded: "wherever you go it is always the Sun's Lodge."[2]

In these trickster narrative is an organic wisdom expressed in a figurative logic. It relies upon reverse psychology exposing the failures of the fool or anti-hero whose the trickster. This logic is mimetic in using a principle of similitude as a means of getting it point across; it serves, however, to present a normative behavioral pattern that is reverse of the trickster. Typically, moreover, the trickster thinks nothing of others and seeks only to fulfill his physical and emotional cravings; hence, he encounters the wonders of the world filled only with his desire. He seeks only to use and abuse others for the sole satisfaction of his desires. In doing so, he commits to a course of action that is obviously inappropriate and absolutely wrong; it is a behavior that can only lead to a moral breach. In the trickster's behavior, there is a reverse barometer of the good; hence, he is an anti-hero or fool. It is in this manner that he conveys the good as a means of disseminating the good. In addition to his gift of a moral insight, when he only makes his plight worse, he often ironically reveals a greater truth that is constituted in the nature thereby conveying an organic *begründen.* This nature referent reveals the deeper eco-centric values at the heart of Pikuni (Blackfeet) traditions that are necessary to live in balance and harmony with their environment; which when discovered are the deepest insights available to appreciating an organic way of life.

Considering this approach to the normative values manifest in Pikuni (Blackfeet) traditions, we can identify several normative values from these selected stories. First, there are societal mores associated with good behavior manifest in D above when N'api steals the man's magical leggings; hence, he is a theft that is the opposite of the social norm. In the incidents of gifting manifest in C and D above: Old Man is a false giver when he takes the coat back from the rock and fails to honor his word. Likewise when he is given the magical leggings he fails to follow the rules and abuses the gift. Repeatedly N'api fails to heed the advice of elders; manifest in particularly in B and C above he ignores the advice of the

Nature Persons and suffers the consequences for his misdeeds. For instance, the nice warn him not to fall asleep but he does so and finds his head stuck in the elk skull thereby paying for his foolishness. In ignoring the warning of the man with the magical leggings, he abuses the gift and looses the power he was given to make life easier while harming himself.

A moral law is affirmed in A when N'api sets out for revenge against the failed warning; he turns the burning willow wan on himself, which suggests wrong doings will come home to roast. Hence, he teaches the law of *karma*; revenge will not make things right only worse as the evil you do comes home to you. Ethical formulations may also be drawn from these stories, particularly in A and D. First, when the Old Man lets the pregnant prairie squirrel escape; she represents the fecundity of the species and its ability to continue its propagation. If you kill them all, there will be no more in that place; hence, the act of letting her go is a conservation ethic whereby you always leave some of your prey for the future good of the species. In the case of the magical leggings, there is warning of waste that likewise is a conservation ethic; in killing the animal you have been gifted by the spirits and you must utilize it fully or otherwise you may become the unlucky hunter or lose the gift in this case. Hence, this is a second form of a conservation ethic. In the case of an environmental ethic, N'api's abuse of the birch tree suggests in reverse that you can harm Nature and you ought not needlessly do so. These stories, moreover, teach the good and provide mores, morals and ethics to the Pikuni (Blackfeet); it is from such teachings that the society finds its norm and generates a moral imperative. In this way, the Pikuni (Blackfeet) story-tellers are expressing wisdom challenging notions of *prima facie* desire and offering the need to take a second considered look at the organic world about us.

Turning to the organic *begründen* or Nature referent, N'api's actions in the first story—A—reveal the origin of the winter wind which in this area is very powerful and demands thoughtful care to those who would live in the region. One is reminded of this strength through the simile of the birch tree's strong roots. Hence, the Pikuni (Blackfeet) way of life is well rooted in this locale. In the second case—B above, the mice dance and sing a curious song—"mice winking their eyes" which by simile of association suggests a kind of equality in orientation to light. During the fall of the year annually, the Pikuni (Blackfeet) disperse along the Rocky Mountain front to hunt elk; this fact is acknowledged in the elk skull which itself makes an ideal nesting site for mice during their hibernation beneath the winter snows. Old Man, as light personified, then appears to have departed the people at the equinox—"mice winking their eyes"—and he is lost until spring when the rivers rise with the snowmelt flooding. Hence, his capture and his freedom from the skull is a symbol of the spring equinox when the light returns and will wax strong again. In this case the *begründen* is one with the light cycle and its eternal return. In narrative—C above, N'api is helped to escape the rock by the curlews or night hawks thereby revealing the power of renewal born in each day as the Old Man is daylight personified and the curlews signify night with immemorial process associated with the rocks; it is thus a tale of process revealing the diurnal—day and night—cycle over the scope of time immemorial. In the last case—D above, the mythologem is associated with the handsome man who shines each day in the Old Man's face waking him and who has the power of fire through the magical leggings adorned with the red tipped plums of the redheaded woodpecker. In simile of association, this man metaphorically represents the sun because as the story concludes: "No matter where you go on earth it is the Sun's Lodge." Acknowledged in this Nature, *begründen* is the force and power of the Sun as it shapes life on earth, we are all beholding to this power and thereby obligated to respect it. It is a poignant acknowledgement of the "earthrise" phenomenon experienced by astronauts seeking to walk on the moon who observed the earth as a green disk rising against the backdrop of space and Sun thereby realizing it fragile and unique role in giving life within our solar system; something that ought to be given the utmost respect which is implied in the Pikuni (Blackfeet) reference—"No matter where you go it is the Sun's Lodge." Hence, the earth referent is a reminder of our place in this fragile terrestrial ecosystem that we know as home and the Pikuni (Blackfeet) qualify with utmost respect as the Sun's Lodge.

Trickster stories such as these serve to reference place creating a mnemonic way of assert morality without the abstraction of literacy. Sites and places where the trickster played become benchmarks of discovery reminding the knower of his or her normative responsibilities and moral obligations in serving the good; for many Native Americans you only need mention the place to assert morality. In this way, place with its organic power, becomes a sacred geography revealing the good in traditional life; however, one must be cautioned that this good is only found where the place and its natural or wild properties remain intact. Should the place be disturbed or otherwise transform and made void of the respective spirits—Nature Persons—the power that gives it meaning is lost and so to the Nature *begründen.* Together these morals and eco-centric value findings are powerful insights demanding respect and consideration be given to the social and natural order; collectively they account for mores, morals and ethics, as well as environmental values that must be acknowledged if the good life is to be realized.

As an engine of irony, trickster narratives encourage listeners to a well-considered opinion with conclusions and ideas ensconced in the ambiguity that is the natural world about us. It is in this way that an *oralcy* based logic acts as an auto-criticism that ultimately discloses the ubiquitous quality and character of life and Nature. The American-Indian author and post-modern theorist, Gerald Vizenor, has used this trickster criticism as a discourse challenging all terminal creeds in his work. He has, moreover, taken the post-modern afield from ideology and oriented it in the sensuous doors of perception, which is called for in attending the organic paradigm and we might well heed such advice when facing the modern world with its eminent disrespect for Nature.

Notes

1. See for example Gladys Reichard, *Dezba: Woman of the Desert.* New York: J.J. Augustin, 1939; Alice Marriott, *Maria: The*

Potter of San Ildefonso. Norman: University of Oklahoma Press, 1948; Nancy Oestrich Lurie, *Mountain Wolf Woman, Sister of Crashing Thunder: Autobiography of a Winnebago Woman*. Ann Arbor: University of Michigan Press, 1961; Lalla Scott, *Karnee: A Paiute Narrative, the Story of Annie Lowry*. Reno: University of Nevada Press, 1966; and accounts recorded by Truman Michelson, "The Autobiography of a Fox Indian Woman" in *Fortieth Annual Report of the Bureau of American Ethnology, 1918-19*. Washington, DC: Smithsonian Institution, U.S. Government Printing Office, 1925: 291-349; ____, "The Narrative of a Southern Cheyenne Woman" in *Smithsonian Misc. Collections*. Washington, DC: Smithsonian Institution, U.S. Government Printing Office, 1932, v87: 5; ____, "Narratives of an Apache Woman," *American Anthropologist*. 35: 595-610; Ruth M. Underhill, *The Autobiography of a Papago Woman*. Memoirs of the American Anthropological Association, No. 46. Menasha, WI: American Anthropological Association, 1936; Jane Holden Kelly, *Yaqui Women: Contemporary Life Histories*. Lincoln: University of Nebraska Press, 1978; as cited in Cruikshank, *Like a Story*, 3, 358.

2. This conclusion reflects the story as related to me by the old story-tellers of my personal experience among the Pikuni (Blackfeet).

Works Cited

Abram, David. *The Spell of the Sensuous: Perception and Language in a More-Than-Human World*. New York: Vintage Books, 1996.

Baudrillard, Jean. *Simulacra and Simulation*. Trans. Sheila Faria Glaser. Ann Arbor: The University of Michigan Press, 1995.

Briton, Daniel G. *Aboriginal American Authors and Their Productions. Especially Those in the Native Language—A Chapter in the History of Literature*. Philadelphia, 1883.

Brown, Joseph E. *The Spiritual Legacy of the American Indian*. New York: Crossroad Press, 1982.

Campbell. *Transformation of Myth*, and Campbell with Moyers, *Power of Myth*. New York: Betty Sue Flowers, 1988.

———. *This Business of the gods...*, ed. Fraser Boa and Jenny Donald. Caledon East, Ontario: Windrose Films Ltd., 1989.

Cruikshank, Julie. *Life Lived Like a Story*. Lincoln: University of Nebraska Press, 1990.

Eric, A., Havelock. *Preface to Plato*. Cambridge, MA: The Belknap Press of Harvard University Press, 1963.

Grinnell, George Bird. Blackfoot Lodge Tales: The Story of a Prairie People. Henry D. Thoreau, A Week on the Concord and Merrimack Rivers. New York: Hurst & Company, 1892.

Hallowell, Irving. "Ojibwa Ontology, Behavior, and World View", in *Teachings from the American Earth: Indian Religion and Philosophy*. Edited by Dennis Tedlock and Barbara Tedlock. New York: Liveright, 1975. Print.

John, C. Ewers. *The Blackfeet: Raiders of the Northwestern Plains*. Norman: University of Oklahoma Press, University of Oklahoma Press, 1958.

Jung, C.G. and Kerényi, C. *Essays on a Science of Mythology: The Myth of the Divine Child and the Mysteries of Eleusis*, 1949. Trans. R.F.C. Hull. Princeton, NJ: Princeton University Press, 1969.

Kerényi in Jung and Kerényi. *Science of Mythology*. Princeton: Princeton University Press.

Lakoff and Johnson. *Metaphors We Live By*. Chicago: University of Chicago Press, 1981.

McClintock, Walter. *The Old North Trail: Life, Legends and Religion of the Blackfeet Indians*, Lincoln: University of Nebraska Press, 1992.

Schultz, J. Willard. *(Apikuni), Blackfeet Tales of Glacier National Park*. Boston: Houghton Mifflin Co. 1916.

Thwaites, R.G. ed., *The Jesuit Relations and Allied Documents*. Cleveland, 1896-1901.

Underhill, R.M. *Singing for Power: The Song Magic of the Papago Indians of Southern Arizona* [1930]. Tucson: The University of Arizona Press.

Vest, Jay Hansford C. "Myth, Metaphor and Meaning in *The Boy Who Could Not Understand*: A Study of Seneca Auto-Criticism," *American Indian Cultural and Research Journal*, 30: 4, 2006.

Walter J. Ong. *Orality and Literacy: The Technologizing of the Word*. New York: Routledge, 1982.

Wissler, Clark and Duvall, D.C., "Mythology of the Blackfeet," American Museum of Natural History, *Anthropological Papers*, New York, 1908.

24

W.B. Yeats and Irish Legends: A Reading of *The Countess Cathleen*

Rashmi Attri

W.B. Yeats was the pioneer in the establishment of the Abbey Theatre, an offshoot of Irish Literary Renaissance. This literary renaissance was itself an integral part of the general movement for freedom from the British rule. Drama being the most effective medium received considerable attention from its pioneers. These playwrights were supposed to write plays dealing either with contemporary life or with legendary past. While Synge opted for Irish peasantry for their dramatic material, Yeats found Irish myths and legends as a rich mine of source-material and thus declared that, "from the great candle of past we must all light our little tapers" (*Letters to New Island,* 158). He thought these legends and myths more relevant for contemporary life of Irish people. Yeats believed that "Of all the many things that past bequeaths to future, the greatest are the great legends; they are the mothers of nation" (*Uncollected Prose,* 104). National myths no doubt create national identity, common shared heroic and subjugated backgrounds serve as focal points around which people can rally to the "common cause". This phenomenon of using mythology to create national identity is not new. Romans used mythology to define them; they attributed both defeat and victories to the whims of the Gods and Heroes. Romans used mythology to extend their heritage of their republic and their right to imperial dominion of the Mediterranean. Irish national history is littered with mythology; Yeats and others felt the need to assert that Irish history and sovereignty was as older as any foreign throne could place its claim. Yeats believed that only Greece could rival Celtic mythology in its exuberance. He further believed that these folk tales represented "an ancient system of belief" which had been overlaid by the later Christianity. Actually in his reaction against realism, Yeats turned towards legends and myths. However, his liking for legends and myths does not imply that Yeats was interested in a retrospective art. In this regard, he clarifies his stand in his letter to Katherine Taynan "I am not very fond of retrospective art. I don't think that pleasure that we get from old methods of looking at things...belongs to the best literature.... I do not mean that we should not go to the old ballads and poems for inspiration, but we shall search them for new methods of expressing ourselves" (*Letters,* 98). Here Yeats was indebted to John O' Leary in his fast increasing interest for legends and Folklore.

Yeats drew inspiration from Irish myths and legends to create Irish literature. During revolution, Yeats particularly wrote in order to revive an interest in history of old Ireland, which during colonial times had been suppressed by the English system. By incorporating Irish legendary and mythological stories, Yeats endeavoured to invoke national character of Ireland. These legends helped to promote his own sense of nationalism as the rich cultural heritage of the heroic legendary past was considered more conducive to re-awakening of the Irish consciousness to its earlier greatness. Yeats preferred to weave these legendary stories with the present political concerns since this legendary material was to be exploited in manner in which it could acquire universal dimensions. In this process, Yeats asserts, poetic imagination plays a primary role. It is only then that it can qualify to be called great literature. Yeats took folklore to be affirmation of the "ancient supremacy of imagination". Yeats firmly believed that "reality" was not in the artificial world of formal literature, but amongst the tales of Irish peasants. World of legends it is needless to say that it offers a fertile soil for imagination to work on. In Yeats' words, these myths and legends were both far from the discussion of our own interests and the immediate circumstances of our life. Yeats believed that remoteness lends charm to the life presented in drama and hence appeals to the audience more effectively than the actual reality around us. Myths and legends would create a world that would transcend topicality and temporality. To quote Ellmann, Yeats wanted that "Theatrist's individualised consciousness must be married to ancient, anonymous, popular, unconsidered images" (*The Identity of Yeats*, 89). But it does not mean that Yeats ignored the world of reality absolutely, rather these legendary stories were to be exploited in such a way that they would have relevance to the immediate life.

Besides this emphasis on the revival of Irish mythology and legendary past was also due to the realisation of the derision in which "Irish Literature" was held in the 19th century. England had even banned the very teaching of the Irish Language. One English historian went on to describe Irish epics as "ridiculous bombast". Robert Atkins, an authority on Middle Irish manuscripts critically said this "It has scarcely been touched by the movement of great literature, it is the untrained popular feeling...it is almost intolerable low in tone...and every now and then...goes down lower that low..." (Skelton, 9). Irish oral traditions were regarded debased superstitions. This entrenched bias against Celtic culture began to unravel, as more and more material about Irish folklore made its way in to the mainstream. This renewed interest resulted in the birth of the Irish Literary Renaissance (Thuente, 39). Yeats along with Lady Gregory and other Irish writers opted for Celtic god over more traditional use of Greek or Roman gods in their writings with the aim of drawing attention towards the Irish my thology in the world literature. As one of the founders of the Abbey theatre, Yeats' aim was "to build up a Celtic and Irish school of dramatic literature". It would not be incorrect to say that these folklores gave Yeats a new voice. His interest in Irish myths and legends increased so much that by 1902, Yeats started comparing Irish folklores and mythology to similar tales in other parts of the world. Apart from finding a political and cultural identity for the Irish people, Yeats' overriding personal interest in mythology of Ireland cannot be ignored. Yeats had grown up in the countryside of County Sligo, which to him was the "country of his heart", replete with Irish legendary, mythological folktales. Since his childhood, he developed love for these and conversing with country people, though he could not understand Irish. During the initial years of his career, there was an immense literary revival of interest in Irish legends and folklore with such books as *Mystic Charms*, *Superstitions of Ireland* and *The Fire Stories of Ireland*, etc. in publication. He stated as early as in 1889 that "[I had] worked my way through most, if not all, edited, Irish Folktales" (Kinhan, 15). We find Yeats being drifted towards a distinctly Irish sensibility with regard to his love for Ireland, quite evident in his poetry and plays. His longing for the unification of present with the legendary past also point towards Yeats' concept of unity of culture and unity of being; as he writes, "Have not all races had their unity from mythology..." (*Autobiographies*, 240).

His interest in mysticism further strengthened his love for these legends and folktales, and Yeats at the age of twenty-two announced "...I have made a new religion, almost an infallible church of poetic tradition; of a fardel of stories, personages and of emotions; inseparable from their first expression, passes on from generation to generation by poets and painters with some help from philosophers and theologians. I wished for a world where I could discover this tradition perpetually" (*The Trembling of the Veil*, 20). In his opinion, there was no separation between Art and Religion. For Yeats, drama was an extension of magic and magic confirmed his faith that mortal mind could transcend its limits and converse with the greater mind. Yeats' lure for these legends and myths saved him from being carried away by "art for the art's sake" philosophy.

The paper attempts to explore how Yeats has used such legends in his play entitled *The Countess Cathleen* written in 1889. Its theme is taken from the legend of Countess Cathleen

O'Shea described in a book of folklore entitled *Fairy and Folk Tales of Irish Peasantry*. The play, Yeats' first fruit of dramatic apprentice, demonstrates Yeats' attempts to transcend his folktale material and his adherence to the manifesto of the Irish Dramatic Movement of reviving Irish legendary and historical past. Convinced that "Supreme art is a traditional statement of certain heroic and religious truths, passed on from age to age..." (*Autobiographies,* 474). Yeats affirmed that Irish writers should go back to their roots in order to move forward.

The Countess Cathleen also illustrates his urge to transcend his folktale material and to show in a vision something of the face of Ireland "the play thus reveals his deep insolvent in Irish nationalism". *The Countess Cathleen,* Yeats' first attempt to unite poetry and drama, is based on simple Irish legend dealing with Irish noblewoman, Countess Cathleen, who sacrifices her love for the poet Aleel in order to serve the people of Ireland during famine. The play deals with the story of Countess Cathleen who happens to visit the famine stricken part of Ireland. Some merchants visit the village to buy the souls of starving villagers at high price, When Countess comes to know of it she orders her steward to sell her entire property and provide food to these famine ridden men in order to save their souls. Towards the end for this national cause, she even barters her own soul and dies. However, there is turn at the climax and contrary to the terms of the barter it is not the demon but the angels who come to her soul.

The play thus besides being relevant to the contemporary Ireland, has the streak of mysticism in depicting countess eager to renounce this materialistic world for some higher spiritual satisfaction. The play conforms to Yeats' declaration that "the real world is not altogether rejected" (*Essays and Introduction,* 243). The world of reality relates only to the contemporary wave of nationalism and patriotism idealistic realised in the nation's readiness for maximum sacrifice. But the mythical and morality model take the play beyond its realistic moorings.

It follows systematically developed plot with conversational verse written in contemporary idiom. Since the main concern is with idea of self-sacrifice, psychological probing into its characters is not attempted. The play opens in the house of Sheamus Rua who is talking to his wife and son about the starvation in the village due to draught. Countess along with Aleel, the poet, reaches this village and distributes money to the villagers after hearing of the plight of the villagers. When she leaves their house, Sheamus is seen inviting two merchants who have come to buy the souls of these villagers at a very high price. Both Sheamus and his father agree to sell their souls to these two demons. In scene five, we find the entire peasantry have agreed for this deal. Countess Cathleen in utter desperation announces to sell her own soul to these merchants, who are actually devils—provided that they return the souls of these peasants. The merchants agree to this and the action of the play moves towards the final conclusion in the fulfilment of the term of the contract. But a big reversal takes place when instead of demons, angels appear to take the glorious soul of Countess to its divine habitat. The play ends with the following lines: "It is because the The light of lights/ looks away on the motive not the deed. Shadow of shadow on the deed alone" (*Collected Plays,* 50). The significance attached to the entity called soul acquires mystical dimension where redemption or damnation is not envisioned in individual term, but as part of a general scheme for the whole humanity.

The mythical and morality motives take the play beyond its realistic moorings. It becomes spiritual sort of drama which involves the didactic whether man's soul is his property or divine means for the welfare of mankind. Countess rises above her personal spiritual concerns and takes her soul as a gift of god to be used for the general humanity. The play thus uses morality pattern of temptation, surrender to or victory over it and eventual damnation or salvation. Yeats has rightly modified the pattern to suit his dramatic needs. Temptation is presented as by the devils, but so far as the Countess' surrender to it is concerned, it is not motivated by any inner weakness or wavering as is the usual pattern in morality play, but necessitated by external exigencies to which her benign soul responds. This corresponds to Yeats' belief that though the action on stage includes fewer characters, it should suggest a lager phenomenon of life. For Yeats a drama "should be extravagant with an emphasis far greater than the life" (*Plays and Controversies,* 157-58). This is in keeping with his views that drama is not mere reality but an imaginative rendering of this reality so that the play gains universal significance. Yeats play is a complex blend of myth, mysticism and patriotism. In this act form Countess has been depicted as an archetype of Ireland as in the plays of Sean O' Casey. The countess exists in our mind as a symbol of Ireland. Yeats has clarified his position saying that:

> The play is symbolic: The two demons that have come to buy the soul are the world and their gold is the pride of the eyes. The Countess herself is soul, a self-denying persona, selling itself into captivity and unrest that it may redeem God's children, finding the peace it has not sought because all high motives are of the substance of peace. (*Letters,* 139)

Though Yeats could explore the psychological probing into the psyche of Countess, he does not exploit this as he wished to have a symbolic drama consisting of characters that are the creations of artists mind existing only as an idea and symbols not as personalities of flesh and blood. So Countess remains in our mind as a symbol of sacrifice of nationhood than as a woman. Yeats does not develop character as in the ordinary plays. Here the characters tend to be abstract, as the play has spiritual thesis. This point towards his future obsession with abstraction. The play turns out to be complex blend of myth, mysticism and patriotism. This complex thematic pattern develops along the lines of conventional realistic pattern since the message was the predominant dramatic concern. The enwrapping of the story of the sacrifice Countess Cathleen in the legendary cover can hardly hide the ghastly reality of Ireland's economic destitution and the urgency of its immediate solution.

Hence, the play apart from its call for patriotism/ nationhood is rooted in abstraction and intellectualism, an important element in Yeats dramaturgy. It was due to his concern with the fusion of myth, realism and mysticism. The play shows how Yeats transcends folktale material and to "show in a vision something of the face of Ireland". The use of the myth here makes the play more effective dramatically.

The blend of the actual and the legend focuses on the intensity of the symbolic tension in the play between the choice of personal life with marriage and family and the choice of the need for national service. This blending corresponds to Yeats own struggle to unite art, politics, philosophy and mythology in order to attain what he calls "the unity of being" and the "unity of culture". He once remarked "Irish had in Ireland imaginative stories which the uneducated classes knew and even sang, and might we not make those stories current among the educated masses, rediscovering for the works sake what I have called "the applied arts of literature" the association of literature, that is with music, speech, dance, etc...." Yeats was sure that by absorbing the ancient Irish legends he could attain "unity of culture". Here Yeats seems to follow the Greek tragedians whose plots were derived from the famous stories of Thebes or the house of Atreus. Yeats thus sets out "to bring again the theatre of Shakespeare or rather perhaps of Sophocles" (*Plays and Controversies,* 209). The advantage of using such stories was that both rich and poor knew these stories. Additionally, such stories could stir both emotions and intellect at the same time. By taking literature to its old source material, Yeats made it extravagant and joyful expression. These legendary stories also supported his romantic and sublime concept of the poet, besides providing him the body of symbols which could help him express his personal emotions without sentimentality and self-pity.

Works Cited

Allt, P. and Alspach, R.K. *The Variorum Edition of the Plays of W.B. Yeats*. New York: Macmillan, 1966.

Ellman, Richard. *The Identity of Yeats*. London: Macmillan, 1949.

Jhon, P. Fryne. Ed. *Uncollected Prose by W.B. Yeats*, Vol. 1. London: Macmillan, 1970.

Kinhana, Frank. *Yeats, Folklore and Occultism: Contexts of the Early Work and Thought*. Boston: Unwin Hymann, 1988.

Kelly, Neil. "The Use of Mythology in the Creation of a National Identity". knol.google.com. Knol: A Unit of Knowledge, 16 Oct. 2008.

Skelton, Robin and Ann, Saddlemayer. *The World of W.B. Yeats*, Seattle: University of Washington Press, 1965.

Thunte, Mary Helen. *W.B. Yeats and Irish Folklore*. Dublin: Gill and Macmillan Ltd., 1980.

Yeats, W.B. *Autobiographies*. London: Macmillan, 1926.

———. *Letters of W.B. Yeats*. Ed. Allan Wade. London: Macmillan, 1954.

———. *Autobiographies*. London: Macmillan, 1955.

———. *Letters to Katherine Tynan*. Ed. Roger McHugh, London: Burns Oates, 1953.

———. *Plays and Controversies*. London: Macmillan, 1923.

———. *Letters to the New Island* Ed. Horace Reynolds. Harvard University Press, 1934.

25

Exploding the Myth of Universal Human Nature: A Critique of William Golding's Fiction

Ravi Bhushan

What is Evil? No single statement can ever really answer this apparently simple question. The ambiguous and ubiquitous nature of evil therefore makes every definition incomplete, if not suspect. Thinkers and theologians throughout human history have grappled with the subject, but the mystery of evil abides.

A simplistic approach to this complex problem may enable us to regard it as an aspect of the eternal clash between illusion and reality. The real contrast is, between those who take evil and suffering as undeniable and those who view evil as a grotesque dream, ugly but unreal. The belief in an all-wise, all-loving, omnipotent and omniscient God seems to negate the existence of evil. If not a blade of grass could stir without His will, as the scriptures say, why hold man responsible for anything at all? The whole and related questions have been expressed powerfully by Persian poet Omar Khayyam in one of his great quatrains: "The moving finger writes and having writ moves on: nor all thy piety nor wit shall lure it back to cancel half a line, nor all the tears wash out a word of it" (Kapoor, 9).

All great writers have been, in the course of their confrontation with reality, obliged to acknowledge the problem of evil. Some of the world's greatest books—*Oedipus*, *King Lear*, *Moby Dick*, *The Brothers Karamazov*, etc. were written as a result of such a long and terrible peep into the heart of reality.

The word "evil" originated from the Anglosaxon term "yfel", the opposite complement of good, the term is almost always defined negatively. Evil is defined as that which is opposed to the divine order of the universe, which is bad or morally wrong or that which causes harm, pain or misery. The important question to be asked is, do people choose evil as such? Giving their arguments, Irish philosopher Francis Hutcheson and English philosopher Joseph Butler said that people don't choose evil as such but rather pursue their own interests at the expense of the interests of the other people and hence evil is a by-product of these pursuits. Another viewpoint suggests that people can choose evil for its own sake and further it says that all human beings have fallen natures and inevitably choose evil, unless given powerful incentives not to do so and are controlled by State or religious sanctions. But the crucial question is how evil is compatible with the existence of omnipotent and loving God. Several metaphysical theories can be cited to account for this question. One of these says that evil does not really exist, it is an illusion. Another says that evil is the necessary part of a good whole, just as a few dark patches in a painting may contribute to the perfection of the whole. But none of these justify the reality of the pain and suffering.

The problem of evil arises in connection with the alleged incompatibility of the following propositions: (a) God is omniscient (all knowing); (b) God is omnipotent (all powerful); (c) God is all good; (d) God exists; and (e) There is evil in the world. According to most religionists, the first three propositions are included in the definition of the concept God. That is, it is impossible that anything could properly be called God which is not all good, all powerful and all knowing. The fourth proposition is believed true by any conventional religionist. The fifth is usually felt to be obviously true. The incompatibility of the five propositions may be expressed in the form of a dilemma which casts doubt on the existence of any God defined with the first three attributes. Against the belief in a perfect God is pitted the belief in a godless universe. There is a theological view that evil is not a negative but a positive concept. It is regarded as a chastening and purifying agent, a detergent of the human soul; evil is the furnace that burns out the element of dross in us. In terms of the commonsensical philosophy, an eternal clash is seen between optimism and pessimism. The above discussion leads us to conclude that evil and good take on a relative hue that the world is neither good nor bad, but thinking makes it so.

According to Existentialists, man is condemned to be free and the problem of evil and of wrong doing is part and parcel of the problem of freedom or of moral choice. Without freedom, evil is inexplicable. For Karl Mark evil and sufferings were the most overbearing aspects of reality and not the kinds of things which could be explained away metaphysically. However, even the socialist Utopia finally gives no solution to the problems arising from within. Man's struggle is not with the outside world alone, but with his inner self also, where his creatureliness is subject to bafflement, pain and death, which are but different aspects of cosmic oppression. Even when man is at peace with the society in which he lives, he is never, without further struggle, at peace with himself. Where else could man find that courage, strength and peace with himself. So the Marxist view of evil is relevant to Joseph Conrad's world view insofar as Marxism talks about social inequalities. The Marxist view finally does not and cannot wholly account for the presence of evil in man's make up.

The most overriding forms that evil has taken are sin (evil that one does), and suffering (evil that one experiences). There are four possible classes of beings, capable of doing sin (evil): human, superhuman, sub-human and nature as the organic world. Both the human and the superhuman can be aware of moral rules and can presumably make choices to act on these rules or not, but in case of sub-human and nature, choices are instinctive or conditioned. Thus, all the moral rules, moral cunning and moral persuasion imaginable, won't prevent a squirrel from eating the forbidden fruit, nor prevent a wind from knocking it from its sacred, lofty perch. Consequently, while the sub-human creatures and nature are capable of causing suffering, they are incapable of doing evil (sin). Now, if sin is the transgression of a moral rule of some sort, it follows that only human and superhuman can commit sins or evils.

God, therefore, is not to be blamed for our misfortunes for there is nothing whimsical or arbitrary in his scheme. The prosperity of the wicked and the misery of the virtuous and the good are usual phenomena of our society. It is not that the reverse does not happen at all, but it seems undeniable that happiness and misery and prosperity and adversity are not proportionate to one's virtues and vices; instances of the suffering of the virtuous and of the prosperity of the depraved are not difficult to find and can easily be cited.

On the other hand, the ubiquitous evil in the form of miseries and sins compels us to suspect the impartiality of God. To buttress the view, here is an example from *The Mahabharata, Vana Parba,* wherein, Draupadi, the wife of Yudhisthira, derides the idea of God as a good and just ruler of the Universe on the ground that Yudhisthira, who was well known to be an embodiment of virtue was subjected to untold sufferings, whereas, Duryodhana, the well-known archfiend was enjoying prosperity.

Unprecedented scale of wars and persecutions of the 20th century undermined the secular belief in inevitable progress and confronted philosophers and theologians with the problem of evil. The First World War not only shattered the psychic confidence of man, but also stripped the world of its intentionality. The whole of the world is thrust into an ominous awareness of men ridden by forces within themselves too destructive to be controlled. Expressing this very idea, W.B. Yeats says in his visionary poem "The Second Coming" "The blood—dimmed tide is loosed, and every where the ceremony of innocence is drowned; the best lack all conviction, while the worst are full of passionate intensity". Man, in the twentieth century, is fascinated by the problem of evil more than ever before, because Freud, Jung and other contemporary psychologists have delved deep into the hidden side of human personality, which, by nature is indeterminate. As a result, there has been a noticeable shift of emphasis from the outward physical nature of evil to the subtler and more intricate one which is intellectually damaging and spiritually demoralizing. Physical pain and moral-cum-spiritual anguish testify to the existence of evil in the world. Physical pain, thanks to advances in medicine and surgery, can be located and often rooted out, but moral and spiritual pain is and will always be inexplicable, mysterious and terrifying.

In the whole range of English literature, poets and writers have shown in their representative works the problem of evil, though with varying degree of emphasis. Between 1952 and 1955 a number of new and articulate voices in British fiction began to claim public attention. Kingsley Amis, Iris Murdoch, John Wain, Doris Lessing, Angus Wilson, Thomas Hinde and Philip Larkin began to be regarded as representatives of a new post-war generation.

One among such writers was British novelist William Golding (1911-93) whose preoccupation with evil is so intense and extensive that no brief is needed to authenticate its presence. He has brought out the varied forms and facets of evil in man, in society, in nature and in universe, tracing at great length the moral repercussions of the discovery of evil in all these forms. For Golding man is an animal of savage impulses and dark powers which may overwhelm him at any confrontation with evil, which in its varied forms—moral, social, natural, physical, etc.—wrings out of man.

The experience of serving British Navy in Second World War became the turning point in Golding's career. It gave him a chance of observing the melee of humanity, at close quarters. War exposed him to the savagery, cruelty and lust inherent in man's nature. The atrocities of war, loss of traditional values and rootlessness of man in a society, constantly under flux are all reflected in Golding's novels. His firm belief that man is tainted with evil became the basis of Golding's novels.

The polarity between the rational and the imaginative or mysterious is always visible in Golding's works. The polarity reflects Golding's early consciousness of experience, and can be connected to both his desire to separate himself from the father he regarded as "incarnate omniscience" and his switch over at

Oxford University from sciences to literature. He does see the two sides of experience as identifiably separate, as pressures that pull the human being in different directions and is a constant source of human pain. According to Golding, we live constantly in two worlds, one physical and the other spiritual, and that the experience of the two worlds is basically emblematic of our nature. For Golding, who most often uses the conventional religious terms; physical and spiritual to identify the polarity, the physical is equated with the rational. He sees the rational view of experience as denying the irrational, the mysterious, or the spiritual. Yet, for Golding the spiritual is always felt. According to him, some sort of bridge between the two separate worlds exists.

Although Golding was not regarded as articulating any doctrine about the modern world, the implications of his metaphors were often felt as requiring no explanation and as uniquely applicable to contemporary experience. British Literary critic Frank Kermode argued convincingly:

> ...the emotion that generated Golding's fiction was less explicable as 'pain' or as 'grief' than as 'guilt'; an emotion contingent on the constant observation that the human being is unable to measure up to his own concept of himself, that the pain is less a matter of the human being as victim of something outside himself than of the human being as both victim and victimizer, the flawed consciousness of his own imagination. Man is, thus, capable of evil, of violation of himself and other human beings, and so deserves the moral judgment that can legitimately both excoriate most human beings most of the time and venerate the occasional 'saint', the savior of the human community, who is most often its scapegoat. (Kermode, 107-20)

Ralf Freedman further said in 1958:

> The eighteenth century contrast of civilization and primitivism is restated in twentieth century terms.... Golding renders a modern interpretation of what is human which could not have been accepted twenty or thirty years ago. (Freedman, 44-53)

William Golding has observed that modern man is appallingly ignorant of his own nature. His first novel, *Lord of the Flies* (1954) is the most famous and perhaps the most disturbing of his books; it reveals the depths of savagery which lie beneath civilization. Golding experienced two things which he counts the greatest influences on his writing—first the war and his service in the Navy, and secondly, his learning ancient Greek. The first confirmed for him the process, begun with the sinking of the Titanic, of shattering the liberal and optimistic image of man. The war and Greek literature together perhaps confirmed the dissociation from current and ephemeral affairs which makes Golding say that

> if the novelist has a serious, an Aeschylian, pre-occupation with the human tragedy...he is committed to looking for the root of the disease, instead of describing the symptoms. (Medcalf, 3)

His novels, therefore, move at the level of phenomena, of things happening in the physical or the spiritual worlds and develop their own forms for experience. One consequence of this is that perhaps more than with any other novelist, the process of reading a Golding novel is overwhelmingly important.

William Golding was essentially the product of two factors in 20th century English social history; firstly, the Second World War, which changed his view of man's nature and from which *Lord of the Flies* was born; and secondly the English State system Grammar school. His own home must have been a wonderful environment in which to grow up, and one wonders perhaps at the black pessimism of many of William Golding's characters. Perhaps it is that, when one has such a secure and happy, background, one can explore the darker sides of human nature with more objectivity than someone. When one recalls him the person who springs to mind is not the extrovert sailor or producer but an observant, reflective, thoughtful man apparently brooding on problems which he did not seem to share with anyone else. Golding could recognize that when he saw original sin "the guilt of Adam's first sin, the want of original righteousness and the corruption of man's whole nature together with all the actual transgressions which proceed from it" (Monteith, 60). In the desperate chase at the end in *Lord of the Flies* when Ralph is being hunted down by Jack and his group, his long, unshorn locks keep falling blindingly over his eyes, symbolizes effectively but perhaps too heavily the descent of irrationality and instinct, over reason and intelligence.

Golding's novels attempt to deal with the essential human condition, with "man at an extremity, man tested like a building material, taken into the laboratory and used to destruction, man isolated, man obsessed, man drowning into a literal sea or in the sea of his own ignorance" (*A Moving Target*, 198-99). Golding sees his statements about the human beings as fundamentally religious. Yet he follows no particular religious doctrine, is in fact skeptical of all doctrines and systems and declares Marx, Darwin and Freud, "the three most crashing bores of the western world" (*A Moving Target*, 186-87). He believes in a God that is beyond the triviality of man, not a God as "confident authority" or system but God as a principle of universal creation. Wayland Young called attention to Golding's frequent use of religious symbols and said in *Kenyon Review*, "though the specifically Christian element in Golding's work is always subordinate to a generalized sense of natural religion" (Nelson, 18-21).

Golding has one of the most powerful imaginations of any living writer, which is why he convinces even at his most obscure. He believes that imagination can sometimes penetrate what in *Darkness Visible* (1979), the Captain who rescues the child Matty calls "the screen that conceals the working of things" (*Darkness Visible*, 16). In *The Inheritors* (1955), the pictures which Lok and his fellow creatures share are both precursors of thought and intimations of a reality which thought cannot penetrate. Golding believes that the violence of our century is at a bottom, a revolt against reductionism. Perhaps this is what he is getting at when, in *Darkness Visible* truth appears in the mind of Sophy, "The way towards simplicity is through outrage" (*Darkness Visible*, 169).

Golding's concern is with larger; more fundamental, abstract issues that may be called metaphysical or theological. Such works ask not, how does man live? But what manner of creature is man? A few precedents of such fiction in English are Bunyan's *Pilgrim's Progress,* Swift's *Gulliver's Travels* and Orwell's *Animal Farm.* But at least since the eighteenth century it has laid at a distance from the mainstream of fictional tradition. Golding's achievement has been to revalidate this alternative tradition for the modern world. In dealing with a deeper sense of evil, and in also providing a character like Simon in *Lord of the Flies* who grasps the truth, Golding for Grande, really points towards a possible salvation that appealed to contemporary youth. Golding insisted on dark human depravity and offered hope for fallen man. Golding's novels assumed values of community and concern for others. Put another way, he is a reactionary in the most basic sense of the word. Reacting strongly to certain disagreeable aspects of life and literature as he sees them, he writes with a revolutionary heat that is contained rather than exploded within his compressed style. Restoration rather than preservation is his aim: he would restore concepts of belief, free will, individual responsibility, sin, forgiveness, vision and divine grace. He would restore principles in an unprincipled world; he would restore belief to a world of wilful unbelievers.

Golding is unlike the modernists in Blakean and Wordsworthian ways; and unlike the Romantics in Joycean and Conradian ways; he is both intensely skeptical and intensely religious; he uses the visionary against the visual and the visual against the visionary. Sight is nothing without insight and may deceive like words; that is only when the physical eye is made quiet by some deeper kind of perception that we can for a moment see into the life of things. Golding is a man in search of cosmological truth; and it might well be argued that—as he himself has often proclaimed in a slightly different context—the names, the labels do not matter. It is only the ultimate reality that counts and must at all costs be communicated. His characters, as Professor Kermode memorably wrote,

> live in a world of rock and sea and amoebae heaving in the pull of the moon, refusing to be locked fast by human imaginings of good or evil, obstinately talking its own language of sucking, plopping and roaring, against the human language which gives it another kind of life. (Norman, 96)

Despite all his self-imposed limitations, Golding remains the most powerful writer, the most original, the most profoundly imaginative, to have turned his hand to fiction since the war. In reply to a literary magazine's questionnaire, *The Writer in His Age,* William Golding wrote

> I believe that man suffers from an appalling ignorance of his own nature. I am fully engaged to the human dilemma but see it as far more fundamental than a complex of taxes and astronomy. (*London Magazine,* 45-46)

Lord of the Flies is probably the most powerful English novel written since the war. Most of Golding's later novels show this same visionary intensity and show him also groping for a form that will contain this kind of tortured moral vision. Golding is a man haunted by his own sense of human inadequacy who, disregarding all novelistic traditions available to him is conducting a bold search for the kind of novel which will contain his own vision of man. Much of Golding's writing explores moral dilemmas at the centre of human existence and he frequently places his characters in extreme situations to suggest a "mythological dimension" to their lives. Profoundly obsessed with the subject of evil and original sin, he treats these subjects in a way that transcends the boundaries of orthodox Christianity. Novels of William Golding disclose him as a writer obsessed with evil and original sin who created a mythology of his own, revealing new depths of both horror and exhilaration in the human condition.

At the heart of all of his works, Golding's belief is that "man produces evil as a bee produces honey" (Hot Gates, 87). His books aim to make man face the sad fact of his own cruelty and lust. Behind their wide diversity of tone and setting lies the fixed conviction that man is a fallen being, he is gripped by original sin, his nature is sinful and his state perilous.

Merging fast paced narrative into a streamlined, semi-allegoric structure that moves with increasing impetus through scenes of savagery to a terminating pessimism about man, *Lord of the Flies* much resembles Golding's second novel, *The Inheritors* another myth-like story that can be glossed in both political and religious terms. These two novels, among Golding's most successful, deal with humanity and evil in a generalized, panoramic way, in each, human malevolence shows itself most fearsomely through mob atrocity and in the arena of power. The subsequent books focus on individuals and private relationships especially sexual ones.

Golding's fiction makes broad use of allusions to classical literature, mythology and Christian symbolism. Although no distinct thread unites his novels and his technique varies, Golding deals principally with evil and emerges with what has been characterized as a kind of dark optimism. Golding has never tried to avert his eyes from such horrifying knowledge of incidents like Nazi extermination camps and of the dropping of the atomic bombs in Japan. All the novels of his first decade as a novelist, up to the superb *The Spire* (1964) are marked by a hard, unflinching view of human history and potential. His novels are indeed so different from one another that it is hard to delineate connecting threads. The studied pastiche of *Rites of Passage* (1980) is remote form the visionary passion of *The Spire*. The ostensibly autobiographical *Free Fall* (1959) has next to nothing in common with *The Inheritors*. Although Golding calls himself an optimist—there is little evidence in his novels to support that claim. The madness of violence, of lust and of fanaticism seems always just below the surface. Like Koestler, Golding sees man as a species which is irredeemably flawed, and which is only too likely to bring about its own destruction.

Golding has a pre-Freudian vision of man in which the notion of repression plays little part. He thinks much more in terms of dissociation and even of possession. Actual loss of consciousness is surprisingly common in the novels. Simon, the

Christ figure in *Lord of the Flies* is an epileptic. He loses consciousness, not only on his first appearance in the book, but also after the pig's head delivers its sermon to him. In *Darkness Visible*, Sophy suddenly loses consciousness at a party when presented with a Rorschach ink blot which everyone else sees as part of a game. She does so again after her terrifying fantasy of murdering the kidnapped boy. Earlier in the same book, Matty loses consciousness twice after his agonizing encounter with the aborigine.

According to Golding, man has grown away both from nature and himself. He is protected from reality not only by city life, labor saving device, canned food, electric light, running water, daily paper, indifference to the seasons, but also by the spiritual blindness which such conditions breed. He is cushioned in smugness; he has become his own god. Nothing can touch him. Golding has made it his task to break down these false illusions. Writing about schoolboys, Neanderthalers and dead sailors appears to him to be a simple means of turning a light on contemporary human nature. He believes the only hope for humanity is self-knowledge. In an interview for *Books and Art* (March 1958), he also made it clear that the basic problem of modern humanity, was that of learning to live fearlessly, with the natural chaos of existence, without forcing artificial patterns on it.

Golding, in fact, is primarily a religious novelist; his central theme is not the relationship of man to man but the relationship of man, the individual to the universe; and ultimately to God. He searches for basic truths that have been obscured by material progress. He is a spiritual cosmologist. Golding says that man and man alone, introduce evil into the world; a view which is hardly separable from the doctrine of original sin. To a critic who suggested that good was equally an exclusive human concept, he replied: "good can look after itself. Evil is the problem". This attitude suggests both the emotional strength of his work and the intellectual paradox underlying it. In a lecture called *Fable* (included in *The Hot Gates*), he revealed how the war transformed him into a moralist. After the war he realized "that man was sick—not exceptional man, but average man". All of his works revolved around the theological truism that man's nature is sinful and his state perilous. Golding's strength lies in the metaphorical and imaginative power brought into play for detailed amplification of moral tension and elaboration of physical background.

Most of the changes that have taken place during the last hundred years or so are, however, improbably, interrelated, they share a common causality. The growth of an urban industrial society, the decay of traditional religious fundamentalism, the dissemination of scientific method, moral uncertainty, technological advance, the artificial retreat to primitivism, the flourishing neuroses which facilitated the development of psychology and psychiatry; automation, logical positivism, thermonuclear deterrents, political propaganda, horror comics, science fiction, rock-n-roll, angst, the death wish, sexual frustration or hysteria: One pattern binds them all together. Several factors have combined to offer us a comforting, but, ultimately dangerous, protection. Foremost among these has been the notion that science could in some mysterious way, be made a substitute for religion. Reason could stick new labels on the emotions, but it could neither argue nor legislate them out of existence. It would rationalize God by discussing religion in terms of personal psychology, but God (under whatever name) remained. This may seem as a long, perhaps an irrelevant introduction to Golding's work, but it is indispensable if we are to understand his works fully. Golding once wrote that the work of the novelist is to scrape the labels off things, to take nothing for granted, to show the irrational where it exists. His novels, demonstrate this process in action.

Many writers have been concerned, with what is rhetorically called the dilemma of modern man and have given us, lectures on the anarchy of a poisoned future. Golding on the contrary, scarcely uses an argument or issues a warning: He simply shakes us until we feel in our bones the perennial agony of our species. Golding gives remarkably full expression to a profound modern need, the need for reassurance in terms of the primitive; the longing to know somehow of a possible humanity that lives equally in the whole world; the need for myths of total and satisfactory explanation. Our developed consciousness, our accumulated knowledge are marks of guilt; the fragmentary nature of our experience is the theme of Golding's novels. He sees the world enormously altered by new knowledge, it is a world you can blame "science" for if you like, a world in which the myth of progress has failed; but the rival myth of necessary evil and universal guilt has come back without bringing God with it. Golding believes in human guilt and the human sense of paradise lost; he also believes in divine mercy. The evidence for holiness lies scattered among the fragments of our world and those fragments are represented in Golding's books; they form part of the whole.

Golding described himself as "a citizen, a novelist and a schoolmaster". The citizen is concerned with the defects of society, the schoolmaster is concerned to correct them by proper instruction; the novelist finds the appropriate forms in which man's own nature may be embodies, that be may learn to know it. One consequence of this will to instruct is that Golding is an unusually disciplined, schematic writer; another consequence is his desire to have his works read with the same kind of conscious intelligence, and his distrust of irrational and intuitive views of literary creation. He clearly thinks of his novels as the expressions of conscious intentions that existed before the writing began. Golding accepts certain traditional ideas about man and his place in the world; that mind, by meditation and speculation may arrive at truth; that it may find in the past, meanings which are relevant to the present, and available through memory; that it may concern itself with metaphysics and with morals. Not all of these ideas are current now, and consequently Golding's work may seem, in the context of his time, more didactic and moralizing. Though Golding is a moralist, he is not a moral maker, and his novels belong, not with Aesop's fables, but with the important symbolic novels of our century with Camus's and Kafka's.

Works Cited

Frank Kermode, *The Novels of William Golding*, International Literary Annual, 1961. Reprinted in William Nelson, *Golding's Lord of the Flies.*

London Magazine, IV, May 1978.

Quoted in Norman Page *William Golding: Novels, 1954-67*, Houndmills, Macmillan, 1985.

Ralph Freedman, *The New Realism: The Fancy of William Golding*, Perspective, Summer—Autumn 1958. Reprinted in Nelson, *Golding's Lord of the Flies*, New York, Odyssey Press, 1963.

Quoted by Ranjit K. Kapoor, *Joseph Conrad: His Theme and Treatment of Evil*, Chandigarh, Bahri Publications, 1987.

Quoted in Stephen Medcalf, *William Golding*, Essex, Longman Group, 1975.

Wayland Young, *Letter from London*, Kenyon Review, Summer 1975. Reprinted in William Nelson, *William Golding's Lord of the Flies: A Source Book*, New York, Odyssey Press, 1963.

Quoted in *William Golding: The Man and his Books, A tribute on his 75th Birthday*, ed. Charles Monteith, London, Faber and Faber, 1986.

William Golding, *Darkness Visible*, London, Faber and Faber, and New York, Farrar Straus, 1980.

William Golding, *A Moving Target*, London, Farrar, Straus & Giroux, 1984.

26

Merging Myth and Contemporary Reality: Ismail Kadare's *Spring Flowers, Spring Frost*

Shahla Gauri

Ismail Kadare has been one of the most prominent Albanian writers since he began publishing his literary works in the 1960s. A prolific author who has composed poetry, short-stories, and volumes of criticism in addition to his many highly regarded novels, Kadare is one of the few Albanian writers whose works have been translated and published in other countries. His novels and stories have been translated into over thirty languages and have seen an increasing amount of critical attention since the 1980s, particularly in France and the United States. In a country rigidly ruled by a Stalinist regime from the end of World War II until the early 1990s, Kadare's writings have stood out as some of the few examples of Albanian literature that did not follow the strictures of social realism, a genre devoted to propagating Marxist ideology. Instead Kadare offers historical and contemporary tales that range from lyrical portraits of the Albanian people, drawing upon both the history and folklore of the culture, to scathing parodies of totalitarian rule.

In *Spring Flowers, Spring Frost* (first English translation published in 2002), Kadare depicts the time following Albania's liberation from the Communist totalitarian government. Albania has come out from the isolation and terror it experienced under communist dictatorship. But this awakening is bittersweet. Along with all the benefits of joining the modern European order come unforeseen problems in the form of taxes, bank robberies, disappearances and the rebirth of the *Kanun*, an ancient system of blood-debt and revenge that was responsible for perpetuating an endless cycle of violence. Kadare has given a very moving account of this custom's impact on the lives of those who have to follow it in his novel *Broken April*. Mark Gurabardhi, an artist and employee of the Arts Centre, is the main character in *Spring Flowers, Spring Frost* who finds himself caught between the jubilation of a tantalizing freedom and the social chaos that has accompanied it. In the Albanian mountain town of B—the relaxation of Communist rigidity has brought both new freedom and a revival of old terrors. A sensitive soul, Mark feels disturbed by the political turn and the bizarre events taking place in his strife-torn country. He tries to understand the contemporary reality through his knowledge of myths, legends and folktales. The contemporary story and folktale appear to be variations on the same theme, and at times they intersect.

There is no plot to speak of in *Spring Flowers, Spring Frost*; rather it structures the jumbled musings of the painter who seems to have great difficulty in reconciling events of the past with those of the present thus reflecting the struggle of his country Albania as it finally shirks the constraints of Communism and begins to bloom yet is still somewhat suffocated by its traditions, particularly the *Kanun*. The metaphor in the title indicates this state of living in two worlds. As Mark says early in the book, Albania is going through a "period of transition" and is in other words hermaphroditic or in the language of the people, "a bitch and a dog". Kadare in his experimental ordering of the story has alternated a regular chapter whose events take place in the present time with a "counter chapter" narrating a myth or a folktale. In the opening chapter some children have dug up a hibernating snake and a crowd is debating what should be done with it. The appearance of a snake at this time of the year is disturbing for the people of Albania. The snake is "neither dead nor alive" and people know that "frozen snakes don't bite and even if you get bitten, it's not dangerous, the venom is too weak, like it's diluted by the cold...." In this very chapter, the folktale of the girl who married a snake is mentioned with reference to the present state of affairs. This same folktale appears in detail in Counter Chapter 1. An ancient Albanian family force their daughter to marry a snake as punishment for some offence against the *Kanun*. The snake turns out to be a man under a spell. The animal slips out of its skin in the night and retreats into it in the morning. The girl is quite satisfied and her happiness is obvious to the people during daytime. Wanting to keep her husband in his human form, one night the girl throws his skin in the fire, and her husband disappears forever. It was Mark's friend Zef who had likened the monstrosities of today's Albania to the ancient tale of the girl who had married a snake, adding that "all these faces that change their masks from one day to the next, like in some Greek drama...they don't inspire a lot of confidence" (3). Reference to this snake further occurs during the course of the novel along with its symbolic snake-skin. The snake can also be taken as representative of the ancient laws of Albanian Highlands which are neither dead nor alive but keep on making their presence felt.

Another shocking incident which occurs at the small town of B is the hold-up of the National Bank. Interrogations are on but the culprits are still not found. Zef has also mysteriously disappeared. Back at his studio, Mark worries about the safety of his paintings, lest a theft occurs. He calls the locksmith to ensure the safety of his locks and door panels. In the Counter Chapter 2, Mark remembers his drawing of Prometheus at the school of Fine Arts, "scuttling away from Mount Olympus with fire clutched under his cloak". It reminds him of the words of the locksmith that civilisation began with a robbery. Leafing through the *Dictionary of Mythology*, Mark comes to know that the theft of fire was the second robbery on Olympus. The first was the theft of immortality. He tries to find the details of this theft but "it was obscure and poorly explained".

In Counter Chapter 2, the myth of the theft of immortality is described. When death goes knocking at the door of a man who was supposed to die, the reply comes: "Go back whence thou came, I have nothing to do with thee" (59). The messenger is dumbstruck and stands rooted to the ground. It's the first time anything like this has happened. Finally, he has to leave without the man's soul as he shows him the symbol of immortality which the messenger himself had never seen but whose power he well recognises. He goes back and reports the matter to the Minister of Death, Erebus who in turn goes to wake the great leader of them all Hades. There occurs a lot of commotion as the seriousness of the matter is realised by one and all: "He (Hades) tells himself that what has just taken place is the most serious, the most extraordinary event imaginable. Death has been struck to the very root, for the first time in a million years. If breach is not closed, Death will never recover. And the whole edifice of the universe will fall apart" (62). He goes down to the earth to meet Zeus on the Olympus. What ensues there is described not in very certain terms, but finally the culprit is caught. It was Tantalus who was responsible for the theft of immortality, the first theft to have been committed in the universe. The interrogating sessions which he is put to could only be guessed as the absolute nature of these questions was known to none.

Kadare's retelling of the Tantalus myth is fantastically absurd and open to confusing interpretations. It portrays the Ministry of Death as a vast bureaucracy with its endless forms and hierarchies. Zeus is a totalitarian dictator who employs spies and agents; and the interrogation of Tantalus is done behind closed-doors in the "Great Prison", burying his crime under state-sponsored propaganda. The entire episode, thus, becomes shrouded in mystery with even the crime of Tantalus not confirmed. It well could have been any other mortal responsible for the crime but probably to hush up the matter in a hurry, it was Tantalus who was penalised. The uncertainty of all the later interrogations which occur in the text whether regarding the bank hold-up, or Oedipus, or the iceberg which sank the Titanic, or finally Angelin, involved in blood-feud, reflect the ambiguity involved in the original theft.

Mark tries to link these two events of theft "that took place in the heavens" with the "pillaging of the pyramids" and the hold-up at the bank of B. The disturbed times in Albania weigh heavily on his mind and his going back to the details of the Greek myths he had heard or read about, help him indulge in "such idle dreams" which provide temporary relief to his mind. However, in trying to understand the present reality Mark, at times, touches upon borders of insanity and "mental muddle" fostered by the "psychotic atmosphere of the times" (56). His narration also, at times, seem untrustworthy as when he assumes that his girlfriend is sleeping with her brother simply because a traditional Albanian woman is more a sister than a girlfriend. This state of muddle is a pointer to the power of the sub-conscious which can never be fully understood.

Modernity as it intrudes in the town of B does so as a mere material reality. During the course of reference to contemporary times, we are constantly told of memos being sent from the Council of Europe to Albania to regulate administrative affairs, and the political parties plotting to exploit the situation. Mark himself, in trying to translate this reality of modernity in his own language, does so by blending events of the past with present times. When thinking about a man drowned beneath the Strait of Otranto, he fantasizes on the ghosts of other drowned people screaming out that the Strait itself must be punished by being damned. All this takes place amidst flashes of objects "drowned" in the sea:

> ..., innumerable inanimate objects and the outlines of animate beings jostle for space: tin crutches, silver neck chains that have slipped off emaciated necks, homosexual in stunning embrace, glass eyes, candles dolls,...a stone from the Berlin Wall inscribed with "A Souvenir of Andy, a refugee", slimy condoms looking like ordinary molluscs, low-denomination dollar bills, hymn books,... and, finally, an unexploded NATO bomb, which will surely spread panic.... (*Spring*, 154)

The main theme of *Spring Flowers, Spring Frost* is the revival of the so-called "blood laws" which dictated the country's medieval past and the Communist Secret Archives which for unknown reasons have incited interest in the present post-communist era. In fact, these two aspects constantly intersect, to the point that the truth about the one seems to hide or to reveal the truth about the other. The *Kanun* or the Book of the Blood is a book where the "debts" of each family are inscribed according to the ancient "an eye for an eye" law. The ambiguity between the ancient code based on the law of the blood and the modern secret archives is deliberate, as if the crimes and the blood staining the pages of Communist archives were but a new version of the same primitive institution. We know from Mark's tale that somewhere in the mountains lies hidden the Book of the Blood. At the end of the novel we are told that Brezhnev, an Albanian leader himself, visited the mountains and tore at the roots but whether it is the Book of the Blood or photos of the central committee killing people, Mark and we do not know. Ultimately, the coming of Communism to Albania eliminated the *Kanun*, but Kadare leaves us in no doubt that it was merely to replace the ancient law with a modern-day code no less bizarre and inexplicable in its operations.

Mark's girlfriend is a source of link to the happenings in the contemporary world. It is she who brings in news from the capital which he finds disturbing. Mark is aware of the widening gulf between himself and his girlfriend, who is also his model for the nude paintings. He is also aware of the fact that his girlfriend had everything to do with the present and the future, "everything with moving forward" whereas he was related to the past, "was turned backwards". What worries him the most at present is the possibility of his girlfriend leaving him for good. She was attracted towards him because of his fame as an artist but in due course realises that "he wasn't as well known as she had imagined". Mark himself is not sure of his worth as an artist during these disturbing times and therefore starts to think of his "second life" as a policeman.

Things take an unexpected turn when Mark comes to know that his girlfriend's brother has got involved in a blood-feud. Mark had wanted her to be "his guide to the new era" but she now turned out to be "held back by an ancient and rusty hook" (*Spring*, 74). When she comes to him for help he imagines his life as a police officer which his father wanted him to become and the line of distinction between his present profession as an artist and his imagined life in the police department becomes more and more blurred. In Counter Chapter 5, Mark imagines himself to be the police officer opening pending files and referring to registered cases. The cases in these files and the ones he thinks about with reference to these cases are all linked, though some date back to thousands of years. Besides the bank hold-up case, he recalls the interrogation of the queen who had made two contradictory confessions:

> In the first set of avowals she had said unambiguously that her husband, Oedipus Rex, had never been her son. In the second confession, she admitted to having married her son, despite having known for many years that he had killed his own father. She had promised to explain everything at the next interrogation, but in the small hours of the appointed day, she managed at last to hang herself. (*Spring*, 130)

Mark thinks of other cases which needed to be solved like the trial of Tantalus, now 102,000 years old; the truth of which had been lost forever. Another case of killing of a house snake considered to be of an endangered species, creates a lot of hue and cry reminding us of the snake in the first chapter and the myth of a girl marrying a snake. Mark tries to divert his mind to less scandalous cases but each time his mind keeps returning to the Secret Archives and to the deep storage business. He imagines interrogating the only worker but to no avail. Even the final questioning to his girlfriend regarding her loss of virginity is not answered. He fails in getting satisfactory answers to any of the cases he investigates. His second life, although an imaginary one, proves to be as futile and unconvincing as his real one. Throughout the tale Mark wonders in darkness seeking out perpetually the reasons for unexplained actions—why has his girlfriend been called home to see an old uncle who has come down from the mountains, why do the inner party seem so interested in this out of the way town, why has his mistress started taking the pill—and he tries to find answers in the myths and swirls of memory about the region.

Mark Gurabardhi also attempts to seek the underlying truth of unsolved cases through his art. He tries to paint the iceberg which sank the Titanic but the most difficult to paint was the submerged part—"the most tragic and sinister". The single shot that had killed his boss Marian Shkreli intended as blood vendetta in which his girlfriend's brother was involved, inspired the painting "Eight Views of the Iceberg that sank the Titanic". He tried to transfer all the human features of this story of the blood-feud to the iceberg but is not satisfied with the exact white colour he wanted. Everything he fantasises or dreams of brings him back to the fear of revival of the *Kanun*. The Secret Archives and the Book of the Blood, supposed to be hidden in the Northern Mountains had taken complete hold of Mark's imagination.

When, in the final chapter, the members of the Arts Centre go to show around the place to a group of delegates from the Council of Europe, the head of the music section tells Mark that the Secret Archives storage depot was somewhere around. It was when Mark sat looking for the entrance to this secret place, straining his eyes through his binoculars, that he sees a procession of the once dominant dictators appear as hazy and distant mythic figures. They were all looking for the entrance to the secret tunnel. It was, however, Mark who finally comes to realise the truth regarding the mystery of human existence: "He immediately realised why the whole world looked suspicious to him. It was because of the dense mass of brambles that hid the tunnel that led to the Secret Archives. As they resembled a woman's entrance, so they spread the awareness of sin far and wide" (*Spring*, 178). He watches Hoxha, Brezhnev, Walter Ulbricht, etc. walk through the Albanian mountains. In the end follows the blind and infirm

Oedipus; the same Oedipus who murdered his father and slept with his mother. But was it really Oedipus who had committed this crime? Mark could plainly make out the pain evident on his countenance as "he continued to turn his empty sockets in all directions". Mark wanted to reach out to him, "to share with him things that were bursting out of his imagination, but he did not know what language to use." In his earnestness to unburden Oedipus of his guilt, he cries out: "O man of mystery, son and father of yourself, why did you shoulder a crime that you did not commit?" (*Spring*, 180). Mark was convinced of his innocence and suddenly the mystery of all other crimes committed in the past became clear. All the happenings around in post-communist Albania seem to metamorphose into myths. The contemporary setting and characters anchored in both mythical, and historical past and a present full of references to the history of Albania provide proof to the ever receding line of distinction between the past and the present, a constant reminder of the burden of history which cannot be wiped off. Kadare artfully portrays how an individual is affected when his society is suddenly released from long oppression. Nothing ever really changes, the past and the present become indistinguishable making all time as T.S. Eliot put it "unredeemable". In this context any idea of man's freedom would only be illusory.

Works Cited

Berlinski, Mischa. *Woman Marries Snake: A Peculiar Indian Love Story*. Harper Publications. Nov. 2007.

Kadare Ishmail, *Spring Flowers, Spring Frost*, London: Vintage Random House, 2003.

27

To Kill a Myth in Harper Lee's *To Kill a Mocking-Bird*

K.B.S. Krishna

Myth, an established story of apparently historical events is used to explain or understand part of the world view of a culture. Legends, parables, and facts combine to form a heady mix, which is used to explain the practices and beliefs of a set of people, or even natural phenomenon. Over a period of time, these oral tales that are handed down from generation to generation crystallize and are almost accepted unquestioningly. Thus, they become an important part of life, and in a sense give an identity to the people of that culture. For instance, the Hindu mythology has become so deeply ingrained in the psychology of most Indians that some of them would argue that the *Ramayana* and the *Mahabharata*, with all their magical elements, happened exactly as they are related in the epics, irrespective of whether there is any historical evidence to warrant such belief. However, in the present times the word "myth" is used in an almost all-encompassing manner, and is used to refer to even folktales or legends. So, to understand the meaning of "myth", it is necessary to explain these terms. If a story, even if it comprises heroic elements, involves humans rather than supernatural beings, it is a legend, and not a myth. Similarly, even if a story has supernatural elements and beings, if it is not part of a systematic mythology, such a story would be considered as a folktale and not a myth. This negative definition shows that myth is a story that involves supernatural beings as part of a systematic mythology. Myths are generally shrouded in mystery. Considering the origin of myths, this is understandable. This mystery element, as well as the heroic quality of most of the stories, makes myths very appealing to writers. In fiction, as well as in poetry and in drama, authors have unsparingly used myths. They do this to either compare the sequences with what is happening in the present day or to contrast the heroism in myths with the lack of heroism in the present day.

Hence, we have novels such as Mary Shelley's (1797-1851) *Frankenstein* (1818), which was published with the subtitle *The Modern Prometheus*. In the novel, Shelley compares Frankenstein to Prometheus. Shelley's protagonist, in a manner similar to the Greek hero who steals fire from Zeus and gives it to humans, brings the knowledge of creation—which is in a sense was patented by gods—to humans. The trials and tribulations that Frankenstein faces due to his act clearly bring out the similarities between him and the Greek hero. Poems such as Percy Bysshe Shelley's (1792-1822) elegy to John Keats (1795-1821) "Adonais" (1821), similarly, contain references to the Greek goddesses Urania and Venus. He refers to Keats as the god of fertility, Adonis, and calls upon Adonis' mother Urania to mourn his death. By such allusions, Shelley suggests that with the death of Keats a death knell has rung for fertility —in other words, creativity.

Similarly, George Bernard Shaw's (1856-1950) play *Pygmalion* (1912) is loosely based on a Greek myth. However, unlike in the myth, where the sculptor falls in love with the statue that he carves, the erstwhile hero in Shaw's play hardly notices the cultured person that he had trained. Through this allusion Shaw contrasts the happenings in mythology with what happens in an unromantic modern world. Thus, authors have used myths regularly in their works, irrespective of whether the genre that they are dabbling in is romantic poetry or problem plays. They have used myths to compare and contrast, and thereby strived to provide a vivid depiction of the various characters in their works. In this context, I attempt to look at how myth is used Harper Lee's (1926-) *To Kill a Mocking-Bird* (1960) in this paper.

Lee's Pulitzer Prize winning novel was later made into an Oscar award winning film (1962) and is considered as a classic of modern American literature. The novel is interesting because of various factors such as the autobiographical elements present in the novel, the style, and the various genres and themes that it encompasses. Set in 1930s America, the novel is a tale of the growing up of Jem and Scout, the children of a white middle-aged lawyer Atticus Finch. Narrated by a now-grown-up Scout in a reflective manner, the novel depicts the adventures and ordeals of the Finch family over a period of three years. The story is seemingly simple. Scout and her brother Jem are fascinated by their reclusive neighbor Boo Radley. They try to know him better, and are rewarded by little gifts left for them by Boo. Meanwhile, the court appoints Scout's father as the lawyer of Tom Robinson. Tom, a black man, is accused of raping a young white woman, Mayella Ewell. This defending of Tom results in a lot of trouble for the Finch family as they are persecuted by the villagers, who do not like the fact that a black man should dare to contest a white man's statement. Despite evidence to the contrary, the white jury convicts Tom, and he is killed while trying to escape from prison. Although Ewell wins the case, Mayella's father considers the court trial an insult and assaults Jem and Scout on Halloween night. However, Boo Radley comes to their rescue. In the ensuing struggle, Ewell is killed. The case is hushed up, and Boo disappears yet again.

Such dry summarizing of the story makes it seem as if the novel is a high octane mindless thriller. On the contrary, the novel is an insightful tale dealing with problems such as discrimination, innocence, guilt, and sin that have been haunting writers since the Old Testament days. These serious motifs, however, do not make the novel forbidding; rather, as they are told from a child's perspective and with deep empathy and humor, they give the novel an endearing quality that attracts even youngsters. Lee looks at various themes in her novel. Similar to another Pulitzer Prize winning novel, Margaret Mitchell's (1900-49) *Gone with the Wind* (1936), this novel too vividly paints the day-to-day life in a small town in South America. Despite the difference in the setting of the period, the other novel being set in the Civil War, both novels show how racial discrimination is calmly accepted by the citizens as they are so used to it. By extension, the citizens are also not bothered by racial injustice.

Another theme that Lee deals with in the novel is class distinctions. She clearly brings out how the Ewell family is looked down upon by the rest of the society as they are "White Trash". Likewise, discrimination based on gender is also touched upon in the novel in the difference in what the elders expect from Jem and Scout. The laws of the country, and the rules of the society of which the Finch family are a part are also an interesting sub-theme in the novel. Along with these themes dealing with injustices of that period, Lee also portrays universally acknowledged good qualities such as courage, compassion, love, empathy, and sacrifice. How the Finch children imbibe these qualities forms the crux of the story, and in that regard this novel can truly be termed as a bildungsroman. Bringing up children is also an important theme in the novel; and the manner in which Atticus trains his kids is not only admirable, but worth emulating.

However, it is the use of myth in this novel that is most interesting. From the title to the references to the various superstitions that are passed on from generation to generation such as how seasons change because of children's poor behavior, the novel uses myth on various levels for myriad purposes. It uses myth in different ways—both as referring to something supernatural, and as a "falsehood" that is believed in by the majority as being true. This use of myth in Harper Lee's *To Kill a Mocking-Bird* is the focus of my paper. One of the main myths in the novel is that of Boo Radley. Always avoided by the people of Maycomb, the Radley house is treated as an "unknown entity" (*To Kill a Mocking-Bird,* 7). Arthur Radley, or Boo Radley, as he is called, is never seen out of the house. According to neighborhood legend, he is supposed to be a delinquent who was shut up in the house after he once came up for trial due to disorderly behavior. Described as having a "long scar" and "yellow and rotten" teeth (*To Kill a Mocking-Bird,* 14), Boo is seen by the townsfolk as a "malevolent phantom" responsible for everything bad that happens in the town: from "frozen azaleas" to "stealthy crimes"—even those confessed to by others (*To Kill a Mocking-Bird,* 9). The Finch children are also influenced by this Radley myth. Jem describes him to his friend, Dill as dining on "raw squirrels and any cats he could catch". The Radley house is considered so scary that Jem even wages a bet with his friend to touch the house; however, he is so terrified on seeing a shadow that he leaves his pants behind (*To Kill a Mocking-Bird,* 60). However, there are indications, right through the novel, that Boo Radley is, perhaps, not as scary as the town makes him out to be. Scout and Jem find gifts such as chewing-gum, figures made of soap resembling themselves, and a watch, in a tree-hollow near the Radley place —ostensibly left by Boo for them. Although Jem still says that even touching the Radley tree is bad, they covet these gifts and feel bad when the tree-hollow is closed up (*To Kill a Mocking-Bird,* 69). Moreover, Boo Radley covers Scout with a blanket when she is out in the cold, watching the fire (*To Kill a Mocking-Bird,* 80).

The myth is busted at the end when Boo Radley saves the lives of Scout and Jem. He risks his own life and saves them from Robert Ewell (288-89). This shows that he likes both of them and is not an evil spirit but just a sad person confined to a house. So, from being the imagined perpetrator of crimes, he becomes their savior. This busting of the myth shows how Harper Lee looks at myths: they are falsehoods propagated out of ignorance, and knowledge naturally puts an end to such myths. Another myth in the novel is the one about negroes. The people of Maycomb are prejudiced against Afro-Americans, and consider them as irresponsible and sub-human savages. Therefore, they immediate believe Bob Ewell when he complains that Tom Robinson raped his daughter (*To Kill a Mocking-Bird,* 136). In fact, they put Tom up for trial, instead of just lynching him, just because they deem it a legal procedure that has to be followed—albeit one that need not be taken seriously. They staunchly believe that a black man is capable of any crime. Therefore, they are flabbergasted when Atticus Finch refuses to toe the line and sincerely tries to defend the black man. Even the children at school tease Scout about Atticus attitude (*To Kill a Mocking-Bird,* 82). The Finches, however, do not believe in the myth about blacks. This is obvious from the fact that not only that they have a black housekeeper, Calipurnia, but she is treated as a member of the family. Despite Aunt Alexandra's statements that Negroes are untrustworthy and backbite whites (*To Kill a Mocking-Bird,* 173), Calipurnia stays in the household.

In Tom's trial, however, the jurors persist in their long-held opinion of blacks and pronounce him guilty (*To Kill a Mocking-Bird,* 233). Tom's attempt to flee prison also proves that he is human and not an animal like the others imagine, as he understands that being in prison would not get him justice (*To Kill a Mocking-Bird,* 259). However, this action is interpreted by the smug town folk as typical irresponsible 'negro' reaction (*To Kill a Mocking-Bird,* 265). All this suggests that the public opinion of blacks is deeply rooted, and the myth has become a part of their daily life. Lee, in her novel, suggests that the myth that negroes aren't humans and are savages is false, and should be busted. This is clear in the scene where Calipurnia takes the Finch children to the Black Church, the two realize that negroes are just like other human beings (*To Kill a Mocking-Bird,* 131-35). Even the rape allegation against Tom proves, in an ironic manner, that negroes are humans, as the allegation is a result of Mayella Ewell acknowledging Tom as a man and desiring his companionship (*To Kill a Mocking-Bird,* 224).

In fact, in the novel, Lee depicts negroes in a better light compared to whites. After the court case is over, the Negroes are shown to be more humane than the whites; Tom's wife sends Atticus gifts, realizing that he had done his best to save her husband; whereas, Robert Ewell spits on Atticus after winning the case. Similarly, it is the white men who behave like savages as they come close to harming Atticus for defending Tom (*To Kill a Mocking-Bird,* 169-70). These scenes suggest that Lee's novel is in a sense a propagandist novel with the sole aim of putting myths to rest—be it the myth of Boo Radley as a bogeyman or blacks as irresponsible savages. Lee, through this novel, suggests that myths, while they might not seem to be harmful, may result in a conservative and closed society that is not open to people who do not live according to their rigid structures. Hence, Boo Radley, who is a recluse, is avoided, and blacks, for being of a different color, are discriminated against, and even Atticus, when he tries to help Tom, is persecuted. Thus, myths even though apparently harmless like the mocking bird that just sings and does no harm, can cause lots of problems (99). In fact, the mocking bird in the title can be seen as a symbolic representation of a myth, as the novel is all about killing myths, and probably it is high time that we started reading the title as not *To Kill a Mocking Bird*, but To Kill a Myth.

Works Cited

Abrams, M.H. *A Glossary of Literary Terms.* London: Thomas Heinle, Prism, 1999.

Baldick, Chris. *The Concise Oxford Dictionary of Literary Terms.* Oxford: Oxford University Press, 1990.

Cunliffe, Marcus. *The Literature of the United States.* Middlesex: Penguin Books Ltd., 1970.

Lee, Harper. *To Kill a Mocking-Bird.* London: Arrow Books Limited, 1960.

Shaw, G.B., *Pygmalion.* New York: Brentano, 1916.

Shelley, Mary. *Frankenstein, or The Modern Prometheus.* New York: Oxford University Press, 1994.

Shelley, Percy Bysshe. *Complete Poetical Works.* New York: Houghton Mifflin, 1901.

Spiller, Robert, E., William Thorp, Thomas H. Johnson, Henry Seidel Canby, Richard, M. Ludwig. *Literary History of the United States.* New York: The Macmillan Company, 1946.

28

Revisiting the Myth of Androgyny in Feminist Writing

Isha Malhotra

Celebrated by some and rejected by others, androgyny is a concept fraught with contradictions. Although it was always present in one form or another in primitive myths, world religions and ancient philosophy, it re-emerged in the twentieth century in a number of psychological, academic and cultural contexts, from sexology and psychology, popular journalism to feminist analyses, gender criticism to literary imaginations, fashion and media. It is very difficult to state what exactly androgyny stands for, the ubiquity of the concept and the ways in which it was deployed have made the term a nebulous one. Etymologically, the term derived from two Greek words *andro* (male) and *gyn* (female), defines a condition under which the characteristics of the sexes, and the human impulses expressed by men and women, are not rigidly assigned. It makes its first appearance as a compound word in Rabbinic Judaism, (Genesis Rabba, 8.1; Leviticus Rabba, 14.1), most probably as an alternative to Pagan related usage of hermaphrodite. Androgyny is not a stable or a transcendent category, but is subject to historical or cultural change. As Tracy Hargreaves puts it in her book *Androgyny in Modern Literature* (2005) "From the late nineteenth to the twentieth century, androgyny has been produced as a shifting category, mobilized in different discourses—literary, sexological, psychoanalytic, sociological, feminist. The meaning of androgyny depends on its function in a given discourse" (3).

Alternatively, androgyny is "a synonym for bisexuality" Stimpson, 54) or else it is "not bisexuality" (June Singer, 11), androgyny is the expression of "a psychic unity, either potential or actual, conceived as existing in all individuals" (Barbara Charlesworth Gelpi) or "an energy between individuals rather than a psychic state locked within" (Tiffany, 13) or "the androgyne is a representation in human form of the principle of wholeness" (Singer, 199) or it is "the blending of positive masculine and feminine characteristics within a given person" (Cook, 9). From the above discussion it can be conferred that androgyny refers to the mixing of both masculine and feminine characteristics. An androgyne, in terms of gender identity is a person who does not fit cleanly into the typical masculine and feminine gender roles of the society. Many androgynes identify as being mentally "between" woman and man, or as entirely genderless. They may identify as non-gendered, genderneutral, agendered, between genders, intergendered, bigendered, pangendered or gender fluid. "Genderqueer" is often used as an umbrella term for the category. The term androgynous is often used to refer to a person whose look or built makes it difficult to determine the gender, but is generally not used as a synonym for actual intersexuality.

The myth of the androgyne goes back into prehistory and is found in one or another form in many primitive societies. From the Jewish Kabbala, the vedic mysteries, Gnosticism, the Orphic mysteries and Christian Hermetic lore, the androgyne is repeatedly cast as central to creation myths, demonstrating the expression of a totality and divine perfection, which human beings have lost and strive to re-attain. Bi-sexuality was institutionalized in ancient Greece and Rome where men practiced homosexuality in the form of pederasty (male mentorship) and simultaneously maintained heterosexual relations with their wives for procreation. Historically, pederastic relationships were prevalent not only in Western cultures but also in non-Western cultures as in China, Japan, South Pacific and Middle East. Even world religions have embraced numerous deities and demi-dieties with androgynous qualities such as Hapi (Egyptian), Dionysus (Greek), Shiva (Hindu) and Obatala (Voudan religion in Africa, South America and the Carribean).

In Greco-Roman mythology, Dionysus, the ancient God of grape harvest and wine is often represented as an androgynous deity. In the Greek epics the *Iliad* and the *Odyssey*, the androgynous Greek goddess Athena is represented in distinct male or female forms. In Hindu mythology, *Ardhanarishvara* is an androgynous deity composed of Shiva and his consort Shakti, representing the synthesis of masculine and feminine energies and is the symbol of cosmic androgyny. In Chinese philosophy, the concept of yin-yang is used to describe how polar or seemingly contrary forces are interconnected and interdependent in the natural world. In gender relations, yin is female and yang is male and they fit together as two parts of a whole. Although androgyny was not popular in the mainstream of dogmatical institutional Christianity, the androgynous ideal has been persistently kept alive in both Jewish and Christian mythical traditions. It was very popular in the circles of artists, liberals, pietists, Rosicrucians, freemasons and alchemists. In the West, Cabalistic mysticism says God made humans in his own image, and as there is only one God, then that makes God an androgyne. It is also believed that Adam was dual sexed before God extracted Eve from his rib cage.

Two significant, but different, myths of a violent metamorphosis sit side-by-side—one of complement, other of competition. One is Aristophanes' story as it is told in Plato's *Symposium* (c. 385 B.C.) in the dialogue on the origin and nature of love. Aristophanes' speech tells the story of humanity's origins as twinned or dual beings. Originally, the sexes were conjoined, with two heads, four arms and four legs. These rotund figures were uniformly male and male, female and female or androgynously male and female, derived cosmologically from the sun (male), the earth (female) and the moon (the androgyne). As punishment for their extravagant pride and ambition, Zeus split the spherical creatures in two, causing each to experience the loss of the other—a loss that human beings long to redeem through sexual union, as the once androgynous couple becomes the procreative heterosexual couple. The other myth is Ovid's story of the female nymph Salmacis and Hermaphroditus, son of Hermes and Aphrodite. Salmacis forces and welds herself to the unwilling male body of Hermaphroditus, a suture that suggests the violent rape of a man by a woman, leaving him weakened by an unsought, and unwanted, femininity, "a fantasy of unity". The double-sexed figure shifted in terms of its representation from classical mythology to discourses of medicine and psychiatry in nineteenth-century sexology.

Psychologists and sexologists of the nineteenth and early twentieth century such as Richard von Krafft-Ebing, Edward Carpenter, Havelock Ellis, and Otto Weininger talked about the concept of the third sex, in which masculine and feminine characteristics come together in a single body. Darwin (*Descent of Man*), Freud (*The Sexual Aberrations*, *Leonardo da Vinci*), Havelock Ellis (*Studies in the Psychology of Sex*) and Richard von Krafft-Ebing (*Psychopathia Sexualis*), as well as Earl Lind (*Autobiography of an Androgyne*) talked about this double-sexed figure in their respective works. While some saw the dual-sexed figure as atavistic, a throwback to an earlier age when vertebrates appeared to be a mixture of both anatomical sexes others like Richard von Krafft-Ebing constructed the androgyne as the womanly man, a pathologised identity. The English writer Edward Carpenter claimed distinguished and heroic figures from Greek and Renaissance histories (Michaelangelo, Alexander the Great, Sappho) to secure lofty precedents for the modern "intermediate type", artists and educators who combined positive elements of traditional male and female characteristics. The androgynous ideal, as Norman O. Brown has shown, comes up in Freud's *Beyond the Pleasure Principle.* Dr. Anduin, as quoted by Freud, asserts that "there are masculine and feminine elements in every human being; but one of these—according to the sex of the person in question—is incomparably more strongly developed than the other, so far as heterosexual individuals are concerned...." This theory was further developed by Carl Jung whose concept of anima (the female within male) and animus (the male within female), was interpreted as the healthy balance for the human psyche.

The myths are moulded and revisioned by contemporary women writers so as to serve their feminist purpose. Feminists latch hopefully onto motifs in ancient myths that seem to indicate a possible past in which women had more agency, perhaps even a central role in society. Many women writers today consciously include mythic tendencies or motifs in their works to make them function similarly to how myths have always functioned—helping to shape (or re-shape) our world views and craft myth-like narratives that feature female heroes and world affirming mythic stories. Feminists look upon the concept of androgyny as a trope that by deconstructing stereotypical gender rules subverts hegemonic binaries of sex/gender in literature and popular culture and enables us to rethink and comprehend the dynamics of fast paced change in society and culture in the new millennium. The desire to reconfigure, rethink, re-experience identity beyond the prescriptive and normalizing hetero-normative binary oppositions found expression in "androgyny", the "androgynous" and the embodied "androgyne". Feminist theorists envisaged a hypothetical future society in which masculinity and femininity are no longer normatively associated with sex.

Much before the herald of the second wave feminism when the concept of androgyny was becoming ubiquitous, Virginia Woolf is the first feminist critic to debate the concept of the androgynous mind in *A Room of One's Own*. Among literary critics—especially feminists—"androgyny" has become virtually synonymous with "Virginia Woolf". For Woolf, androgyny was a theory that aimed to offer men and women a chance to write without being conscious of their sex, the effect of which would ideally result in an uninhabited creativity. The foundation of Woolf's androgyny and Bloomsbury's sexual liberation can be found in the social, cultural and academic milieu of the time. Despite its problematic origins androgyny was for Woolf, a way of liberating women from the negativism of patriarchy. Woolf's novels *Mrs. Dalloway*, *To the Lighthouse* and *Orlando: A Biography*, are a record of this search for the elusive unity of being, which she refers to as the androgynous mind in which masculine and feminine elements unite in perfect harmony. Virginia Woolf's sixth novel *Orlando* engaged with androgyny as both an oscillatory identity (Orlando is first a man, then a woman, and cross-dressing, is able to re-inhabit masculinity) and as the product of complementary union. When Orlando marries, she recognizes that her husband is also a woman, just as he recognizes that Orlando is also a man.

By the 1970s, androgyny was "an idea whose time had come" as social scientists "rediscovered" (Cook, 15) the concept. It was "in the head, on the body, an attitude, a way of being, in the psyche, cosmic, unisex, bisex" (Hargreaves, 97). It wasn't just social scientists who had rediscovered it though within the second-wave feminism (1960s to 1990s) and in literature, androgyny heralded the possibility of a much broader range of sex-role possibilities for members of both the sexes. The term "androgyny" re-acquired greater cultural currency across the second wave, the increasingly broad use of "androgyny" and "androgynous" mcant that its application was extensive as the term underwent a series of paradigm shifts. Even a brief glance at books and articles written between the 1960s and 1990s tells us that androgyny was a protean concept whose function shifted according to the discourse that constructed it.

During the second wave feminism, the androgynist position was initially articulated by Mary Ellman in *Thinking About Women* (1969), Carolyn Heilbrun in *Toward a Recognition of Androgyny* (1973), Mary Daly in *Beyond God the Father* (1973), Andrea Dworkin in *Woman Hating* (1974) and June Singer in *Androgyny: The Opposites Within* (1976). Besides that a number of important essays and articles were written on this subject. Following a forum on androgyny held at the Modern Language Association in 1973, the journal *Women's Studies* devoted a special issue, "The Androgyny Papers", to the topic. The edition included papers that were both for and against androgyny. The MLA's Commission on the Status of Women in the Profession prompted the edition, making it clear that androgyny was vetoed less as a mystical or sexual ideal, and more as a pragmatic and realiasable possibility. Nancy Topping Bazin and Alma Freeman argued in "The Androgynous Vision" that "just as we must go beyond our own past, we must go beyond past definitions of androgyny" (185). In other words, its historically specific meanings needed to be re-attuned as a motif for, or index of, equal opportunities which can bring social transformation.

Joyce Carol Oates in her essay titled "Woman Writer: Theory and Practice" (1986) says, "Subject-matter is culture-determined, not gender-determined. And the imagination, in itself genderless, allows us all things" (142). Helen Haste in her thought provoking essay, "The Sexual Metaphor" (1993), analyses the social construction of gender. She defines the aim of "socialist" feminism as a kind of "rational androgyny"—to which all, regardless of sex, can aspire. She argues that dualistic thought is only capable of a single perspective since it casts one side of each dichotomy as "ideal" and its opposite as "other". In contrast to the "writer only" problems of androgynist poetics, therefore, most feminist critics insist that the way to contend with patriarchal bias against women is not to deny sexual difference but to dismantle gender hierarchies. Therefore, social feminists try to transfer the perceived polarities, differences and conflicts between female and male into the entire world and everything in it.

The main characteristics of androgyny that have come up in second-wave feminism can be stated as follows:

(1) There could be no question, though, that the promotion of an androgynous ontology was part of emerging feminist debates. Mary Daly argued that androgyny and feminism were crucially linked, stating in *Beyond God the Father* (1973) that radical feminism would give rise to an "initiation of androgynous existence." In her introduction to *Women Studies*' special edition of "The Androgyny Papers", Cynthia Secor expressed the hope that the

collection of writings would "be a tool for the feminist classroom where we strive collectively to articulate and document the necessary complex relations between literature and life" (163).

(2) Feminists look upon the concept of androgyny as a trope that by deconstructing stereotypical gender rules subverts hegemonic binaries of sex/gender in literature and popular culture and enables us to rethink and comprehend the dynamics of fast paced change in society and culture in the new millennium. The desire to reconfigure, rethink, re-experience identity beyond the prescriptive and normalizing hetero-normative binary oppositions found expression in "androgyny", the "androgynous" and the embodied "androgyne." Feminist theorists envisaged a hypothetical future society in which masculinity and femininity, are no longer normatively associated with sex. To many feminists, androgyny has come to represent escape from the prison of gender, that is, from socially enforced preconceptions of ways in which women and men should differ in their psychology and behaviour. Feminists were breaking "the dam of sex stereotyping" that stops men and women from becoming integrated, androgynous personalities.

(3) Barbara Charlesworth Gelpi considered contemporary theories of androgyny as "useful and potentially liberating" and suggests that it is good for women to begin speculating for themselves on the reintegration of the masculine principle into the feminine psyche...as a potential which they posess and should use. Heilbrun's literary and cultural study invoked androgyny as a liberating (often strategically feminizing) ideal which offered recuperation from an overly masculinised culture. Androgyny could be, she argued, a palliative for an era that she defined as "an age of manliness." She believes that "our future salvation lies in a movement away from sexual polarization and the prison of gender toward a world in which individual

roles and the modes of personal behaviour can be freely chosen. The ideal toward which I believe we should move is best described by the term Androgyny". Mary Daly in *Beyond God the Father* suggested that as women acquired liberation through feminism, men might experience liberation too, so that the becoming of the androgynous human persons implies a radical change in the fabric of human consciousness and in the styles of human behaviour. Mary Daly says that androgynous integrity and transformation will require that women cease to play the role of "complement" and struggle to stand alone as free human beings.

(4) Most discussions in second-wave feminism focused on "androgyny" or the "androgynous" rather than on the embodied figure of the "androgyne". Men and women would not necessarily be re-embodied as androgynes through feminism, but could become androgynous in their behavior, "one need not be male to be a priest, or female to be a nurturer," as Heilbrun put it. Sexual dissolution or the abolition of sexual difference was never really under discussion, we would function as men and women but non-hierarchically, and perhaps importantly, still retain the appearance of "men" and "women" whilst all behavioural characteristics might be open to us, not assigned on the basis of our anatomical difference.

(5) Many feminists like Carolyn Heilbrun, Mary Anne Warren and Mary Daly recognized that androgyny could only ever be a temporary solution to the perceived socio-sexual crisis highlighted by second-wave feminism. For Heilbrun the word androgyny is "only to get on with". Once the stage of dominant and aggressive masculinity is broken, the term may no longer be either useful or appropriate. Mary Anne Warren says that once the old stereotypes of femininity and masculinity are thoroughly broken down, and people find it bizarre to speak of rationality as

masculine or intuition as feminine, the concept of psychological androgyny will have served its purpose. Daly anticipated a point at which androgyny would become meaningless once the androgynous world had been established.

In the literary imagination, androgynous and androgyne ontology were achieved through the destabilizing effects of various literary strategies rather than through realism, either through the genre of fantasy (Virginia Woolf's *Orlando,* Ursula le Guin's *The Left Hand of Darkness*), science fiction (Marge Piercy's *Woman on the Edge of Time*), poetic imagination (Adrienne Rich's *Diving into the Wreck*), post-modern play (Jeanette Winterson's *Written on the Body*) or through alchemy (Lindsay Clarke's *The Chymical Wedding*, Angela Carter's *The Passion of New Eve*). These texts gesture less to the possibility of a newly realized and material androgynous identity, and more to concerns with how representation is mediated visually and in language.

Works Cited

Bazin, Nancy Topping and Alma Freeman. "The Androgynous Vision." *Women's Studies*. 2. 1974.

Bem, Sandra L. "The Measurement of Psychological Androgyny." *Journal of Consulting and Clinical Psychology*. 42 (1974).

Butler, Judith. *Gender Trouble: Feminism and the Subversion of Identity*. London: Routledge, 1990.

Chodorow, Nancy. "Heterosexuality as a Compromise Formation." *Literary Theory: An Anthology*. Ed. Julie Rivkin and Michael Ryan. Massachusetts: Blackwell, 2002.

Cook, Ellen Piel. *Psychological Androgyny*. Oxford: Pergammon. 1985.

Daly, Mary. *Beyond God the Father: Towards a Philosophy of Women's Liberation*. London: The Women's Press. 1973.

De Beauvoir, Simone. *The Second Sex*, trans. Parshley, H.M., London: Pan Books, 1988.

Feldman, Stephe. *Androgyne Online*. Transgender Tapestry. N.p. 2004. Web. 20 Sept. 2010.

Foucault, Michel. *The History of Sexuality: Volume One: An Introduction*, trans. R. Hurley, London: Penguin Books, 1979.

Fuss, Diana. *Inside/Out: Lesbian Theories, Gay Theories*. New York: Routledge Press, 1991.

Gelpi, Barbara Charlesworth. "The Politics of Androgyny." *Women's Studies*. 2. 1974.

Hargreaves, Tracy. *Androgyny in Modern Literature*. New York: Palgrave Macmillan, 2005.

Heilbrun, Carolyn G. *Toward a Recognition of Androgyny*. New York: Knoff, 1973.

Liquori, Cristina E. "Woolf, Le Guin and Winterson: Androgyny as a Literary Strategy in Twentieth Century Womens Writing." Union College English Thesis. 9 July 2010. Web. 1 Oct 2010.

Paglia, Camille. *Sexual Personae in Art and Literature*. Yale Dissertation, 1974.

Plato. *Symposium*. Trans. Walter Hamilton. London: Penguin Books, 1951.

Rich, Adrienne. "Compulsory heterosexuality and Lesbian Existence." *Blood, Bread, and Poetry*. New York: Norton Paperback, 1994.

Sedgwick , Eve Kosofsky. *Between Men: English Literature and Male Homosocial Desire*. New York City: Columbia University Press, 1985.

Singer, June. *Androgyny: Toward a New Theory of Sexuality*. Garden City, N.Y: Anchor Press, 1976.

———. *Androgyny: The Opposites Within*. Boston: Sigo Press, 1976.

Stimpson, Catherine R. *The Androgyne and the Homosexual*. New York and London: Methuen, 1988.

Tiffany, Grace. *Erotic Beasts and Social Monsters: Shakespeare, Jonson and Comic Androgyny*. Newark: University of Delaware Press, 1995.

Warren, Mary Anne. *'Femininity', 'Masculinity', and 'Androgyny': A Modern Philosophical Discussion*. New Jersey: Littlefield, Adam and Co., 1982.

Woolf, Virginia. *A Room of One's Own*. Oxford: Oxford University Press, 1988.

———. *Orlando: A Biography*. London: Penguin, 1993.

Zhou, Zuyan. *Androgyny in Late Ming and Early Qing Literature*. USA: University of Hawaii Press, 2003.

29

Myth of a Doomed Woman Artist in Margaret Atwood's *Surfacing* and *Lady Oracle*

Sonia Khajuria

This paper explores Margaret Atwood's ability to deconstruct the power of mytho-culture in order to expose its impact on the psyche of an individual. *Surfacing* and *Lady Oracle* bring to light the struggle of women artists who are victimized in phallocentric society. Both the novels expose the roots of sexual colonization, and deconstruct the societal apparatus that reinforce female subordination and servitude. Atwood has tried to explore Eurocentric myths designed to confine women's access as contributors in the world of art and literature, where they are mere spectators, rather than an agent of cultural evolution. Atwood has exposed the dualities that exist in the society, through the use of the myth of a "doomed woman artist" and ways in which the protagonists of *Surfacing* and *Lady Oracle* have internalized this myth.

I have divided this paper into two parts. The first part analyzes Atwood's *Surfacing* as a site of oppression of a woman artist and the second part explores the impact of the myth of a "doomed woman artist" on the psyche of a woman artist in Atwood's *Lady Oracle*.

The unnamed narrator in *Surfacing* does not get any recognition for her work by her lover, rather he exploits her sexually and convince her to undergo an abortion. Unable to cope with the guilt of killing her unborn child, she takes up a spiritual quest. While undergoing the transformation she exposes the split between masculine principle and the feminine principle. Her external struggle is a direct result of a serious internal struggle that has roots in her past. Through stream of consciousness, the protagonist retraces her own retreat from, and rejection of, patriarchy.

Joan, the protagonist, in *Lady Oracle* is another woman artist, who struggles to live her life as a wife and a published writer, and thus challenges the patriarchal definition of womanhood. She revolts against the patriarchy by writing under a pen-name. Joan, takes her inspiration by Tennyson's heroine in his poem "The Lady of Shalott". In the novel, the condition of the Lady of Shalott can be seen as a metaphor for the woman artist's imprisoned potential. Joan's life echoes the myth of a doomed woman artist—that a woman cannot be both an artist and a wife. Ultimately, the myth becomes Joan's source of enlightenment as she creates multiple identities with mutually exclusive lives to defy patriarchy.

Both the novels by Atwood reflect a dilemma many women face: choosing between professional satisfaction and the confined life within patriarchal norms. Atwood's female protagonists in their own ways, find the means to seize the metaphorical pen to carve out an identity for them. By allowing her protagonists the ability to express through art and literature, Atwood has revealed her own ability to seize the "pen".

Through her writings Atwood expose that "the world is masculine on the whole; those who fashioned it, ruled it, and still dominate it today are men" (Beauvoir, 298). The unnamed narrator of *Surfacing* "had an experience of sexual colonialism when she was just a school going child" (Kaur, 20). She grew up with bitter memories of her childhood where:

> the boys chased and captured the girls after school and tied them up with their own skipping ropes. I was the one they would forget on purpose to untie. I spent many afternoons looped to fences and gates and convenient trees, waiting for a benevolent adult to pass and free me;

> later I become an escape artist of sorts, expert at undoing knots. (*Surfacing*, 77)

She realized quite early in the childhood that she is an female alien in a masculine world. Throughout the novel her alienated female consciousness is in conflict with male authority. From the beginning to the middle of the novel she sees herself as a non-entity in a powerful phallocentric world. Long back in her childhood she had stopped fighting back because she "never won" (*Surfacing*, 155).

When she grew up she became illustrator of children's book and falls in love with her art teacher, who was a married man:

> For him I could have been anyone but for me he was unique, the first, that's where I learnt. I worshipped him, non-child bride, idolater, I kept the scraps of his handwriting like Saint's relics, he never wrote letters, all I had was criticisms in red pencil he paper-clipped to my drawings. CS and DS, he was an idealist, he said he didn't want our relationship as he called it to influence his aesthetic judgement. He didn't want our relationship to influence anything: it was to be kept separate from life. A certificate framed on the wall, his proof that he was still young. (*Surfacing*, 158)

Her art teacher emotionally exploited her and did not let her grow professionally out of his own insecurity about her. She wanted to be a real artist but "he thought that was cute but misguided, he said I should study something I'd be able to use because there have never been any important woman artistes...but he was right, there never have been any" (*Surfacing*, 56).

Her lover convinced her to go for an abortion without any remorse. He acts like an emotionally callous controller:

> He said, I should do it, he made me do it; he talked about it as though it was legal, simple, like getting a wart removed. He said, it wasn't a person, only an animal; I should have seen that was no different, it was hiding in me as if in a burrow and instead of granting it

> sanctuary, I let him catch it.... After the slaughter, the murder, he couldn't believe, I didn't want to see him anymore; it bewildered him, he resented me for it.... (*Surfacing*, 155)

The protagonist suffers from a strong sense of guilt. The abortion had a psychological effect on her and in order to forget that she starts repressing its memories "a section of my own life sliced off from me like a Siamese twin, my own flesh cancelled. Lapse, relapse, I have to forget" (*Surfacing*, 52). The negative impact of the abortion takes its toll on the protagonist and she is doomed with the painful memories of her abortion. She is unable to concentrate on her profession and turns into an "escape artist"—she leaves her married lover and make up a false story of her marriage. Her fake marital status gave her some solace as she was brought up in a society where:

> Women are still expected to be better than men, morally that is, even by women, even by some branches of the women's movement; and if you are not an angel, if you happen to have human feelings, as most of us do, especially if you display any kind of strength or power, creative or otherwise, then you are not human. You're worse than human, you are a witch, a Medusa, a destructive powerful scary monster. (Atwood, 25)

The unnamed protagonist starts believing her own fake story and it becomes an escape route for her from her painful past to a socially defined "peaceful world". Towards the end of the novel she again decides to be pregnant, and this time she accepts Joe, her friend as a partner. When the body of the protagonist's father is discovered in the woods, the confirmation of his death pushes the protagonist beyond her breaking point. At this point she begins to abandon the rationalizing process of her false self and give herself over to the logic of the transformative space. In the woods she dives into the lake and her diving into the lake leads her to an awareness of a new child to protect and she begins to make changes in her life by asserting her power. In the end she affirms that she will not return to her status as a victim. She creates a divine self out of her divided self:

> This above all, to refuse to be a victim. Unless I can do that I can do nothing. I have to recant, give up the old belief that I am powerless and because of it nothing I can do will ever hurt anyone. A lie which was always more disastrous than the truth would have been. (*Surfacing*, 206)

Atwood's another novel *Lady Oracle* has taken the myth of a doomed woman artist to another level. The protagonist of the novel Joan Foster, creates fake multiple identities to live her life to its fullest "the plurality and juxtaposition of different styles in the novel appear than to find a correspondence in the scattered identification of its character" (Rao, 146).Written in the earlier days of second wave feminism, *Lady Oracle* resonates with issues of importance during that phase such as exposing sexual discrimination and deconstructing the societal apparatus that reinforce female subordination and servitude.

Atwood has used the protagonist of the novel Joan, to allude vicariously the obstacles that she herself faced as a female writer in a patriarchal culture. In *Second Words* she writes that:

> the woman writer, then ,exists in a society that, though it may turn certain individual writers into revered cult objects, has little respect for writing as a profession, and not much respect for a woman either. (Atwood, 204)

Sandra M. Gillbert and Susan Gubar argue that throughout history, patriarchy has perpetuated a phallocentric myth of creativity in which literary production is a male prerogative, and they respond by arguing that "women must escape just those male text which...deny them the autonomy to formulate alternatives to the authority that has imprisoned them" (Madwoman, 13).

Lady Oracle follows the life of Joan Foster, from an obese child and adolescent to a secret costume Gothic writer, and author of an acclaimed book of poetry called *Lady Oracle*. When a blackmailer threatens to expose her secrets Joan fakes her own death with the help of her friends, and escapes to Terremoto, Italy.

In the novel, Atwood challenges literary protocol and disrupts conventional linear form by interweaving diverse genres such as letters, gothic romances, nursery rhymes, visions and dreams into Joan's meandering story, which begins shortly after her staged "suicide". Thus, Joan revisits the circumstances and influences that led her to view death as a viable solution to her dilemma revealing the effects of "interior colonization", and illustrating multiple ways in which this innate sexism plays itself out in Joan's affluent Anglo-urban echelon of Canadian society.

Atwood's *Lady Oracle* re-construct narrative patterns, words and metaphors to speak the unspeakable, the denied and taboo. In *Lady Oracle* Atwood has internalized the myth of a doomed artist. There are intertextual influences of Tennyson's character the Lady of Shalott, on Joan's life. There are many other characters in the novel which are from the ancient myths, fairytales that contain a dark interconnecting thread—that of the myth of a doomed woman artist.

Atwood's allusions to Tennyson's Lady of Shallot brings out the fact that a woman cannot be both an artist and a wife. This core belief is problematic for Joan as she—an artist/writer/weaver of words—must suppress or conceal her artist self, first from Paul, for whom she is a mistress, and later from Arthur, whom she marries. For Joan "this is yet another rendering of the story in which a woman is offered a choice, between love and art, that is not really a choice because either alternative entails disaster" (Fenwick, 6).

The story of the magical weaver in *The Lady of Shalott* romanticizes the imprisoned artist, her unrequited love and subsequent death, and thus reinforces the concept of suicide as a culturally condoned option for "unhappy women", it perpetuates a belief system so long held in Western culture that its gynocidal underpinning may go unnoticed, exemplifying what Kate Millet describes as "perhaps patriarchy's most powerful psychological weapon...its universatility and longevity...when a system of power is thoroughly in command, it has scarcely to speak itself aloud" (81). The success of this process of internalized colonization is evident in Joan's high school teaching into the world view of Tennyson: she recalls first reading The *Lady of Shalott* in a Grade Nine textbook, narrative poems for juniors: "I was a romantic despite myself, and I really wanted, then, to have someone, anyone, say that I had a lovely face, even if I had to turn into a corpse in a barge bottom first" (*Lady*, 150).

Joan, as a young teenager, was already willing to sacrifice her life in order to fulfill her fantasy of being the object of a handsome man's desire; as an adult, the story of the Lady of Shalott becomes a powerful template for Joan's life. For example, after graduation, Joan travels to England chasing dreams of Camelot—looking for her knight in shining armour. She is disappointed, however, when she discovers that, in reality, London "is not as romantic as she expected it to be" (Jensen, 32). Expecting "castles and princesses, the Lady of Shalott floating down a winding river in a boat" (*Lady*, 150), Joan finds instead "a lot of traffic and a large number of people with bad teeth" (*Lady*, 150). Not dwelling on her disillusionment, Joan romantically links herself with "royalty", a Polish Count named Paul, but Joan soon begins to feel restricted by his control of her life.

Through Paul, however, she discovers her love of writing. Paul is a writer of "nurse romances" (*Lady*, 162), and becomes Joan's connection both with the publishing world (*Lady*, 164-65) and with the formula—framework or loom—to weave her own "trashy novels". As novice writer of Gothic romances, Joan delights him in spinning the prescribed yarns and becomes an enthusiastic weaver of words. Successful at her task, Joan is soon fulfilling requests from her publisher for more material "Material, they called it as if it came by the yard" (*Lady*, 165). Especially, she delights in creating clothing for her characters and spends "whole afternoons in the costume room of the Victoria and Albert Museum...thought that if she could only get the clothes right, everything else would fall into line. And it did" (*Lady*, 164-65).

Unwilling to give up either her husband or her writing, and attempting to avoid living out the myth of the doomed woman artist, Joan creates two mutually exclusive identities. At home she is Joan Foster, Arthur's wife; to the publishers she is someone else completely: Joan had submitted both the name and photo of the overweight, but flamboyantly dressed Louisa Delacourt/, Joan's deceased spinster aunt:

> I was two people at once, with two sets of identification papers, two bank accounts, two different groups of people who believed I existed...as long as I could spend a certain amount of time each week as Louisa, I was all right, I was patient and forbearing, warm, a sympathetic listener. But if I was cut off, if I couldn't work at my current Costume Gothic, I would become mean and irritable, drink too much and start to cry. (*Lady*, 225-26)

Keeping balance, for Joan, is an ongoing struggle that becomes compounded when, while working through a scene in her current gothic romance, she begins to explore automatic writing, a technique she had first attempted as a teenager (*Lady*, 117-18). Like the Lady of Shalott, Joan weaves the vision she sees in her mirror and some of her poetic images eerily, or perhaps ironically, echo Tennyson; also like the lady, when Joan offers her vision to the world, she meets with dire consequences. Unlike the lady, however, Joan does not die; instead her personality fragments once again, creating space in her life to embrace another aspect of herself as a prophet-poet.

In an interview Joan confesses that the poems were "dictated...by a spirit hand" (*Lady*, 253), thus increasing her mystique and accenting her role of prophet/poet. This is quite a different Joan Foster from her role as wife to Arthur—the supportive listener to a man either preoccupied by political involvement or depressed by defeat. Joan appeases Arthur by playing the role of the inept housewife:

> Arthur enjoyed my defeats. They cheered him up. He loved hearing the crash as I dropped a red hot platter on the floor...he liked to hear me swear in the kitchen...my failure was a performance and Arthur was the audience. His applause kept me going. (*Lady*, 222-23)

At home Joan does what she can to please Arthur, even to her own degradation; however, Joan Foster as poet is the center of attention, a celebrated artist, and soon gets romantically involved with the Royal Porcupine, also an artist, and every bit as theatrically bent as Joan. They begin a playful affair through which Joan leaves out her romantic and sexual desires (*Lady*, 271), and yet another secret life is born: Joan is no longer living a double life; she has become triplicate "I was triple, multiple, and now I could see that there was more than one life to come, there were many. The Royal Porcupine had opened a time space door to the fifth dimension" (*Lady*, 261). Joan, to express herself more fully, creates separate lives and multiple personalities; she has chosen to be a doting wife, gothic romance novelist/spinster, prophet/poet/lover. These characters are woven on separate looms with distinctly different patterns/cultural roles, and "none is completely real" (*Lady*, 230). In time Joan feels the strain of maintaining these separate lives, and, aware of more repressed identities waiting in the wings, Joan plots suicide as a means of escaping her predicament—thus activates the myth of a doomed woman artist just like the Lady of Shalott.

After her staged death, Joan flies to Rome, ends up in the village of Terremoto where she buries her funeral clothes "her former self" (*Lady*, 17), then cuts and dyes her trademark red hair, thereby transforming her appearance so she can "pass for a secretary on vacation" (*Lady*, 11). Once again Joan is re-defining herself by re-weaving her appearance and, thus, her personality. Joan is now the Lady of Shalott reborn; an unfinished revision of the old myth for which Joan can create the conclusion. When Joan can no longer maintain her separate lives as wife or poet or lover, she activates the myth of a doomed woman artist.

In addition to the character of the Lady of Shalott, Joan is also related to the mythic figure of Penelope, whose name means "she with a web on her face". Penelope must weave a death shroud in memory of her husband King Odysseus who is missing from war and assumed by many to be dead. Once her tapestry is completed, his death will be official, and a new king proclaimed. As long as her work is in progress, however, Penelope's autonomy is assured; therefore, as a survival mechanism she weaves during the day and unravels her work at night. Atwood's heroin maintains her autonomy in another unique way: Joan manipulates the threads of identity needed for her various roles; thus, she weaves new identities on demand, re-invents the tapestry of her body, her clothes, her lifestyle. But, less meticulous than Penelope, Joan does not unravel the previous identity/identities but creates double/binds until her life has become "a rat's nest of dangling threads and loose ends" (*Lady*, 313), and she begins to consider suicide as a means of liberation.

Through *Surfacing* and *Lady Oracle* Atwood has logically illustrated the power of myth to shape an individual's life.

Works Cited

Atwood, Margaret. *Lady Oracle*. 1976. Toronto: Mc Celland & Stewart, 1998.

———. *Second Words: Selected Critical Prose*. Toronto: House of Anansi Press, 1972.

———. *Surfacing*. 1973. Mc Celland & Stewart, Canada, 1992.

Beauvoir, Simone de. *The Second Sex*. Tr. and Edited by H.M. Parshley, Penguin Books, 1949.

Gilbert, Sandra M. and Gubar, Susan. *The Mad Woman in Attic*. New Heaven: Yale University Press, 1979.

Jensen, Emily. "Margaret Atwood's *Lady Oracle*: A Modern Parable". *Essays in Canadian Writing*, 33 (1986).

Kaur, Iqbal. *Margaret Atwood's Surfacing: A Critical Study*. Arun Publishing House. Chandigarh, 1994.

Millet, Kate. *Sexual Politics*. 1969. New York. Doubleday and Company Inc., 1978.

Rao, Eleonora. "Margaret Atwood's *Lady Oracle*: Writing against Nations of Unity", in *Margaret Atwood: Writing and Subjectivity*. Org. Colin Nicholson, St. Martin's Press, New York, 1994.

Tennyson, Lord Alfred. *Poems of Tennyson*. Edited by Jerome H. Buckley. Cambridge: The Riverside Press, 1955.

Wikipedia. "Weaving (mythology)" http://en.wikipedia.org/wiki/weaving.Web

30

Mythical Effects of Calvinism on Canadian Consciousness: A Study of Hugh MacLennan's *Each Man's Son*

Reena Salaria

Myth is a usually traditional story of ostensibly historical events that serves to unfold part of the world view of a people or explain a practice, belief. Calvinism is the theological system designed by John Calvin (1509-64). John Calvin was an important figure in the protestant Reformation and created in the city of Geneva, Switzerland, a theocratic state ruled entirely by his own ideas of what a Christian state should be. Calvinist theology is often labeled "Federal" or "Covenantal". According to their belief, God has made to arguments or covenants with humanity.

The first was the covenant of works made with Adam and Eve in the Garden of Eden. It is called a covenant of works because it was based upon behavior—Adam and Eve adhered to the agreement so long as they refrained from one particular action: eating the fruit of a particular tree. Nothing else was forbidden. Unfortunately for Adam and Eve, they didn't obey this one command and so "fell", being subject now to disease and death. God, however, took pity on them and so entered into a new covenant with humanity. This time it wasn't based upon obedience because that is simply beyond humans;

instead, the new covenant is based upon confessing their faults and having faith in God through Jesus Christ.

Calvinist theologian believed because of the myth of the Original Sin and fall of man, man is unable of himself to saintly believe the gospel. Human sin has affected every aspect of the human character—thought, emotions, will, etc. The sinner is dead, blind and deaf to the things of God; his heart is deceitful and desperately corrupt. His will is not free, it is in bondage to his evil nature, therefore he will not—indeed he cannot—choose good over evil in the spiritual realm. Consequently, it takes much more than spirit's assistance to bring a sinner to Christ—it takes regeneration by which the spirit makes the sinner alive and give him a new nature. God's choice of certain individuals unto salvation before the foundation of the world rested solely in his own sovereign will. He gives faith and repentance to each individual whom He selected. Christ's redeeming work was intended to save the Elect only and actually secured salvation for them. All those who were chosen by God, redeemed by Christ, and given faith by the spirit are eternally saved. They are kept in faith by the power of Almighty God and thus preserve to the end.

The Reformation spread rapidly to Scotland, largely under the leadership of John Knox (1513-72), who served nineteen months as a galley slave before he went to England and then to Geneva. Knox brought the Reformation's principles from Geneva to Scotland and became its most notable spokesman there. In 1560, the Scottish reformed "kirk" or church was reorganized. In ensuing generations, many Scots became Stalwart Calvinists.

The Jacobite Rebellion of 1745 ended the traditional patterns of life in the Highlands. The clan system was destroyed. The chiefs, who were previously the administrators of justice, were removed and the title was given to the crown. The Scots were forbidden to bear arms or to wear the kilt or tartan. In the wake of this development, the chiefs were no longer able to command the loyalty of their people who faced poverty because, "the value of men declined, the value of money went up" (Cockburn, 11). The infamous Highland clearances became the answer to the problem. This deplorable situation lasted into the first half of the nineteenth century.

The displaced Highlanders, crammed into emigrant ships, sailed from their homeland to North Carolina, New Zealand, Australia and Canada. The Scots brought with them a myth of an ancient curse,—the belief that man has inherited from Adam a nature, so sinful, there is no hope for him and that furthermore, he lives and dies under the wrath of an arbitrary God who will forgive only a handful of his Elect on the Day of Judgment. As no normal human being can exist in constant awareness that he is sinful and doomed, through no fault of his own, the Highlanders behaved outwardly as other men do who have softened the curse or forgotten its existence. They lived with this myth of guilt even in Cape Breton.

In *Each Man's Son,* Hugh MacLennan effectively portrays effect of the myth of Original Sin and the theme of Calvinist guilt which afflicts the people of the little Cape Breton mining town of Broughton. There is the sense of a fate hanging over the inhabitants which makes ill-luck expected and good fortune suspect. It is a setting where Violence, superstitions and a consciousness of guilt and doom prevails. In this novel, MacLennan is writing about his ancestral consciousness, the spirit of his inheritance. Although a third-generation Canadian, "he never needed to go to the Highlands to understand whence he came or what he was" (*Scotchman's Return*, 1) and MacLennan has said of himself that the knowledge of his heritage "seems like a kind of doom from which I am too scotch even to think of praying for deliverance. I can thank my father for his last-ditch neurosis" (*Scotchman's Return*, 1).

In *Each Man's Son*, MacLennan attempts to demonstrate the terrible mythical effects Calvinism could have on man and illustrate those who tried to live by such ethics were as much victims as torturers. He explores the corrosive effects of the myth of Original Sin and guilt on the inhabitants of Cape Breton. He equates the Calvinist religion with a joyless, repressed Puritan mentality, a result of his peculiar upbringing. He believes that the Canadian society has been conditioned from the beginning by Calvinist forces' effect of Original Sin and concept of guilt that prevailed long after the waning of established religion, enormously inhibiting the Canadian Consciousness in the process.

The novel portrays the mythical curse of Puritanical religion which induces a haunting sense of guilt as the principal internal enemy of Western civilization. The central protagonist, Mollie Mac Neil, lives alone with her eight year old son. MacLennan says of Mollie at the beginning that she is a "woman who has lived for years with a child and for a child" (*Each Man's* Son, 4). Alan's father is a prize fighter who has been away from Cape Breton for four years fighting in the States. Mollie is ashamed of the brutal way in which her husband earns her living that is why she never revealed anything to Alan.

The novel focuses on a father/son situation to present his theme of myth of Calvinist guilt of Original Sin which haunts the entire Scottish Cape Breton community like a doom. Because of the effects of myth of Original Sin, the society is to subconsciously guilt-ridden to live fully or love well. It focuses on Daniel Ainslie's journey to self-knowledge and self-understanding. MacLennan shows the influence of Original Sin on Daniel Ainslie—"that every day of his life was haunted by sense of sin, a legacy of the ancient curse" (*Each Man's Son,* 9).

Ainslie is a splendid doctor and it is in the hospital only, where he does not feel sadness and frustration, where he does not seem to others masterful and inconsiderate and where he does not feel the fear of the curse that "led directly to the fear of love itself" (*Each Man's Son,* 219). The curse takes material form in Ainslie's personal life. It has created a gulf between him and his wife. The gulf, however, is much more the fault of Ainslie, who is unable to show emotions, including love, without guilt and who is too proud to make concessions.

Because of his religion, Daniel feels guilty. Douglas Mackenzie clarifies his marital troubles by saying: "As long as you've been married to Margaret, you've resented her because she hasn't been able to wash away your sense of sin" (*Each Man's Son*, 63). The curse has totally dominated Daniel's life;

"He was past forty, he had no children, he was in a treadmill, which he could neither slow down nor escape by jumping off, and marriage's unhappiness made him feel increasingly day by day" (*Each Man's Son,* 54). Alan's life totally revolves around religion. Dr. Mackenzie remarks: "Dan, you haven't forgotten a single word you've ever heard from the Pulpit or from your own Presbyterian father. You may think you've rejected religion with your mind, but your personality has no more rejected it than dyed cloth rejects its original colour" (*Each Man's Son,* 63). The myth of Original Sin has engulfed their entire being.

Ainslie also suffers from the pangs of guilt. He thought "was there no end to the circle of Original Sin?" (*Each Man's Son,* 64). Ainslie decides young Alan will fill the role of his own son to fulfill his need for a son. He thinks that he may be able to find a new meaning in life by centering his hopes and ambitions on the prizefighter's son, Alan. During Alan's illness, the feelings came to his mind, it seems as though he has made him his own, and here is the answer to all his longings. He arranges for Alan to go to his house for meals and tuition after he is discharged from hospital.

Mollie, succumbs to the advances of a Frenchman named Louis Camire, in the absence of her husband. To placate his own guilt, Ainslie tries to seduce Alan away from his mother. The doctor causes Mollie to write her equally lonely husband that she never wants to see him again. Eventually, fearing Ainslie's influence will alienate Alan from her, Mollie opposes continuation of the education plan, and listens to her other tempter; Camire, who is all set to take Mollie and her son to France.

Ainslie finally acknowledges his latest show of guilt, admits to himself that it was he who drove Mollie to extremes with Camire. The night Mollie gives herself to Camire is also the night when Archie returns home, a loser, a wretched man going blind. He kills both Camire and Mollie and also loses his own life. Dr. Ainslie can at last claim the boy as his own. Mackenzie tells him he is not looking for a son, but for a God.

He ultimately finds that the causes of all his trouble are guilt of myth of Original Sin which he was feeling.

After the violent climax of the novel, Ainslie realizes that his separate peace with life has still not freed him from the consequences of sin and guilt. But he finally understands that the circle of Original Sin that has caused this tragedy is the reality of human selfishness, which Calvinism with its vengeful father Jehovah has simply magnified into a terminus.

MacLennan has convincingly embodied his religious concerns of myth of Original Sin and guilt and the influence of Calvinism in the existential struggle of his protagonist and the consequent drama of human conflict. He has portrayed the impact of the mythical perception of the Original Sin in the lives of the Canadian people and how it completely dominates their consciousness.

Works Cited

Cockburn, Robert. *The Novels of Hugh MacLennan.* Canada: Harvest, 1969.

MacLennan, Hugh. *Scotchman's Return and Other Essays.* Toronto: Macmillan, 1960.

MacLennan, Hugh. *Each Man's Son.* Boston: Little, 1951.

31

Myth and Orality in Gloria Naylor's *Mama Day* and *Baileys' Café*

Jatinder Kaur

Africa being the second largest continent in the world is home to 46 clans and tribes and can boast of being treasure house of 7000 myths, legends and folktales, developed in oral tradition. This tradition of orality, i.e. verbal handing down of the tradition and ancient rites and rituals was the precise reason of their survival and revival by the African Diaspora who survived the brutal and inhuman treatment meted out to them. When millions of Africans—young and old, men and women were chained, tortured and hurled headlong into the abyss of non-existence, they became totally oblivious of their "selves", their roots, their rich cultural heritage. The African slave families, through their verbal art of story-telling nurtured and re-established their connection with their own native culture and roots. The African slaves were forced to rely on their voice and language as the only outlet to express the emotions of their souls. Their voices became the forms through which they expressed their acts (Atkinson, 13). During the years of slavery orality also came to be a source of strength and a medium for resistance; courage and hope to struggle for the cultural identity.

Black American writers especially women writers who had inherited the art of story-telling incorporated the traditional black female activities of root working, herbal medicine, conjure, mid-wifery and quilt making into the fabric of their stories to convey their special knowledge. The stories evoke images that help the listener to internalize the particular idea or concept. The striving for Racial Solidarity interests in the revision of Black antiquity, i.e. tracing their racial roots to African history and reach a final climax in Harlem Renaissance. Writers like Langston Hughes, Zora Neale Hurston, and her contemporary Anne Petry sought to celebrate the rich oral and musical culture of Black masses that reached the epitome of "New Negro". An heir to the southern folk tradition, Hurston used the common rural Negro speech (dialect) folklore, folk history and developed a thematic pattern so well supported by the folkloric oral tone and language which is authentic dialect of black rural life, thereby, creating a bridge between the primitive authority of folk life and the literary powers of written text. The presence of mythologies in Black women writers points towards the element of myth—metaphor, spirituality, memory.

In the modern times in Gloria Naylor one comes across not only coming of age in African-American literature but that she sculpted these new moulds of characters in relation to the black culture and community. It is the black collective history and black cultural past that Gloria Naylor wants to recover and aims at the reclamation of her fictional canon. In *Mama Day*, the power comes from folk tradition, from fore-mothering and from nature, as Naylor moves into the realm of "matriarchal mythmaking". Gloria Naylor belongs to Black Novelistic Literary Tradition, goes beyond the established shorelines and as one of the major African-American authors of the past two decades, Naylor herself becomes what Marjorie Pryse terms "a metaphysical conjure woman"—a medium who like Morrison, Walker and others makes it possible for readers —to recognize their common ancestors.

Naylor's *Mama Day* not only gives her concrete presence but she goes on to suggest Miranda Day's connection to the history, legend and myth that constitute the collective imagination of Willow Springs. A narrative communal voice uses, "We" and "Our" and "Us" to retell the story of Willow Springs and involve the readers in its simultaneous recall of historical, spiritual and physical events (*Mama Day*, 5). "Think about it...ain't nobody really talking to you..... Really listen this time, the only voice is your own.... You done heard it without a single living soul really saying a word" (*Mama Day,* 10). This voice ancient, aware and able to bridge the subjective and the objective worlds and to match the imagination with magic—connects the story's disparate events and maintains the presence over all of them. In addition to the ancestral narrative voices of the island itself—its dust, purple flowers, the gardens, cemeteries, etc. abandoned houses and remembered, rituals gather to tell Naylor's story.

The ancestral voices in this story are primarily the voices of the island's generations. All of them mediate the text, bridging the events of Naylor's contemporary story of the lovers Cocoa and George with the haunting presence of Sapphira Wade. Cocoa's grandmother of five generations past, whose propensity for conjuring permeates into the present-day world. The result is a text where voices of both the present and the past texture the narrative structures of the novel and culminate in a resonant confusion of mythology and reality. Naylor's choice of location, i.e. Willow Springs—the island on the border between Georgia and South Carolina—is represented as a place not charted in any map. Her choice has been dictated by the historical relationship of the island to the perpetuation of African culture for these places with the exception of New Orleans, the most African of places in Africa. The distinctive Gullah heritage, which is both social and cultural, makes the Sea Island an actual symbolic African presence, rich with magico-religious beliefs that ultimately serve signifying systems.

Also important to Naylor are Gullah beliefs about the spirit world, originating from the African religion. For African especially Bakongo groups the afterlife was a reality, death was a journey to the spirit world, which nonetheless did not constitute a break with on earth rather these ancestors serve as guardians of the living. Naylor's ancestors are conjurors, "Sapphira.... Could grab lightening in the palm of her hand and use the heat of lightening to start the kindling under the medicinal pot" (*Mama Day,* 1). It is culturally appropriate that

Naylor has Mama Day inherit her powers from Sapphira wade. Mama Day during the course of the novel causes lightening to strike enemy's house, uses chickens to impregnate barren friend and ultimately saves her great niece cocoa from an early death.

Commenting on women power in the novel Andrews states:

> Female power and wisdom are vividly incarnated in Miranda. Forced prematurely into a nurturing role in her family after her mother's Suicide, Miranda eventually becomes not only the community's midwife but also its guardian of tradition and its central authority; Mama say no, everybody say no. (*Mama Day*, 6)

Miranda's woman, however, is presented as an expression of natural forces and as an inheritance from the legendary mother of community. Miranda's communication with ancestral voices seems genuine and usually occurs during the solitary walks in the woods and reflective of Bakongo belief in the ancestors (dead)[1] "Miranda's family graves are also in the woods and are arranged in groups of seven, old graves and little ways off seven older again, All erected by them live Oaks and hanging moss..." (*Mama Day,* 10). The narrator tells us Oaks are also important features of Bakongo beliefs. Trees were planted directly on graves in order to guide the spirits on their journey into the earth; her connection with the movement of air has more to do with the unusual perception and her ability to listen.

Naylor writing about Georgia, South Carolina Sea Island in 1980's also posits African-American orality as an integral part of lives of characters in *Mama Day*. The fates of some of her characters are linked to their ability to listen to the voices of their culture, and to understand them once they hear them. Only a communal voice—for linguistic content—can tell the story of Willow Springs because it is only within a community of speakers that the tale can be voiced or understood. The narrative Naylor uses—the collective voice of Willow Springs—is proof or evidence that even one such as Reema's boy an ethnographer doomed not to understand the people, he has moved through Eurocentric Education and Geography—outside of his linguistic community. When he returns to the island to "study" the culture, he focuses on the meanings of an important expression: 18 and 23. The collective voice which serves as a frame for the individual voices introduced later explains in the introduction. "If the boy wanted to know what 18 and 23 meant why didn't he just ask? When he was running around sticking his that machine in everybody's face; we were sitting right here—every one of us—and his being Reema's we would oblige him. He could ask Cloris about the curve in her spine that came from planting season when their mule broke his leg and she took up the reins and kept pulling the plough with her own back. Winky would have told him about the hot tar that took out the corner of his right eye the summer we had only seven days to rebuild the bridge so the few crops that we had left after the storm could be gotten over before rot set in" (*Mama Day,* 8). The collective voice insinuates here that 18 and 23 is metaphor for the survival skills of the community, however, in earlier passages the voice that has used 18 and 23; a synonym for the conjure powers of Mama Day, for the flirting rituals of island's teenagers, for the film flam attempts of the hotel manager, for the unforgettable summer when a storm blew down the bridge and for the mysterious relationship between Bascombe Wade, the white owner of the island and the African born captive [slave woman] he married Sapphira Wade also. 18 and 23 is identified as the year when Sapphira Wade either smothered, stabbed or poisoned Bascombe Wade bearing him seven sons in just one thousand days and after persuading him to free all of his slaves and deed the land to them. The ambiguities in the ancestral voice match the linguistic ones. When she compels us to hear and believe the personal narrative of George who is already dead. Cocoa has been talking to him in her family graveyard in Willow Springs. The man has found his spiritual home in the Southern Graveyard among ancestral voices of the past—voices he resisted hearing in his passion to emphasize the "Now" while present on earth.

Although George immediately takes to Willow Springs can see himself staying there forever, he is also distressed when the bridge is destroyed and unable to leave the island when Dr. Buzzard approaches him after the funeral of Bernice's child telling him. "...we got us a bridge to build" (*Mama Day*, 269). It is understood that it is metaphorical bridge building which is needed, between the scientific and the intuitive; the rational and the non-rational; the secular and the sacred. Miranda's need of George is determined by the past events in the lives of the Days, the suffering of the other Day men, by crosses that have been endured, and the issue of the binding and releasing of the women beginning with the ancestral matriarch Sapphira. When Ophelia's life is threatened by Ruby's nightshade, Miranda herself gains knowledge of this tradition. She sees Cocoa's position in terms of the whole tradition of suffering women from Sapphira's slavery to Miranda's mother grief. After finding Bascombe Wade's ledger, Miranda is impelled to uncover the well where her sister Peace had died, in order to confront and understand her mother's tragic sorrow and suicide. Miranda depends on George's belief in himself and his resolve to "hold on to what was real" (*Mama Day*, 291) and craves to feel those oars between (his) hands "as he fantasizes about rowing Cocoa across the Sound" (*Mama Day*, 282-83). Miranda knows that to help Cocoa George must handover his belief to her "of his own accord" he had to hand it over to her. She needs his hands in hers—his very hand—so she can connect it up to all the believing that had gone before. So together they could be the bridge for Baby girl to walk over.

By placing his hand in Miranda's by joining the secular with the sacred, the real with the magical, they can save Cocoa, like many other initiates he is asked to perform certain tasks which seem quite irrational to him. Armed only with Miranda's walking stick (symbol of power) and the ancient Ledger which contains within it the partially erased bill of sale (history and knowledge], he is to go to the nest of the brooding, hen ,the object he most fears—and "bring back to Miranda whatever he finds" (*Mama Day*, 300). George fails Miranda's riddling test because his fear and disbelief got the better of him, although as he battles the enraged hen, he glimpses something of Miranda's meaning: "Could it be that she wanted nothing but my hands" (*Mama Day*, 300). While he does save Cocoa because he intuits something about the connection between speech and act, he is unable to make a genuine surrender of belief to Miranda and hence loses his life. *Mama Day* remarks frequently about hands and their power, not only in relation to the instructions she gives to George but in relation to her own gifts and those of all the Day men. However, the subject of hands also appears in the single fragment of myth—the story of origins of Willow Springs, "The Island got spit out from the mouth of God, and when it fell to the earth it brought along an army of stars. He tried to reach down and scoop them up, and found Himself shaking hands with the greatest conjure woman on the earth, "Leave them here Lord," she said, "I ain't got nothing but these poor black hands to guide my people but I can lead on with light"" (*Mama Day*, 110). This mythical story, during the course of the novel is enacted in the form of a ritual which is gradually losing its folkloric significance. It is observed on 22nd December, the longest night of the year. Candle walk is symbolic of rebirth of the terrestrial world. The candles carried by each islander in night procession across the island configure a winding stream of light, which in its zig-zag movement becomes a signature of all the elements—air, earth, fire and water (*Mama Day*, 110). The exchange of gifts "from the earth" that are "the work of your own hands" points to the importance of making and of need of each individual to imitate the creative act which created the island itself (*Mama Day*, 110). To that end the candles—used to welcome and accompany the spirit—represent the spirit of the Great Mother who has returned in a ball of fire to Africa, and also stand for "the light that burned in a man's heart" (*Mama Day*, 110).

Thus, Naylor's text, the story of the conjure women, is also the story of "the beginning of the Days'—a story that includes a goddess who must be recovered—as Sapphira will be recovered by Cocoa. It is also the story of the spirit of Africa that has travelled to the New World on wind and water. It affirms the staying power of the oral tradition, and although it is written down, it still must be "heard" although listened to in the way the communal voice has demanded.... Listen... Really listen this time" (*Mama Day*, 10), it must be read in Esu's way.

Bailey's Café, woven along with *Mama Day* through the character of George is profoundly spiritual and normatively powerful. Unlike *Mama Day*, where focus is on rich rural community celebratory of its origins and ways of life, *Baileys Café* takes place in an unnamed city on a mystical street "sits right on the margin between the edge of the world and infinite possibility" (*Bailey's Café*, 76), accessible only to those who are at the bottom or edge of despair. The lonely, the absurd, the dispossessed can have a clear perception of their tortured pasts and shattered dreams. But both of her novels highlight a locale that shapes and in itself is created by the characters that inhabit it. The boundaries between the real and the magical are blurred and therefore more akin to the works of magical realism in that the scientific works of time, space and probability are unraveled. The neighborhood, in particular the café is on metaphorical crossroads.

It exists nowhere and everywhere like Willow Springs, it is not on any map, and yet "you can find it in any town" (*Bailey's Café,* 112). It is a spiritual way station, a place to "take breather for a while" (*Bailey's Café,* 28), a place you have to already know about in your soul before you can find it. "If they can't figure out, we are only here when they need us, they don't need to figure out" (*Bailey's Café,* 28). As the epigraph "Hush! Now you can hear it can't be far away" (*Bailey's Café,* 21) harks back to the novel's antecedent beginnings in oral and from here "the choices have always been clear; you eventually go back and resume your life hopefully better off than when you find us or you head back to the back of cafe and end it" (*Bailey's Café,* 221). Behind the café is the well. It is a "void" (*Bailey's Café,* 76), an "endless plunge", (*Bailey's Café,* 76) "black empty space", where many visitors come to commit suicide. But once the well is accepted, that is the implacable harshness of life, including death, is accepted-out back is also where dreams come true. Sadie and

Jones "dance under the stars" (*Bailey's Café,* 40) out back. There Jesses Bell at first sees nothing but upon Eve's insistence looks again and sees her dream of "the simple bedroom she'd had as a girl" (*Bailey's Café,* 137). There Eve creates the dream setting for Mariam. "The void out back produced exactly what (Mariam's) child-like mind called up; endless water" (*Bailey's Café,* 228). Miss Maple is liberated from the confirming improbabilities of real life.

Using seven as recurring number, Naylor has seven stories to tell about the women who come to the café, each' one representing note on chromatic scale. The unifying thread is the narrative of Bailey himself, the fatherly war veteran and café proprietor, who gives a clue to the vernacular and its role in allowing access to the places through which these characters must pass in the journey toward self-identity. It is Bailey whose veiled comments offer insight into the close relationship between the text and distinctly black oral forms of expression which it evolves, "Anything really worth hearing in this greasy spoon happens under the surface. You need to know that if you plan to stick around here and listen while we play it all out" (*Bailey's Café,* 35). While café welcomes everyone, Eve's boarding home offers sanctuary to only those women, who truly need help or in whom she sees promise. Eve, whose name means "mother of all living" is essentially self-generated, "She is what Karla Holloway describes as the ancestor". She is the most mythical, becoming one with the delta dust as if to convey her close affinity with African traditions involving magic, mysticism and the supernatural "Eve's song evolves out of the oral and written lore surrounding the exploits of extraordinary women who had turned their backs on the world" Eve relies upon her magic the power of conjure in curing Jesse's addiction of heroin by crafting a series of illusions which allow Jesse Bell to be cured within a month. Her ability to manipulate reality and her close affinity with the supernatural are qualities reminiscent of figures such as revered conjure figure on the lines of Sapphira Wade or Mama Day. She gets the fragmented lives and returns them whole, "Go home my friend"; Eve says "leave your daughter here, and I'll return her to you whole" (*Mama Day,* 113-14).

Well or abyss at the back is both suggestive of womb and tomb that is birth and death. In *Mama Day* as well as *Bailey's Café*, Naylor establishes a community of characters who have not resisted the abyss of devastating world and therefore are secure in their identities and roles. They emerge stronger because they have learnt to accept the brutality of African-American life in a racialised society and because they have transformed their double consciousness into an advantage. To that community she brings an assortment of persecuted refugees each of whom has struggled in vain in his or her well of torment. Together the privileged—Bailey, Nadine, Eve and Gabe and these waifs Jesse Bell, Peaches, Mariam transcend their narrow confinements and along with the novel itself, celebrate a broader community based on openness, tolerance, psychic interconnection and telling and hearing their life stories. The abyss is not threatening to Miss Maple or the four proprietors because they are accustomed to it. They have no illusions about life, expecting little from it, "Life is (not) supposed to make you feel good, or to make you feel miserable either. Life is just supposed to make you feel" (219).

The refugees in *Bailey's Café* have been denied not only place but any meaningful past, since their African past was repudiated by White Americans, negating their identities to mere slaves, reducing them to nothing. Ellison contends that "Negro Americans are in desperate search for identity". The occasion of George's miraculous birth from the womb of Mariam restores a sense of cosmic harmony to the novel's characters, establishes for them living and livable African American space, thereby, restores a sense of the past and provides a hope for the present, if not the future.

Works Cited

Montgomery, Maxine L. 1996. "Authority, Multivocality; and The New World in Gloria Naylor's *Bailey's Café*". *African American Review*, Vol. 29, No. 1995.

Naylor, Gloria. *Bailey's Café*. New York: Harcourt, 1992.

———. *Mama Day*. New York: Ticknor and Fields, 1988.

Tucker, Lindsay. "Recovering the Conjure Women: Texts and Contexts in Gloria Naylor's *Mama Day*". *African American Review*, Vol. 28, No. 2, 1992.

Whitt, Margaret Earley. *Understanding Gloria Naylor*. New York: Harcourt Press, 1999.

6. Wilson, E. Charles JR. Gloria Naylor: *A Critical Companion*. London: Greenwood Press, 2011.

32

Unveiling the Myth of Harem: A Study of Fatima Mernissi's *Dreams of Trespass*

Rupali Gupta

One aspect of Islamic civilization which cannot be ignored is "Harem". The concept of Harem is the most misunderstood facet of Arab life. A Harem is a space set aside in a home specifically for the use of women and young children and men are not allowed to enter, it is considered as a private or forbidden area. Harems vary widely in size and composition, from the palatial complexes of the Ottoman sultans to a simple private room for women. The etymology of the word "harem" metaphorically refers to a jail, which is the slight variation of the word harem means "the forbidden" in Arabic.

Muslims have traditionally separated women from men, as they believe that this separation is ordered by the Qur'an and other religious authorities. The institution of harem was first mentioned within the Islamic text of the Qur'an. It was common throughout the Ottoman Empire to take women from conquered territories as—slaves for the royal harem. Graham-Brown claims, "The harem...was identified with complete male domination over women's lives and the apparently untrammeled sexual pleasures of four wives and unlimited numbers of concubines" (*Feminist Postcolonial Theory*, 503). The Imperial Harem of the Ottoman Sultan was typically housed with several dozen women, including wives, Sultan's mother, daughters and other female relatives, as well as eunuchs and servant girls to serve the aforementioned women.

During the later periods, the sons of the Sultan also lived in the Harem until it was considered appropriate for them to appear in the public and administrative areas of the palace. The harem was, in some cases, merely the private living quarters of the Sultan and his family within the palace complex. Some women of Ottoman Harem, especially wives, mothers, and sisters of Sultans played important political roles and at times it was said that the empire was ruled from harem. Lewis states, "The harem as an experimental domestic system of segregated living was the very real terrain on which Ottoman women fought for liberation" (*Rethinking Orientalism*, 101).

Long viewed by the West, harem simply as a place of sensual abandon, promiscuity, and overall languor, has suffered denigration and misrepresentation based largely on supposition alone. Most Westerners take harem as hundreds of women floating around large tiled rooms waiting to serve the lord and master. The harem in West is known as "seraglio", literally means "a cage for wild animals". The East was subjected to the most extensive mispresentation by eighteenth and nineteenth century Europeans. Oreintalist's depiction of harems tends to share a range of distinctive features which include paintings on the harem; emphasized woman's nudity, eroticism and exoticism. The Western image of the harem is an exotic paradise as a brothel consisting of many sensual young women lying around pools with oiled bodies, with the sole purpose of pleasing the powerful man to whom they had given themselves.

This perception of the harem as paradise becomes an ideological fantasy when it is collated with the reality of the harem life as depicted in Fatima Mernissi's *Dreams of Trespass: Tales of a Harem Girlhood* where she depicts the East that stands in opposition to the Western understanding of the Orient. As Edward Said claims the Orient was a European invention, the harem, as an integral part of this invention, was a Western construct as well. Mernissi adroitly deconstructs the myth of the harem as paradise, an exotic place populated by nude, voluptuous women, as perpetuated in Orientalist literature and paintings. Lewis asserts that, "Mernissi reads seclusion of women as part of a Muslim binarism which divides space into the public, men's space of the umma—the community of believers in which women only exceptionally had a justifiable place—and the women's space of the home, in which men were not encouraged to linger" (*Feminist Postcolonial Theory*, 525).

An internationally distinguished Moroccan feminist, Fatima Mernissi has written extensively on the status of women in Islam and the Arab world. Mernissi examined the differences between traditional Western and Muslim notions of female sexuality, drawing attention to the cultural roots of women's oppression in the Islamic world. She has explored the historical links between the religion of Islam, the societal oppression of women, and suppression of democracy in predominantly Muslim nations.

Mernissi belonged to a family of wealthy landowners and agriculturists and raised in privileged surroundings, her childhood was spent in the confines of harem. Contrary to Western notions of the harem, Mernissi's harem, consists of extended family and is designed to keep women sheltered from men outside of the family and the public sphere in general. At times, this highly circumscribed upbringing promoted feelings of frustrating isolation which impacted her later development as a scholar.

In *Beyond the Veil: Male-Female Dynamics in a Modern Muslim Society* (1987), Mernissi examines differences between Western and traditional Muslim conceptions of female sexuality and gender. In *The Veil and the Male Elite: A Feminist Interpretation of Women's Rights in Islam* (1991), she turned to the Qur'an and other traditional Islamic text to examine how the emancipatory aspects of early Islam were overridden or forgotten due to the efforts of Mohammed's critics and emphasizes the prominent roles played by Mohammed's wives and other women in the early years of Islam.

When Benazir Bhutto became Prime Minister of Pakistan in 1988, many claimed that it was a blasphemous assault on Islamic tradition since no Muslim state, had ever been governed by a woman. In *The Forgotten Queens of Islam* (1997), Mernissi documents the lives of a number of notable women—queens, wives, and mothers from the eighth century to the present who attained considerable political power in Muslim states. Thus, she argues strongly against the common misconception that Muslim women have never played eminent positions in the political arena. Unlike her previous studies, *Islam and Democracy: Fear of the Modern World* (2002) focuses not only on women's issues but also addresses the broader issue of the role of democracy in Muslim nations. Mernissi suggests that Muslims must re-examine their values and perspectives on the West—a task that Mernissi herself begins by deconstructing Muslim myths and the roots of Islamic fundamentalism. Mernissi argues, "The seclusion of women, which to Western eyes is a source of oppression, is seen by many Muslim women as a source of pride. In rural Morocco, seclusion is considered the privilege of women married to rich men. Harems...were considered even more prestigious since they required huge economic assets" (*Feminist Postcolonial Theory*, 493).

Being a native informant, Mernissi describes a world few people have ever seen and gives a voice to the countless powerless women who were kept as prisoners in a man's world and reflects many universals about Arab women. In this autobiographical account, Mernissi's captures her childhood experiences of harem life, where an extended family arrangement keeps the women mostly apart from the society, who are confined to their shared home, a dull space that allows few freedoms; and the frustrations felt by these inhabitants as well as her own efforts to subvert them, as opposed to the more stereotypical "imperial harem", which historically provided sex for sultans and other powerful court officials.

The primacy of the harem myth is illustrated even by Ellison, who has shown the operation of harem as a sign within the Orientalist discourse; she wrote:

> I asked Halide-Hanoum, perhaps the most active and best known of modern Turkish women in the name of one of our prominent suffrage societies, how we English women could help the Turkish women in their advancement. "Ask them", she said, "to delete for ever that misunderstood word "harem", and speak of us in our Turkish 'homes'". "Ask them to try and dispel the nasty atmosphere which a wrong meaning of that word has cast over our lives. Tell them what our existence really is." (*An Englishwoman in a Turkish Harem*, 17)

In *Dreams of Trespass: Tales of a Harem Girlhood,* Mernissi elaborates a highly Orientalist representation of the lives of Arab and Muslim women as oppressed victims of notorious institution, "The Harem" which is always surrounded by gates; guarded by door keepers which were usually black eunuchs. Mernissi describes the gate of her harem, which separates women from the male strangers walking in the streets and, even children could not step out of the gate without taking permission. Not only this, Mernissi informs, "What is the color of the morning in the deserted, silent streets? no one answered. In a harem you don't necessarily ask questions to get answers.... Roaming freely in the streets was every woman's dream" (*Dreams of Trespass,* 22). Mernissi's women too were not allowed to go to the city without protection and girls after completing their Koranic education are confined within the harem.

Moreover, she emphasized, "WHAT EXACTLY is a harem?" (*Dreams of Trespass,* 39) is not the kind of question grownups volunteered to answer and acknowledges the women of the harem were struggling to cope with the life in a traditional harem when such practices were rapidly changing. The tension between cultural change and family tradition in the Mernissi harem created a strangely exciting, and fragile atmosphere of progress and regression simultaneously.

In an effort to explicate the term, and to insist on its connection with the Arabic, Mernissi breaks it down to its roots, "The word 'harem,'...was a slight variation of the word haram, the forbidden, the proscribed. It was the opposite of halal, the permissible" (*Dreams of Trespass,* 61) and she goes on to present, "Once you knew what was forbidden, you carried the harem within. You had it in your head" (*Dreams of Trespass,* 61). Even Graham-Brown claims, "One of the arguments of those who campaigned against the harem system was that the boundaries imposed on women by seclusion were not just physical, but mental and spiritual" (*Feminist Postcolonial Theory,* 512).

Questions about the "harem" continue even towards the end of the book: "Is a harem a house in which a man lives with many wives?" (*Dreams of Trespass,* 150), and "Did you need to have slaves to have a harem?" (*Dreams of Trespass,* 155). By raising these questions, Mernissi puts forward the facts about the harem life and moreover, she asserts harem means living according to the rhythm of the group and household tasks are performed according to a strict rotation system. Mernissi recites, "Women organize themselves into small teams formed along friendship and interests lines, and split chores among them" (*Dreams of Trespass,* 69). This clearly refers to the association of women who follow the stringent conventions of the harem.

Mernissi represents herself as the "Other"; that takes us back to a colonial situation as being narrated from a postcolonial space, which opens with the lines, "I WAS BORN in a harem in 1940 in Fez, ninth century Moroccan city...one of the dangerous capitals of the Christians. The problems with the Christans start, said Father, as with women, when the hudud, or sacred frontier, is not respected" (*Dreams of Trespass,* 1). The narrative is not only an Orientalist, but also patriarchal, it is the father who associates women with the aggressive Christians one form of the other. Mernissi defines, "Harem was the place where a man sheltered his family, his wife or wives, and children and relatives" (*Dreams of Trespass,* 61). By which she means women's seclusion rather than the building in which women are kept.

Patriarchal discourse is not only associated with the men but even with the women themselves, particularly the older women such as Fatima's paternal grandmother, Lalla Mani.

She is the patriarchal wife, and mother who uploads the status quo which is evident in her comment to Mernissi's mother, "You know dear,".... "You are lucky to have married such an easygoing man as my son. Others would have cast out a wife who disobeyed.... Besides, don't forget Allah has given the right to have four wives" (*Dreams of Trespass,* 234). This shows Mernissi's harem is monogamous; rather than polygamous. At another occasion when Mernissi's father dislikes putting henna by her mother and runs away; and she chases father until Lalla Mani appears, imposing her authority and pronounces, "You know, Madame Tazi, in this respected household, husbands are not terrorized...this very religious city,...women behave by the book. They are obedient and respectful" (*Dreams of Trespass,* 232). The stated fragment shows not only grandmother's imperial power but reminds that the Mernissi's mother is new arrival in the family as grandmother summons mother with her family's name. Mernissi claims, "The spatial division according to sex reflects the division between those who hold authority and those who do not, those who hold spiritual powers and those who do not" (*Feminist Postcolonial Theory,* 490).

Mernissi understands the misconceptions about female domesticity—within Morocco specifically and the Middle East in general. She employs diverse voices to express the words, thoughts, and hopes of many of the women in the harem; thereby, she breaks the silence by giving a louder voice to its various inhabitants depicting them not solely as victims or odalisques but as complex human beings. Each of these women maintains a distinct position within the harem hierarchy, and despite the fact that they are all stuck in the harem. Mernissi communicates their powerful qualities of dignity and hope, including her mother, desperate for reform and modernity; Yasmina, her maternal grandmother who lives in a farm harem with neither doors nor walls; a cousin Chama, keen about her identity; Aunt Habiba, a divorcee whose powerlessness and need to please make her a figure of a great pathos and admiration; and Mina, an Ethiopian farmer slave.

The most rebellious character in Mernissi harem is her mother; who rebels against the traditions often. She becomes angry at seeing her daughter with a scarf tied around the head; she reprimands her as, "don't you ever cover your head!" and says further, "Do you understand me? Never! I am fighting against the veil, and you are putting one on?!" (*Dreams of Trespass,* 100). From an urge to break the convention of daily domestic co-existence, Mernissi's mother often refuses to eat meals with the group. Instead, she insists on deciding for herself when and what she would like to eat, as Mernissi notifies, "Eating at fixed hours was what Mother hated most about communal life" (*Dreams of Trespass,* 75). Sometimes, she would skip eating altogether, especially when she wanted to annoy her father, as skipping a meal was considered "terribly rude and too openly individualistic" (*Dreams of Trespass,* 76). However, such behavior means trouble from Mernissi's grandmother who wants to maintain the traditional harem rules. Her mother attempts to remind father constantly to live apart but father always feels guilty about the breaking up of family's solidarity as to him, "harem life particularly... fast becoming relics of the past" (*Dreams of Trespass,* 76).

Even Mernissi's uncles felt constrained by the discipline of harem life too and left the house one by one, it was only Uncle Ali and her father were left. Her father's departure would mean the death of his large family, and he declares, "As long as [my] mother lives, I wouldn't betray the tradition" (*Dreams of Trespass,* 77) and further articulates, "We live in difficult times, the country is occupied by foreign armies, our culture is threatened. All we have left is these traditions" (*Dreams of Trespass,* 78). But her mother argues that by sticking in the big house will never gain the strength they need to throw the foreign armies. Father tries to pacify her, but she explodes, "This tradition is choking me" (*Dreams of Trespass,* 78) with tears in her eyes which shows how much she has been frustrating with the existing pattern of harem.

Graham-Brown argues, "the desire to control women was often expressed in terms of safeguarding family honour and was manifested primarily in the physical segregation of women's space from that of men" (*Feminist Postcolonial Theory,* 504). Though Mernissi's father is loving and liberal husband who, to certain extent, is willing to meet his wife's needs, yet not much able to do anything as he too is restrained within the rigorously designed custom. Even further Graham-Brown claims, "Although it is clear that changes in men's attitudes were crucial to the relaxation of women's seclusion, women themselves played a part in pressing men to allow these changes" (*Feminist Postcolonial Theory,* 512).

For children, learning their position in this rapidly changing world was especially challenging, and it is the pivotal figure of Mernissi's maternal grandmother, Yasmina, who embodies the notion that the progress made within the mind and spirit can go a long way toward bringing down the walls. She expresses the kind of post-feminism while inspiring the hopes and ambitions of the future generations. Since Yasmina lives in the countryside and does not appear to young Mernissi to be locked in a harem at all, she innocently asks her grandmother to explain how such a life could be considered a harem. Grandmother gives several different answers to the question which bewilders Mernissi more. The first part of the answer is that in a harem women have "lost the power of movement," and the second is that "a harem meant misfortune because a woman had to share her husband with many others" (*Dreams of Trespass,* 34).

On her farm, Yasmina is one of eight co-wives. Despite being a traditional, illiterate woman, she yet desires for a different future to be achieved through local, native means. She expresses faith in women's right to education, the banning of polygamy and slavery. She pronounces this hope triumphantly, "Morocco has changed quickly little girl" and "and it will keep on doing so" (*Dreams of Trespass,* 37). Throughout the text, grandmother and mother will repeat the assertion and anticipate that Mernissi and the girls of her generation will benefit from these changes and that their lives will thus be substantially poles apart from their own.

The imbalanced burden placed on women in maintaining cultural identity is strongly felt among Mernissi's female relatives, especially seventeen-year-old cousin, Chama. Women's efforts to come into contact with the Western world, is also illustrated; which they associate with freedom. They try to smoke cigarettes, chewing gum, and learn foreign languages. Excited about the possibility of acquiring foreign languages and knowing other cultures, the women listen to the radio, the only opportunity they have to widen their horizons. However, Mernissi informs, "The men were the only ones in the house supposed to have access to a huge cabinet radio which they kept...locked when the radio was not in use...Father...and Uncle had the only keys to the radio" (*Dreams of Trespass,* 7).

When Chama discusses the issue of men and women adopting Western-style dress, with Mernissi's father, the father affirms, "if Arab women started imitating European ones by dressing provocatively, smoking cigarettes, and running around with their hair uncovered, there would be only one culture left. "Ours would be dead" and further Chama argues, "if that is so," "then why can my male cousins run around dressed like so many imitating Rudolph Valentinos and cut their hair like French soldiers, with no one screaming at them that our culture is about to disappear?" (*Dreams of Trespass,* 181).

Mernissi's father's insistence that culture itself is dependent on women's behavior is an amazingly widespread trend. Even some women share the attitude of Mernissi's father about women's role in protecting such traditions as they are not keen on changing traditions pertaining to veiling and sequestering. Graham-Brown again asserts, "The strict control of women's appearance and behavior in public was assumed to be the corollary of unbridled license within the harem" (*Feminist Postcolonial Theory,* 503). Although Mernissi and her cousins sought explanation and clarification of the harem, these urban women had no distinct answer either, as she discloses "But whenever I tried to find out more about the word 'harem,' bitter arguments ensued" (*Dreams of Trespass,* 40). Indeed, the women of the Fez Harem fell into two camps with opposing views—leaving the children in a dilemma. The debates for and against harems proceed logically on both sides until Chama explains her theory about how harems first got started.

Chama proclaims that it was the Emperor of the Byzantines who conquered the world and caught a huge number of women to whom he put in his harem to prove that he was the chief; that made East and West scared of him. After that Arabs improved their techniques until, she further informs:

> They became very good at it and dreamt of conquering the Byzantines. Finally, Caliph Harun al-Rashid had that privilege. He defeated the Roman Emperor in the Muslim year 181 (A.D. 798), and then went on to conquer other parts of the world. When he had gathered one thousand jayra, or slave girls, in his harem, he built a big palace in Baghdad, and put them in it, so no one would doubt he was the Sultan.... Everyone was very impressed after that—the Arabs gave orders, the Romans bowed. (*Dreams of Trespass,* 44)

The portraits of the Fez and farm harems complement the message of Chama's story, bears an uncomfortable note of reality to it. In the beginning, woman is a warrior, Chama narrates, fierce and difficult to catch, but, in time, the warrior woman is rendered to be nothing but a Jarya, a slave to the Muslim man who is used and exploited, and the fundamental insanity of the entire enterprise is satirized.

Among the harem inhabitants, reactions to Chama's tale range from delighted agreement to outrage over the ridicule of the customs, the latter attitude expressed most vehemently by Mernissi's paternal grandmother. Contrasted with the country grandmother, Mernissi's paternal grandmother is grand, urbane, and infinitely conservative, choosing to support the perpetuation of the harem system. Chama's story certainly appeals to Mernissi's imagination which she reiterates to grandmother, Yasmina. The ensuing conversation balances very serious issues with a lightheartedness that characterizes her grandmother's wisdom. She continues, "Wherever there are human beings, there is a qaida, or invisible rule. If you stick to the qaida, nothing bad can happen to you...unfortunately, most of the time, the qaida is against women" (*Dreams of Trespass,* 62). Although this concept is alarming to Mernissi, yet grandmother assures her, "You will be a modern, educated lady...even I, as illiterate and bound by tradition as I am, have managed to squeeze some happiness out of this damned life" (*Dreams of Trespass,* 64).

Aunt Habiba, a divorcee and the other story-teller is the least powerful, unlike Fatima's mother, whose married status confers on her the right to partake in rebellions acts and it was upstairs where stories are told; the place where Habiba has her room, which allows her to take transgressive flight of fantasy. She is, "certain that we all had magic inside, woven into our dreams" (*Dreams of Trespass,* 114). But the claims that Habiba makes do not enable her to escape the confines of the household in which she is reduced to one of the less prestigious and more confining positions.

A similar role played by the only person in the household with even less overt power than Habiba is the Ethiopian former slave Mina, whose experience of kidnapping and resistance inspires the children to always hope and dream for a better future. The lessons of Habiba and Mina point strongly to the idealistic notion that life for women will be improved by dreams which provides powerless wings and therefore liberty. Thus, the telling of tales is another remarkable feature that is closely associated with the woman of harem. In this way, women pass time creatively, and the younger generation is educated to see the possibilities beyond their own limited experiences in harem.

Mernissi describes different aspects of Moroccan traditions and women's ambivalent relationships with them. The community of women living in Mernissi's harem succeeds in establishing atmosphere of nurturing guidance, exercising a kind of power in defiance of their seeming powerlessness. Among the harem women themselves, some were throbbing for transformation, whereas others were among the most virulent reactionaries. Despite the frustrations experienced by them, they manage to cope with the limitations of the harem by utilizing the powerful tools of speech, stories, and role-playing.

Each one promises in her own way that modernizes its Islamic heritage. Sarah-Brown too, opines, "One of the results of sexual segregation in all classes of society was the creation of largely separate women's worlds, not necessarily confined to the four walls of the home, with their own culture—songs, stories, religious practices—overlapping at times with that of men, but seen by both sexes as different and distinct" (*Feminist Postcolonial Theory*, 518). Even de Burgh in her famous work, writes:

> Unlike in Ingre's paintings and Flauberts' imagery, where the harem is depicted as sexually charged with lesbian overtones and boundless eroticism, Loti shows the harem to be a domestic space. Bereft of the lesbian orgies and flagrant nudity imagined in the mythology evoked by Ingres and Flaubert, Loti's harem is a site of stories and card games. Thus exposes the sexual myth of the harem as baseless, leaving a cornerstone of Orientalism irreversibly de-mystified. (*Sex, Sailors and Colonies*, 62)

The memoir stated many of the inequalities women in harems had to deal with. When the preadolescent Mernissi begins to take interest in love chants and amulets, it causes a rift between her and her much-loved cousin Samir who was born the same day as Mernissi. The difference between Samir and Mernissi becomes evident at puberty when he starts reminding of her status as woman in relation to that of a man. It is at this stage Mernissi is reduced to silence by his comments. At one point we are acquainted with:

> There was nothing I could say because I realized that for the first time in our children's games, all that Samir had said was right, and that whatever I said did not matter that much. Suddenly, it all seemed to strange and complicated, and beyond any grasp. Could I feel that I was crossing a frontier, stepping over a threshold, but I could not figure out what kind of new space I was stepping into. (*Dreams of Trespass*, 241)

By wrestling the definition of a harem throughout her childhood and her narrative Mernissi is able to reveal what a true harem is—the pure companionship of women, who dreamed moving beyond the walls, but did not even have the privilege of simply walking down the street. She relates her life and the events of her world in an innocent fashion, to understand women living in harem struggle between boundary and freedom. With deep feelings and compassionate understanding for the Arab world, Mernissi breakdowns common stereotypes and shows that binaries between "Western civilization" and "Eastern primitivism" are false and destructively counterintuitive by demystifying the concept of harem.

Works Cited

Alloula, Malek. *The Colonial Harem.* USA: University of Minnesota, 1986.

Booth, Marilyn, ed. *Harem Histories: Envisioning Places and Living Spaces.* USA: Duke University Press, 2010.

Bullock, Katherine. *Rethinking Muslim Women and the Veil.* UK: Biddles Limited, Guildford and King's Lynn, 2002.

De Burgh, Helene. *Sex, Sailors and Colonies: Narratives of Ambiguity in the Works of Pierce Loti.* Germany: European Academic Publishers, 2005.

Delplato, Joan. *Multiple Wives, Multiple Pleasures: Representing the Harem, 1800-1875.* USA: Rosemount, 2002.

Essed, Philomena, Goldberg David Theo and Kobayashi Audrey, ed. *A Companion to Gender Studies.* USA: Blackwell, 2005.

Ellison, Grace. *An Englishwoman in a Turkish Harem.* New York: Methuen, 1915.

Gauch, Suzanne. *Liberating Shahrazad Feminism, Postcolonialism and Islam.* USA: University of Minnesota Press, 2006.

Graham-Brown, Sarah. "The Seen, the Unseen and the Imagined: Private and Public Lives." *Feminist Postcolonial Theory: A Reader.* Ed. Reina Lewis and Sara Mills. Edinburgh: Edinburgh University Press, 2003.

Hodgson, Barbara. *Dreaming of East: Western Women and the Exotic Allure of the Orient.* Canada: Greystone, 2006.

Mehta, Brinda. *Rituals of Memory in Contemporary Arab Women's Writing.* New York: Syracuse University Press, 2007.

Mernissi, Fatima. *Dreams of Trespass: Tales of a Harem Girlhood.* USA: Basic Books, 1994.

———. "The Meaning of Spatial Boundaries." *Feminist Postcolonial Theory: A Reader.* Ed. Reina Lewis and Sara Mills. Edinburgh: Edinburgh University Press, 2003. 489-501.

———. *Scheherazade Goes West: Different Cultures, Different Harems.* New York: Washington Square Press, 2001.

———. *Beyond the Veil: Male-Female Dynamics in Modern Muslim Society.* USA: Indiana University Press, 1987.

———. *Islam and Democracy: Fear of the Modern World.* New York: Perseus, 2002.

———. *The Forgotten Queens of Islam.* USA: University Minnesota Press, 1997.

———. *The Harem Within.* Bantan, 1996.

———. *The Veil and the Male Elite: A Feminist Interpretation of Women's Rights in Islam.* New York: Perseus, 1991.

Moghissi, Haideh. Feminism and Islamic Fundamentalism: The Limits of Postmodern Analysis. New York: Zed books, 1999.

Lewis, Reina. "On Veiling, Vision and Voyage: Cross-Cultural Dressing and Narratives of Identity." *Feminist Postcolonial Theory: A Reader.* Ed. Reina Lewis and Sara Mills. Edinburgh: Edinburgh University Press, 2003. 520-41.

Rethinking Orientalism: Women, Travel and the Ottoman Harem. New York: I.B. Tauris, 2004.

Peirce, Leslie P. *The Imperial Harem: Women and Sovereignty in the Ottoman Empire.* New York: Oxford University Press, 1993.

Rhouni, Raja. *Secular and Islamic Feminist Critiques in the Work of Fatima Mernissi.* Netherlands.

Roberts, Mary. *Intimate Outsiders: The Harem in Ottoman and Orientalist Art and Travel Literature.* USA: Duke University Press, 2007.

Said, Edward. *Orientalism.* London: Penguin, 1985.

Salhi, Kamal, ed. *Francophone Postcolonial Cultures: Critical Essays.* USA: Lexington, 2003.

33

Ogun Myth as a Paradox of Creation and Destruction in Wole Soyinka's *A Dance of the Forests*

Vishali Sharma and *Vandhana Sharma*

Myths are multi-dimensional, ever-present and all-pervading component of all cultures and with the evolution of mankind have emerged as a significant phenomenon in world literature. Claude Levi-Strauss says, myth makes people aware of their roots and gives them a "tool with which to face human existence" (*The Raw and the Cooked*, 27). The sophists of Greek enlightenment interpreted myth as "allegories revealing naturalistic and moral truth" (*Folk and Myth*, 35). Writers worldwide have used myths to show the flow of the past into the present as Wole Soyinka, one of the most powerful voices of Nigeria asserts, "The old must flow into the new" (*The Lion*, 54). Hence, myth-making becomes an essential part of any artist's creativity more so in the tradition-bound African society embedded in myths, rituals and folklore.

Wole Soyinka, whose own life has been an intriguing admixture of Western and African way of living, as his father was a Yoruba and his mother a "wild Christian", has always shown a unique fascination for Yoruba mythology. The most spectacular feature of his oeuvre is the depiction of gods as descending to the earth to be reunited with the human essence. The first according to Soyinka is the one who bridged the gulf of separation and emerges as the leader of the gods is Ogun who possesses immense power of will. Ogun's nature as

Soyinka mentions in "The Fourth Stage" is most clearly revealed in three actions: "The crossing of the primordial marsh", "the disastrous battle on behalf of the people of Ire", and "his descent and settlement in Ire". But, though Soyinka refers to all three, it is the first which he regards as central to the Yoruba concept of tragedy. The Yoruba myths tell how, when the gods came to earth intent on taking up their appointed places, they found themselves separated from man by chaotic growth—a primordial marsh. Of all the gods only Ogun, the hunter who had visited earth before and who knew how to smelt iron, was able to make an axe and cut a path through the growth. His action united gods and men, and he was rewarded by being given the title "Chief among the Divinities". But he was too restless and violent to dwell in the human community and preferred to live apart on the top of a hill, whence he hunted and fought. On one occasion, fighting for Ire, he became drunk and slew friend and foe indiscriminately. Eventually, he decided that the time had come for him to live a settled life among men, but his appearance "of fire and blood" so terrified the people that they fled from him. Ogun then covered himself in palm-fronds, entered Ire, and was made king. In his interpretation of the Ogun myth, Soyinka emphasizes that Ogun is the first darer and explorer. The Ogun myth is explored to the very depth in Soyinka's poem "Idanre", where the concept is elevated to the heights of universality. In *Ogun Abibiman*, Ogun becomes "not merely the god of war but the god of revolution in the most contemporary context" (Soyinka, 54).

The present paper aims at analysing the Ogun myth in Wole Soyinka's *A Dance of the Forests* with an emphasis on the hero of the play who embodies the creative and destructive aspect of the Yoruba god Ogun. Commenting on the hero of the play, Gerald Moore writes, Demoke from Soyinka is "the only occasion in Soyinka's work when his Ogunian hero is distinctly portrayed as an artist" (*Twelve African Writers,* 219). *A Dance of the Forests* is Soyinka's first play that defines "both the Yoruba world view and the playwright's own artistic vision in relation to the myth and metaphysics of Ogun"

(Nasidi, 46). The play is based on the myth and metaphysics of Ogun. In doing this, Ogun becomes the exemplary paradigm of heroism. In Wole Soyinka's famous book *Myth, Literature and the African World,* Soyinka discusses at length the nature of Yoruba myth and in particular, the symbolic import of Ogun, who, for Soyinka, is the most significant of the Yoruba gods. Ogun, the Yoruba god of iron, however, is Soyinka's idol god in the theatre. For Soyinka, Ogun is the moral standard for mankind. Ogun is a god of multiple meaning in the Yoruba mythology. In the mythology, he is the pathfinder, the terrible guardian of the sacred oath and a shield to the orphan. In *Myth, Literature and the African World,* Soyinka describes Ogun as:

> ...the embodiment of challenge, the Promethean instinct in man, constantly at the service of society for its full self-realisation. Hence his role of explorer through primordial chaos, which he conquered, then bridged, with the aid of the artifacts of his.... Only Ogun experienced the process of being literally torn as under in cosmic winds..... (30)

Demoke in *A Dance of the Forests* is an embodiment of "the Promethean instinct in man" and according to Soyinka this instinct is most predominant in the artist. As an artist he carves the totem and as an *alazon* he possesses the courage to take the Half-child who symbolises man's future as he stands at the threshold of two ages—traditional Africa and the modern Africa, since it has witnessed the violent past when its innocent mother was killed and the present, which does not seem very promising. As an artist, Demoke is carrying out Aroni's design to let the future decide its course by reversal of its path or by stubborn continuation. The visionary artist in Demoke forces that the power of will is not yet strong enough for a reversal of the cycle of destruction which has plagued mankind. He has any rate been cautioned that the Abiku child, symbol of the future, is a "doomed thing" which he cannot dispense with lightly. Nor does the artist have the transcendental force of will that is required to challenge established powers. This kind of energy Soyinka makes clear in

"The Fourth Stage", is in Hellenic terms "a totality of the Dionysian, Apollonian and Promethean virtues" which enabled Ogun to bridge the gulf of transition.

Soyinka has argued that it is only the person "whose spirit has been tested and whose psychic resources laid under stress by the forces most inimical to individual assertion...[who] can understand and be the force of fusion between the two contradictions" (*Myth,* 150). "The resulting sensibility", he goes on to say, "is also the sensibility of the artist, and [one] is a profound artist only to the degree to which he [or she] comprehends and expresses" (*Myth,* 150). This paradoxical truth of the good/evil duality in man especially in the artist has always fascinated Soyinka.

Demoke in *A Dance of the Forests* is the only character over whom Ogun exercises and even openly admits his tutelage. Demoke reflects the Ogun essence. In his previous existence, he is a court poet in the service of a medieval African tyrant, Mata Kharibu, whose queen, Madame Tortoise, is Rola in the present existence. It is in his present life as carver that we see him as a true surrogate of the god that creates and kills.

Ogun is the creative and yet destructive god and so is the protagonist of the play. The creative character of Ogun is one that should be emulated by any human entity. Ogun symbolizes man's quest for life and meaning and for this reasons man's attempt to achieve a meaning for a life that has none, should be based on the qualities of Ogun. According to Soyinka, "Ogun is the embodiment of will, and the will is the paradoxical truth of destructiveness and creativeness in acting man" (*Myth,* 150).

Ostensibly, Demoke combines the destructive and the creative capabilities of man. His very act of creation involves destruction too. Destruction is often necessary for creation. In Demoke's earlier existence—as the court poet—he had also lived as an artist. Yet he too involves contradiction. Being human, even this extraordinary artist is susceptible to jealousy and vertigo; he is capable of destruction as well as creation; of murder as well as the production of an extraordinary work of art—"the kind of action that redeems mankind". The majestic

Araba has to be destroyed in order to produce the Totem. A Totem was required as a symbol for the gathering of the tribes. The Totem emerges as a multi-faceted symbol. Its violent and bestial theme is, as we have seen, no accident since it represents the inherent properties of human nature. The Totem is a symbol of regeneration, recollection and solidarity. But the paradox is that Demoke who carves the Totem symbolizing the spiritual regeneration is himself subject to deep envy and causes the death of Oremole. As Eldred Jones aptly points out:

> Demoke's Totem in *A Dance of the Forests* towers above both the vandalism of the councillors and his own petty human jealousy. There seems to be a persistent hint that the world could be saved only through the artistic, the creative spirit, but spiritual progress is slow. (*Perspective on African Literature,* 135)

Further destruction of the forest by the townspeople, and the resulting vulgarization of his work, disgusts Demoke as he condemns it, ".... When I finished it, the grove was cleared of all the other trees, the bush was razed and a motor road built right up to it. It looked different. It was no longer my work. I fled from it" (*A Dance,* 11). Unlike the destruction of the Araba tree, the murder of Oremole is not necessary; it is a crime, and the memory of it plagues Demoke's soul until he confesses it. At first he skirts round his crime. He mentions the death of his apprentice as though it had nothing to do with him:

> The knife doesn't carve its own handle you know. There were Others who looped off the branches and skinned the trunk. In fact it took quite a few of us to do it. And one man fell to his death. (*A Dance,* 6)

The growing uneasiness of his conscience is dramatized by his compulsive urge to question the dead—he is the only one of the protagonists who takes any real interest in them. But what begins as an anxiety that his crime might be revealed by the voices of the dead, becomes—with the help of forest head's gentle prodding—an irresistible urge to make an open confession which leaves the way open for the regeneration which is forest head's purpose in ordering the welcome ceremony. Soyinka dramatizes the murder in a verbal flashback heightened by poetry. The narration highlights the mixture of jealousy and humiliation which motivated Demoke to murder his apprentice because he could climb higher than his master:

> I plucked him down
> Demoke's head is no woman's cloth, spread
> To receive wood shavings from a carpenter.
> Down, down I plucked him, screaming on Oro.
>
> (*A Dance,* 27)

This act of murder is immediately succeeded by a frenzied act of creation no less vividly described. Demoke is the one who precipitates a conflict between the two gods Eshuoro and Ogun. As a part of the celebration, he carves a gigantic "Totem" which is the centre-piece of "the Gathering of the Tribes", out of an "Araba" (the silk cotton tree) tree, which is sacred to the god Eshuoro. Thus, his very first role as a carver and a creator is highly symbolic:

> Before he made hard obeisance to his earth,
> My axe was executioner at Oro's neck. Alone,
> Alone I cut the strands that mocked me, till head
> And boastful slave lay side by side, and I
> Demoke, sat in the shoulders of the tree,
> My spirit set free and singing, my hands
> My father's hands possessed by demons of blood
> And I carved three days and nights till tools
> Were blunted, and these hands, my father's hands
> Swelled big as the tree- trunk. (*A Dance,* 27)

In the scenes showing his earlier existence, his work as a poet is not highlighted—except in the fulsome poetic phrases with which he praises Madame Tortoise—but his dual nature is even there suggested by the contrast between the deep contempt which he feels at Madame Tortoise's callousness, and the flattery which he lavishes on her hearing:

> Your hair is the feathers my lady.... Your forehead my lady—is the inspiration of your servant. Madame, you must not say you have lost your canary—[aside] unless it be your virtue, slut! (*A Dance,* 52)

He possesses the audacity to defy Madame Tortoise and forbid his novice to go on the hazardous errand to recover the canary—"I forbid him to go" (*A Dance,* 53). And his innuendoes almost bring down the wrath of his callous mistress on his head: "and look out, my poet: sometimes, you grow wearisome" (*A Dance,* 63). But it is Demoke the carver who has the greater significance for the play. Both acts—of destruction and creation- are essentially Demoke's. In spite of Ogun's attempts to take over the responsibilities of his protégé's crime: "In all that he did, he followed my bidding. I will speak for him" (*A Dance* 66).

Soyinka's *A Dance of the Forests* is a complex fusion of Yoruba festivals and traditions with the African spiritual cosmology. In this play, the author uses the Yoruba myth, especially the myth of *Abiku* child as an embodiment of Soyinka's belief that the new born nation, Nigeria, like the wanderer child is born with death in the soul. The child that has to be born has to be welcomed in a special ceremony after he is a few days old and only then he is properly a member of this world. That is why we can say that the dance of the half-child is as obscure as the future itself:

> Feel this dread,
> I who flee from womb
> To branded womb, cry it now
> I'll be born dead
> I'll be born dead.
>
> (*A Dance,* 74)

The Half-child is a symbol for man's future. That this future is doomed is clear in the Half-child chorus. The fate of the Half-child is for sometime in the balance, with Eshuoro and his jester trying to win him to one side, while his mother, Demoke and Ogun all seem to fight on the other side to save the child. These forces are the natural mother, and the artist representing the noble side of man's nature, and the god of creativity. The peril of the Half-child is vividly dramatized in the dance in which it is tossed between Eshuoro, the third triplet (posterity) and Eshuoro's jester, while Demoke tries to rescue the child from the obvious peril represented by the knives. It is Ogun, however, who intervenes, rescues the child, and passes him to Demoke. It is evident that the individualism of the Ogun-possessed and Ogun-enabled hero makes collective societal salvation an impossible task.

Thus, Soyinka uses the *Abiku* motif not only to show the fate of Africa wedged in a bondage imposed by the exigencies of greed, tyranny, corruption and prostitution but also to give his vision of a "New Africa" that would escape its colonial past by grafting the technical advances of the present onto the stock of its own ancient traditions. Aspects of the native life were to be reformulated to integral elements of the recent history to form a solid foundation for the future. The vision of the writer lies with Demoke who with his creative-destructive capabilities possesses the potential to regenerate the mankind.

In *A Dance of the Forests*, Demoke re-enacts Ogun's "crossing of the primordial marsh". Demoke is first "stripped of his excrescences" or, in Forest Head's words, "shown the mirror of original nakedness". He has to become aware that, like Ogun, he is both creative and destructive, both carver and murderer. He is then drawn into the abyss, in the form of the "Welcome of the Dead", at which point he becomes the unresisting mouthpiece of the god, uttering visions symbolic of the transitional abyss. During the "Dance of the Half-Child" he asserts his will and impulsively enters the dance. Moments later, during the "Dance of the Unwilling Sacrifice" he again asserts himself, this time to such good effect that the forces of destruction are thrown into disarray. He falls from the totem and cleansed by the air, is preserved to stand "as it were beside himself, observant, understanding, and creative", blessed with "supernal insight".

The final dance in *A Dance of the Forests* is supposed to bring about a spiritual realization and give a new birth as it were to them. Out of darkness and wilderness, there is expected an emergence of light and order. They learn the lesson of sacrifice and expiation and wish to know the future. But the future is not clear to them. Wole Soyinka seems to suggest through the ritual sacrifice and expiation supervised by the forest head that although the Africans have a rich religion, mythology and a pantheon of gods, they have to rely upon themselves for their actions.

Soyinka's fascination with the Ogun transcends the metaphysics of the deity to a trenchant evocation of the deity's mythic capacity for shaping and transforming society. Through this subtle mythic evocation he gives active voice and teeth to his sense of commitment. The playwright aims at re-educating the minds of his compatriots especially in shaping their ways of looking at social processes and in taking their collective destiny in their hands.

Works Cited

Gibbs, James. *Critical Perspectives on Wole Soyinka.* Ed. Bruce, Kings. London: Heinemann; New York: Africana: Twayne Publishers, 1980.

Jones, Eldred. "Progress and Civilization in the Work of Wole Soyinka", *Perspective on African Literature.* Ed. Christopher, Heywood. London: Heinemann; New York: Africana: Twayne Publishers, 1971.

Lalit, Handoo. *Folk and Myth.* Mysore: Central Institute of Indian Language, 1988.

Levi-Strauss, Claude. "Introduction to a Science Mythology", *The Raw and the Cooked.* Volume 1. New York: Harper and Row, 1969.

Moore, Gerald. *Twelve African Writers.* London Melbourne Sydney Auckland: Hutchinson University Library for Africa, 1980.

Nasidi, Yakubu. *Beyond the Experience of Limits.* Ibadan: Caltop Publications, 2001.

Soyinka, Wole. "A Dance of the Forests", *Collected Plays.* Volume 1. London: Oxford University Press, 1973.

———. *Myth, Literature and the African World.* United Kingdom: Cambridge University Press, 1976.

———. *The Lion and the Jewel.* London: Oxford University Press, 1963.

———. *Idanre and Other Poems.* London: Methuen, 1967.

Contributors

Ajay B. Kukade, Professor, M.Fua Mahavidyala, Warud.

Alan Johnson, Senior Professor, Department of English and Philosophy, Idaho State University, USA.

Anita Bhela, Associate Professor, Delhi College of Arts and Commerce, University of Delhi.

Catherina Moss, Researcher and Teacher, Don Bosco School Park Circus, Kolkata.

Geetanjali A. Rana, Associate Professor, Govt. College for Women, Gandhi Nagar, Jammu & Kashmir.

Geetanjali Multani, Associate Professor, Govt. College for Women, Gandhi Nagar, Jammu, Jammu and Kashmir.

Indira Nityanandam, Principal, Smt. S.R. Mehta Arts College.

Indranath Choudhari, Former Sectretary, Sahitya Akademi, New Delhi.

Isha Malhotra, Assistant Professor, Central University of Jammu. Jammu & Kashmir.

Jasbir Jain, Director, Institute for Research in Interdisciplinary Research, Jaipur.

Jatinder Kaur, Assistant Professor, Govt. College for Women, Gandhi Nagar, Jammu, Jammu & Kashmir.

Jay Hansford C. Vest, Ph.D., Senior Professor, Department of American Indian Studies, University of North Carolina at Pembroke, One University Drive at Pembroke, North Carolina, USA.

K.B.S. Krishna, Assistant Professor, Department of English, GITAM University, Hyderabad.

K.S. Vaishali, Associate Professor, Department of English, Banglore University, Banglore.

Mahua Mukherjee, Director, Centre for Studies in Dance Forms of Bengal and Professor, Dept. of Dance, Rabindra Bharati University, Kolkata, West Bengal.

Mohit K. Ray, Professor (Retd.) of English, Burdwan University, Burdwan.

Mrinalini Atrey, Assistant Professor, The Law School, University of Jammu, Jammu and Kashmir.

Neeru Tandon, Associate Professor, V.S.S.D College, Kanpur.

Prakash Chandra Pradhan, Associate Professor, Banaras Hindu University, Varanasi.

Pulakesh Ghosh, Assistant Professor and Head of Department of English at APCR Govt. College, Siliguri, West Bengal.

Rashm Attri, Associate Professor. Department of English. Aligarh Muslim University, Aligarh.

Ravi Bushan, Assistant Professor, Department of English, Bhagat Phool Singh Mahila Vishwavidayala Khanpur Kalan (Sonipat), Haryana.

Reena Salaria, Assistant Professor, Department of English, G.G.M. Science College. Jammu, Jammu and Kashmir.

Rupali Gupta, Research Scholar, University of Jammu, Jammu and Kashmir.

Saiket Banjerjee, Research Scholar, Central University of Haryana.

Samina Khan, Associate Professor. Department of English, Aligarh Muslim University, Aligarh.

Sanjoy Saksena, Professor of English, University of Allahabad.

Santosh Gupta, Professor (Retd.), University of Rajasthan, Jaipur.

Shahla Ghauri, Assistant Professor, Department of English, Aligarh Muslim University, Aligarh.

Shashi Khurana, Associate Professor, Satyawati College, Delhi University, Delhi.

Sonia Khajuria, Assistant Professor, Department of English, Govt. Degree College, Kathua, Jammu and Kashmir.

Vandhana Sharma, Director, School of Languages and Literature, Shri Mata Vaishno Devi Universty, Katra, Jammu and Kashmir.

Vishali Sharma, Research Scholar, School of Languages and Literature, Shri Mata Vaishno Devi Universty, Katra, Jammu and Kashmir.